What's New

Microsoft Project 2013

Dale A. Howard
Gary L. Chefetz

What's New

Microsoft Project 2013

Publisher: Chefetz LLC dba MSProjectExperts
Authors: Dale A. Howard and Gary L. Chefetz
Cover Design: Emily Baker
Copy Editor: Rodney Walker
Cover Photo: Chuck Baker

ISBN: 978-1-934240-26-7

Library of Congress Control Number: 2013935537

Published and distributed by Chefetz LLC dba MSProjectExperts, 90 John Street, Suite 404, New York, NY 10038. (646) 736-1688 http://www.msprojectexperts.com

Contents

Introduction

What's New Microsoft Project 2013 is a quick learning guide to get you up to speed with the new features in Microsoft Project 2013. The content of this book derives from the *Ultimate Study Guide: Foundations Microsoft Project 2013*, (ISBN: 978-1-934240-27-4). Consider obtaining *The Ultimate Study Guide: Foundations* for a complete learning experience and reference manual, which includes the new features in Project 2013 presented in context with Project Management Institute (PMI) best practices and project management cycle.

Microsoft Project 2013 introduces exciting new features representing profound changes to reporting, including the ability to easily create dashboard style reports, a complete replacement for the built-in reports that had not changed much in many years. From the new getting started story, to the amazing new integration with SharePoint, Microsoft Project 2013 is packed with new features and changes that you can use to enrich your scheduling experience.

The 2013 edition introduces the concept of apps. You can already purchase apps from the Microsoft Office Apps store and the number and the breadth of these is expected to grow rapidly. Numerous smaller and more subtle enhancements round out the changes in Project 2013, making this version the most important ever. This book covers all of these changes in depth. Be sure to download the practice files and work your way through the hands-on lessons to be up to speed in no time. Enjoy!

Download the Sample Files

Before working on any of the Hands On Exercises in this book, you must download and unzip the sample files required for each exercise. You can download these sample files from the following URL:

http://www.msprojectexperts.com/whatsnew2013

Module 01

User Interface Changes to Project 2013

Learning Objectives

After completing this module, you will be able to:

- Use the Welcome to Project tutorial
- Use the new Start Experience when launching Microsoft Project 2013
- Understand changes to the Backstage
- Understand new options in the Project Options dialog
- Experience changes to visuals in Task and Resource views

Inside Module 01

Using the Welcome to Project Tutorial

The very first time that you launch Project 2013 after installation, the software displays the *Welcome to Project* tutorial shown in Figure 1 - 1. Aimed primarily at new users, this tutorial helps you to learn how to plan and manage your projects effectively.

Figure 1 - 1: Welcome to Project tutorial on first launch of Project 2013

To start the tutorial, click the *Start* button in the middle of the *Welcome to Project* page. The software displays the *Schedule your work* page of the tutorial shown in Figure 1 - 2.

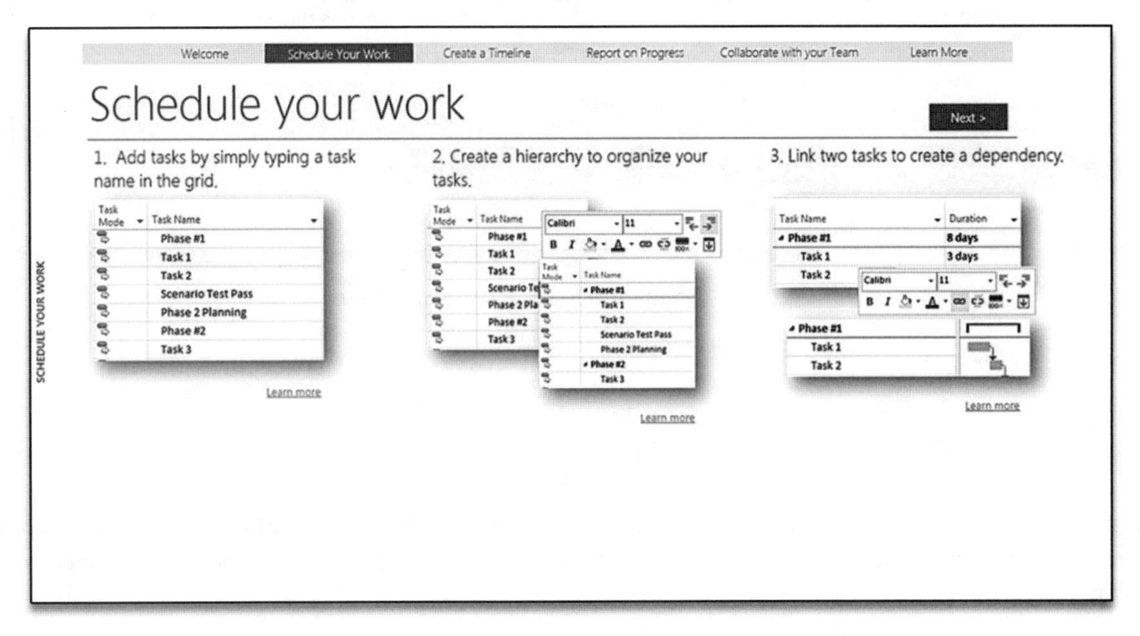

Figure 1 - 2: Schedule your work page of the tutorial

The *Schedule your work* page of the tutorial includes three steps to effectively plan the task work in your projects. At the bottom of each step, you can click the *Learn more* hyperlink to learn more about how to schedule your work in Project 2013. If you click any of the *Learn more* hyperlinks, the software launches Internet Explorer and navigates to the *Video: Schedule your work* page in the *Microsoft Office Support* web site shown in Figure 1 - 3. On this page, you can watch a video about how to schedule your work, and you can click on any of the links at the bottom of the page to learn more about task planning or to watch a video about the new features in Project 2013. Close the Internet Explorer when you finish using the support page.

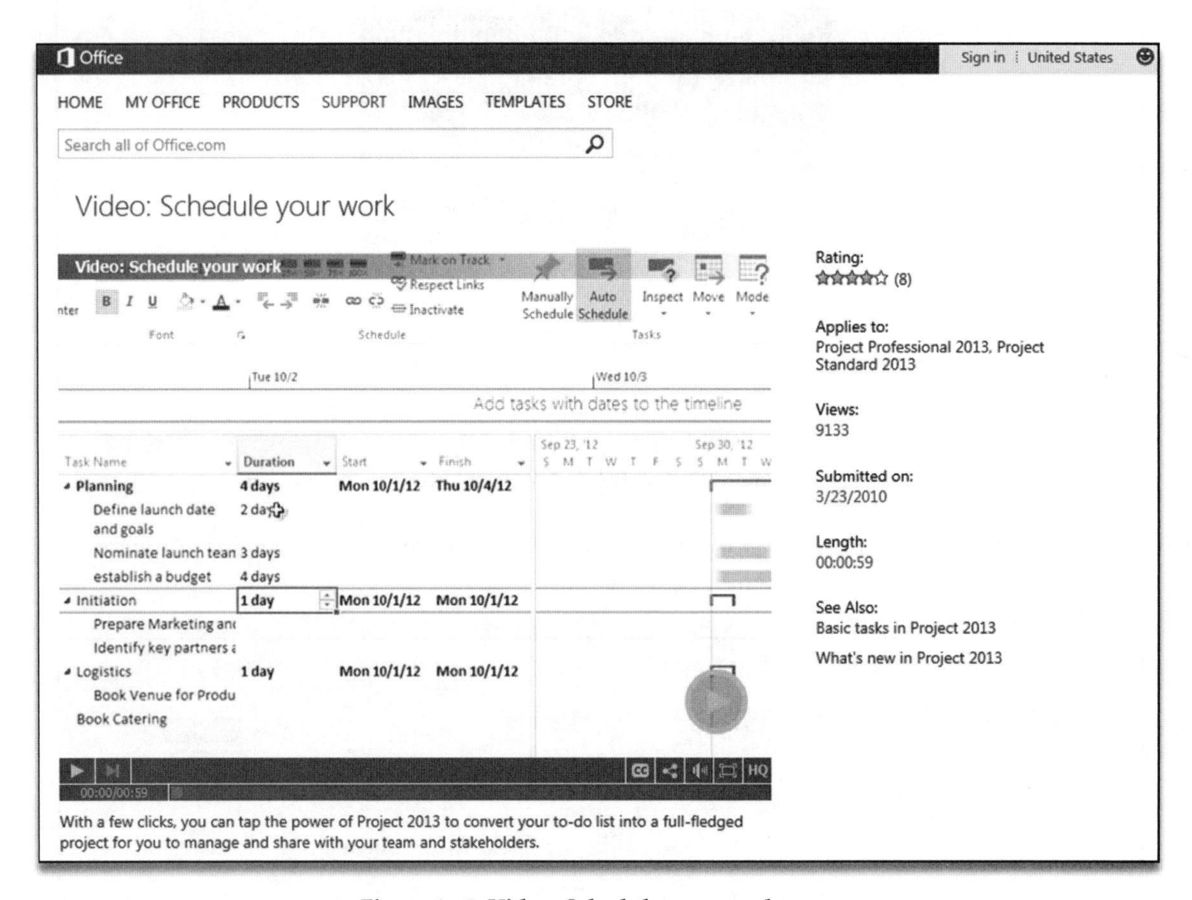

Figure 1 - 3: Video: Schedule your work page

To navigate to the next page in the tutorial, click the *Next* button in the upper right corner of the *Schedule your work* page as shown previously in Figure 1 - 2. Project 2013 displays the *Create a timeline* page shown in Figure 1 - 4.

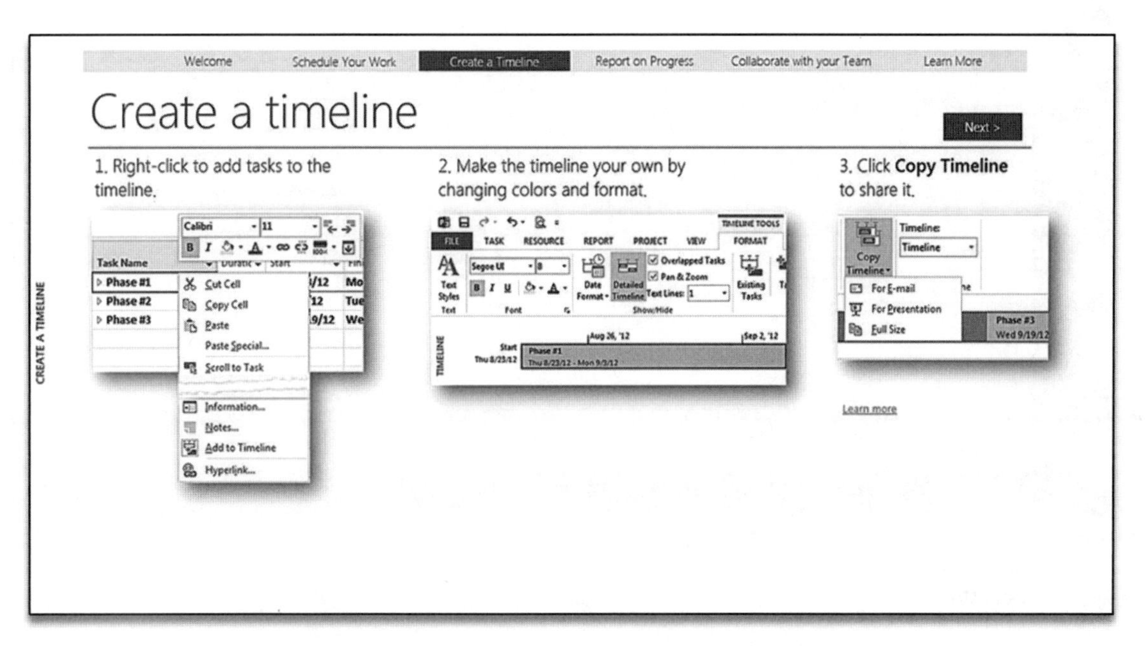

Figure 1 - 4: Create a timeline page of the tutorial

The *Create a timeline* page of the tutorial includes three steps to create a *Timeline* view to report about your project. At the bottom of the third step, you can click the *Learn more* hyperlink to learn more about creating a *Timeline* view. If you click the *Learn more* hyperlink, the software launches Internet Explorer and navigates to the *Video: Create a timeline* page in the *Microsoft Office Support* web site shown in Figure 1 - 5. On this page, you can watch a video about how to create a *Timeline* view, and you can click on either of the links at the bottom of the page to learn more about creating a *Timeline* view or to watch a video about the new features in Project 2013. Close the Internet Explorer when you finish using the support page.

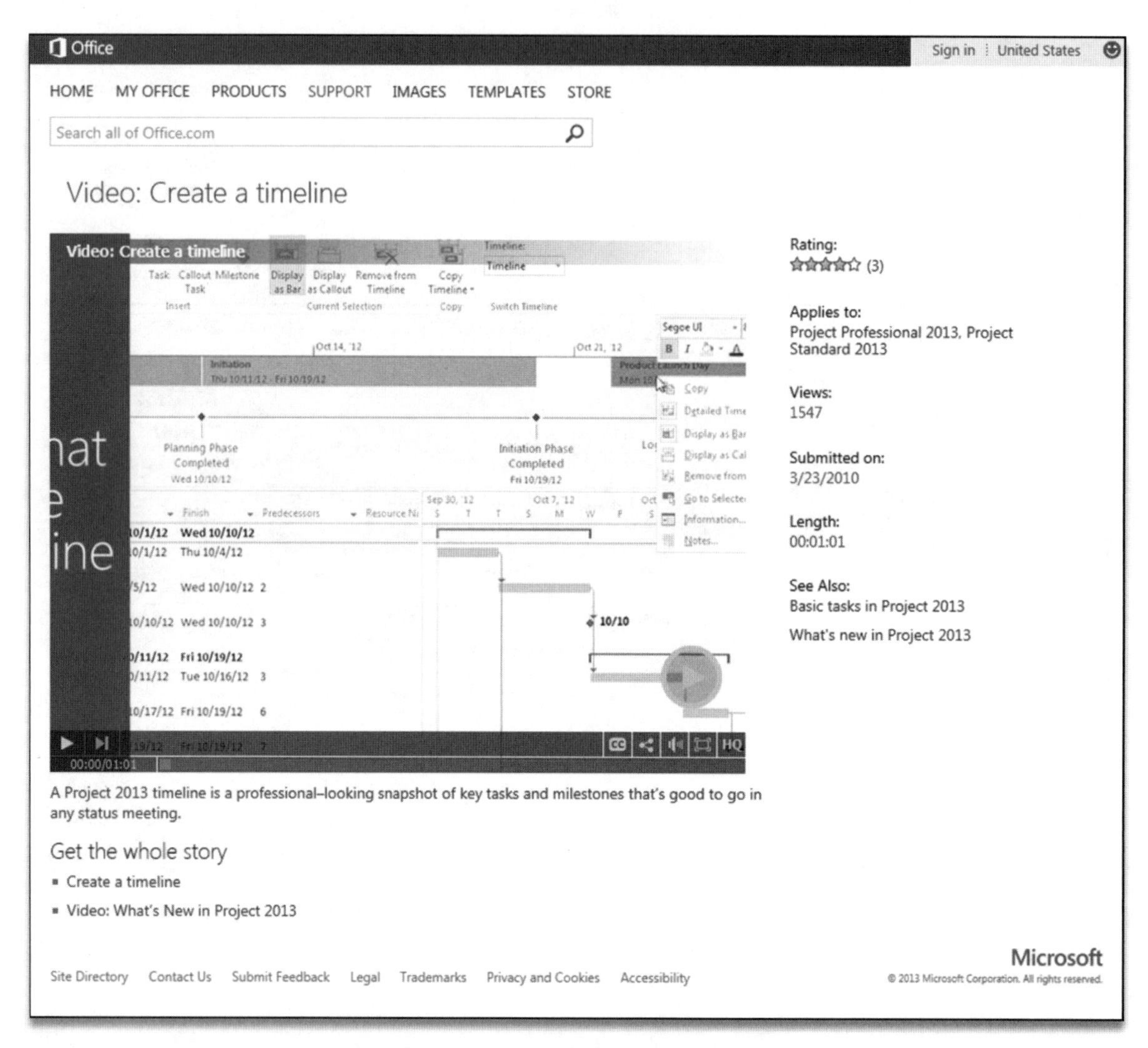

Figure 1 - 5: Video: Create a timeline page

To navigate to the next page in the tutorial, click the *Next* button in the upper right corner of the *Create a timeline* page as shown previously in Figure 1 - 4. Project 2013 displays the *Report on progress* page shown in Figure 1 - 6.

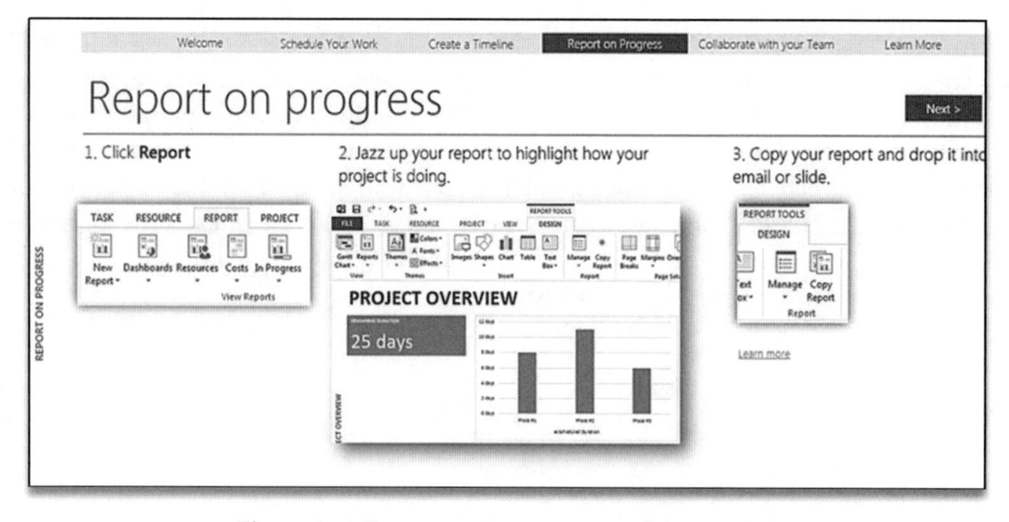

Figure 1 - 6: Report on progress page of the tutorial

The *Report on progress* page of the tutorial includes three steps to report progress about your project. At the bottom of the third step, you can click the *Learn more* hyperlink to learn more about reporting progress. If you click the *Learn more* hyperlink, the software launches Internet Explorer and navigates to the *Video: Report on progress* page in the *Microsoft Office Support* web site shown in Figure 1 - 7. On this page, you can watch a video about how to report on progress, and you can click any of the links at the bottom of the page to learn more about reporting on progress or to watch a video about the new features in Project 2013. Close the Internet Explorer when you finish using the support page.

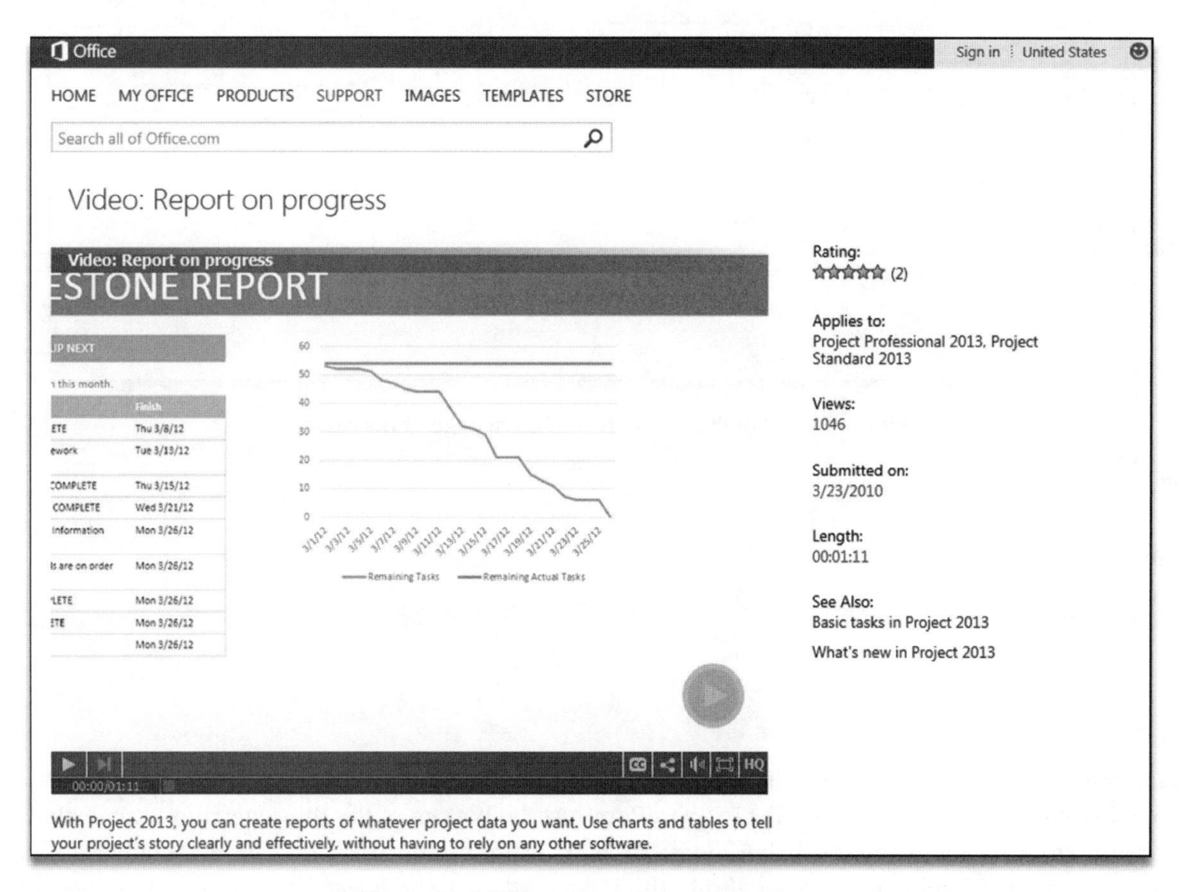

Figure 1 - 7: Video: Report on progress page

To navigate to the next page in the tutorial, click the *Next* button in the upper right corner of the *Report on progress* page as shown previously in Figure 1 - 6. Project 2013 displays the *Collaborate with your team* page shown in Figure 1 - 8.

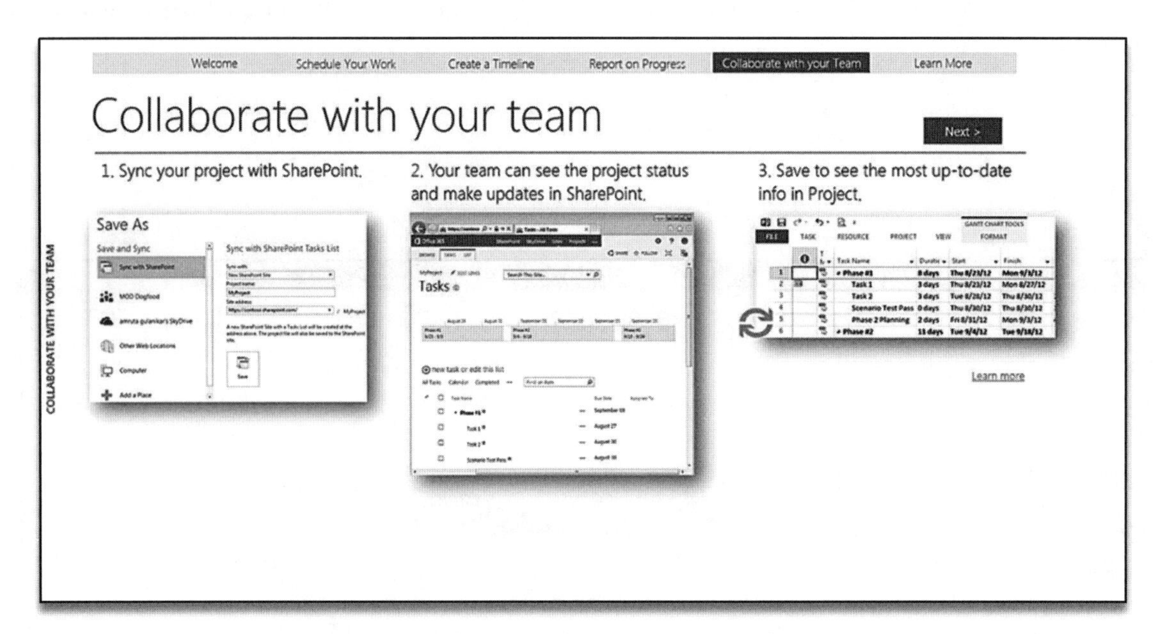

Figure 1 - 8: Collaborate with your team page of the tutorial

The *Collaborate with your team* page of the tutorial includes three steps to collaborate with your project team by synchronizing your project with a *Tasks* list in SharePoint. At the bottom of the third step, you can click the *Learn more* hyperlink to learn more about collaborating with your team. If you click the *Learn more* hyperlink, the software launches Internet Explorer and navigates to the *Video: Collaborate with your team* page in the *Microsoft Office Support* web site shown in Figure 1 - 9. On this page, you can watch a video about how to use SharePoint to collaborate with your team, and you can click either of the links at the bottom of the page to learn more about using SharePoint to collaborate with your team or to watch a video about the new features in Project 2013. Close the Internet Explorer when you finish using the support page.

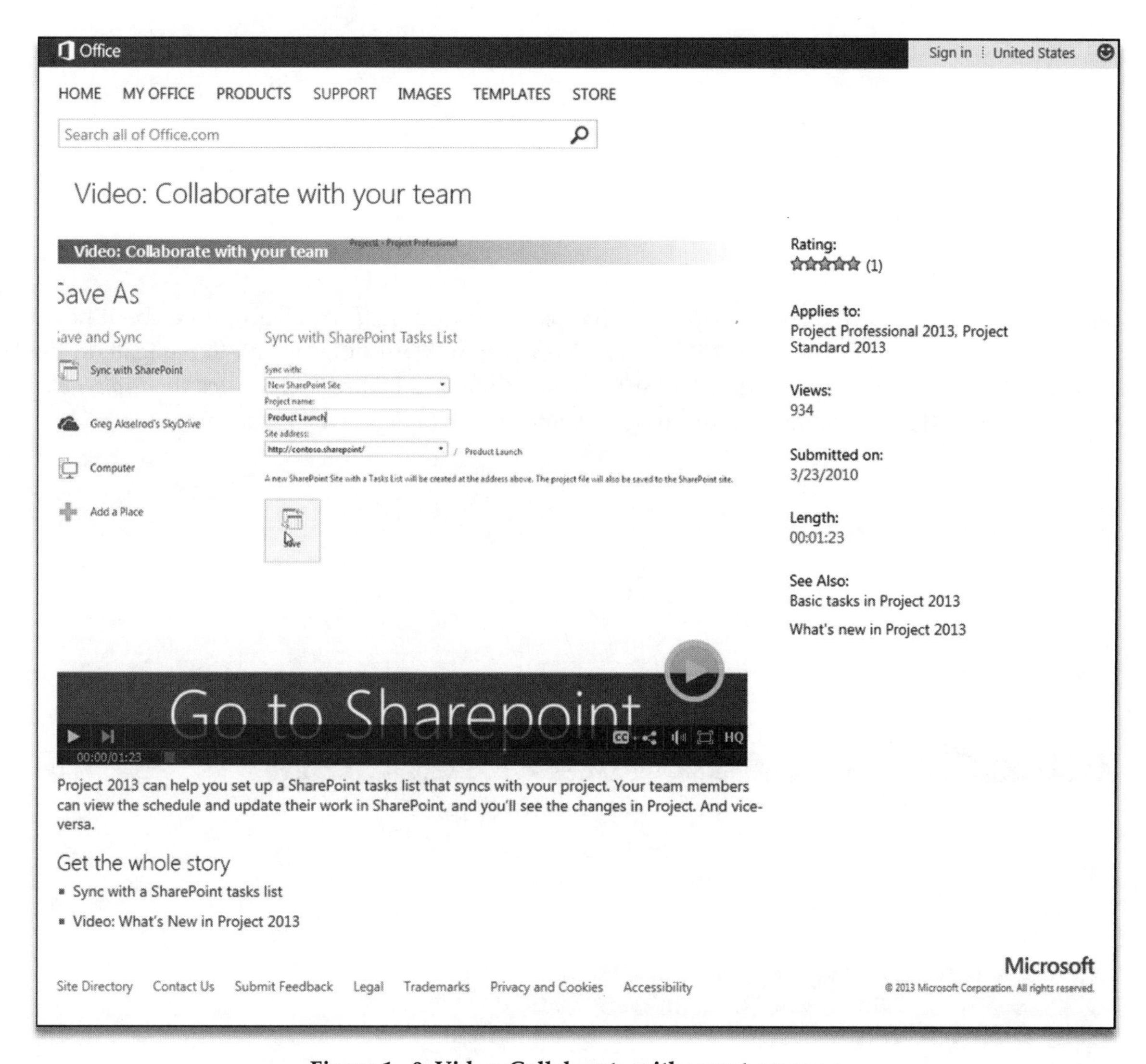

Figure 1 - 9: Video: Collaborate with your team page

To navigate to the final page in the tutorial, click the *Next* button in the upper right corner of the *Collaborate with your team* page as shown previously in Figure 1 - 8. Project 2013 displays the *Keep going* page shown in Figure 1 - 10.

Welcome | Schedule Your Work | Create a Timeline | Report on Progress | Collaborate with your Team | Learn More

Keep going. There are lots more new features and ways to work in Project.

See the Project 2013 Getting Started Center

Visit the Project blog

Try out the new features

LEARN MORE

Figure 1 - 10: Keep going page of the tutorial

The *Keep going* page offers you several hyperlinks to web pages that can help you learn more about how to manage projects effectively in Project 2013. Click the *Project 2013 Getting Started Center* link to navigate to the *What's new in Project 2013* page in the *Microsoft Office Support* web site shown in Figure 1 - 11. Click the *Project blog* link to navigate to the Project 2013 development team's blog web site shown in Figure 1 - 12.

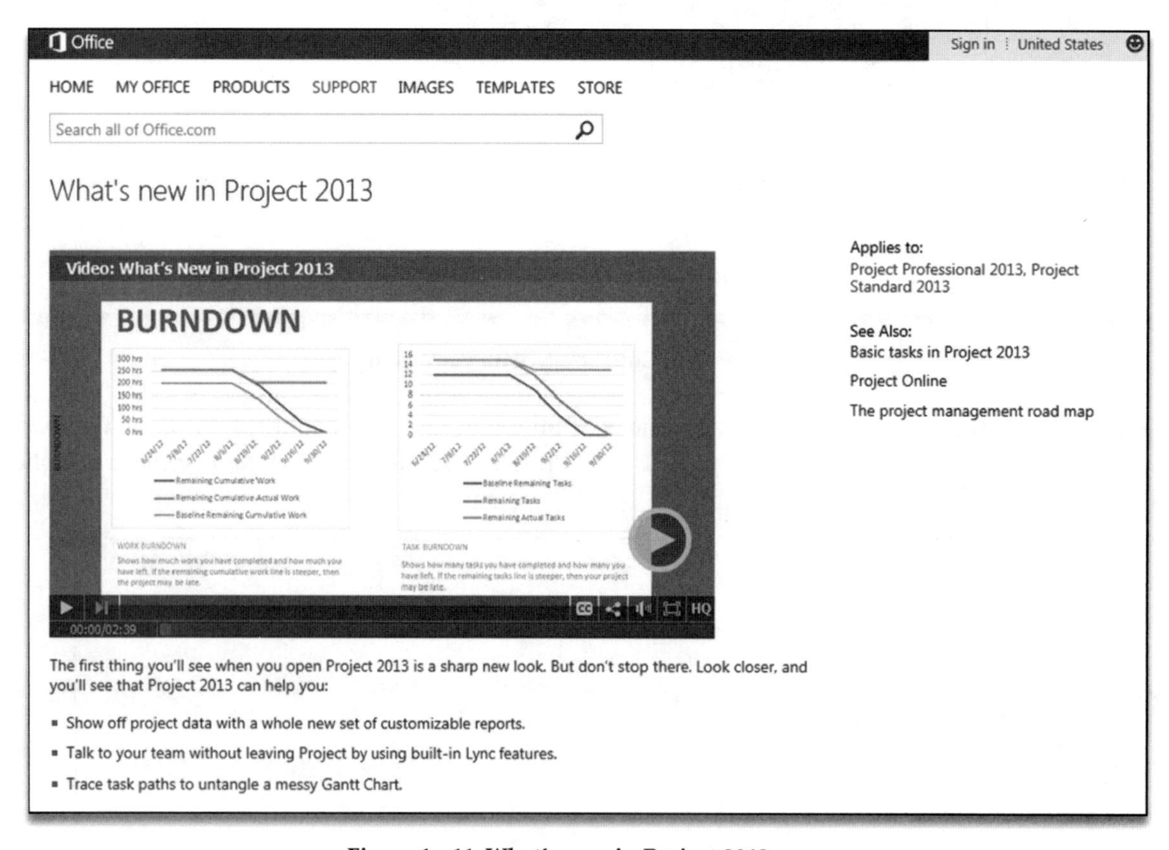

Figure 1 - 11: What's new in Project 2013 page

Figure 1 - 12: Project 2013 team blog web site

When you click the *Try out the new features* link on the *Keep going* page of the tutorial, the software displays the sample project shown in Figure 1 - 13. This project demonstrates the results of following the steps documented in the tutorial. Study this sample project to learn more about the project management process using Project 2013 and then close the file when finished.

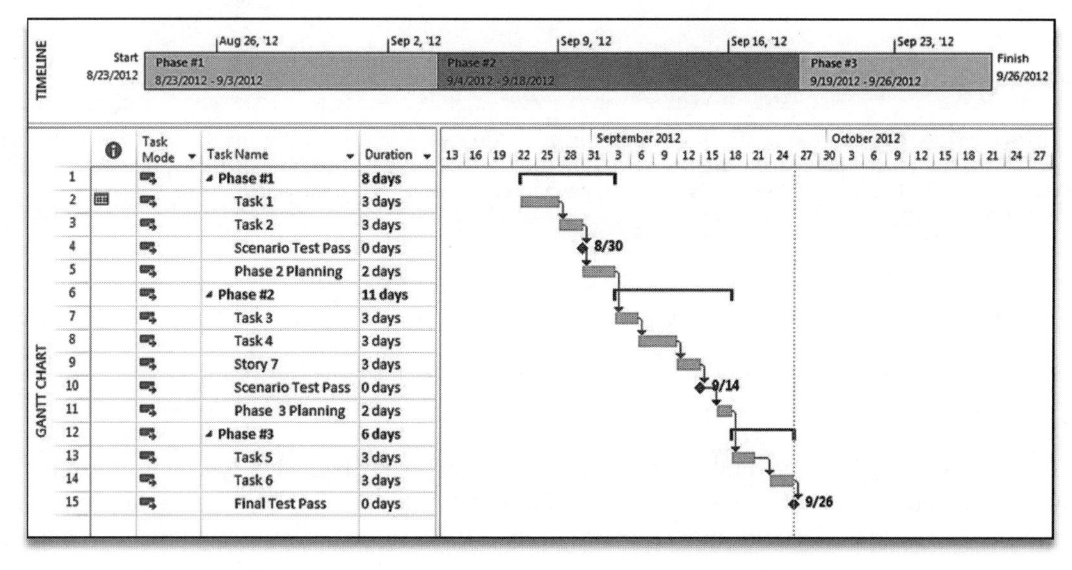

Figure 1 - 13: Sample project created at the end of the tutorial

Information: If you want to skip the tutorial entirely, click the *Skip Intro* link on the *Welcome* page of the tutorial. The system skips all of the steps in the tutorial and takes you directly to the sample project shown previously in Figure 1 - 13.

Introducing the New Start Experience

After launching Project 2013 for the very first time, every future time you launch the software, you see the new *Start* page of the *Backstage* shown in Figure 1 - 14. Notice that this page contains a list of recently opened project files in the *Recent* section of the sidepane on the left side of the page. To open one of the recently opened projects, click the name of project file you want to open. To open any other project, click the *Open Other Projects* button in the sidepane on the left side of the page. The software displays the *Open* page of the *Backstage* where you can open a project file from your computer, or from a cloud-based location such as a Windows Live SkyDrive folder. I discuss the features of the *Open* page in the *Introducing the Open Page* topical section later in this module.

Information: Notice in the *Start* page shown in Figure 1 - 14 that the *Recent* section contains the *Welcome to Project.mpt* template used to create the *Welcome to Project* tutorial you see the very first time when you launch Project 2013 after installation. To run the tutorial again, simply click this project in the *Recent* section of the *Start* page.

Information: If you float your mouse pointer over the name of a recently used project in the *Recent* section of the sidepane, the software displays a floating tooltip that reveals the file path and the complete file name for the project. This functionality is new behavior when compared with a similar feature available in the *Backstage* in Project 2010.

Notice also that the main content area of the *Start* page contains an extensive list of templates from which you can create a new project. Because the *Start* page is very similar to the *New* page in the *Backstage*, I present an in-depth discussion on how to create a project from a template in the *Introducing the New Page* topical section later in this module.

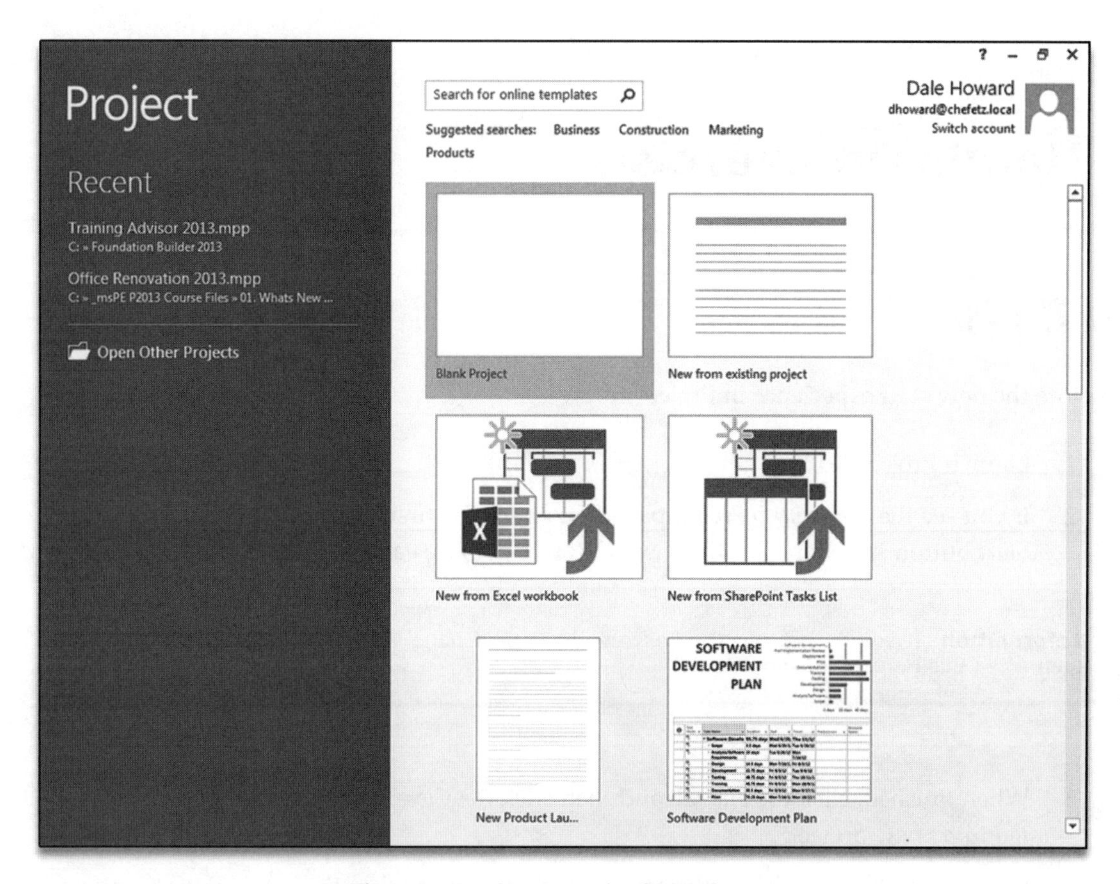

Figure 1 - 14: Start page in the Backstage

To navigate to the *Open* page in the *Backstage* from the *Start* page, click the *Open Other Projects* button in the sidepane on the left side of the page. To return to the *Start* page, click the *Back* button (large left-arrow button) at the top of the sidepane in the *Backstage* (not shown).

To exit the *Start* page and navigate directly to the main user interface of Project 2013, press the **Escape** key on your computer keyboard. The software automatically opens a new blank project file named *Project1*.

Information: To prevent Project 2013 from displaying the *Start* page every time you launch the software, press the **Escape** key to exit the *Start* page and create a new blank project. Click the *File* tab, and then click the *Options* button in the sidepane of the *Backstage*. On the *General* page of the *Project Options* dialog, **deselect** the *Show the Start screen when this application starts* option and then click the *OK* button.

Hands On Exercise

Exercise 1 - 1

Explore the new start experience in Project 2013.

1. Launch Project 2013.
2. If you see the *Welcome to Project* page that opens the first time you launch the software, click the *Start* button and then click the *Next* button to explore each page of this brief tutorial.

Information: If you do not see the *Welcome to Project* page when you launch Project 2013, skip ahead to step #7 in this Hands On Exercise.

3. When finished, click the *File* tab and then click the *Close* tab in the *Backstage* to close the *Welcome to Project* new project.
4. Click the *No* button when prompted to save changes to the *Welcome to Project* new project file.
5. Click the *Close* button (**X**) in the upper right corner of the *Backstage* to exit Project 2013, and then relaunch the software.
6. Examine the new *Start* page in the *Backstage*.
7. Click the *Open Other Projects* link at the bottom of the sidepane in the *Start* page to display the *Open* page in the *Backstage*.
8. Click the *Options* tab at the bottom of the sidepane in the *Backstage* to display the *Project Options* dialog.
9. In the *Start up options* section of the *General* page in the dialog, deselect the *Show the Start screen when this application starts* option, and then click the *OK* button.
10. Click the *Close* button (**X**) in the upper right corner of the Project 2013 application window to exit the software.

Changes to the Backstage

To access the new features of the *Backstage* in Project 2013, click the *Open Other Files* link in the sidepane on the left side of the *Start* page. The software displays the *Open* page of the *Backstage* by default, shown in Figure 1 - 15. New features in the *Backstage* include the *New* page, the *Open* page, the *Save As* page, the *Export* page, the *Account* page, plus changes to the options available in the *Project Options* dialog. I discuss each of these changes individually.

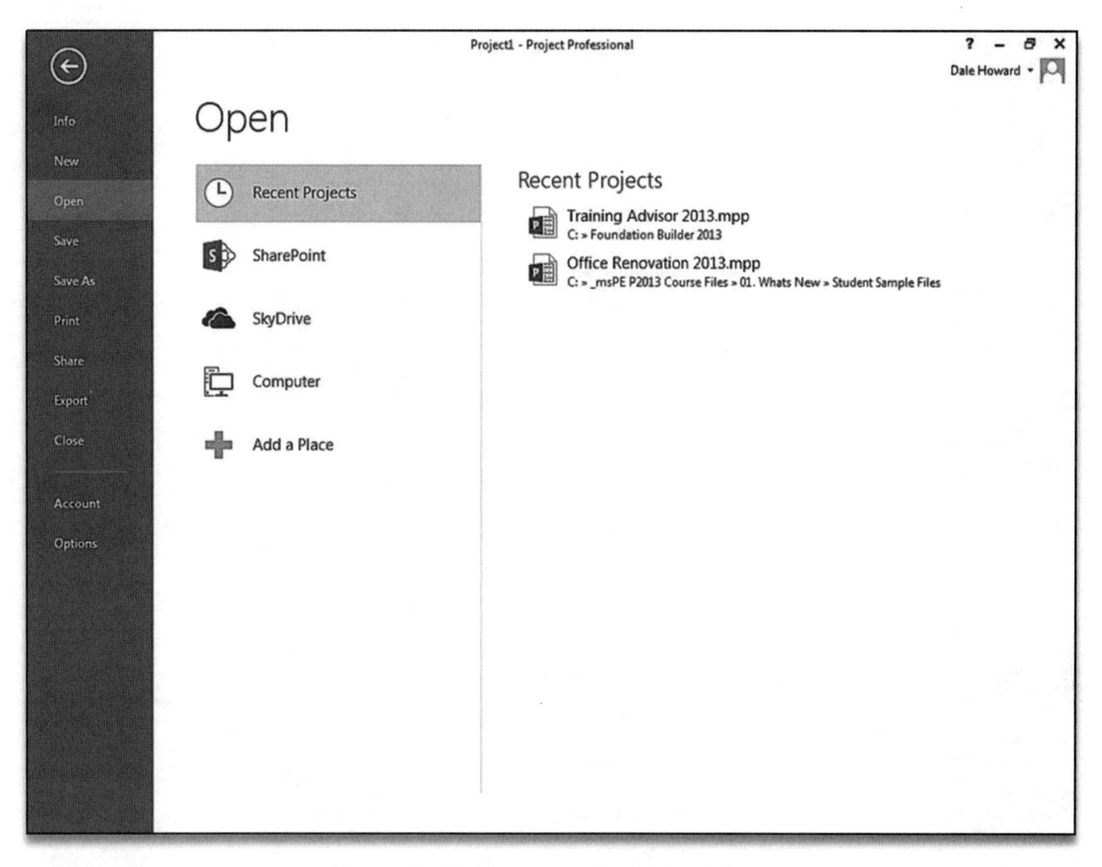

Figure 1 - 15: Open page in the Backstage

Introducing the New Page

Click the *New* tab in the *Backstage* and the software displays the *New* page shown in Figure 1 - 16. Notice that the *New* page appears very similar to the *Start* page shown previously in Figure 1 - 14.

In the main content area of the *New* page, notice that the first four buttons offer you four methods for creating a new project, including the *Blank Project, New from existing project, New from Excel workbook,* and *New from Share-Point Tasks List* buttons. Keep in mind that none of these four methods are new in Project 2013.

In addition, notice that the main content area also shows you a selection of additional project templates available in the *Office.com* web site. Notice finally that the top of the *New* page offers you a *Search for online templates* field in which you can search for other project templates in the *Office.com* web site, along with four links on the *Suggested searches* line to allow you to search for commonly used templates such as business or construction templates.

Information: To pin one of the *Office.com* templates so that Project 2013 always displays the template at the top of the *Start* page and the *New* page in the *Backstage*, float your mouse pointer over the template icon and then click the *Pin to list* button (pushpin button) in the lower-right corner of the icon. To unpin a pinned template, float your mouse pointer over the pinned template icon and then click the *Unpin from list* button (pushpin button) in the lower-right corner of the icon.

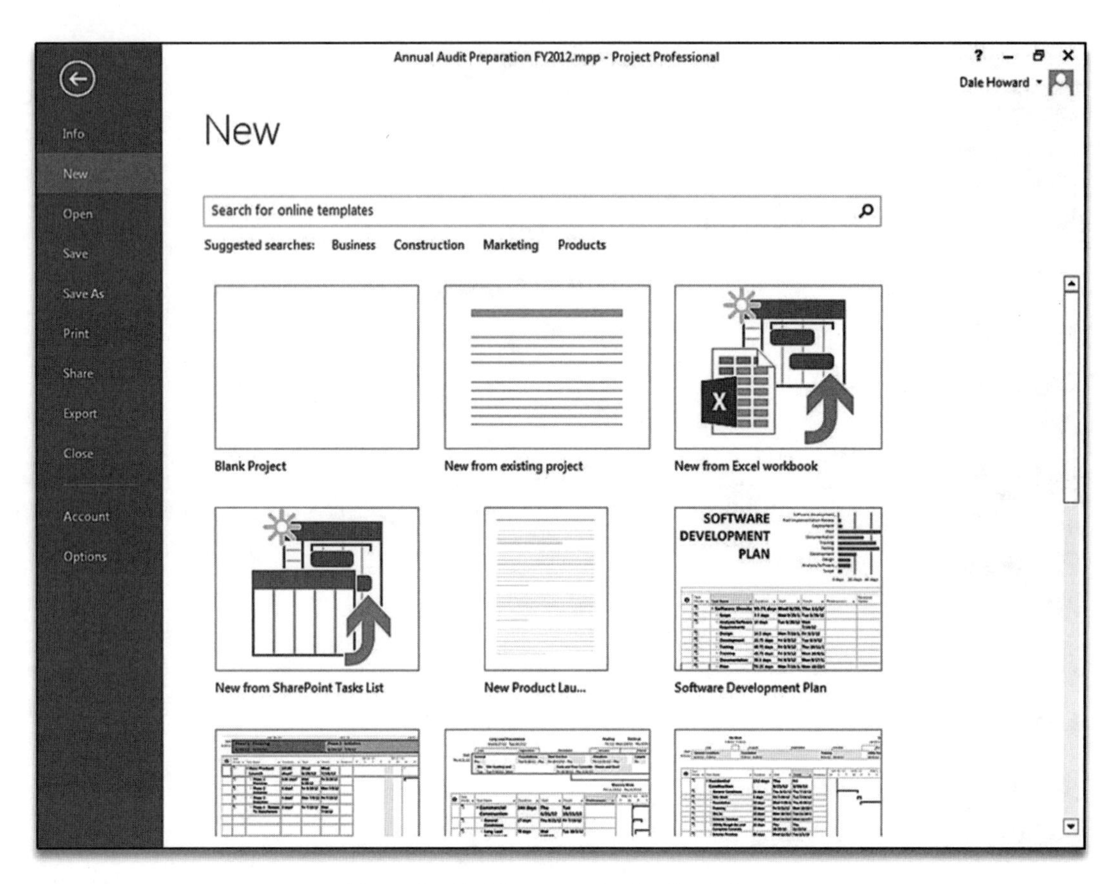

Figure 1 - 16: New page in the Backstage

If the *New* page does not display the type of template you want to use to create a new project, you can use the search features on this page to locate an appropriate template in the *Office.com* web site. To search for a project template, enter your search term in the *Search for online templates* field and then click the *Start searching* button at the right end of the field. Alternately, you can click one of the links in the *Suggested searches* line, such as the *Marketing* link. During the search process, Project 2013 briefly displays a *SEARCHING THOUNDS OF ONLINE TEMPLATES* message, and then reveals the search results on the *New* page as shown in Figure 1 - 17. Notice that using the search term *Products* yielded three project templates.

In addition, the *Category* sidepane on the right side of the page displays sub-categories of templates available in the *Office.com* web site. For example, notice that the *Office.com* web site includes ten *Analysis* templates. To further filter the list of templates, click one of the template categories shown in the *Category* list. Project 2013 shows you all of the templates that match the category you selected in the *Search for online templates* field or in the *Suggested searches* line, and the sub-category you selected in the *Category* list. After conducting a search for templates in the *Office.com* web site, you can return to the unfiltered *New* page by clicking the *Home* button to the left of the *Search for online templates* field.

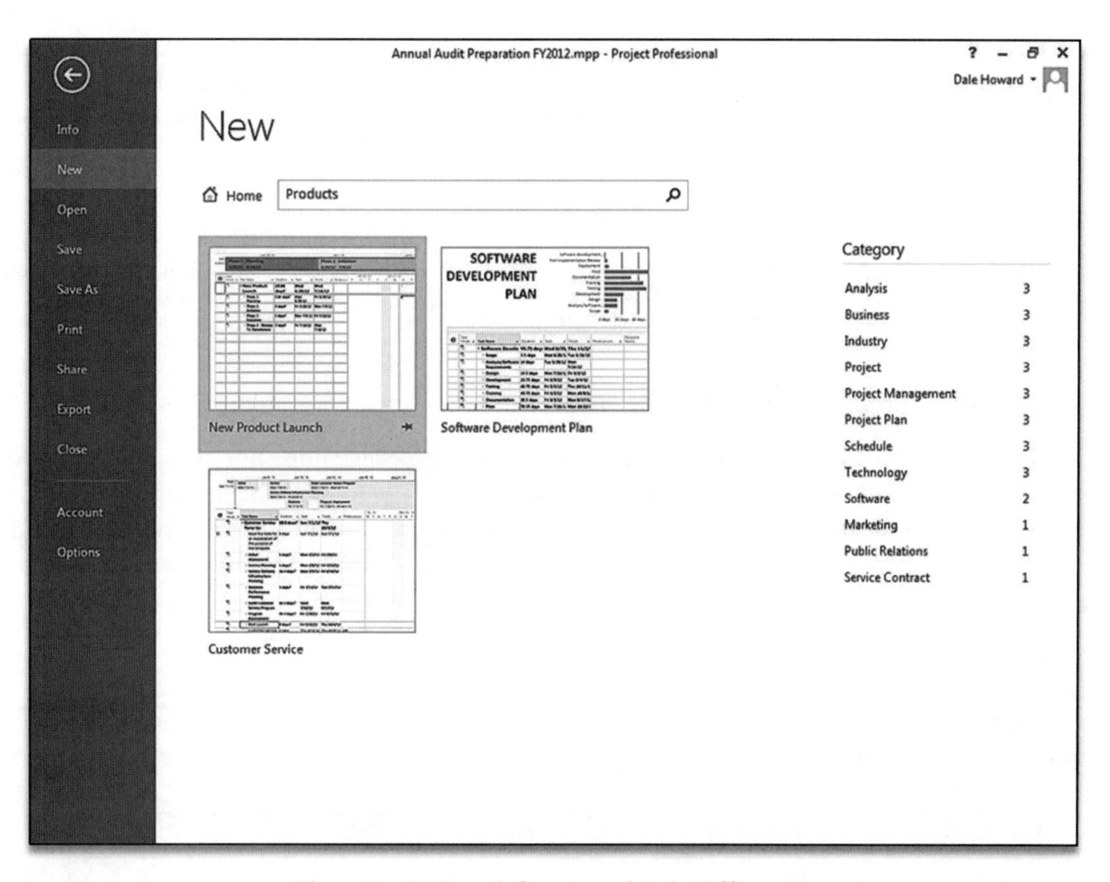

Figure 1 - 17: Search for a template in Office.com

To create a new project from one of the *Office.com* templates, click the name of the template you want to use. Project 2013 displays a preview dialog for the selected template similar to the one shown in Figure 1 - 18.

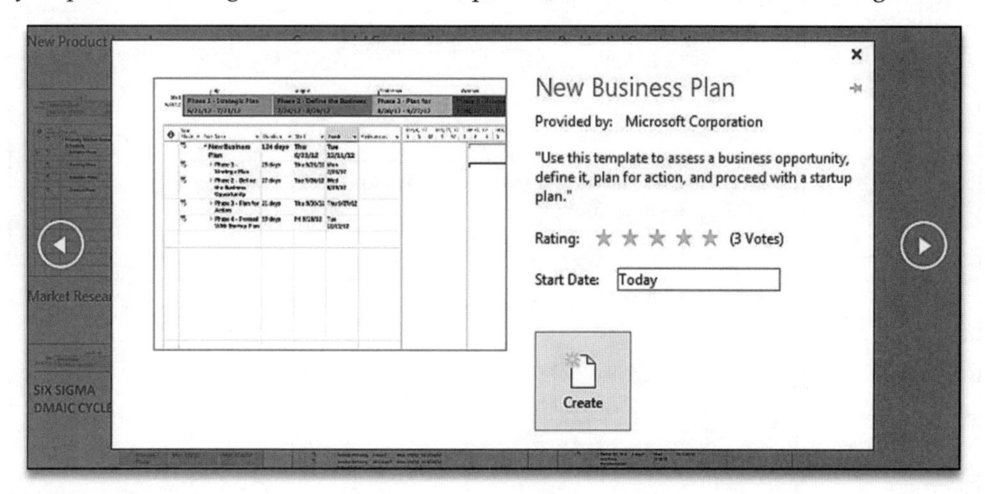

Figure 1 - 18: New Business Plan template preview dialog

Notice that the preview dialog shown in Figure 1 - 18 displays a preview of the *New Business Plan* template, which includes a pre-built *Timeline* report at the top of the template. The dialog also includes additional information about the template, including the name of template creator (in this case, Microsoft), a description of when and how to use the template, and the rating of the template by members of the user community. For some of the templates, the preview dialog also displays the download size of the template.

To create a new project from the selected template, enter the *Start* date of the project in the *Start Date* field and then click the *Create* button. Project 2013 downloads a copy of the template, saves it in the default *Templates* folder on your computer's hard drive, and then creates a new project from the selected template, ready for you to use to plan your project.

Information: To navigate in the preview dialog to the previous template or the next template on the *New* page, click the *Previous* or *Next* buttons (big white arrow buttons) on either side of the preview dialog.

Accessing Templates Stored in Your Templates Folder

Because of new functionality in Office 2013, the *New* page in the *Backstage* **does not** automatically allow you to create a new project from any template stored in your default *Templates* folder. This includes templates that you download from the *Office.com* web site and templates that you create personally and save in your *Templates* folder. If you want to create a new project from any template stored in your *Templates* folder, you must complete the following steps first:

1. Click the *File* tab and then click the *Options* button in the *Backstage*.

2. Click the *Save* tab in the *Project Options* dialog. The software displays the *Save* page of the *Project Options* dialog shown in Figure 1 - 19.

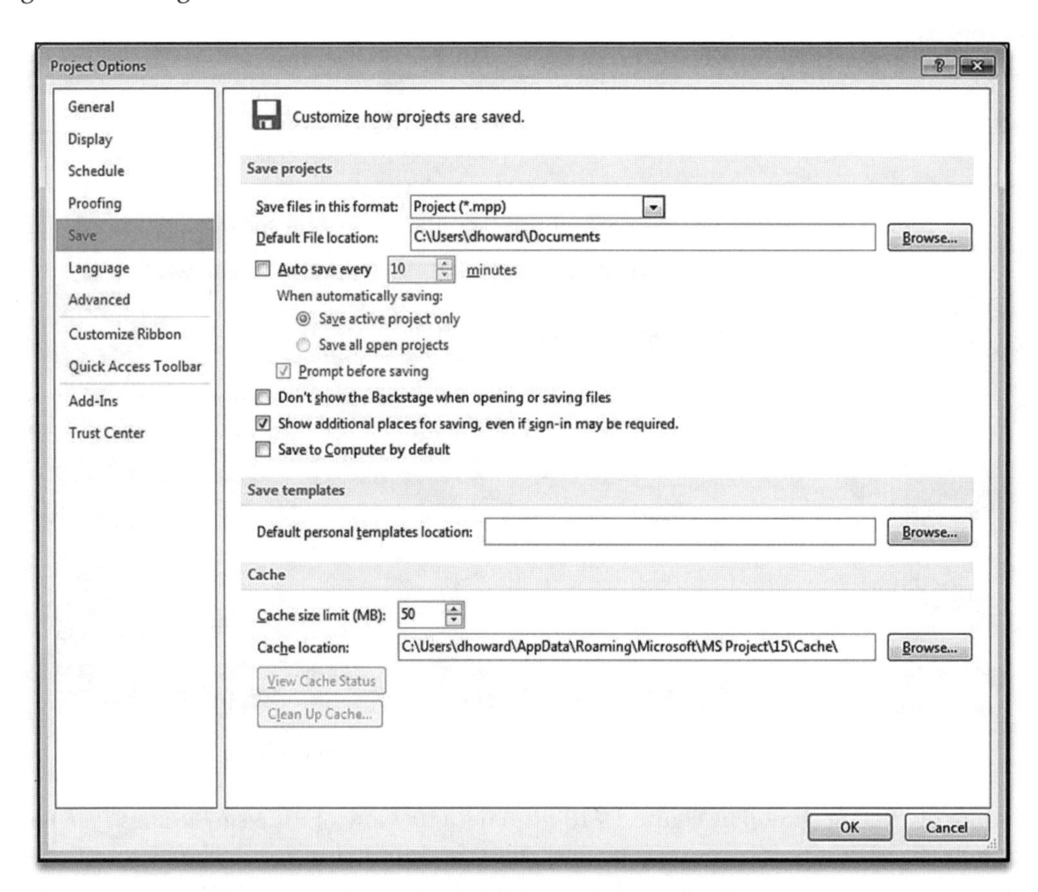

Figure 1 - 19: Project Options dialog, Save page

3. In the *Default personal templates location* field in the *Save templates* section of the dialog, manually enter the path for your default *Templates* folder based on the example below, or use the *Browse* button to navigate to your default *Templates* folder.

   C:\Users\YourUserID\AppData\Roaming\Microsoft\Templates

4. Click the *OK* button.

The next time you navigate to the *Start* page or to the *New* page in the *Backstage*, Project 2013 displays two new links in the upper left corner of the page: the *FEATURED* link and the *PERSONAL* link. When selected, the *FEATURED* link displays *Office.com* templates plus the four default template types. Click the *PERSONAL* link to view project templates stored in your default *Templates* folder, as shown in Figure 1 - 20. Notice that I have four templates available for use in my default *Templates* folder, all downloaded from the *Office.com* web site.

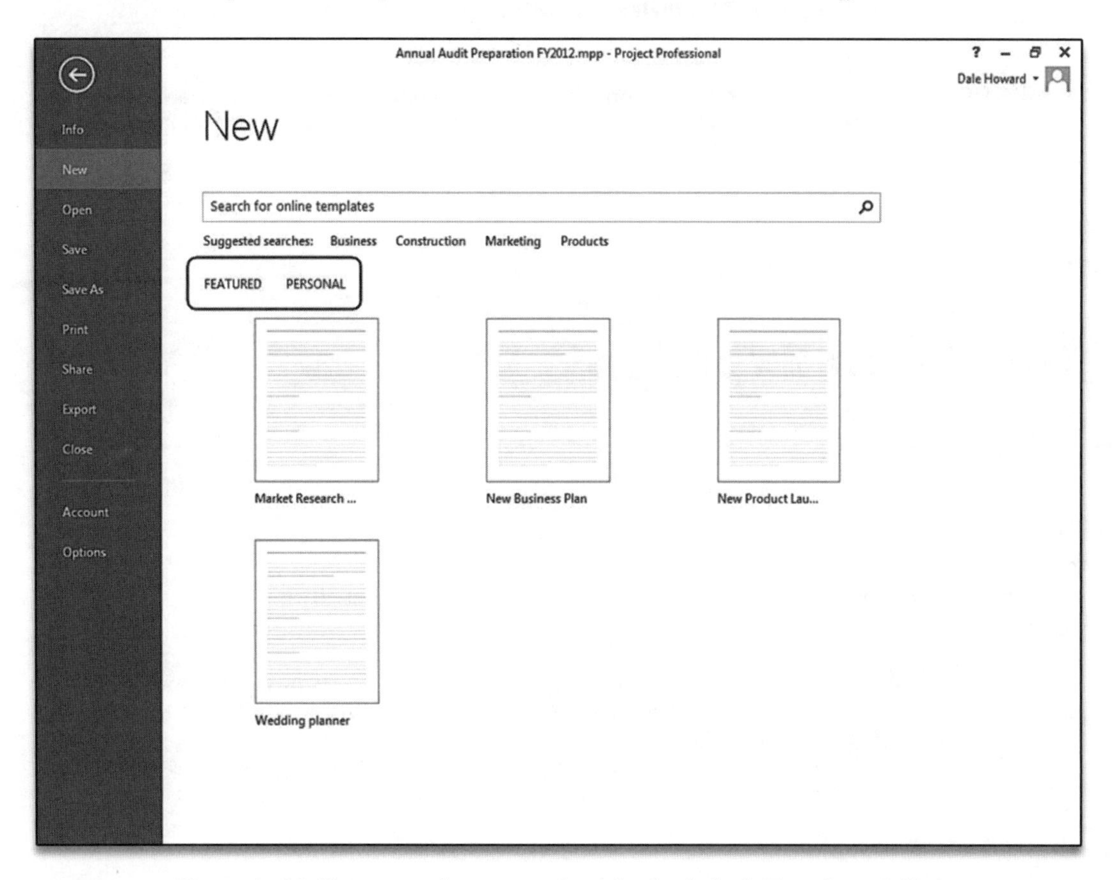

Figure 1 - 20: New page shows templates in the default Templates folder

Warning: If you want to use templates in the default *Templates* folder with any of your other Office 2013 applications, you must repeat the same process detailed above **in each of these applications individually**. There is currently no way to specify the default *Templates* folder for all of the Office 2013 applications simultaneously.

To create a new project from a template stored in your default *Templates* folder, click the *PERSONAL* link on the *New* page of the *Backstage* and then click the icon for the template you want to use. Project 2013 displays the dialog shown in Figure 1 - 21. In this dialog, enter a date in the *Start Date* field and then click the *Create* button. The software creates the new project as a copy of the template you selected.

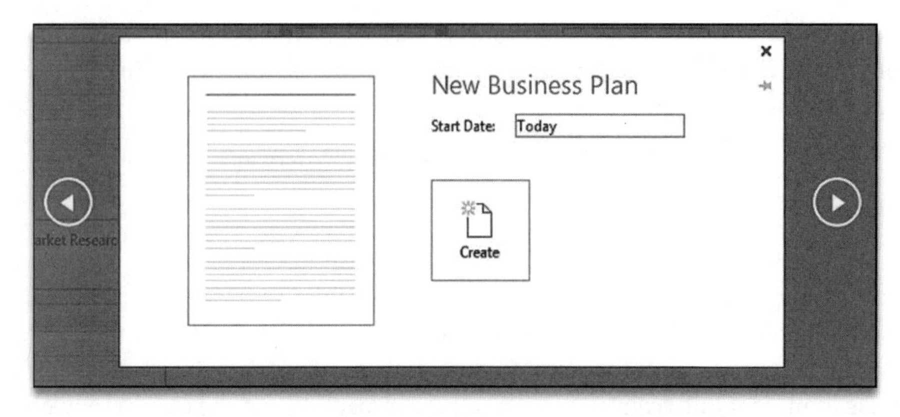

Figure 1 - 21: Preview dialog for a personal template

Information: To navigate in the dialog to the previous template or the next template on the *New* page, click the *Previous* or *Next* buttons (big white arrow buttons) on either side of the preview dialog.

Hands On Exercise

Exercise 1 - 2

Explore the new features on the *New* page in the *Backstage* in Project 2013.

Warning: Before you work this Hands On Exercise, confirm that you do have Internet access. You must have Internet access to view and download available templates from the Office.com web site.

1. Launch Project 2013.
2. Click the *File* tab and then click the *New* tab to display the *New* page in the *Backstage*.
3. Examine the list of project templates available from the *Office.com* web site.
4. In the *Search* section at the top of the page, click the *Marketing* link to search for marketing templates.
5. In the *Category* sidepane on the right side of the page, click the *Software* item to limit the search to software-related templates.
6. Click the *New Product Launch* template.
7. In the *Start Date* field in the *New Product Launch* dialog, enter a date **3 months in the future**, and then click the *Create* button.

8. Leave the new project open, click the *File* tab, and then click the *Options* tab in the *Backstage*.
9. In the *Project Options* dialog, click the *Save* tab to display the *Save* page of the dialog.
10. In the *Save Templates* section of dialog, enter the path of your default *Templates* folder in the following form (or click the *Browse* button and browse to the *Templates* folder):

C:\Users\YourUserID\AppData\Roaming\Microsoft\Templates

11. Click the *OK* button to close the *Project Options* dialog.
12. Click the *File* tab and then click the *New* tab again in the *Backstage*.
13. At the top of the *New* page, notice the new *FEATURED* and *PERSONAL* links.
14. Click the *PERSONAL* link to see your saved templates.
15. Click the *Back* button (big left-arrow button) in the upper left corner of the *Backstage* to return to the project you created in this exercise using the *New Product Launch* template.

Introducing the Save As Page

After creating a new project, you are ready to save the project by clicking either the *Save* tab or the *Save As* tab in the *Backstage*. In either case, Project 2013 displays the new *Save As* page shown in Figure 1 - 22. Using the features on this page, you can synchronize your project with a *Tasks* list in SharePoint, save your project file to a SkyDrive folder, or save your project files to a folder on your computer. I provide an in-depth discussion of the *Sync with SharePoint* feature in Module 02, *Using the Synch with SharePoint Tasks List Feature*.

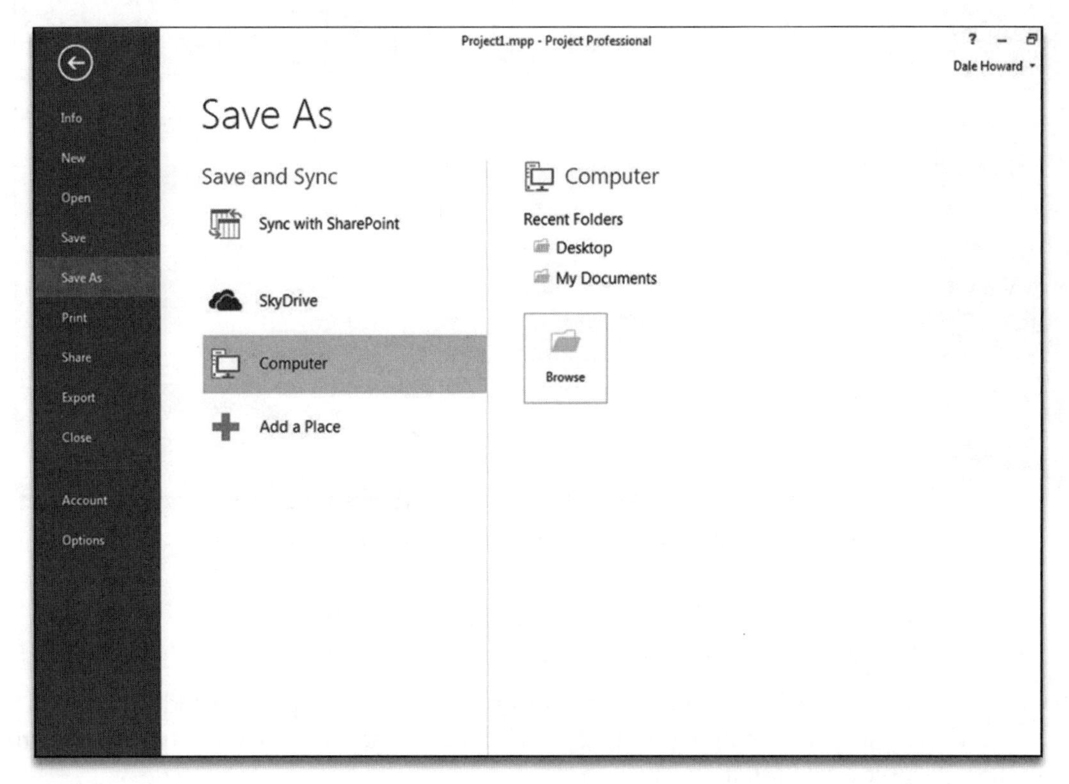

Figure 1 - 22: Save As page in the Backstage

Saving a Project File to a SkyDrive Folder

When you click the *SkyDrive* link on the *Save As* page, the software displays the *Save As* page with the *SkyDrive* options enabled, as shown in Figure 1 - 23. On this page you see a new feature that allows you to save your current project to a SkyDrive folder. SkyDrive is a cloud-based file storage system offered by Microsoft as a part of the Windows Live feature.

Before you can use the SkyDrive feature, however, you must have a valid Windows Live ID, and you must activate the SkyDrive file system by logging in to Windows Live through your web browser. If you do not have a Windows Live ID, click the *Learn more* link to learn about SkyDrive, or click the *Sign up* link to create a new Windows Live ID.

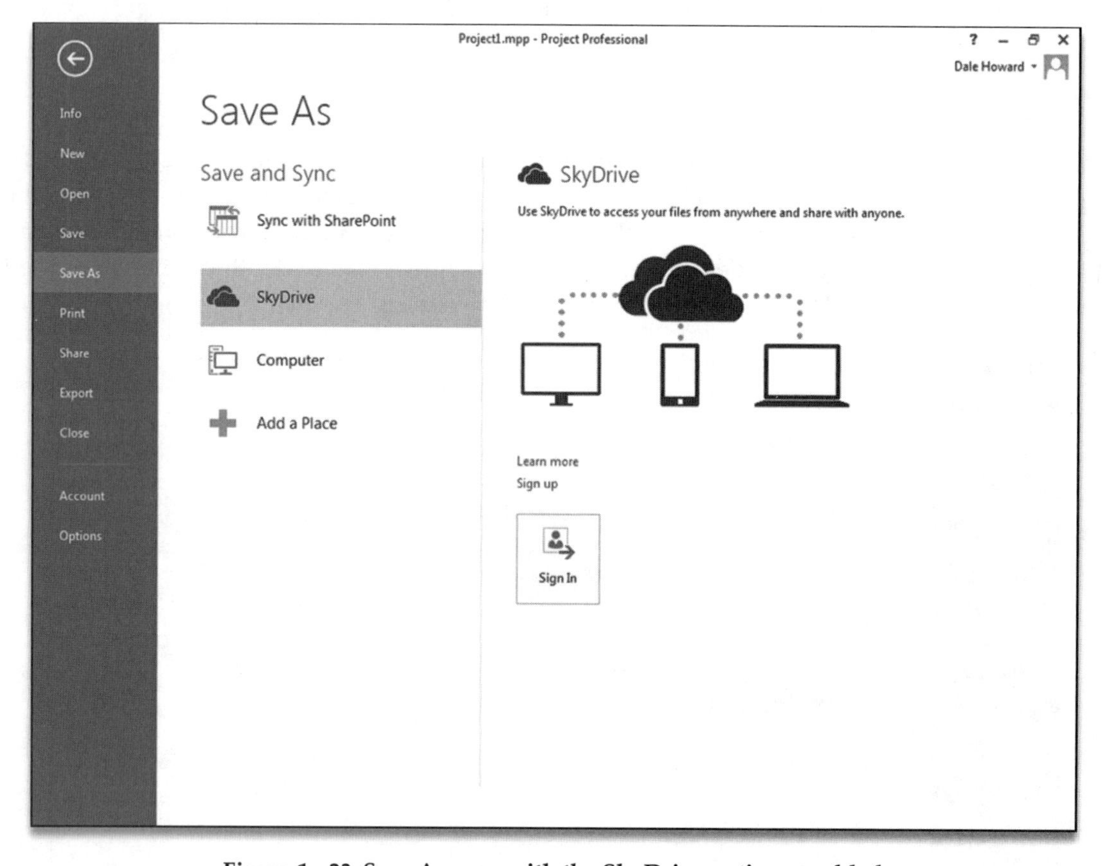

Figure 1 - 23: Save As page with the SkyDrive options enabled

Once you have a Windows Live ID, click the *Sign In* button on the *Save As* page of the *Backstage*. The software displays the *Add a service* dialog shown in Figure 1 - 24. Enter your Windows Live e-mail address in the *Add a service* dialog and then click the *Next* button.

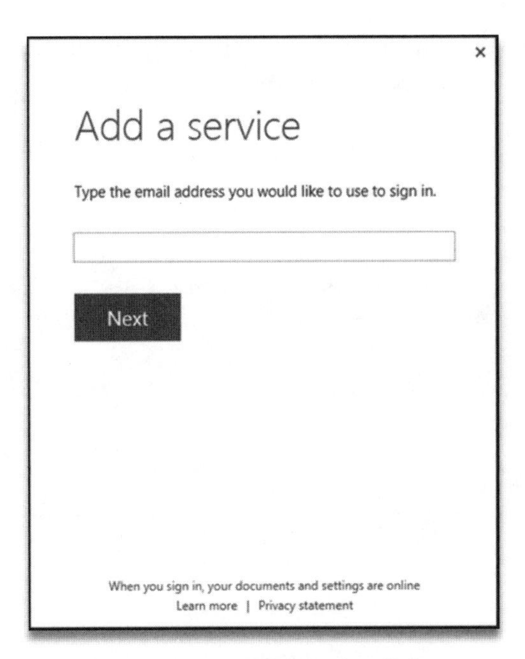

Figure 1 - 24: Add a service dialog

The software displays the *Sign in* dialog with your Windows Live e-mail address entered in the *Microsoft account* field shown in Figure 1 - 25. Enter your password in the *Password* field and then click the *Sign in* button.

Figure 1 - 25: Sign in dialog

After you successfully log in to Windows Live using your Windows Live ID, the software refreshes the *Save As* page to show your SkyDrive account, as shown in Figure 1 - 26. Notice that the software displays the name of your SkyDrive account at the top of the page.

Notice also that the *Dale Howard's SkyDrive* section of the page includes the *Get SkyDrive for Windows and take your files with you anywhere* section at the bottom. If you click the *Learn More* link, the software launches your Internet Explorer and navigates to the *Microsoft SkyDrive* web page. On this page, you can learn how to download and use the free SkyDrive desktop app for Windows from Microsoft. To hide the *Get SkyDrive for Windows and take your files with you anywhere* section in the *Save As* page, click the *Don't show this message again* (**X**) button at the right end of the section.

Information: When you log in to Windows Live to access a SkyDrive location in Project 2013, the system automatically logs you in to Windows Live in all of the other applications in the Office 2013 family of software tools.

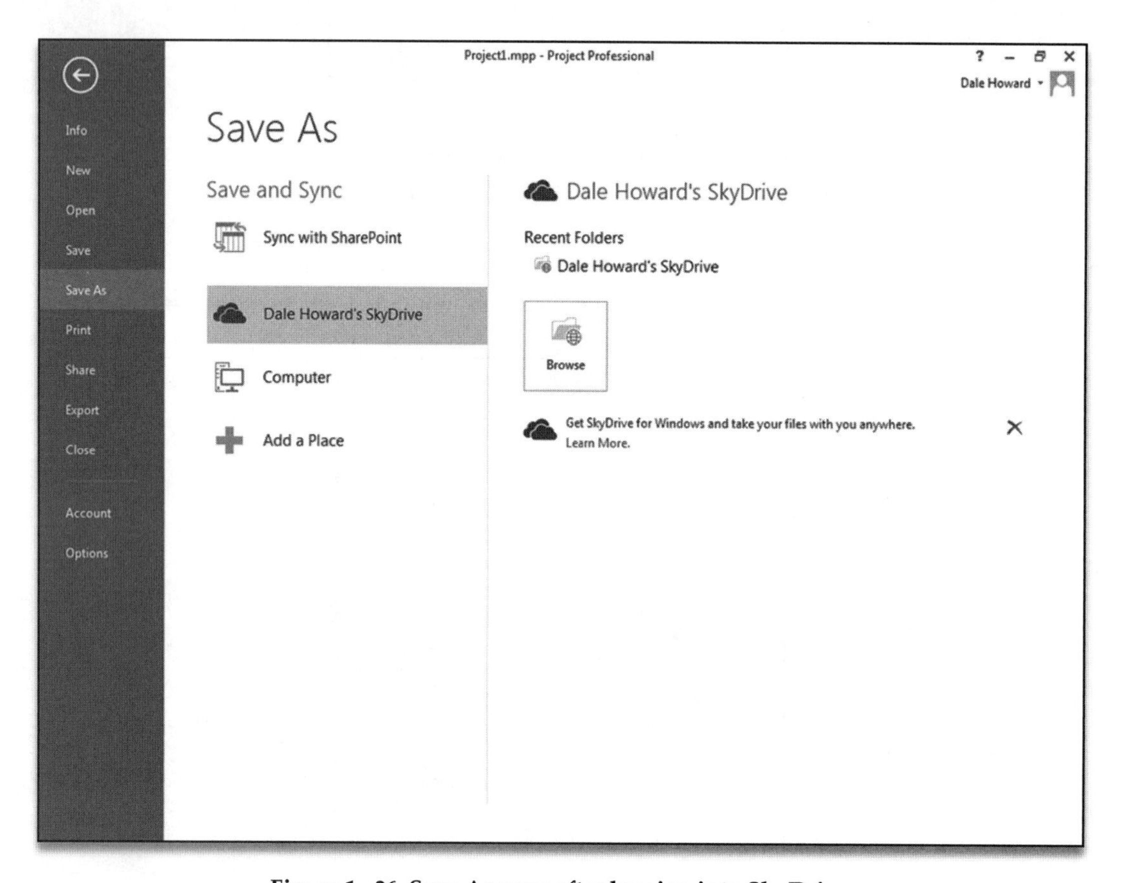

Figure 1 - 26: Save As page after logging into SkyDrive

To save the active file to a SkyDrive folder, select one of the folders shown in the *Recent Folders* section. If you click the *Browse* button, Project 2013 displays the *Save As* dialog and navigates to the top level of your SkyDrive location where you can see all of the available folders. For example, in the *Save As* dialog shown in Figure 1 - 27, notice that my SkyDrive location offers three folders: the *Documents, Pictures,* and *Public* folders. To create a subfolder in the *Documents* folder, click the *New folder* button near the top of the *Save As* dialog. Select a folder in your SkyDrive location, enter a name for the project in the *File Name* field, and then click *Save* button.

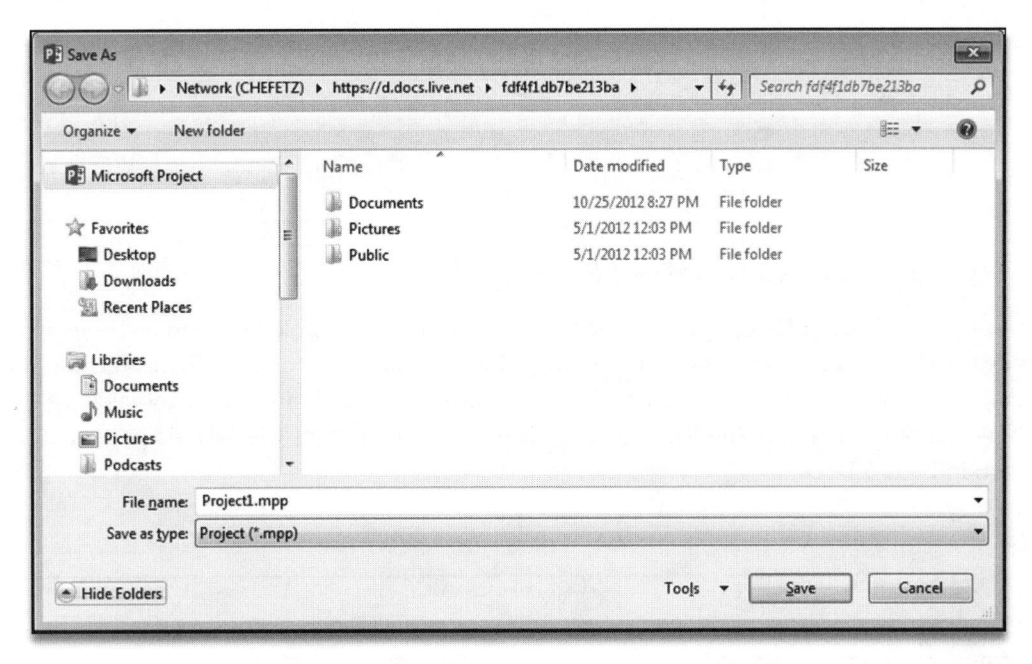

Figure 1 - 27: Save As dialog shows SkyDrive folders

Saving a Project File to Your Computer

To save the current project file to a folder on your computer, click the *Computer* link on the *Save As* page. The software displays a *Save As* page similar to the one shown previously in Figure 1 - 22. The *Computer* section of the *Save As* page shows the list of recently used folders in which you saved project files. Select one of the recently used folders or click the *Browse* button to display a *Save As* dialog similar to the one shown previously in Figure 1 - 27. In the *Save As* dialog, navigate to the folder where you want to save your project, enter a name for the project in the *File name* field, and then click the *Save* button.

By the way, the *Save As* dialog offers you a number of additional ways to navigate to a folder and to save an existing project, including each of the following:

- Click one of the folders shown in the "Breadcrumb" bar at the top of the dialog.
- Click the *Previous Locations* pick list button at the right end of the "Breadcrumb" bar.
- Enter a search term in the *Search* field in the upper right corner of the dialog.
- Click the *New Folder* button at the top of the dialog and then create a new folder.
- Select a folder in either the *Favorites* list or the *Libraries* list on the left side of the dialog.
- Select a computer drive and folder in the *Computer* list on the left side of the dialog.
- Click the *Save as type* pick list at the bottom of the dialog, and choose an alternate file type to save, such as an a file.
- Click the *Tools* pick list button at the bottom of the dialog and select the *Map Network Drive* option to map a network drive and assign it a drive letter.

Information: After you save the project initially, you can click the *Save* button to save the latest changes to the project.

Saving a Project to an Office 365 SharePoint Folder

Another new feature on the *Save As* page in Project 2013 allows you to save your project files in an Office 365 SharePoint folder. To use this feature, however, you must already have an existing Office 365 SharePoint account. If you have an account, you can save your project in an Office 365 SharePoint folder by clicking the *Add a Place* option in the *Save and Sync* section of the *Save As* page. The software updates the *Save As* page with an *Add a Place* section, as shown in Figure 1 - 28.

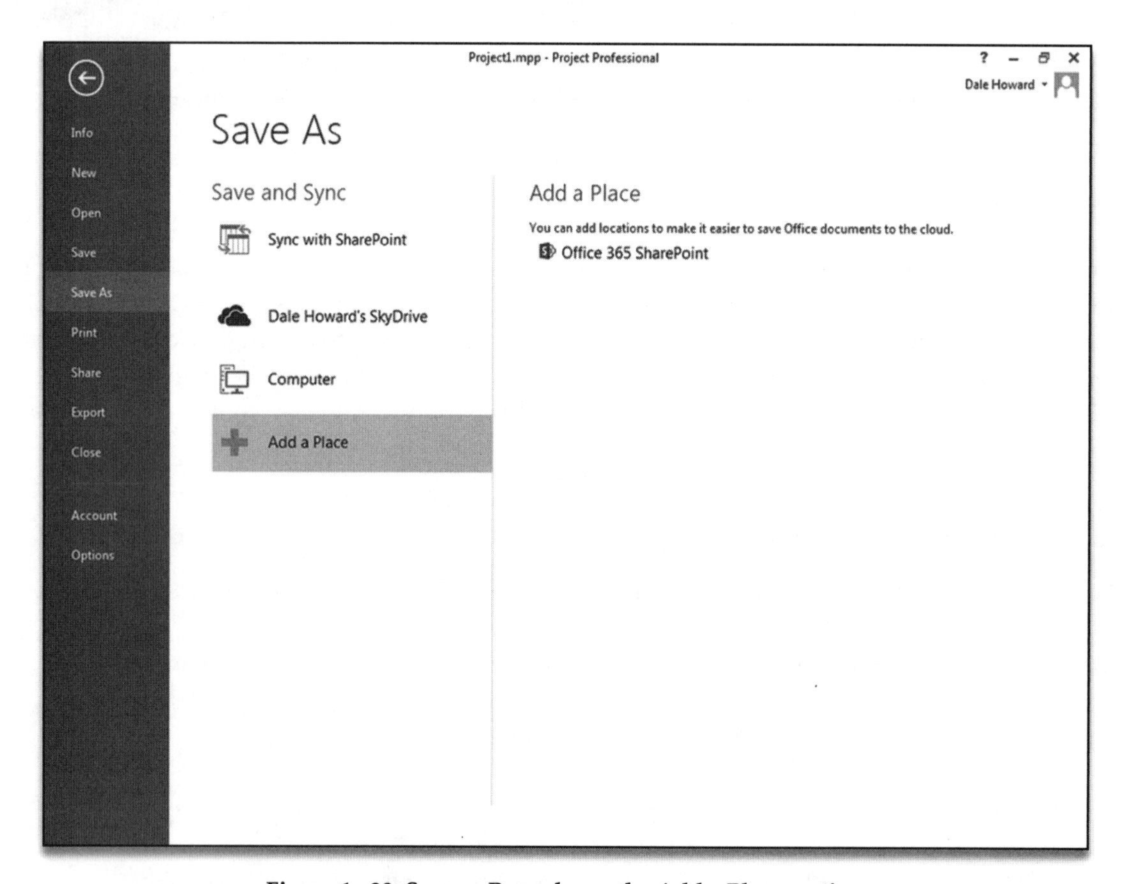

Figure 1 - 28: Save as Page shows the Add a Place section

If you click the *Office 365 SharePoint* link, Project 2013 displays the *Add a service* dialog shown previously in Figure 1 - 24. Enter your Office 365 SharePoint e-mail address in the *Add a service* dialog and then click the *Next* button. The software displays the *Sign in* dialog with your Office 365 SharePoint e-mail address entered in the *User ID* field, as shown in Figure 1 - 29. Enter your password in the *Password* field, leave the *Keep me signed in* option selected, and then click the *Sign in* button.

Figure 1 - 29: Sign in dialog

After you successfully log in to Office 365 SharePoint, the software refreshes the *Save As* page as shown in Figure 1 - 30. Notice that Project 2013 displays the name of the Office 365 SharePoint location at the top of the page and shows a new Team Site in the *Recent Folders* list.

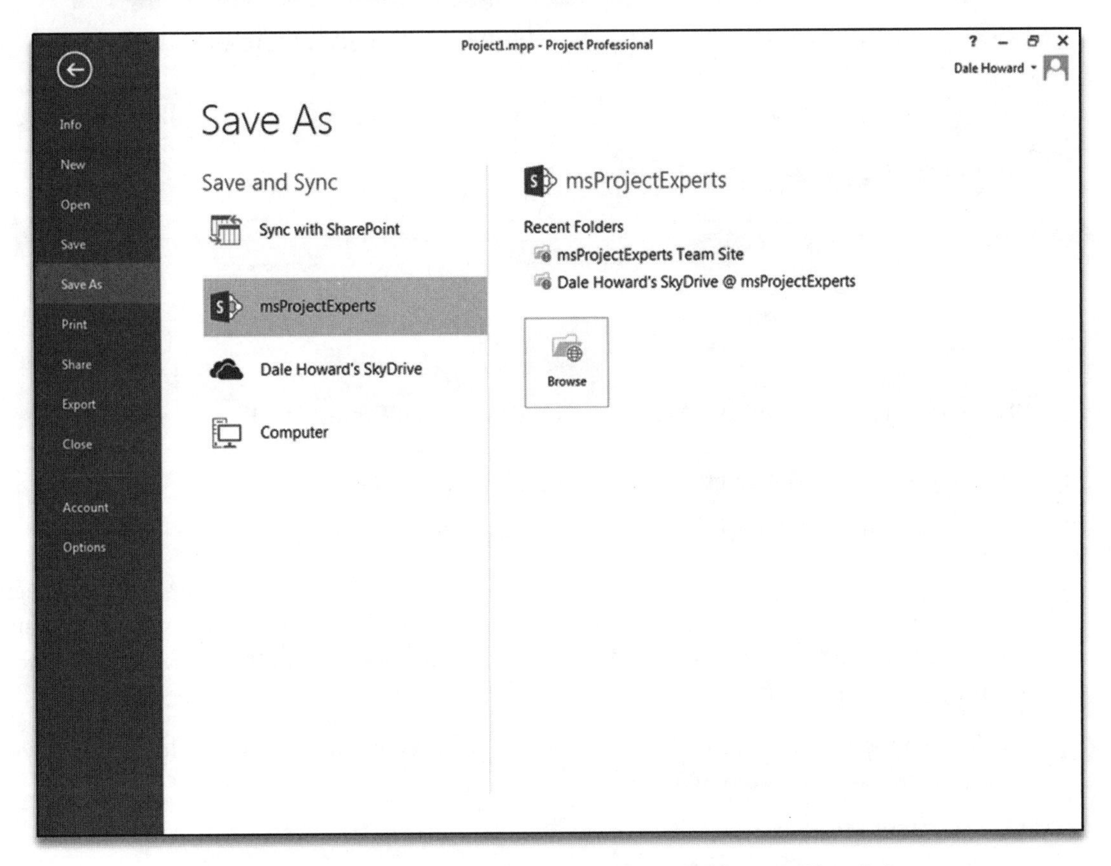

Figure 1 - 30: Save As page after logging into Office 365 SharePoint

To save the current project in the Office 365 SharePoint location, click the *Team Site* link in the *Recent Folders* section or click the *Browse* button. In the *Save As* dialog shown in Figure 1 - 31, double-click the *Documents* folder or navigate to the folder where you want to save your project, enter a name for your project, and then click the *Save* button.

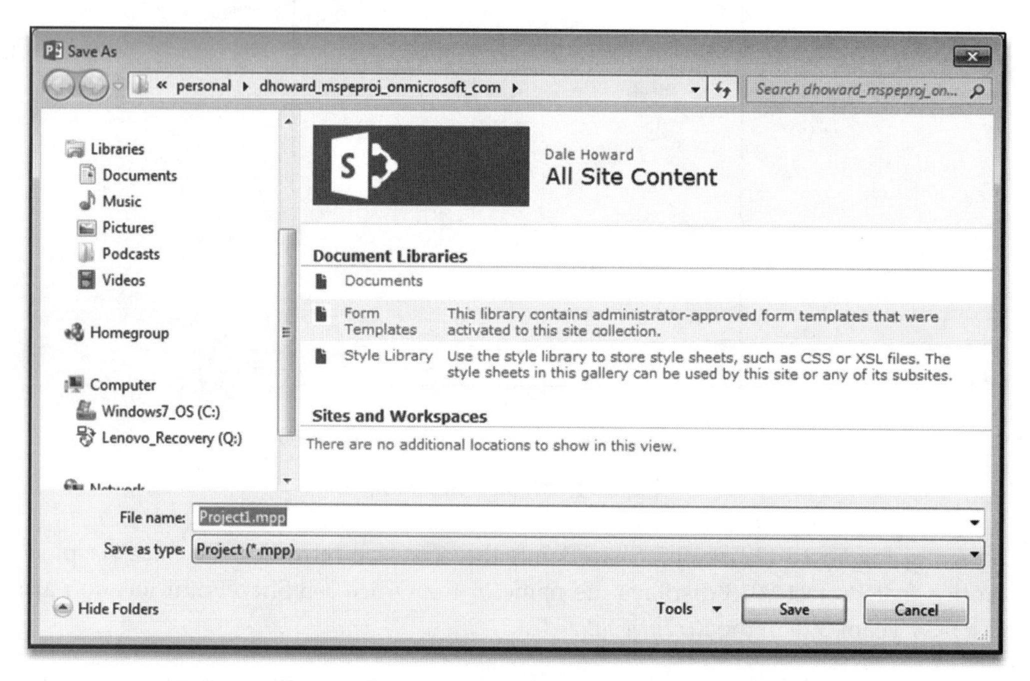

Figure 1 - 31 : Save As dialog shows Office 365 SharePoint folders

Hands On Exercise

Exercise 1 - 3

Explore the new features on the *Save As* page in the *Backstage* in Project 2013.

1. Click the *File* tab and then click the *Save As* tab in the *Backstage*.
2. Notice the new *SkyDrive* and *Add a Place* items on the *Save As* page.
3. If you have an existing Windows Live SkyDrive account, click the *SkyDrive* item, and then click the *Sign In* button. Enter your Windows Live e-mail address in the *Add a service* dialog and then click the *Next* button. In the *Sign in* dialog, enter your password in the *Password* field and then click the *Sign in* button.
4. Click the updated *SkyDrive* item on the *Save As* page to see the available folders where you can save your project in your SkyDrive location.
5. Click the *Add a Place* item.
6. If you have an existing Office 365 SharePoint account, click the *Office 365 SharePoint* link. Enter your Office 365 SharePoint e-mail address in the *Add a service* dialog and then click the *Next* but-

ton. In the *Sign in* dialog, enter your password in the *Password* field, leave the *Keep me signed in* option selected, and then click the *Sign in* button.

7. Click the updated *Office 365* item on the *Save As* page to see the available folders where you can save your project in your Office 365 SharePoint location.
8. Click the *Computer* item.
9. In the *Computer* section in the middle of the *Save As* page, click the *My Documents* item.
10. In the *Save As* dialog, enter the name **Killer Software Application Product Launch** in the *Field name* field, and then click the *Save* button.
11. Click the *File* tab and then click the *Close* tab in the *Backstage* to close your project file.
12. Notice how Project 2013 returns to the *New* page in the *Backstage* automatically.

Introducing the Open Page

Click the *Open* tab to see the *Open* page in the *Backstage*. If you previously signed in to a SkyDrive location or an Office 365 SharePoint location, Project 2013 displays an *Open* page similar to the one shown in Figure 1 - 32. Notice in my example that the *Open* page contains four links: the *Recent Projects* link, the *msProjectExperts* link for the Office 365 SharePoint location, the *Dale Howard's SkyDrive* link for the Windows Live SkyDrive location, and the *Computer* link. If you did not log in to a SkyDrive location or an Office 365 SharePoint location, the *Open* page omits these two links, and shows only the *Recent Projects, Computer,* and *Add a Place* links instead.

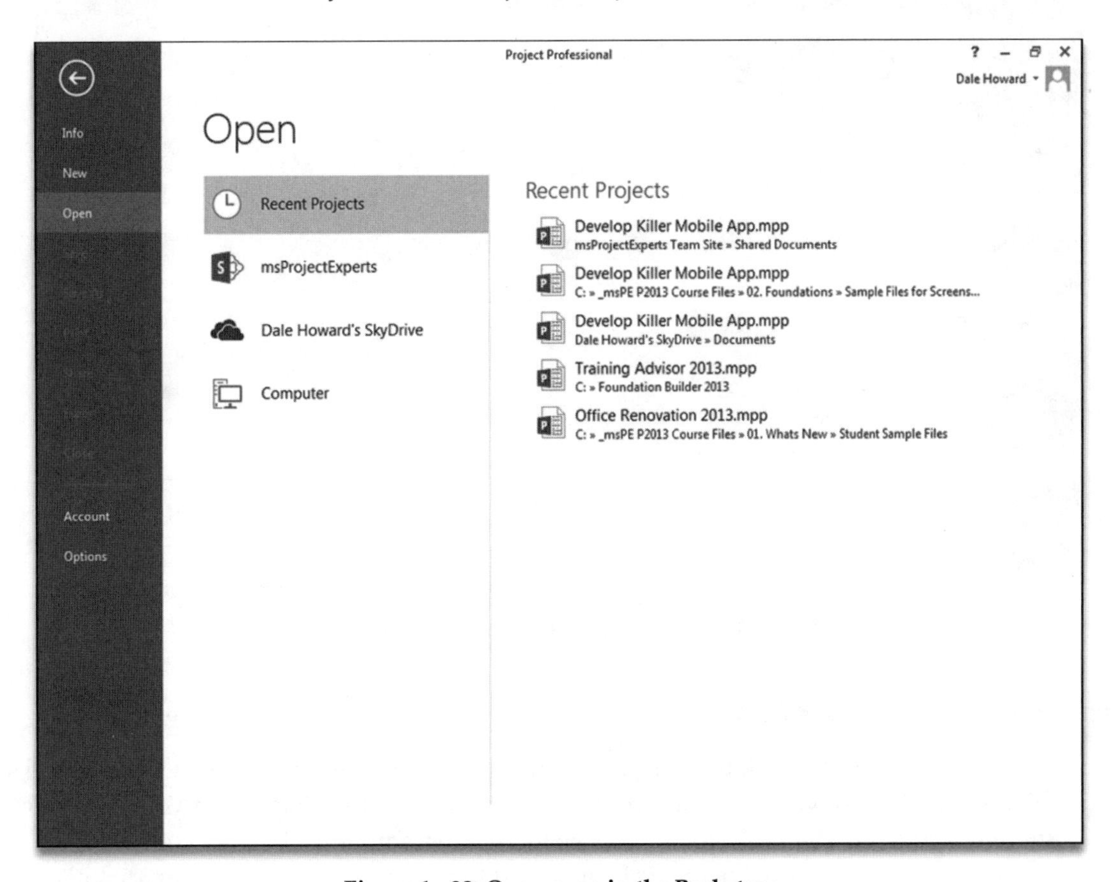

Figure 1 - 32: Open page in the Backstage

By default, the *Open* page selects the *Recent Projects* item in the list on the left side of the page, and displays the recently opened projects in the *Recent Projects* list in the middle of the page. To open a recently opened project, click the name of the project in the *Recent Projects* list. To pin any recently opened project to the top of the *Recent Projects* list, float your mouse pointer over the file, and then click the *Pin this document to the Recent Projects list* button (pushpin button) at the right end of the file name. To unpin a pinned document, float your mouse pointer over the file, and then click the *Unpin this document from the Recent Projects list* button (pushpin button) at the right end of the file name.

Opening a Project File from a SkyDrive or Office 365 SharePoint Location

To open a file from a SkyDrive location or an Office 365 SharePoint location, click the name of the location in the list on the left side of the *Open* page. Project 2013 updates the *Open* page similar to the one shown in Figure 1 - 33. Notice that the *Recent Folders* list in the middle of the page shows a list of recently used folders in the selected location. To open a project file, click the name of the recently used folder or click the *Browse* button, and then open the project file in the *Open* dialog.

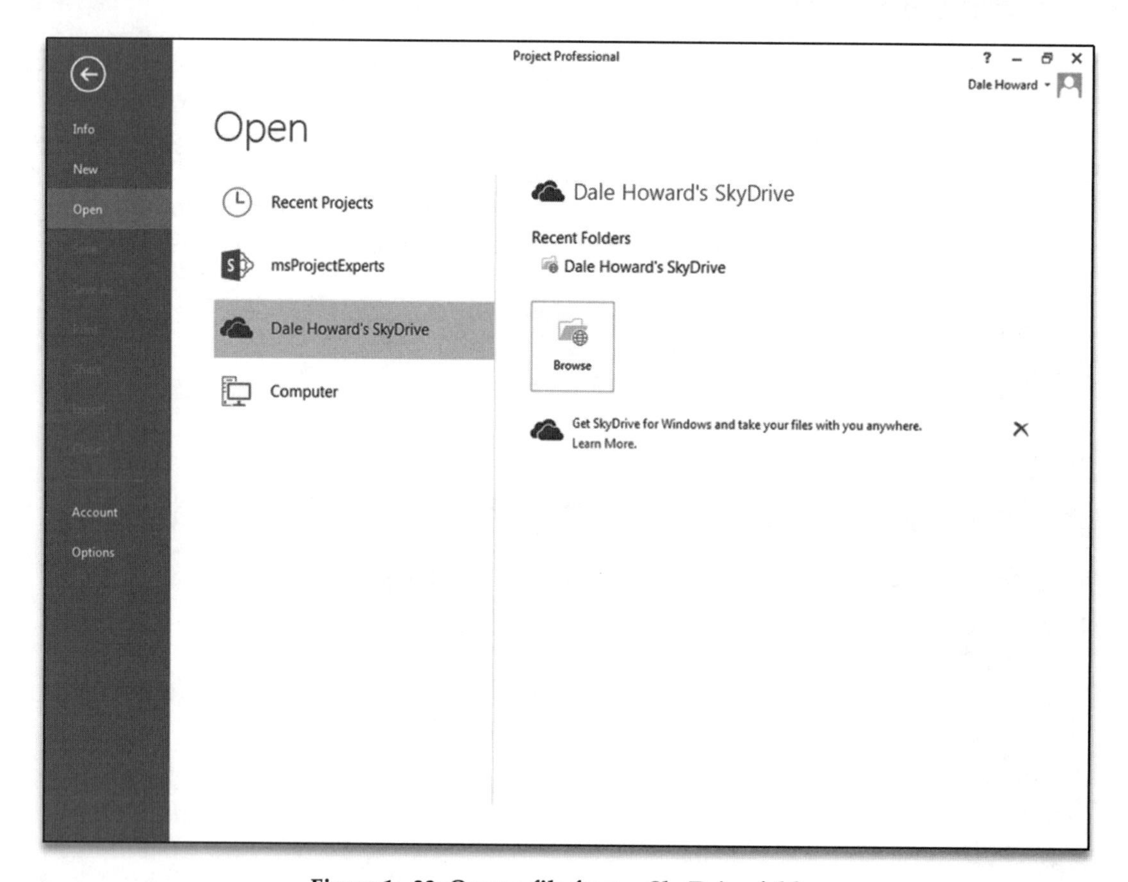

Figure 1 - 33: Open a file from a SkyDrive folder

Opening a Project File from Your Computer

To open a file from your computer, click the *Computer* option. The software updates the *Open* page as shown in Figure 1 - 34. Notice that the *Recent Folders* list shows a list of recently used folders on your computer, and includes the *Documents* folder and the *Desktop* folder as well. To open a project file from your computer, click the name of the recently used folder or click the *Browse* button, and then open the file in the *Open* dialog.

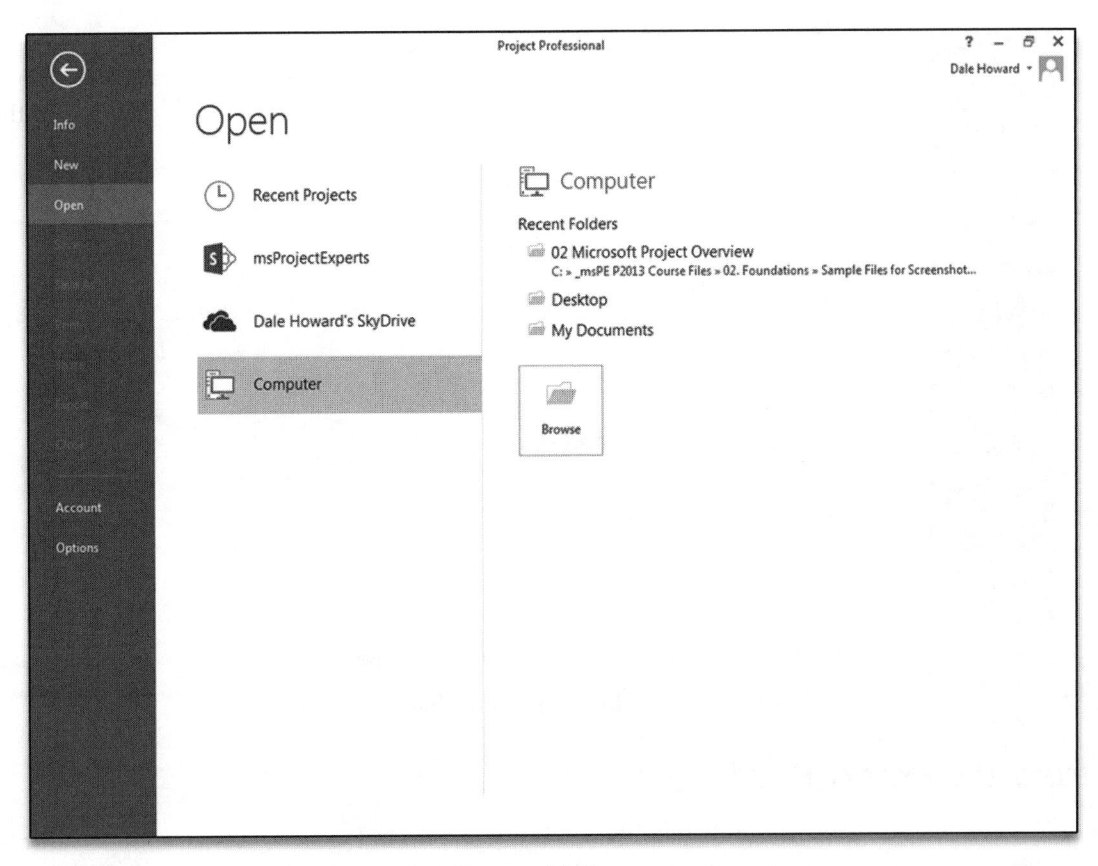

Figure 1 - 34: Open a file from your computer

Introducing the Share Page

Open any project file and then click the *Share* tab to see the new *Share* page in the *Backstage* shown in Figure 1 - 35. The *Share* page in Project 2013 replaces the *Save & Send* page found previously in the 2010 version of the software. The *Share* page offers only two options: the *Sync with SharePoint* and *Email* options.

Click the *Sync with SharePoint* option and then click the *Go to Save As* button in the *Sync with SharePoint Tasks List* section on the right side of the page. The software displays the *Save As* page in the *Backstage* and selects the *Sync with SharePoint* option, which you can synchronize your project file with a *Tasks* list in SharePoint.

Click the *Email* option and then click the *Send as Attachment* button in the *Email* section of the page. Project 2013 creates a new e-mail message in your default e-mail application, and then adds a copy of the active project as an attachment to the e-mail message.

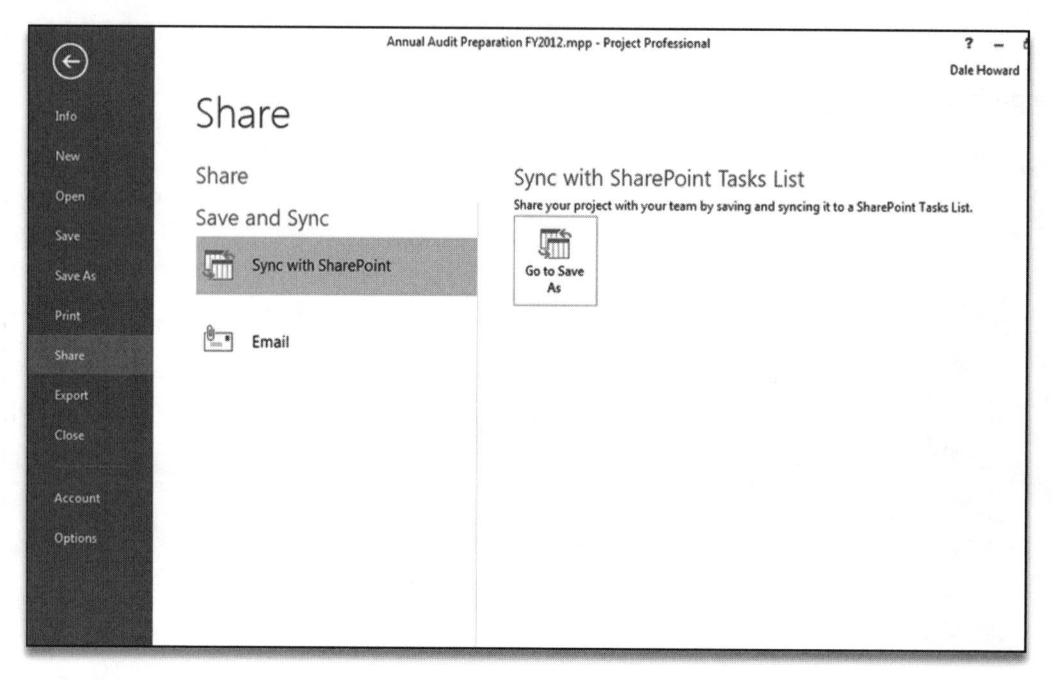

Figure 1 - 35: Share page in the Backstage

Introducing the Export Page

Click the *Export* tab to see the new *Export* page in the *Backstage* shown in Figure 1 - 36. Use the *Export* page to export a project file to a PDF file or XPS file, or to export the project file to another file format.

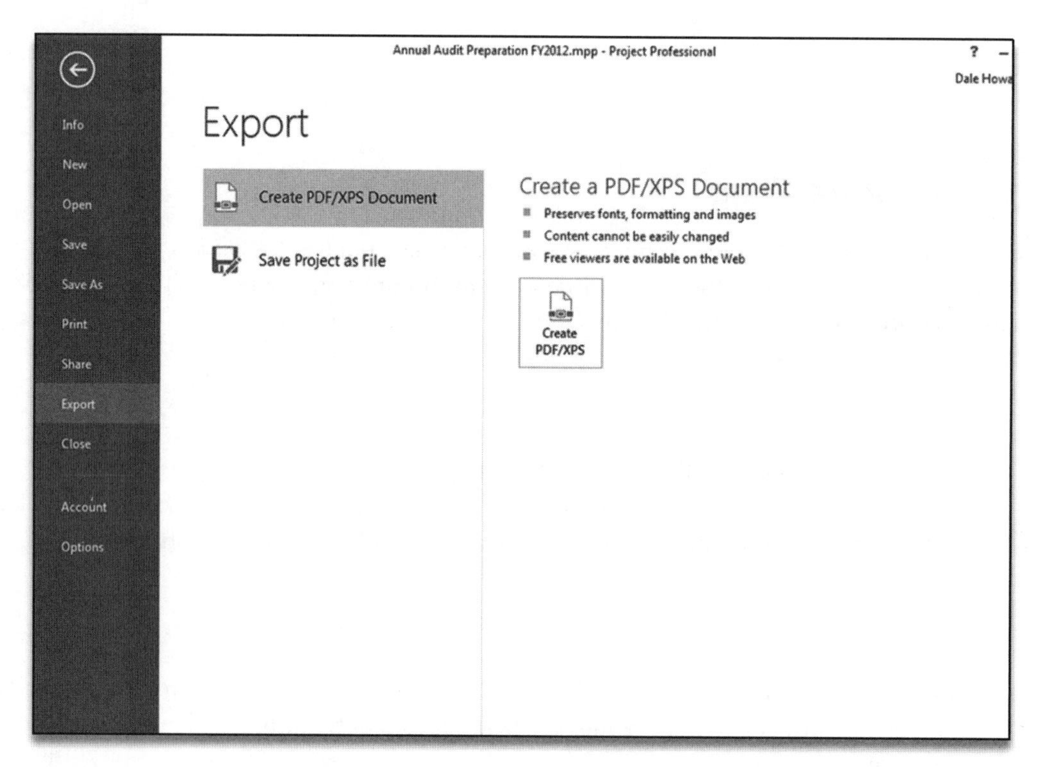

Figure 1 - 36: Export page in the Backstage

Exporting a Project File to a PDF or XPS Document

To export a project file to a PDF file, select the *Create PDF/XPS Document* option on the *Export* page and then click the *Create PDF/XPS* button. Project 2013 displays the *Browse* dialog shown in Figure 1 - 37. Notice that the software selects the *PDF Files (*.pdf)* format by default on the *Save as type* pick list in the *Browse* dialog. In the *Browse* dialog, navigate to the folder where you want to export the project file. Optionally, you may also click the *Save as type* pick list and select the *XPS Files (*.xps)* format, if needed. Click the *OK* button to export the project file to a PDF or XPS document.

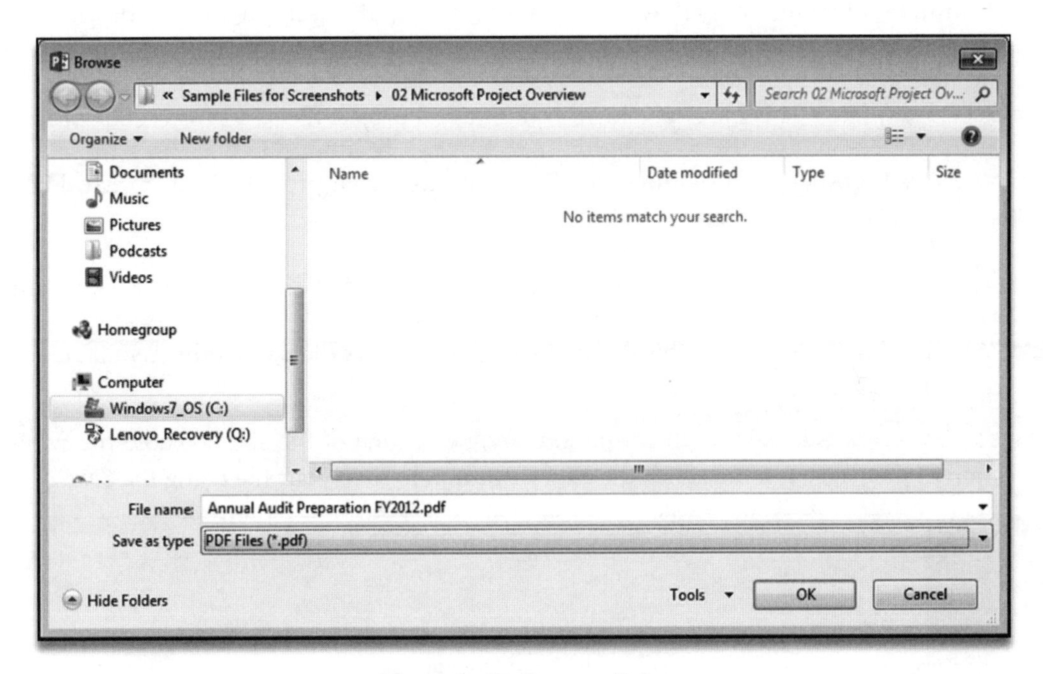

Figure 1 - 37: Browse dialog

Project 2013 displays the *Document Export Options* dialog shown in Figure 1 - 38. Select your desired options for exporting the project file to a PDF for XPS document and then click the *OK* button.

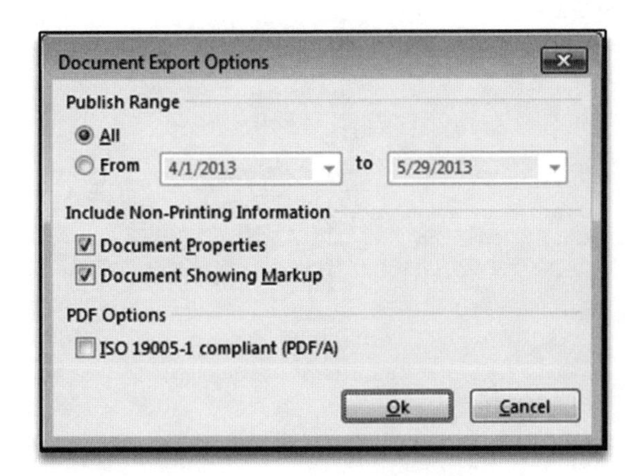

Figure 1 - 38: Document Export Options dialog

Exporting a Project File to an Alternate File Type

When you click the *Save Project as File* option in the *Export* page in the *Backstage*, Project 2013 updates the page with *Save Project as File* section shown in Figure 1 - 39. Using the options in the *Save Project as File* section of the *Export* page, you can immediately export your project file to the following file types:

- **Project** – This is the default Project 2013 file type which is also compatible with Project 2010.
- **Project 2007 Project** – This file type provides backwards compatibility with Project 2007.
- **Project Template** – This file type allows you to save a project file as a Project 2013 project template which is also compatible with Project 2010.
- **Project 2007 Template** – This file type allows you to save a project file as a Project 2007 project template.
- **Microsoft Excel Workbook** – This file type allows you to save a project file as an Excel 2013 workbook which is also compatible with Excel 2007 and 2010.
- **XML Format** – Select this file type to save your project file as an Extensible Markup Language (XML) file.
- **Save as Another File type** – Select this option to save the project file using other available file types, such as a Text file, for example.

By default, the software selects the *Project* file type initially. Select one of the six available file types in the *Save Project as File* section of the page, and then click the *Save As* button to save your file using the *Save As* dialog.

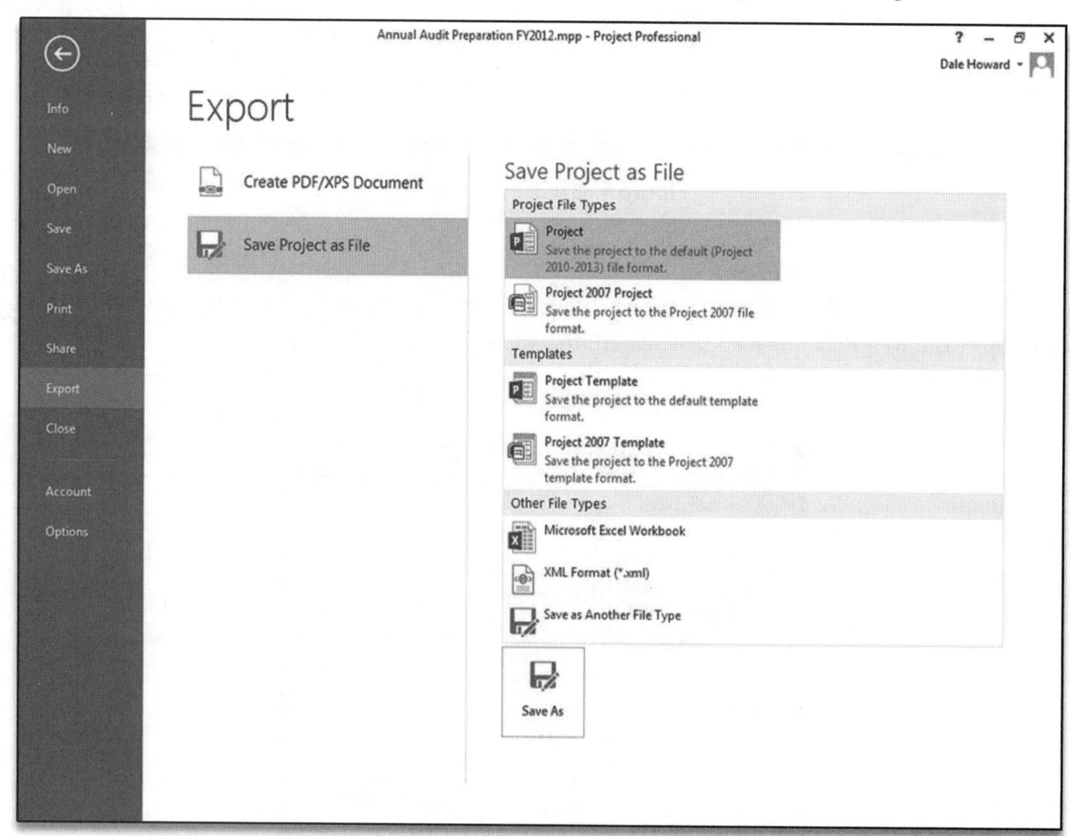

Figure 1 - 39: Export page, Save Project as File selected

In addition to the default list of file types, you can also select the *Save as Another File Type* option and then click the *Save As* button to display the *Save As* dialog. In this dialog, click the *Save as type* pick list where you can select one of these additional file types:

- **Project 2000-2003 Project** – This file type provides backwards compatibility with the 2000, 2002, and 2003 versions of Project.
- **PDF File** – Select this file type to save a project file as a Portable Document Format (PDF) file. Using the PDF file type allows you to share project information with users who do not have any version of Project installed on their workstations.
- **XPS File** – Select this file type to save a project file as an XML Paper Specification file. Using the XPS file type allows you to share project information with users who do not have any version of Project installed on their workstations.
- **Excel Binary Workbook** – Select this file type to save the project file as a Macro-Enabled Excel workbook file stored in Binary format rather than saving it in the XLSX format. Use this file format to save a very large Project file quickly and efficiently. This file type is compatible with Excel 2013, 2010, and 2007.
- **Excel 97-2003 Workbook** – Select this file type to save a project file as an Excel workbook using a format that allows Excel 97 through Excel 2003 to open the workbook directly without using a converter.
- **Text File** – Select this file type to save your project file as a Tab Delimited text file.
- **CSV File** – Select this file type to save your project file as a Comma Delimited text file.

Select one of the file types on the *Save as type* pick list and then click the *Save* button. Because there is no new behavior in saving files to an alternate file type in Project 2013, I do not discuss this topic any further.

Information: You can also save a project file using an alternate file type by clicking the *File* tab and then clicking the *Save As* tab in the *Backstage*. On the *Save As* page, click the *Computer* option and then click the *Browse* button. In the *Save As* dialog, click the *Save as type* pick list, select an alternate file type, and then click the *Save* button.

Hands On Exercise

Exercise 1 - 4

Explore the new features on the *Open, Share,* and *Export* pages in the *Backstage* in Project 2013.

1. Click the *Open* tab in the *Backstage*.
2. If you signed in to a Windows Live SkyDrive account and an Office 365 SharePoint account in Exercise 1 - 3, notice these two items on the left side of the *Open* page.
3. Click the *Office 365 SharePoint* link to see the folders where you can open a project from the Office 365 SharePoint location.

4. Click the *SkyDrive* link to see the folders where you can open a project from the SkyDrive location.

5. Click the *Computer* item.

6. In the *Recent Folders* list in the middle of the *Open* page, click the *My Documents* item.

7. In the *Open* dialog, select the **Killer Software Application Product Launch.mpp** project file and then click the *Open* button.

8. Click the *File* tab and then click the *Share* tab in the *Backstage*.

9. Click the *Email* item and then click the *Send as Attachment* button in the middle of the *Share* page.

Notice that Project 2013 launches your Outlook application and creates a new e-mail message for you with the project file added as an attachment.

10. Enter **your own** e-mail address in the *To* field and then click the *Send* button to send the e-mail message to yourself.

11. Return to your Project 2013 application window, click the *File* tab, and then click the *Export* tab in the *Backstage*.

12. Click the *Create PDF/XPS* button in the middle of the *Export* page.

13. Click the *OK* button in the *Browse* dialog and then click the *OK* button in the *Document Export Options* dialog as well.

Introducing the Account Page

Click the *Account* tab to display the *Account* page in the *Backstage*. If you did not log in to Windows Live SkyDrive account or an Office 365 SharePoint account on the *Save As* page, the *Account* page appears as shown in Figure 1 - 40. The *Account* page contains a *User Information* section on the left and a *Product Information* section on the right. Use the features in the *User Information* section to change the background pattern and theme colors used in Project 2013 or to connect your software to services such as Windows Live SkyDrive, Office 365 SharePoint,

Flickr, YouTube, Facebook, LinkedIn, or Twitter. Use the features in the *Product Information* section to determine the activation status of your software or to learn more about your version of the software.

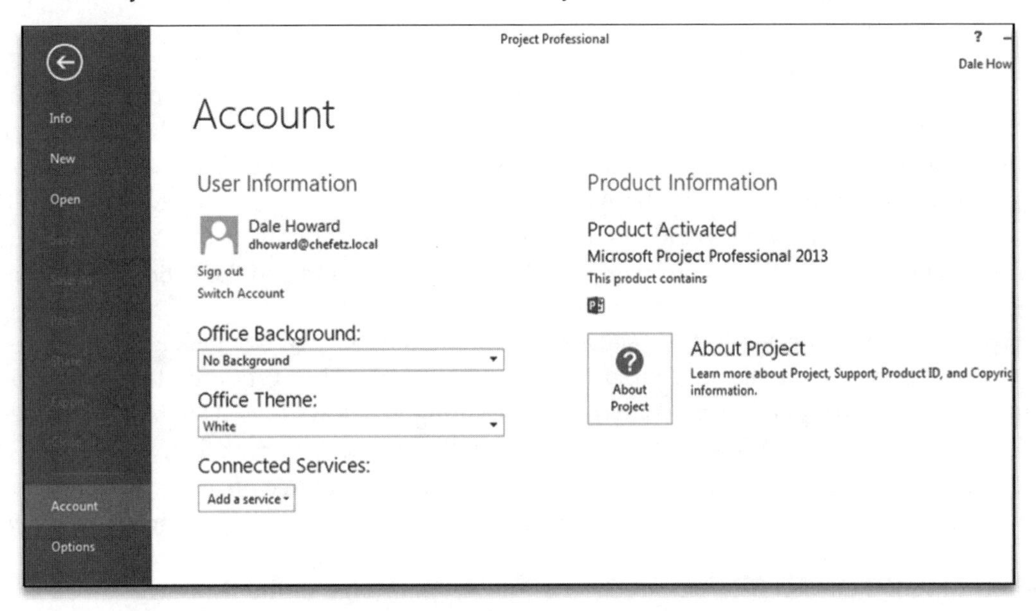

Figure 1 - 40: Account page in the Backstage without logging in to Windows Live or Office 365

Adding Connected Services to Project 2013

To log in to a Windows Live SkyDrive location, an Office 365 SharePoint location, or any other connected service, click the *Add a service* pick list button in the *Connected Services* section of the *Account* page. The software displays the *Add a service* pick list shown in Figure 1 - 41. If you select the *Storage* item, notice that the software allows you to log in to an Office 365 SharePoint location or a Windows Live SkyDrive location. If you select the *Other Sites* item, the software allows you to log in using your *Windows Live Connect* information so that you can connect with services such as Flickr, LinkedIn, Facebook, Twitter, and YouTube. If you select the *Office Store* item, the software allows you to log in to the Office Store web site so that you can connect to Office Apps.

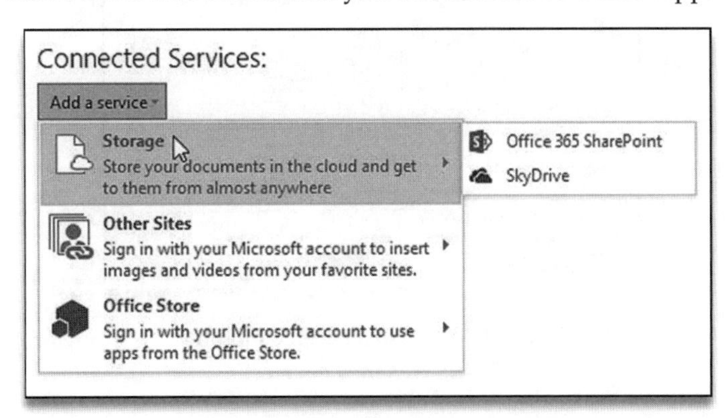

Figure 1 - 41: Add a service pick list

To log in to an Office 365 SharePoint location, select the *Storage* item on the *Add a service* pick list, and then click the *Office 365 SharePoint* item on the flyout menu. Project 2013 displays the *Add a service* dialog shown previously in Figure 1 - 24. Remember that you must already have an existing Office 365 account to use this feature. Enter your Office 365 SharePoint e-mail address in the *Add a service* dialog and then click the *Next* button. The software displays the *Sign in* dialog with your Office 365 SharePoint e-mail address entered in the *User ID* field, as shown previously in Figure 1 - 25. Enter your password in the *Password* field, leave the *Keep me signed in* option selected, and then click the *Sign in* button.

To log in to a Windows Live SkyDrive location, select the *Storage* item on the *Add a service* pick list, and then click the *SkyDrive* item on the flyout menu. Project 2013 displays the *Add a service* dialog shown previously in Figure 1 - 24. Remember that you must already have an existing Windows Live ID to be able to use this feature. Enter your Windows Live e-mail address in the *Add a service* dialog and then click the *Next* button. The software displays the *Sign in* dialog with your Windows Live e-mail address entered in the *Microsoft account* field, as shown previously in Figure 1 - 25. Enter your password in the *Password* field and then click the *Sign in* button.

To log in to Windows Live Connect, select the *Other Sites* item on the *Add a service* pick list, and then click the *Microsoft account* item on the flyout menu. Project 2013 displays the *Add a service* dialog shown previously in Figure 1 - 24. Keep in mind that you must already have an existing Windows Live ID to be able to use this feature. Enter your Windows Live e-mail address in the *Add a service* dialog and then click the *Next* button. The software displays the *Sign in* dialog with your Windows Live e-mail address entered in the *Microsoft account* field, as shown previously in Figure 1 - 25. Enter your password in the *Password* field and then click the *Sign in* button.

The software refreshes the *Connected Services* section of the *Account* page in the *Backstage*. If you click the *Add a service* pick list shown in Figure 1 - 42, you see several new items on the pick list, including the *Images & Video* item and the *Sharing* item. The items on the *Images & Video* flyout menu connect you to Flickr or YouTube so that you can access your stored pictures and videos. The items on the *Sharing* flyout menu connect you to Facebook, LinkedIn, or Twitter so that you can share documents with other users. When you connect Project 2013 to any of these services, remember that you also connect every other application in the Office 2013 suite of tools to these services as well. This might allow you to embed a photo from Flickr to a presentation in PowerPoint 2013, for example.

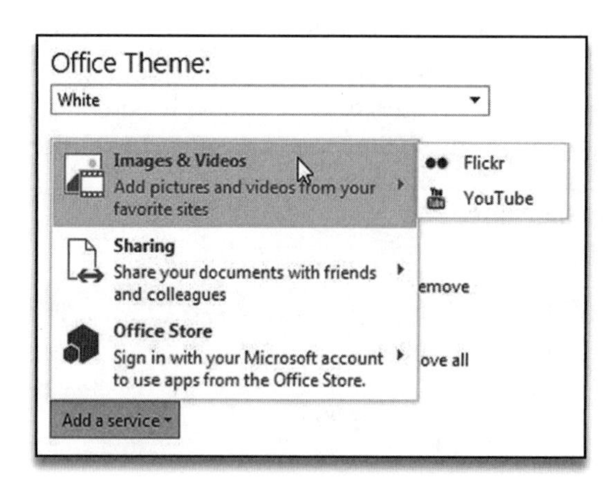

Figure 1 - 42: Add a service pick list shows two new services

To add the Flickr connected service, select the *Images & Videos* item on the *Add a service* pick list, and then click the *Flickr* item on the flyout menu. The software displays the *All your photos in one place* dialog shown in Figure 1 - 43. To use this feature, you must have an existing Flickr account, or you can create a new Flickr account during the connection process. To connect Project 2013 and the rest of your Office 2013 software applications to Flickr, click the *Connect* button in the dialog.

Figure 1 - 43: All your photos in one place dialog to add photos and videos from Flickr

The software displays the *Sign in to Yahoo* dialog shown in Figure 1 - 44. If you do not already have a Yahoo user account, click the *Create New Account* button at the top of the dialog and create a new user account. Otherwise, enter your Yahoo user account and password in the dialog and click the *Sign In* button.

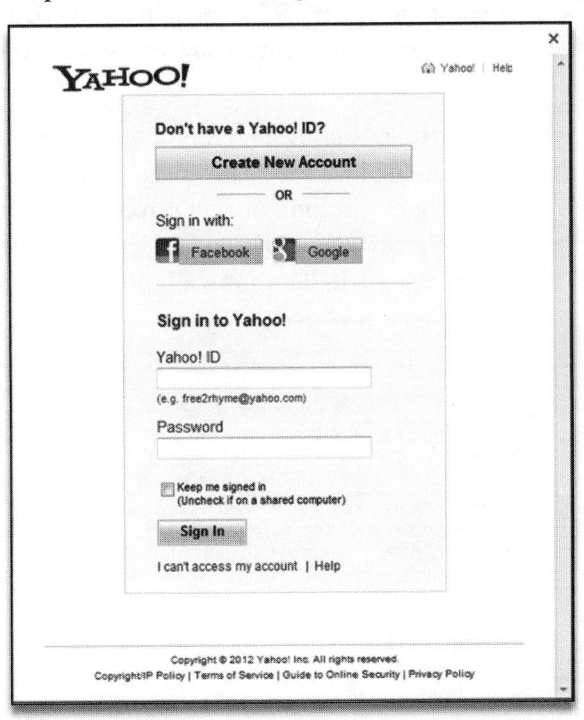

Figure 1 - 44: Sign in to Yahoo dialog

When the software completes the sign in process, you see the Flickr confirmation dialog shown in Figure 1 - 45. To change your Flickr connection settings, click the *connection settings* hyperlink in the dialog. Otherwise, click the *Done* button to close the dialog.

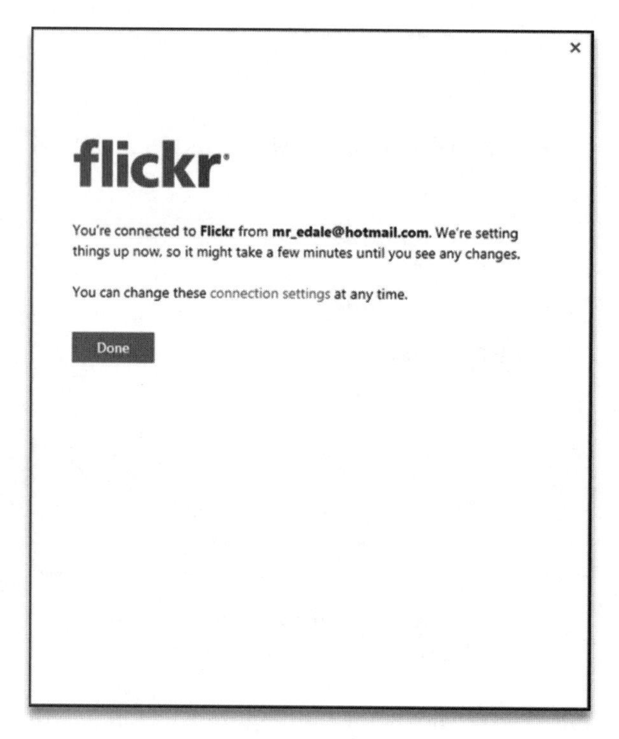

Figure 1 - 45: Flickr confirmation dialog

To add the YouTube connected service, select the *Images & Videos* item on the *Add a service* pick list, and then click the *YouTube* item on the flyout menu. The software adds the YouTube service immediately and does not prompt you to log in to YouTube.

To add the Facebook connected service, select the *Sharing* item on the *Add a service* pick list, and then click the *Facebook* item on the flyout menu. The software displays the *Share to Facebook* dialog shown in Figure 1 - 46. To use this feature, you must have an existing Facebook account, or you can create a new Facebook account during the connection process. To connect Project 2013 and the rest of your Office 2013 software applications to Facebook, click the *Connect* button and then log in to Facebook in the *Facebook Login* dialog.

Figure 1 - 46: Share to Facebook dialog

To add the LinkedIn connected service, select the *Sharing* item on the *Add a service* pick list, and then click the *LinkedIn* item on the flyout menu. The software displays the *Share to LinkedIn* dialog shown in Figure 1 - 47. To use this feature, you must have an existing LinkedIn account. To connect Project 2013 and the rest of your Office 2013 software applications to LinkedIn, click the *Connect* button and then sign in to LinkedIn in the *LinkedIn* dialog.

Figure 1 - 47: Share to LinkedIn dialog

To add the Twitter service, select the *Sharing* item on the *Add a service* pick list, and then click the *Twitter* item on the flyout menu. The software displays the *Share on Twitter* dialog shown in Figure 1 - 48. To use this feature, you must have an existing Twitter account. To connect Project 2013 and the rest of your Office 2013 software applications to Twitter, click the *Connect* button and then sign in to Twitter in the next dialog.

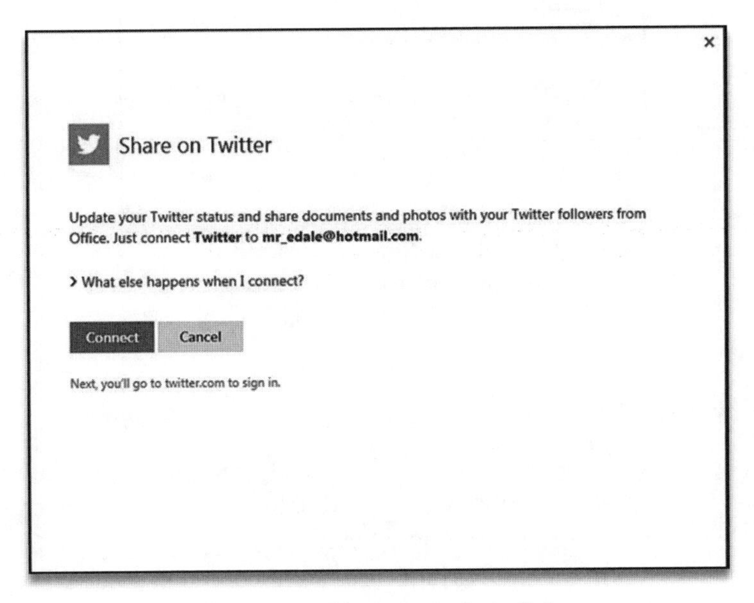

Figure 1 - 48: Share on Twitter dialog

To add the Office Store service, select the *Office Store* item on the *Add a service* pick list, and then click the *Office Store* item on the flyout menu. The software displays the *Add a service* dialog shown previously in Figure 1 - 24. To connect Project 2013 and the rest of your Office 2013 software applications to the Office Store, you must have an existing Microsoft account. Enter your Windows Live e-mail address in the *Add a service* dialog and then click the *Next* button. The software displays the *Sign in* dialog with your Windows Live e-mail address entered in the *Microsoft account* field as shown previously in Figure 1 - 25. Enter your password in the *Password* field and then click the *Sign in* button.

Figure 1 - 49 shows the *Account* page in the *Backstage* after adding several new services. Notice that my *Connected Services* list displays the Windows Live SkyDrive, Office 365 SharePoint, Office Store, Flickr, LinkedIn, and YouTube connected services.

Figure 1 - 49: New services added to the Connected Services list

Changing the Office Background and Theme

To change the background pattern used in all of your Office 2013 applications, click the *Office Background* pick list shown in Figure 1 - 50. The software offers you 14 background patterns from which to choose. To see a preview of each background pattern, float your mouse pointer over the name of a pattern in the *Background Pattern* pick list and then look at the pattern preview in the upper right corner of the *Account* page in the *Backstage*. When you select a background pattern on the *Office Background* pick list, the software applies a light gray pattern in the upper right corner of every application in the Office 2013 family of software tools.

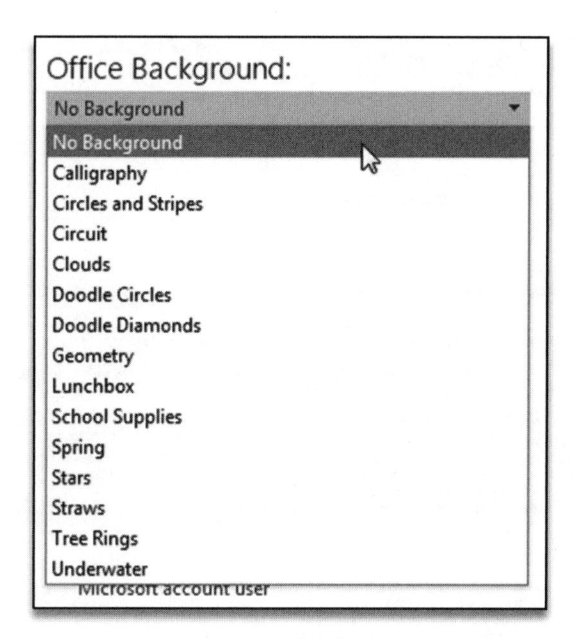

Figure 1 - 50: Office Background pick list

To change the color theme used in all of your Office 2013 applications, click the *Office Theme* pick list. The software offers you three color themes from which to choose: *White* (the default), *Light Gray*, and *Dark Gray*. The color theme you select controls the colors of all items in the user interface of your Office 2013 applications, such as color of the buttons in the *Ribbon*, the colors used in the *Backstage*, and the color of the background pattern.

Information: You can also specify the background pattern and the color theme you want to see in Office 2013 by clicking the *Options* button in the *Backstage* to navigate to the *General* page of the *Project Options* dialog. To specify the background pattern or color theme, select the *Always use these values regardless of sign in to Office* checkbox, select a background pattern in the *Office Background* pick list, and select a color theme in the *Office Theme* pick list. Click the *OK* button when finished.

The *Product Information* section of the *Account page* shows you the activation status of your copy of Project 2013. Notice in Figure 1 - 40 shown previously that I properly activated my copy of the software. You can also click the *About Project* button to display the *About Microsoft Project* dialog found in previous versions of the software, as shown in Figure 1 - 51.

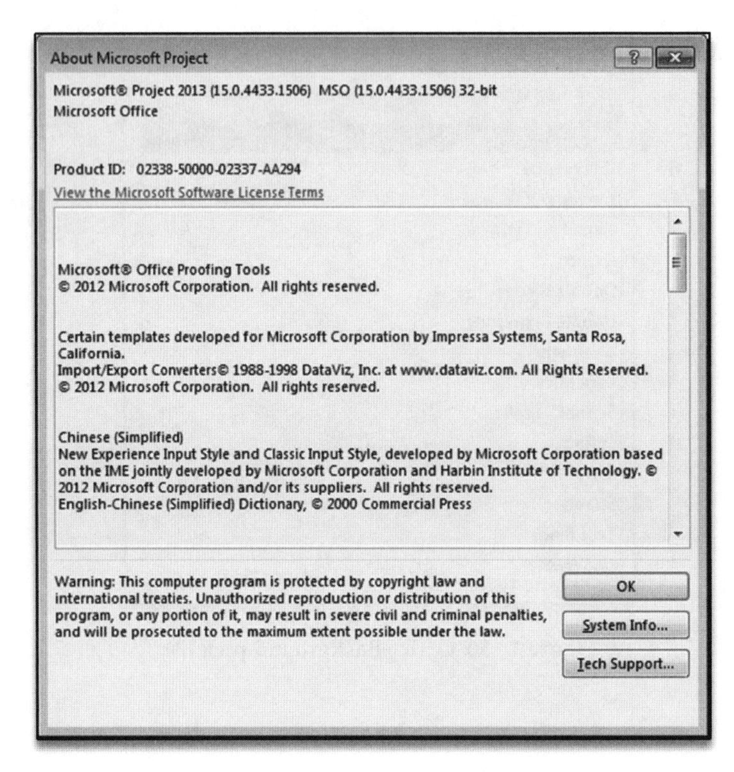

Figure 1 - 51: About Microsoft Project dialog

Hands On Exercise

Exercise 1 - 5

Explore the new features on the *Account* page in the *Backstage* in Project 2013.

1. Click the *File* tab and then click the *Account* tab in the *Backstage.*

2. If you signed in to a Windows Live SkyDrive account and an Office 365 SharePoint account in Exercise 1 - 3, notice these two items in the *Connected Services* section at the bottom of the *Account* page.

3. In the *Connected Services* section, click the *Add a service* pick list button, select *Other Sites* on the pick list, and then click the *Sign in with your Microsoft account* item in the flyout menu.

4. Click the *Sign In* button in the *Sign in to Office* dialog, enter your Microsoft user account information in the *Microsoft account Sign in* dialog, and then click the *Sign in* button.

5. If you connected your Microsoft user account with other services like Flickr or LinkedIn, click the *Add a Service* pick list button again and connect to one of those services in Project 2013.

6. Click the *Office Background* pick list.

7. On the *Office Background* pick list, float your mouse pointer over each of the background names individually, and examine the background pattern in the upper right corner of the *Backstage*.

8. Select the *Underwater* item on the *Office Background* pick list.

9. Click the *Office Theme* pick list and select the *Dark Gray* item.

10. Click the *Back* button (big left-arrow button) in the upper left corner of the *Backstage* to return to your **Killer Software Application Product Launch.mpp** project.

11. At the top of your Project 2013 application window, notice how the software applied the office background and office theme you just selected on the *Account* page of the *Backstage*.

12. Click the *File* tab and then click the *Account* tab again.

13. Click the *Office Background* pick list and select the *No Background* item.

14. Click the *Office Theme* pick list and select the *White* item.

15. Click the *Back* button (big left-arrow button) in the upper left corner of the *Backstage* to return to your **Killer Software Application Product Launch.mpp** project.

Changes to the Project Options Dialog

Click the *Options* tab in the *Backstage* to display the *Project Options* dialog shown in Figure 1 - 52. By default, Project 2013 selects the *General* tab to display the options on the *General* page of the dialog. The *Project Options* dialog in Project 2013 is nearly identical to the same dialog in the 2010 version of the software, including the same set of eleven pages in the dialog, but it does include several important changes.

Changes on the *General* page of the *Project Options* dialog include:

- Microsoft removed the *Color scheme* option in the *User interface options* section of the dialog.

- The *Personalize your copy of Microsoft Office* section contains three new options that allow you to change the background pattern and background theme colors. These options include the *Always use these values regardless of sign in to Office* checkbox, the *Office Background* pick list, and the *Office Theme* pick list. I discussed these options previously in the *Changing the Office Background and Theme* sub-topical section of this module.

- The new *Start up options* section contains a single option called *Show the Start screen when this application starts*. By default, the software selects this option, which forces Project 2013 to display the *Start* page every time to launch the software. If you disable this option, every time you launch Project 2013 the software opens a new blank project file and applies the *Gantt with Timeline* view to the project.

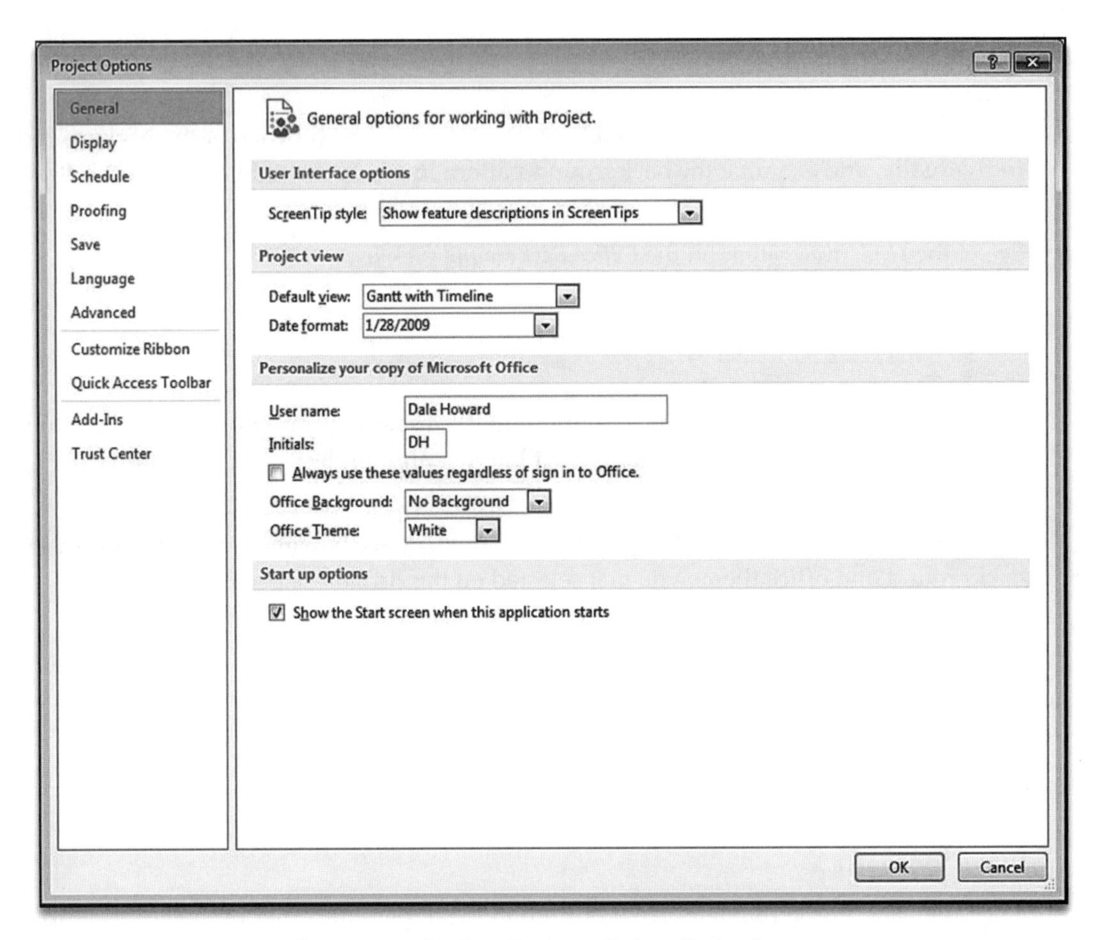

Figure 1 - 52: Project Options dialog, General page

Changes on the *Save* page of the *Project Options* dialog include:

- The *Save projects* section contains three new options. The *Don't show the Backstage when opening or saving files* option forces Project 2013 to hide the *Backstage* whenever you open or save a project file using the *Open* or *Save* buttons on your *Quick Access Toolbar*. When you click the *Open* button or the *Save* button with this option selected, the software displays the *Open* or *Save As* dialog instead of displaying the *Backstage*. By default, the software deselects this option. The *Show additional places for saving, even if sign in may be required* option forces the software to display the *SkyDrive* link on the *Save As* page in the *Backstage*. By default, the software selects this option. The *Save to Computer by default* option forces the software to select the *Computer* link on the *Save As* page every time you save a new project file. By default, the software deselects this option.

Information: In order to fully use the *Don't show the Backstage when opening or saving files* option on the *Save* page of the *Project Options* dialog, you must customize the *Quick Access Toolbar* by adding the *Open* button. To perform this customization, click the *Quick Access Toolbar* tab in the *Project Options* dialog, select the *Open* button in the list of commands on the left side of the dialog, and then click the *Add* button.

- The *Save templates* section is entirely new in Project 2013 and contains only a single option, the *Default personal templates location* option. Remember that you must manually enter the path for your default *Templates* folder if you want to create new projects from templates you downloaded from the *Office.com* web site or templates you created and saved. Refer back to the *Accessing Templates Stored in Your Templates Folder* section of this module for more information about using this option.

Changes on the *Language* page of the *Project Options* dialog include:

- The *Choose Editing Languages* section includes a new option called *Let me know when I should download additional proofing tools*. By default, the software selects this option, which forces Project 2013 to warn you when you open a project file created in a language different from your selected editing languages.

Changes to the *Advanced* page of the *Project Options* dialog include:

- The *Display* section contains three options. The *Show this number of Recent Projects* option determines the number of recent projects displayed in the *Recent Projects* section of the *Open* page in the *Backstage*. By default, the software specifies *25* projects in this option. The *Quickly access this number of Recent Projects* option forces the software to display the names of the selected number of projects at the bottom of the sidepane on the left side of the *Backstage*. By default, the software does not select this option. The *Show this number of unpinned Recent Folders* option determines how many unpinned folders you see in the *Recent Folders* section of either the *Save As* page or the *Open* page in the *Backstage*. By default, the software specifies *5* folders in this option.

- Microsoft removed the *Show bars and shapes in Gantt views in 3-D* option in the *Display* section of the dialog.

- The *Display* section contains a new option called *Disable hardware graphics acceleration*. By default, the software does not select this option. Depending on the graphics hardware in your computer, you may see this option as disabled (grayed out) so that you cannot change the option.

When you click the *Trust Center Settings* button on the *Trust Center* page of the *Project Options* dialog, Project 2013 displays the *Trust Center* dialog. In the *Trust Center* dialog, Microsoft removed the *DEP Settings* page and added the new *Trusted App Catalogs* page shown in Figure 1 - 53.

Use the options on the new *Trusted App Catalogs* page to manage your Office Apps for all of the applications in the Office 2013 suite of tools. Office Apps are web pages loaded inside an Office 2013 application and displayed in a pane. In Project 2013, you can only use task pane Office Apps to help you work with a project file.

To trust an Office App catalog in Project 2013, enter the URL for the Office App catalog in the *Catalog URL* field and then click the *Add Catalog* button to add the Office App to the list in the *Trusted Catalogs Table* section of the dialog. To remove any existing Office App catalog, select the catalog and then click the *Remove* button. In addition, you can disable Office App catalogs by selecting either the *Don't allow any apps to start* option or the *Don't allow apps from the Office Store to start* option in the *Trusted App Catalogs* section at the top of the dialog.

Information: When you specify any of the preceding settings in the *Trust Center* dialog, the Office 2013 system saves these settings in the *Trust Center* dialog for every application in the Office 2013 suite of tools.

Information: I discuss how to use task pane Office Apps for Project 2013 in the *Using Task Pane Office Apps* topical section of Module 03, *Using Microsoft Project 2013 Day to Day*.

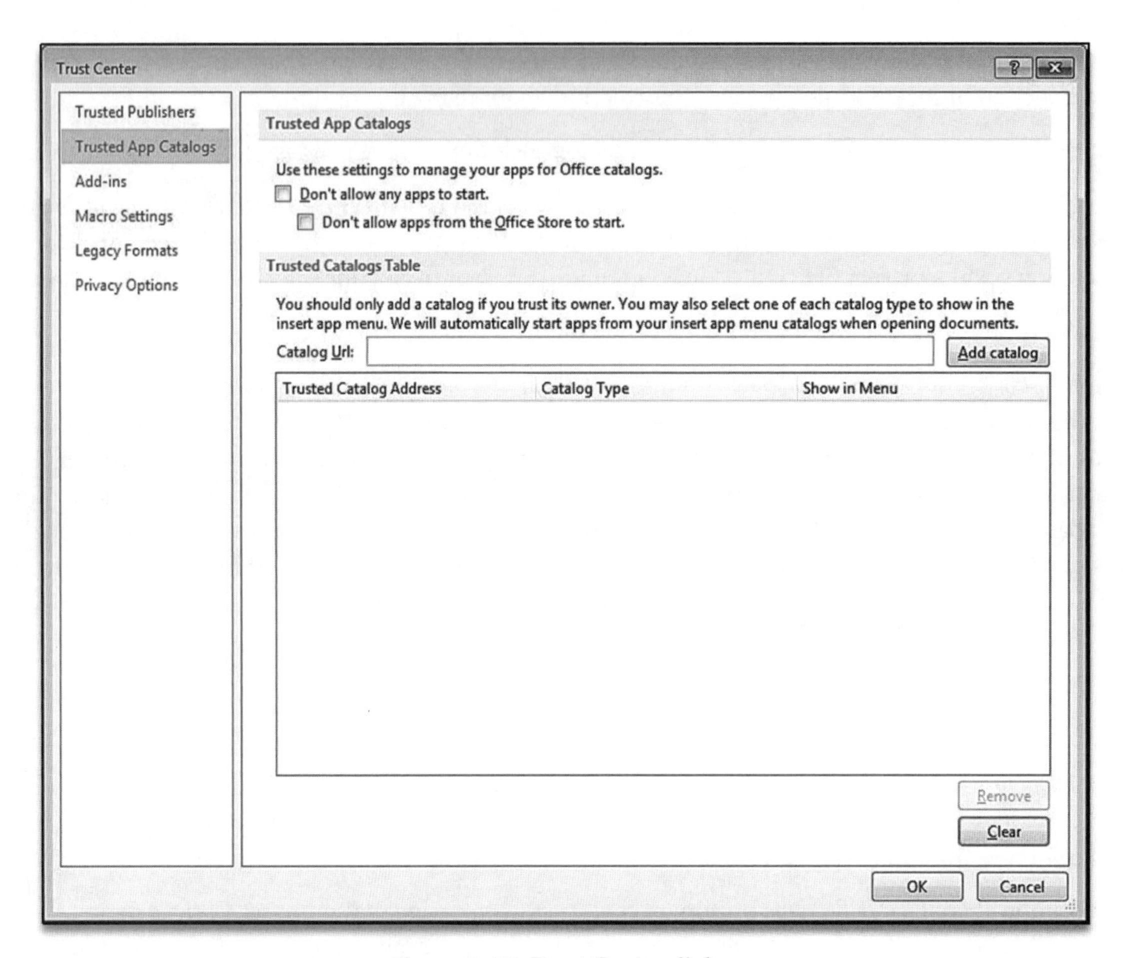

Figure 1 - 53: Trust Center dialog

On the *Privacy Options* page of the *Trust Center* dialog, Microsoft removed the *Connect to Office.com for updated content when I'm connected to the Internet* option and the *Automatically detect installed Office applications to improve Office.com search results* option, and added two new options. The new *Allow Office to connect to the Internet* option allows the Office 2013 application to use online services and to find the most recent online content if you are connected to the Internet. By default, the software selects this option. The other new option is the *Turn on the Office Feedback Tool (Send a Smile) so that I can send feedback to help improve Office* option. By default, the software disables (grays out) this option.

Click the *OK* button to close the *Trust Center* dialog and then click the *OK* button to close the *Project Options* dialog as well. The software returns you to the Project 2013 user interface.

Hands On Exercise

Exercise 1 - 6

Explore the new features in the *Project Options* dialog in Project 2013.

1. Click the *File* tab and then click the *Options* tab in the *Backstage.*

2. On the *General* page of the *Project Options* dialog, notice the new options in the *Personalize your copy of Microsoft Office* section and notice the new *Start up options* section containing the new *Show the Start screen when this application starts* option.

3. Click the *Save* tab to display the *Save* page in the *Project Options* dialog.

4. On the *Save* page of the dialog, notice the three new options at the end of the *Save projects* section of the dialog.

5. If you do not intend to save projects to a Window Live SkyDrive location or an Office 365 SharePoint location, **deselect** the *Show additional places for saving, even if sign in may be required* option and then **select** the *Save to Computer by default* option.

6. Notice the new *Save templates* section of the *Save* page in the dialog.

7. Click the *Advanced* tab to display the *Advanced* page in the *Project Options* dialog.

8. Notice the three new options at the top of the *Display* section of the *Advanced* page of the dialog.

9. Click the *Trust Center* tab and then click the *Trust Center Settings* button on the *Trust Center* page of the *Project Options* dialog.

10. Click the *Trust App Catalogs* tab to display the *Trusted App Catalogs* page in the *Trust Center* dialog.

11. Examine the options available on the *Trusted App Catalogs* page of the dialog.

12. Click the *OK* button to close the *Trust Center* dialog.

13. Click the *OK* button to close the *Project Options* dialog as well.

Changes to the Ribbon and Quick Access Toolbar

Project 2013 includes no changes to the default buttons on the *Quick Access Toolbar,* includes a new *Report* ribbon and a new *Design* ribbon, along with a handful of other minor changes to the *Ribbon.* Click the *Report* tab to display the new *Report* ribbon shown in Figure 1 - 54. Features on the new *Report* ribbon include the *Compare Projects* button, eight buttons in the *View Reports* section of the ribbon, which you can use to work with all types of new reports in the software, and the *Visual Reports* button.

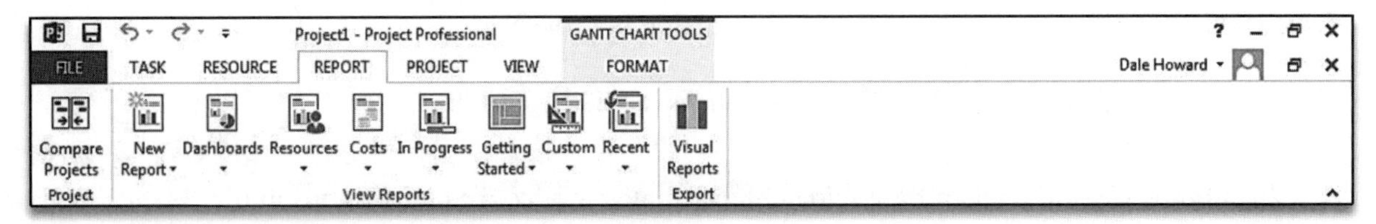

Figure 1 - 54: Report ribbon

You see the new *Design* ribbon when you display any of the new reports included in Project 2013. When you display one of these new reports, the software displays the *Design* ribbon with the *Report Tools* applied, as shown in Figure 1 - 55. You use the new *Design* ribbon to create and edit reports.

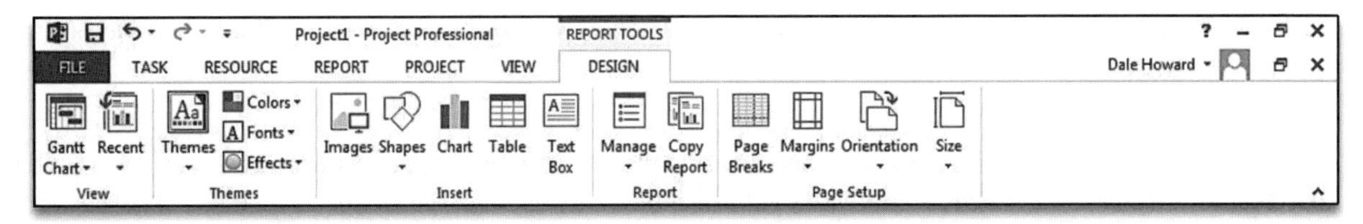

Figure 1 - 55: Design ribbon

Other minor changes to the *Ribbon* include each of the following:

- In the *Assignments* section of the *Resource* ribbon, Microsoft removed the *Substitute Resources* button. This change only affects users who have the Professional version of Project 2013 and use it with Project Server 2013.
- In the *Apps* section of the *Project* ribbon, Microsoft added the *Apps for Office* pick list button that allows you to load task pane Office apps into Project 2013.
- In the *Status* section of the *Project* ribbon, the *Status Date* field displays an *NA* value by default, and only displays a date if you specify a *Status Date* value. In Project 2010, the *Status Date* field displays the *Current Date* value by default until you specify a *Status Date* value.
- In the *Status* section of the *Project* ribbon, Microsoft removed the *Sync to Protected Actuals* button. This change only affects users who have the Professional version of Project 2013 and use it with Project Server 2013.
- Microsoft removed the *Reports* section of the *Project* ribbon, moving the *Visual Reports* button and the *Compare Projects* button to the new *Report* ribbon.
- In the *Bar Styles* section of the *Format* ribbon with the *Gantt Chart Tools* applied, Microsoft added a new *Task Path* pick list button.

You find the final new *Ribbon* feature immediately above the far right end of the *Ribbon*. This new feature is the *User Name* pick list. If you are not already logged in to Windows Live or Office 365 SharePoint, click the *User Name* pick list and select the *Account settings* item on the menu. Project 2013 displays the *Account* page in the *Backstage*, shown previously in Figure 1 - 40. Click the *Add a service* pick list button and log in to a Windows Live SkyDrive location and/or an Office 365 SharePoint location, as needed. After you log in to either a Windows Live SkyDrive location or an Office 365 SharePoint location, Project 2013 refreshes the *User name* pick list to show your connected services, as shown in Figure 1 - 56.

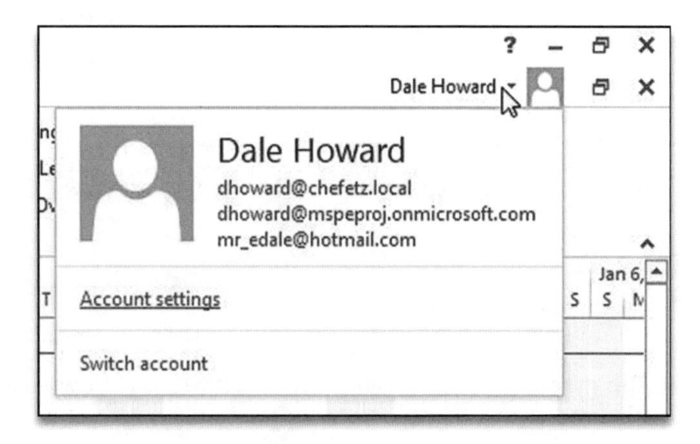

Figure 1 - 56: User Name pick list menu

Updated Visuals in Task and Resource Views

Intended to give the software a more modern appearance, Project 2013 includes updated graphics used in most task and resource views. The software includes updated graphics shown in frequently used views such as the *Gantt Chart, Timeline,* and *Team Planner* views. For example, Figure 1 - 57 shows the updated Gantt bar graphics in the *Gantt Chart* view. Notice that the updated graphics include new graphical symbols for summary Gantt bars, along with a new default color scheme. In addition, the software includes new color schemes in the *Gantt Chart Style* section of the *Format* ribbon when you have any Gantt-based view applied.

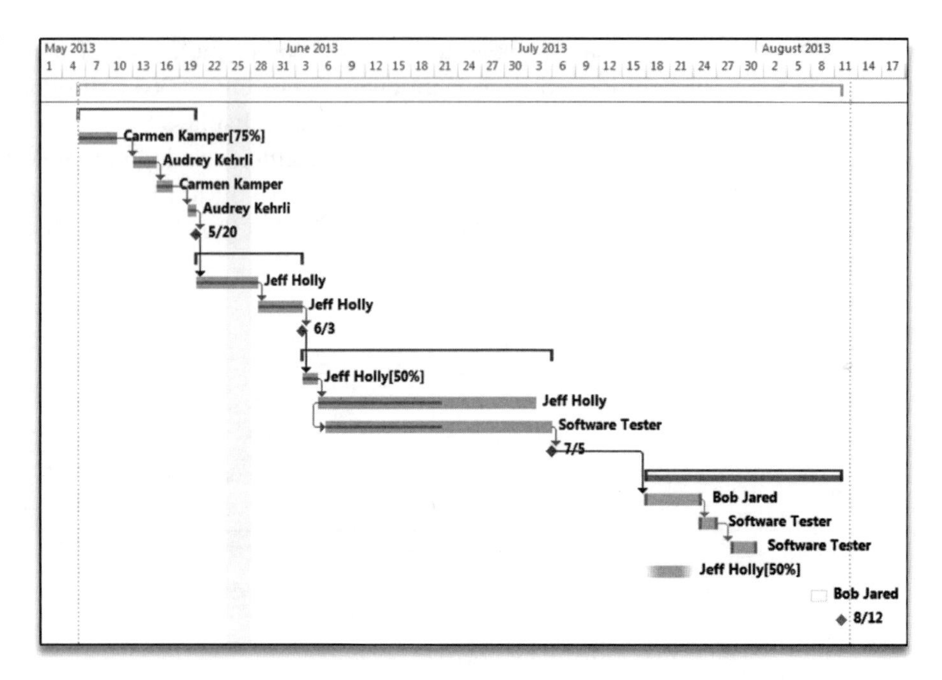

Figure 1 - 57: Updated graphics in the Gantt Chart view

Using another improvement to the graphics used in Gantt-based views, it is now easier to align each Gantt bar with its corresponding task name on the left side of the view. If you select any task in the task sheet portion of the *Gantt Chart* view, for example, Project 2013 displays a set of horizontal gridlines running across the entire screen to show you the selected task. For example, notice in Figure 1 - 58 that I selected the *Develop budget* task, and that Project 2013 draws a pair of horizontal gridlines around the selected task's Gantt bar in the *Gantt Chart* portion of the view.

		Task Mode	Task Name	Duration
0			◢ CRM Software Development	68 d
1	✓		◢ Analysis/Software Requirements	11 d
2	✓		Conduct needs analysis	5 d
3	✓		Draft software specifications	3 d
4	✓		Develop budget	2 d
5	✓		Develop delivery timeline	1 d
6	✓		Analysis complete	0 d
7	✓		◢ Design	9 d
8	✓		Develop functional specifications	5 d
9	✓		Develop prototype based on functional specifications	4 d
10	✓		Design complete	0 d

GANTT CHART

May 2013 | June 2013
1 4 7 10 13 16 19 22 25 28 31 3 6 9 12
Carmen Kamper[75%]
Audrey Kehrli
Carmen Kamper
Audrey Kehrli
5/20
Jeff Holly
Jeff Holly
6/3

Figure 1 - 58: Horizontal gridlines show selected task

Hands On Exercise

Exercise 1 - 7

Explore the new features in the *Ribbon*, along with updated visuals in Project 2013.

1. Click the *Report* tab to display the new *Report* ribbon.
2. In the *View Reports* section of the *Report* ribbon, click the *Dashboards* pick list button and select the *Project Overview* report, if necessary.
3. Examine the buttons available in the new *Report* ribbon.
4. Click the *Design* tab to display the *Design* ribbon with the *Report Tools* applied.
5. Examine the buttons available in the new *Design* ribbon.
6. Click the *Project* tab to display the *Project* ribbon.
7. In the *Apps* section of the *Project* ribbon, notice the new *Apps for Office* pick list button.
8. Click the *View* tab to display the *View* ribbon.
9. In the *Task Views* section of the *View* ribbon, click the *Gantt Chart* button to display the *Gantt Chart* view.
10. Examine the updated graphics for the Gantt bars shown in the *Gantt Chart* view.
11. Select task ID #12, the *Obtain launch budget approval* task, and notice the new set of horizontal gridlines surrounding the select task and the task's Gantt bar.
12. Save but do not close your **Killer Software Application Product Launch.mpp** project.

Module 02

Using the Sync with SharePoint Tasks List Feature

Learning Objectives

After completing this module, you will be able to:

- Understand how to synchronize your project with a new or existing SharePoint site
- Include additional fields in the synchronization process
- Add users to your SharePoint site
- Collaborate on a project in a SharePoint Site

Inside Module 02

Understanding the Updated Sync with SharePoint Tasks List Feature

Project 2013 offers an improved version of the Sync with SharePoint Tasks list feature introduced previously in Project 2010. This feature leverages the power of SharePoint by publishing your project file to a SharePoint site as a *Tasks* list, and then synchronizing your project tasks with the *Tasks* list. This feature enables two-way communication between you and your project team members, as it allows you to display the current task schedule to all team members, and allows your team members to submit task updates for their assigned tasks.

To use this improved Sync with SharePoint Tasks list feature, open a project that you want to synchronize with a *Tasks* list in SharePoint. Click the *File* tab and then click the *Save As* tab to display the *Save As* page in the *Backstage*. In the *Save As* page of the *Backstage*, click the *Sync with SharePoint* icon in the *Save and Sync* section of the page. The software refreshes the *Save As* page as shown in Figure 2 - 1.

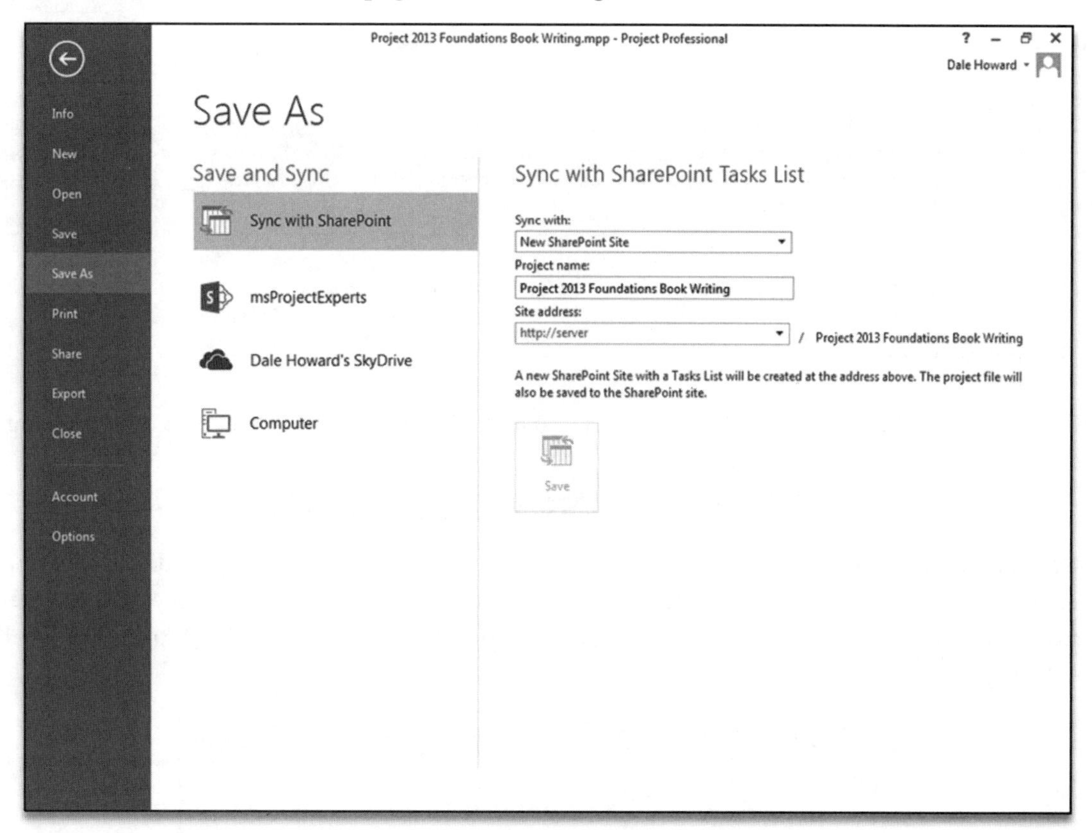

Figure 2 - 1: Save As page in the Backstage

Notice that the *Sync with a SharePoint Tasks List* pane in the right half of the page includes three fields in which you must select an option or enter information. Using the improved Sync with SharePoint Tasks list feature, you can do one of the following:

- Create a new SharePoint site, save the project to the site, and then use the site to collaborate with your team members.
- Save your project to an existing SharePoint site and then use the existing site to collaborate with your team members.

Warning: Before you can perform either of the above actions, your SharePoint administrator must provide you with access to SharePoint, and must provide you with either the URL of the SharePoint server (to create a new site) or the URL of the existing SharePoint site.

By default, Project 2013 selects the *New SharePoint Site* item on the *Sync with* pick list and displays the name of the project in the *Project name* field. If you previously logged in to an Office 365 SharePoint location in Project 2013, the software also displays the URL of the Office 365 SharePoint site in the *Site address* field.

Creating a New SharePoint Site

To create a new SharePoint site in which you and your team can collaborate on the project, complete the following steps:

1. Click the *Sync with* pick list and select the *New SharePoint Site* item on the list, if necessary.

2. Edit the name of the project in the *Project name* field, if necessary.

Warning: If you use spaces in the name of your project in the *Project name* field, the software substitutes the *%20* text string for each space when creating the URL for the new SharePoint site. If you do not want to see the *%20* text string in the URL, replace the space characters with the underscore (_) character instead.

3. Enter or edit the URL of the SharePoint server in the *Site Address* field.

4. Click the *Save* button.

Project 2013 creates the URL of the new SharePoint site using the URL of the SharePoint server, along with the name of the project, in the following form:

http://SharePointServerName/ProjectName

As the software creates the new SharePoint site, it displays a series of *Sync with Tasks List* dialogs, such as the one shown in Figure 2 - 2. The dialogs allow you to monitor the progress as the software creates the site, verifies that the list exists, reads the list properties, reads the list items, and then updates the SharePoint site and the active project.

Figure 2 - 2: Sync with Tasks List dialog

During the synchronization process, the software may display a resource error dialog similar to the one shown in Figure 2 - 3. The message in this dialog indicates that a resource assigned to tasks in the project, Myrta Hansen, does not have access to the SharePoint site. To resolve this problem, I must manually share the site with this resource. I discuss how to add resources to the SharePoint site in the *Adding Users to the SharePoint Site* section of this module.

Figure 2 - 3: Sync resource error dialog

When the software completes the process of creating the new SharePoint site, it launches the Internet Explorer and navigates to the *Home* page of the new SharePoint site. Figure 2 - 4 shows the *Home* page of the new SharePoint site for my project.

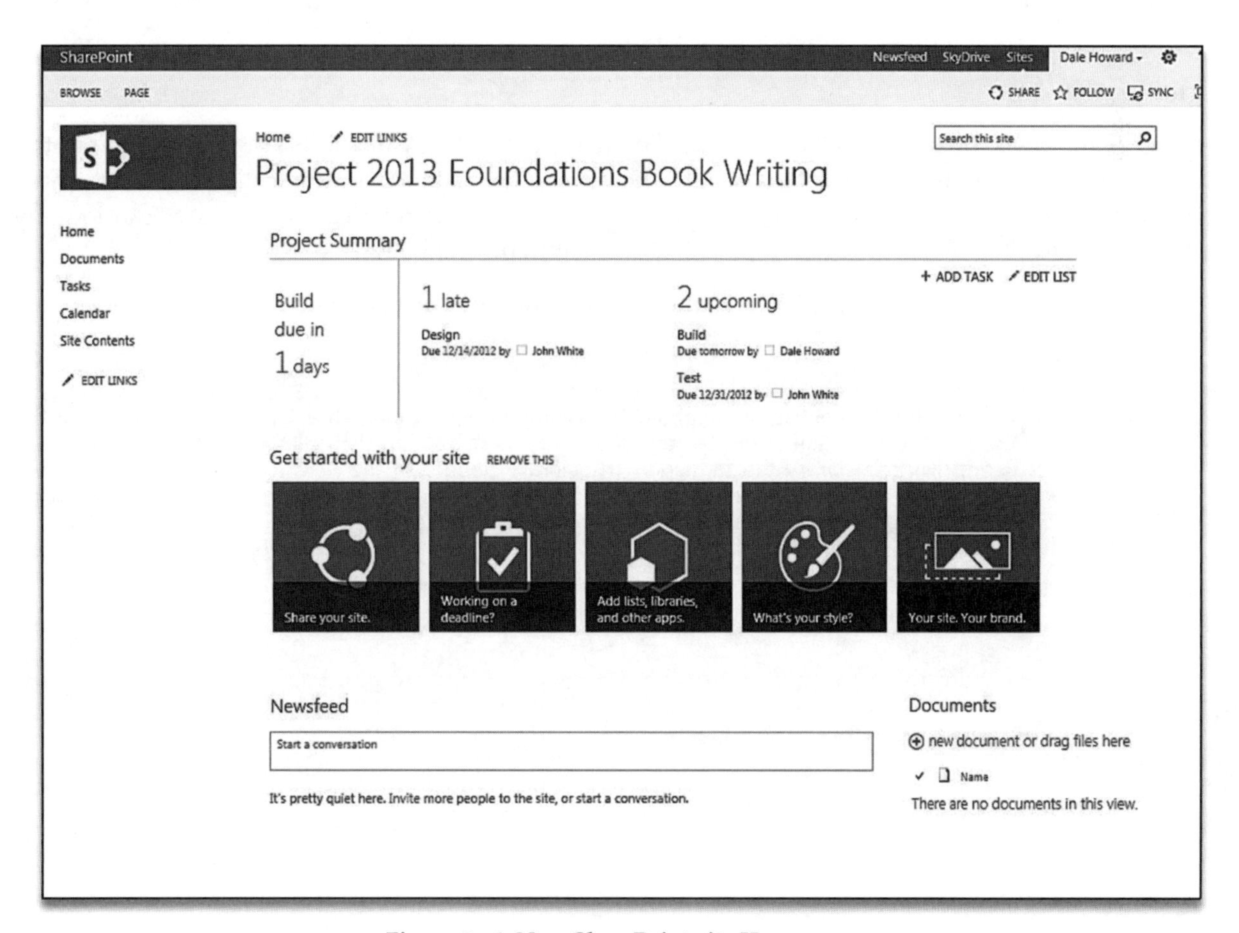

Figure 2 - 4: New SharePoint site Home page

Information: When Project 2013 creates the new SharePoint site, the software creates the site using the *Project Site* template.

Notice that the *Home* page includes each of the following elements:

- The *Quick Launch* menu on the left side of the page offers links for *Home, Documents, Tasks, Calendar,* and *Site Contents.*
- The *Project Summary* section at the top of the page displays late tasks that are overdue, along with upcoming tasks in the project that due in the current week or during the next week. Notice that the *Project Summary* section shows 1 late task and two upcoming tasks. The *Design* task is late, the *Build* task is due in 2 days, and the *Test* task is not due until next week.
- The *Getting started with your site* section in the middle of the page displays a carousel of commands helpful to a new SharePoint user. If your team members are experienced SharePoint users, you can hide the carousel by clicking the *REMOVE THIS* link immediately above the carousel.
- The *Newsfeed* section at the bottom of the page allows you and your team members to hold a conversation about any subject related to the project.
- The *Documents* section in the lower right corner of the page allows you to upload documents related to the project.

When Project 2013 saves the project in the new SharePoint site, the software appends *-Tasks* to the end of the file name, and saves the file in the *Site Assets* library of the new SharePoint site. For example, the name of the project I saved in the new SharePoint site is **Project_2013_Foundations_Book_Writing-Tasks.mpp**. You can locate your project file in the new SharePoint site by entering a URL similar to the following:

http://ServerName/ProjectName/SiteAssets

Warning: By default, the new SharePoint site does not display a link for the *Site Assets* library in the Quick Launch menu on the left side of the *Home* page. To display the *Site Assets* library as a link in the Quick Launch menu, click the *Site Contents* link to display the *Site Contents* page, and then click the *Site Assets* icon. On the *Site Assets* page, click the *Library* tab to display the *Library* ribbon. In the *Settings* section of the *Library* ribbon, click the *Library Settings* button. In the *General Settings* section of the *Settings* page, click the *List name, description, and navigation* link. On the *General Settings* page, select the *Yes* option in the *Navigation* section of the page, and then click the *Save* button.

Hands On Exercise

Exercise 2 - 1

Prepare a project to synchronize with a new SharePoint site.

Warning: Before you can work the following Hands On Exercises, your organization must use SharePoint 2013, and you must have access to an existing SharePoint site. If you do not have access to an existing SharePoint site, ask your SharePoint administrator to create a new site for you and to supply you with the URL for the site. As you work through this exercise, Project 2013 will create a new SharePoint site that is a sub-site of the existing SharePoint site.

1. Open the **Training Advisor 2013.mpp** sample file from your sample files folder.
2. In the *Resource Sheet* view of the project, replace the *Resource 1* resource with yourself.
3. Replace the *Resource 2*, *Resource 3*, and *Resource 4* resources with the names of real people who work with you in your organization.
4. In the *User Logon Account* column, enter the Windows network user ID for each of the four resources in the form of **DomainName/UserName**.
5. In the *Initials* column, enter the 2-letter initials for each of your four resources.
6. In the *View* section of the *Task* ribbon, click the *Gantt Chart* pick list button and select the *Gantt Chart* view.
7. Click the *Project* tab to display the *Project* ribbon.
8. In the *Properties* section of the *Project* ribbon, click the *Project Information* button.
9. In the *Project Information* dialog, click the *Start* date pick list and select the date of *Monday* of the **previous week** (not Monday of the current week), and then click the *OK* button.
10. In the *Schedule* section of the *Project* ribbon, click the *Set Baseline* pick list button and then select the *Set Baseline* item on the pick list.
11. In the *Set Baseline* dialog, leave all of the default settings in place and then click the *OK* button.
12. Click the *File* tab and then click the *Save* button in the *Backstage*.

Exercise 2 - 2

Synchronize a project with a new SharePoint site.

1. Click the *File* tab and then click the *Save As* tab in the *Backstage*.
2. On the *Save As* page in the *Backstage*, click the *Sync with SharePoint* icon.
3. In the *Sync with SharePoint Tasks List* section of the *Save As* page, do the following:
   - Click the *Sync with* pick list and select the *New SharePoint Site* item, if necessary.
   - In the *Project name* field, replace the spaces in the project name with the underscore character (_).
   - In the *Site address* field, enter the URL of the existing SharePoint site.
4. In the *Sync with SharePoint Tasks List* section of the *Save As* page, click the *Save* button.
5. In the *Sync with Tasks List* dialog, monitor the progress as Project 2013 works with SharePoint to create a new SharePoint site and to synchronize your project with the site.
6. If you see a warning dialog about resources that do not exist in the SharePoint server, click the *OK* button.
7. Maximize the new Internet Explorer window, if necessary, to see the new SharePoint site for your project.

Exercise 2 - 3

Create a link for the *Site Assets* library in the *Quick Launch* menu on the *Home* page SharePoint site.

1. Click the *Site Contents* link in the *Quick Launch* menu.
2. On the *Site Contents* page, click the *Site Assets* icon.
3. At the top of the *Site Assets* page, click the *Library* tab to display the *Library* ribbon.
4. In the *Settings* section of the *Library* ribbon, click the *Library Settings* button.
5. In the *General Settings* section of the *Settings* page, click the *List name, description, and navigation* link.
6. On the *General Settings* page, select the *Yes* option in the *Navigation* section of the page, and then click the *Save* button.
7. In the *Quick Launch* menu, click the new *Site Assets* link.

Notice that the Project 2013 saved your project in the *Site Assets* library in the SharePoint site.

8. Click the *Home* link at the top of the *Quick Launch* menu to return to the *Home* page of your SharePoint site.
9. Examine the *Project Summary* section at the top of the *Home* page, looking for any late tasks and upcoming tasks. Ideally, you should see at least one late task and several upcoming tasks.

Using an Existing SharePoint Site

Project 2013 also allows you to use an existing SharePoint site where you and your team can collaborate on the project. Ideally, you should use a SharePoint site created using the *Project Site* template, but you can use any existing SharePoint site and then customize it as needed. To collaborate using an existing SharePoint site, complete the following steps:

1. Click the *Sync with* pick list and select the *Existing SharePoint Site* item on the list. The software updates the *Sync with a SharePoint Tasks List* section of the *Save As* page in the *Backstage*.

Information: By default, the *Site Address* pick list contains the URL of every SharePoint site accessed by Project 2013. Click the pick list and select the URL of a previously used SharePoint site, or manually enter the URL of a new SharePoint site.

2. Enter the URL of the existing SharePoint site in the *Site address* field similar to the one shown in Figure 2 - 5.

Information: If you previously logged into an Office 365 SharePoint location in Project 2013, the software displays the URL of the Office 365 SharePoint site in the *Site address* field by default. In addition, the software displays a list of all recently used SharePoint sites in the *Site Address* field. You have the option, therefore, to manually enter a URL in the *Site Address* field or to click the *Site Address* pick list and select a URL in the list.

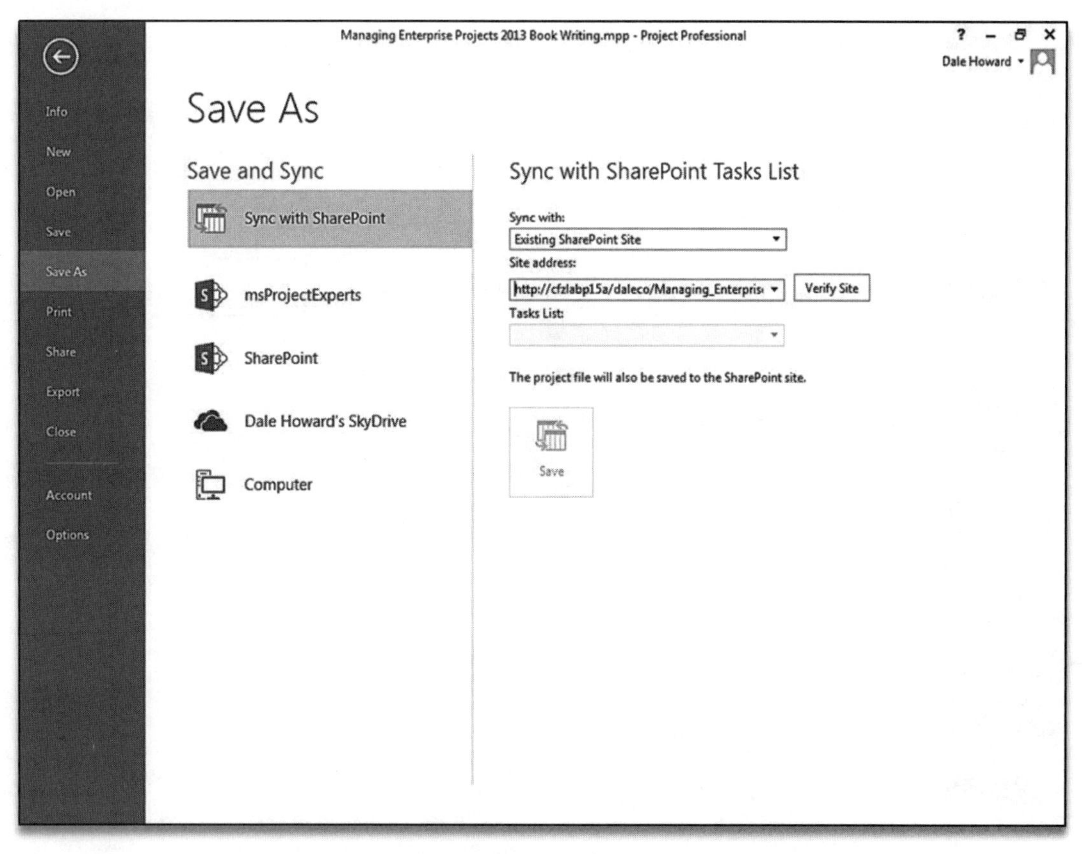

Figure 2 - 5: Updated Sync with SharePoint Tasks List section of the Save As page in the Backstage

3. Click the *Verify Site* button to confirm that the existing SharePoint site contains at least one *Tasks* list. If successful, the *Sync with SharePoint Tasks List* section of the *Save As* page appears similar to the one shown in Figure 2 - 6.

Warning: If your existing SharePoint site does not already contain an existing *Tasks* list, the software **does not** allow you to continue to the synchronization process. To create a *Tasks* list, navigate to the *Home* page of the SharePoint site and click the *Add lists, libraries, and other apps* button in the *Get started with your site* carousel. On the *Add an App* page, click the *Tasks* button, enter a name for the new *Tasks* list in the *Adding Tasks* dialog, and then click the *Create* button.

Warning: If you want to synchronize more than one project in an existing SharePoint site, you must create a *Tasks* list for each project. Remember to give each *Tasks* list a unique name so that you can easily select it in the next step listed below.

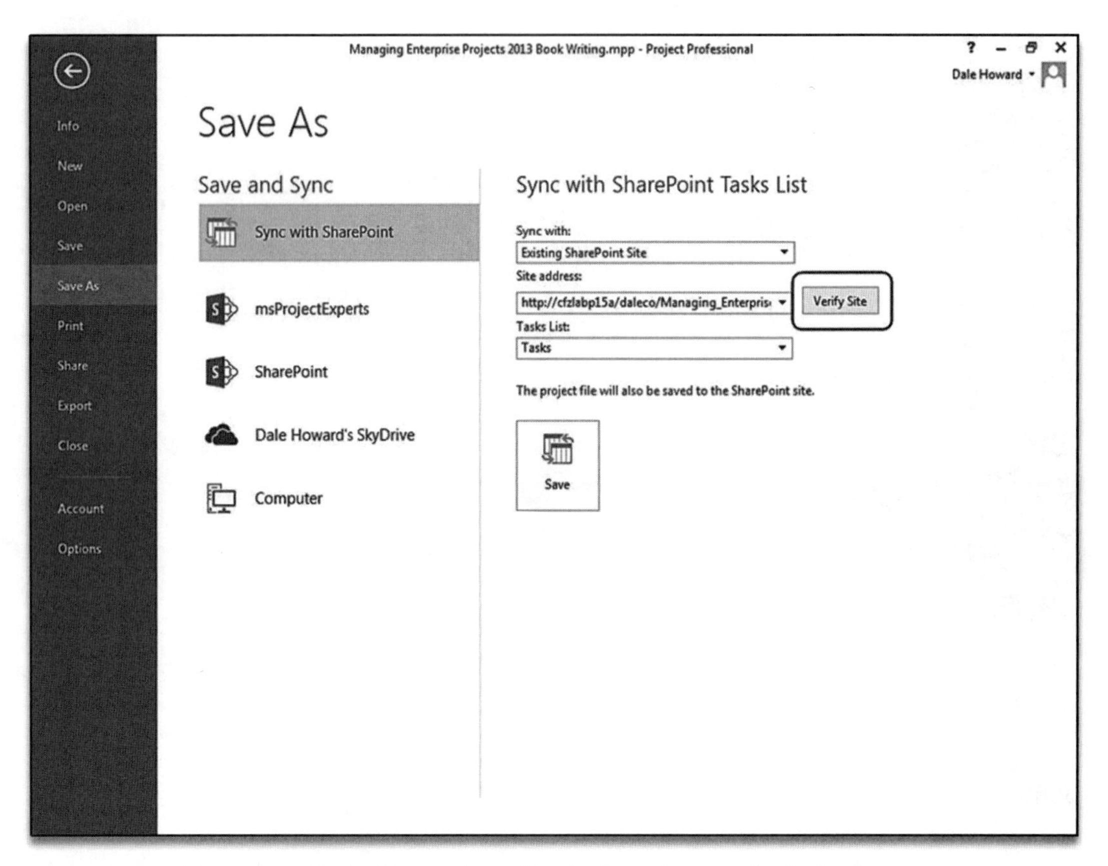

Figure 2 - 6: Tasks list confirmed in the Save As page in the Backstage

If you incorrectly enter the URL of an existing SharePoint site, Project 2013 displays the error dialog shown in Figure 2 - 7. Notice that the dialog lists three possible reasons why it cannot verify the site, including the possibility that the URL for the site is not correct.

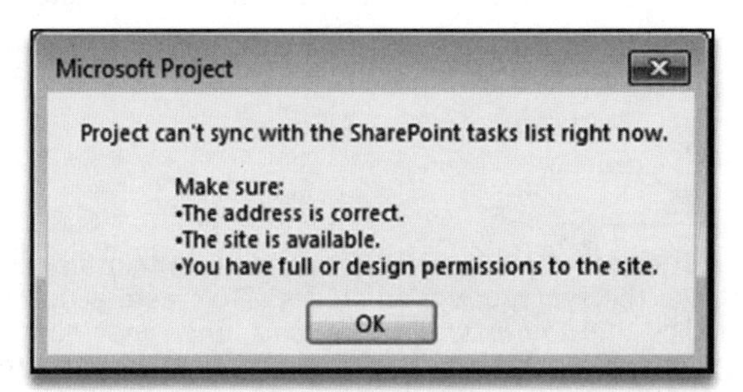

Figure 2 - 7: SharePoint Tasks list error dialog

4. Click the *Tasks List* pick list and select the desired *Tasks* list, if necessary.

5. Click the *Save* button.

As the software saves the project in the existing SharePoint site, it displays a series of *Sync with Tasks List* dialogs, such as the one shown previously in Figure 2 - 2. The dialogs allow you to monitor the progress as the software creates the site, verifies that the list exists, reads the list properties, reads the list items, and then updates the SharePoint site and the active project.

During the synchronization process, the software may display a resource error dialog similar to the one shown previously in Figure 2 - 3. This message in the dialog indicates that a resource assigned to tasks in the project does not have access to the SharePoint site. To resolve this problem, you must manually share the site with this resource. I discuss how to add resources to the SharePoint site in the *Adding Users to the SharePoint Site* section of this module.

After the process completes, you must navigate manually to the *Home* page of the existing SharePoint site and then click the *Tasks* link in the *Quick Launch* menu to see the updated *Tasks* list, such as the list shown in Figure 2 - 8. Notice that the *Tasks* page contains a list of tasks from the active project, along with a timeline at the top of the page.

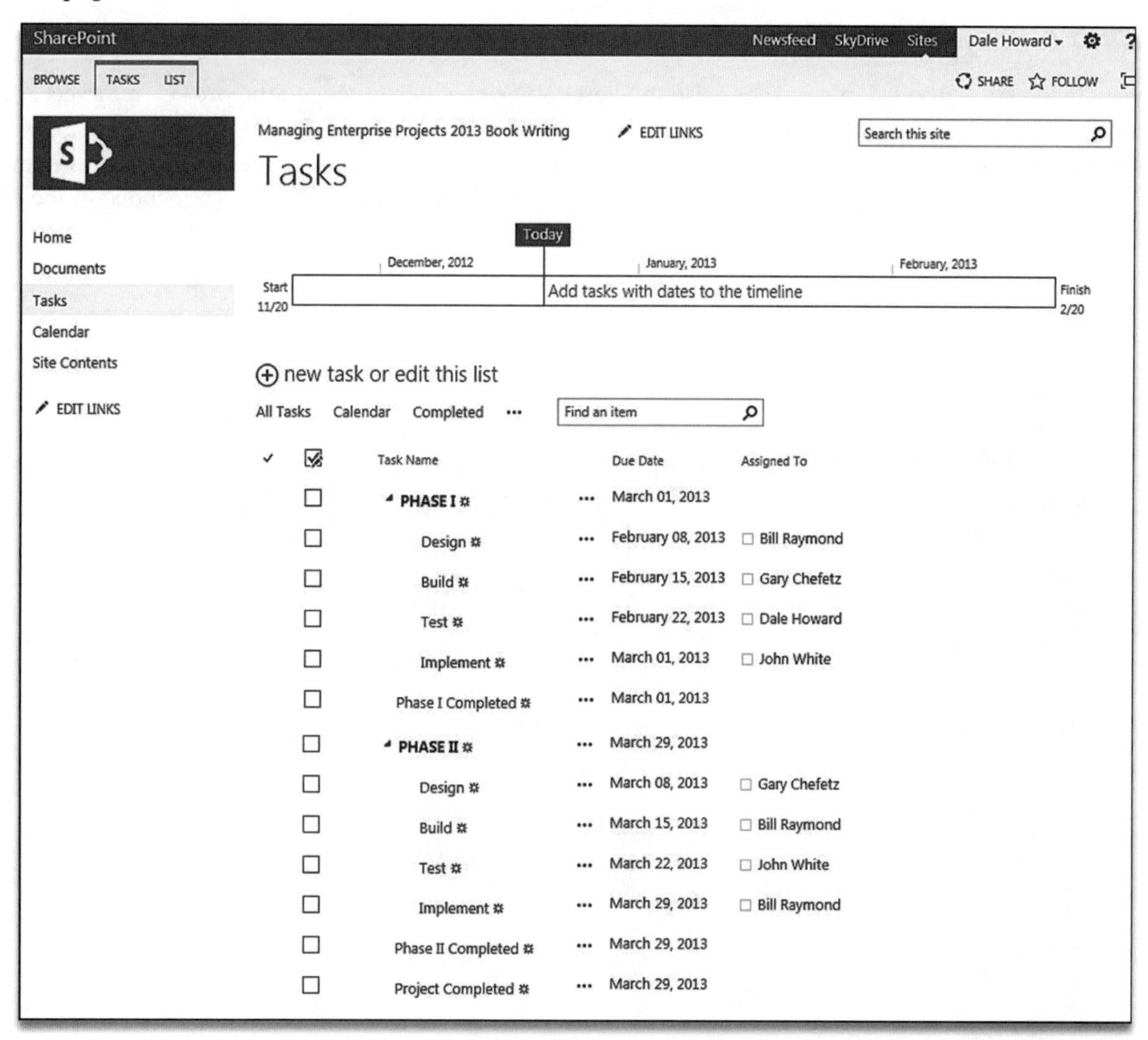

Figure 2 - 8: SharePoint Tasks list contains tasks from the project

Notice in steps #1-5 listed previously in this topical section that Project 2013 **does not** allow you to enter a name for your project. When the software saves your project in the existing SharePoint site, the software applies a generic name for the project based on the title of existing SharePoint site, and then appends *"-Tasks"* to the end of the file name. For example, the software names the project I synchronized with the existing site shown in Figure 2 - 8 as **Managing Enterprise Projects 2013 Book Writing-Tasks.mpp**, and saves the file in the *Site Assets* library of the SharePoint site. You can locate your project file in the SharePoint site by entering a URL similar to the following:

http://ServerName/SiteName/SiteAssets

Warning: By default, an existing SharePoint site does not show the *Site Assets* library in the *Quick Launch* menu on the left side of the *Home* page. To display the *Site Assets* library as a link in the *Quick Launch* menu, click the *Site Contents* link to display the *Site Contents* page, and then click the *Site Assets* icon. On the *Site Assets* page, click the *Library* tab to display the *Library* ribbon. In the *Settings* section of the *Library* ribbon, click the *Library Settings* button. In the *General Settings* section of the *Settings* page, click the *List name, description, and navigation* link. On the *General Settings* page, select the *Yes* option in the *Navigation* section of the page, and then click the *Save* button.

Opening a Project Saved in a SharePoint Site

After you close a project saved in a new or existing SharePoint site, you can reopen the project in Project 2013 by clicking the *File* tab and then clicking the *Open* tab in the *Backstage*. In the *Recent Projects* section of the *Open* page, the software displays all recently opened projects, including projects saved in a SharePoint site, as shown in Figure 2 - 9. Notice the two projects saved in SharePoint sites, each indicated with *–Tasks* appended at the end of the file name.

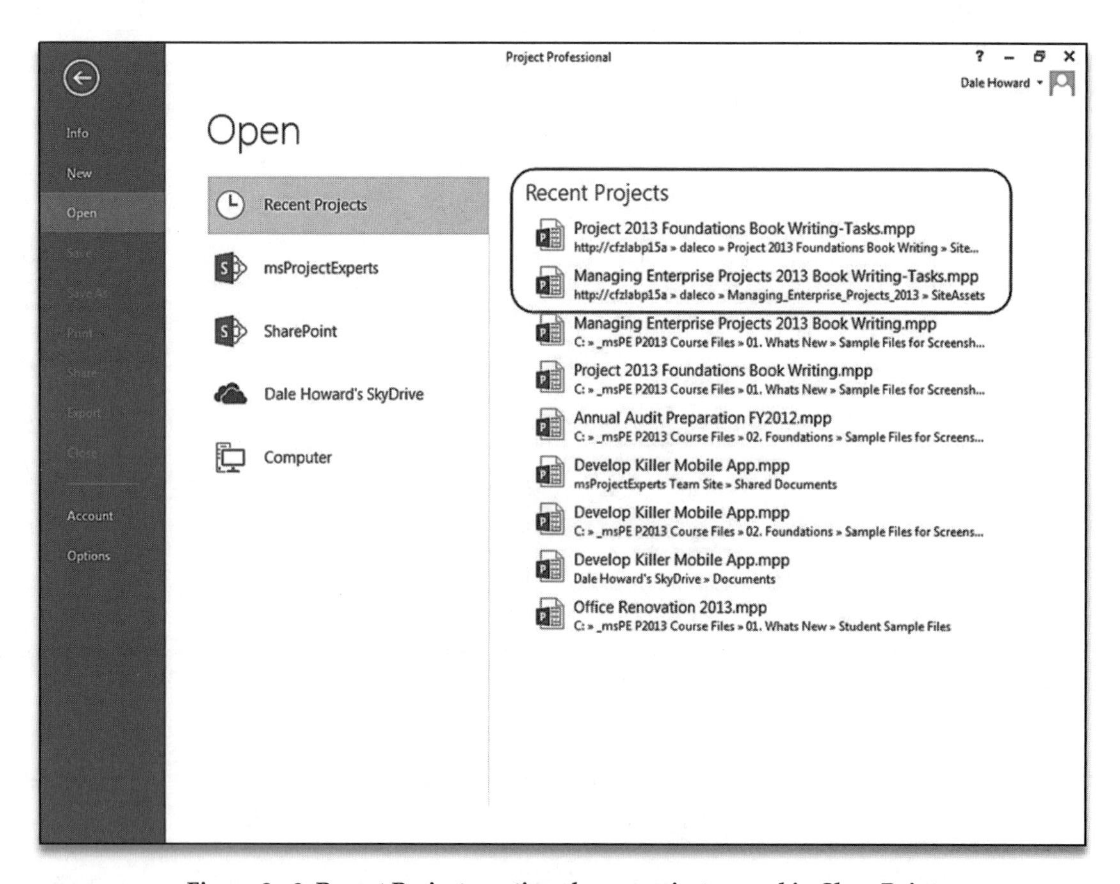

Figure 2 - 9: Recent Projects section shows projects saved in SharePoint

Notice also that of the *Open* page displays a new link named *SharePoint*. Click the *SharePoint* link and the software refreshes the *Open* page as shown in Figure 2 - 10. Notice that the *SharePoint* section displays two recent folders named *SiteAssets*, each representing a SharePoint library in which I saved a project.

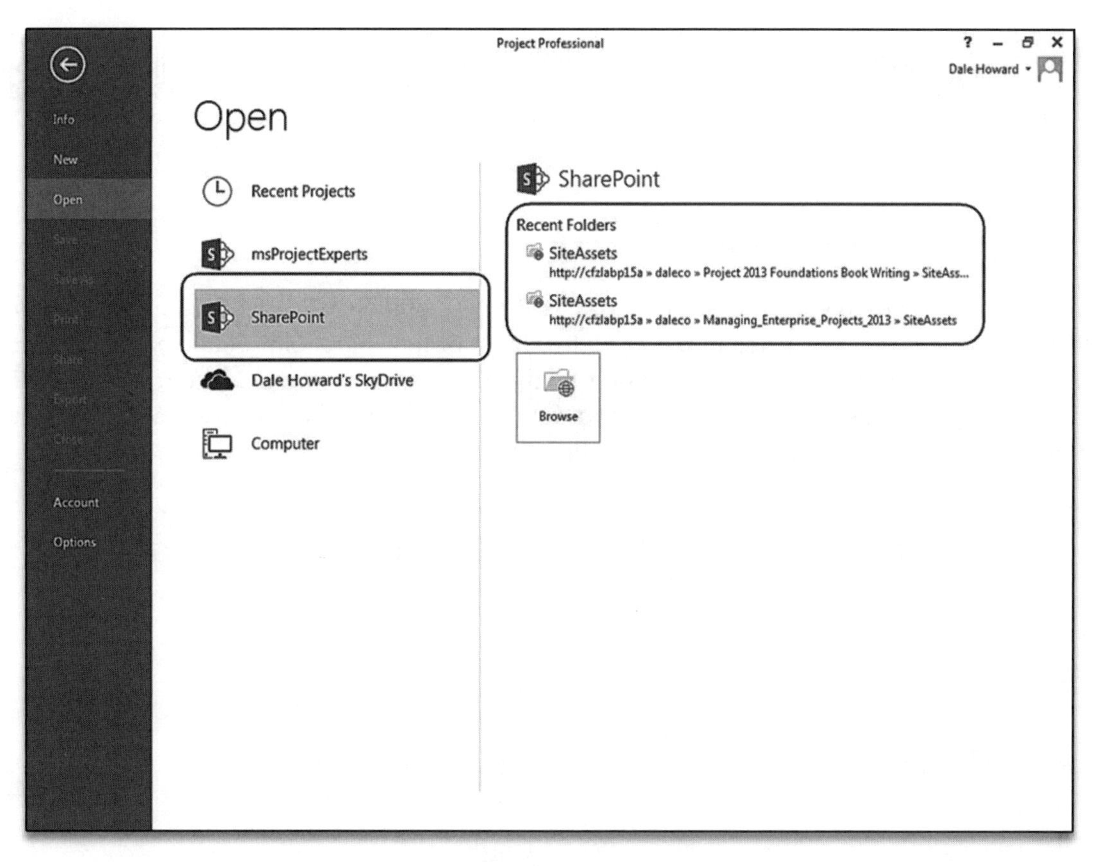

Figure 2 - 10: Open page shows recent SharePoint folders

To open a project saved in a SharePoint site, click the name of the project in the *Recent Projects* section of the *Open* page in the *Backstage*. Alternately, you can click one of the folders in the *SharePoint* section of the *Open* page and then open the project using the *Open* dialog. As the software opens the project, it displays a *Downloading* dialog similar to the one shown in Figure 2 - 11, and then displays a series of *Sync with Tasks List* dialogs such as the one shown previously in Figure 2 - 2.

Figure 2 - 11: Downloading dialog

Information: You can also open the project file directly from the SharePoint site by navigating to the *Site Assets* library in the SharePoint site. Click the *Open Menu* button (the **...** symbol) to the right of the project file name and select the *EDIT* item in the shortcut menu.

Warning: If you attempt to open the project file by clicking the name of the project in the *Site Assets* library, the SharePoint software system opens the project in *Read-Only* mode in Project 2013. To open the project in *Read/Write* mode, you must follow the steps listed in the previous informational note.

Updating the Fields Synchronized with SharePoint

When you initially synchronize your project with a *Tasks* list in SharePoint, Project 2013 uses the information in the project file to create a series of fields in the *Tasks* list. Most of the SharePoint fields map to a corresponding field in the project file, but several of the SharePoint fields do not map to any field in Project 2013. Table 2 - 1 shows the list of SharePoint fields and the corresponding fields in Project 2013. Notice that the *Priority* and *Task Status* fields in SharePoint do not have any corresponding fields in Project 2013.

SharePoint Tasks Field	Project 2013 Field
Title	Name (Task Name)
Start Date	Start
Due Date	Finish
% Complete	% Complete
Assigned To	Resource Names
Predecessors	Predecessors
Priority	No corresponding Project field
Task Status	No corresponding Project field

Table 2 - 1: Corresponding fields in a SharePoint tasks list and a Project 2013 file

In addition to the standard fields included in the synchronization process, Project 2013 allows you to add other fields, including both standard fields and custom fields. You can add these additional fields for reporting purposes or give team members additional information about their task assignments. To add other fields to the task synchronization process, complete the following steps:

1. Click the *File* tab and then click the *Info* tab to display the *Info* page in the *Backstage.* Notice that the *Info* page shown in Figure 2 - 12 includes a *Save and Sync Your Project* section at the top of the page.

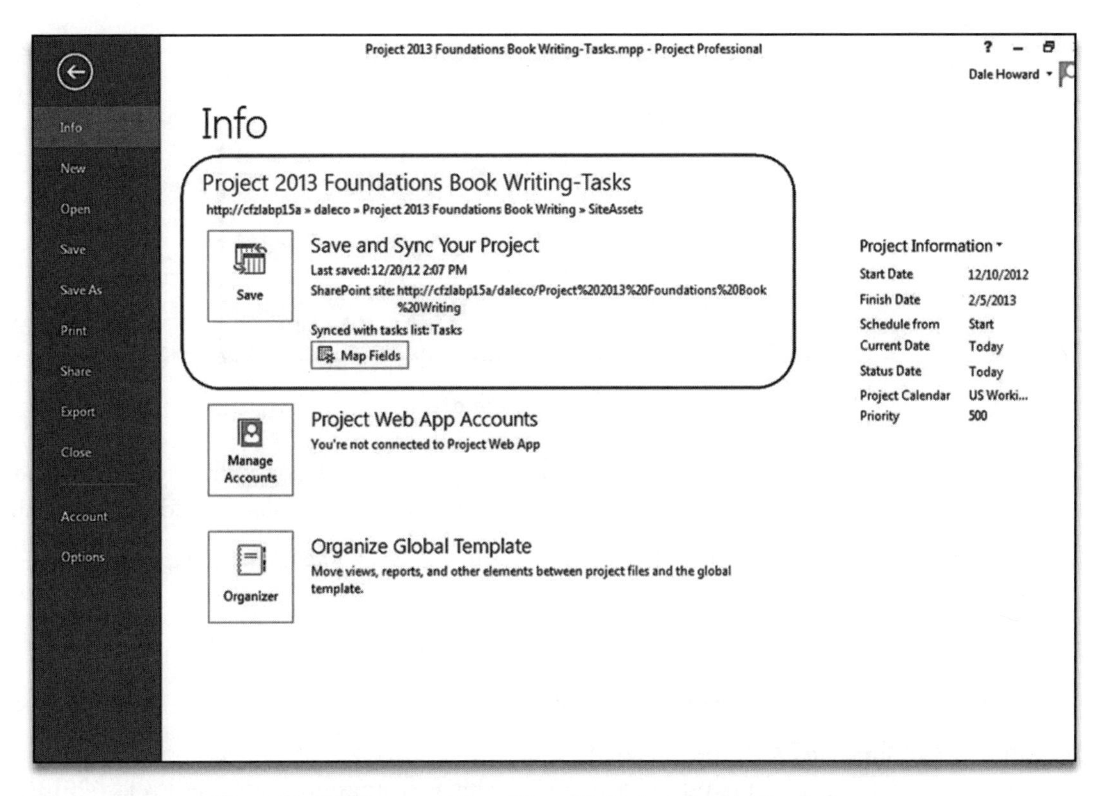

Figure 2 - 12: Save and Sync Your Project section in the Info page

2. In the *Save and Sync Your Project* section of the *Info* page, click the *Map Fields* button. The software displays the *Map Fields* dialog shown in Figure 2 - 13.

Information: In the *Map Fields* dialog shown in Figure 2 - 13, notice the list of fields used for the synchronization process, including the *Priority* and *Task Status* fields created in a *Tasks* list in SharePoint. Notice also that Project 2013 does not allow you to select the *Sync* checkbox for the *Priority* and *Task Status* fields in the *Map Fields* dialog. This is because there are no Project 2013 fields that correspond to these two SharePoint fields; therefore, you must leave them unmapped.

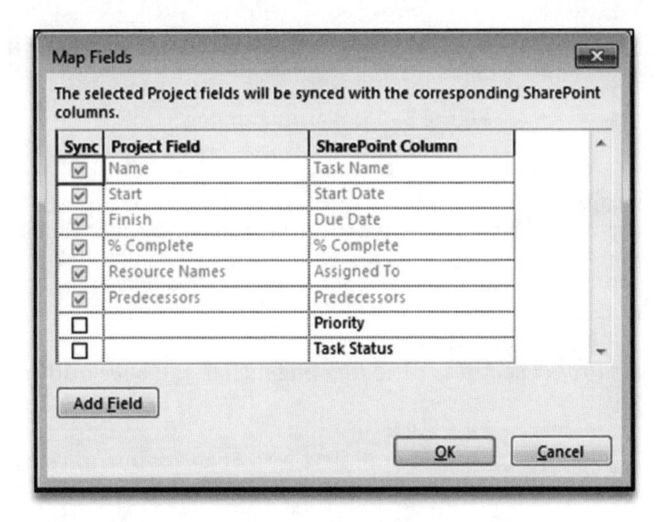

Figure 2 - 13: Map Fields dialog

3. In the *Map Fields* dialog, click the *Add Field* button. The software displays the *Add Field* dialog shown in Figure 2 - 14.

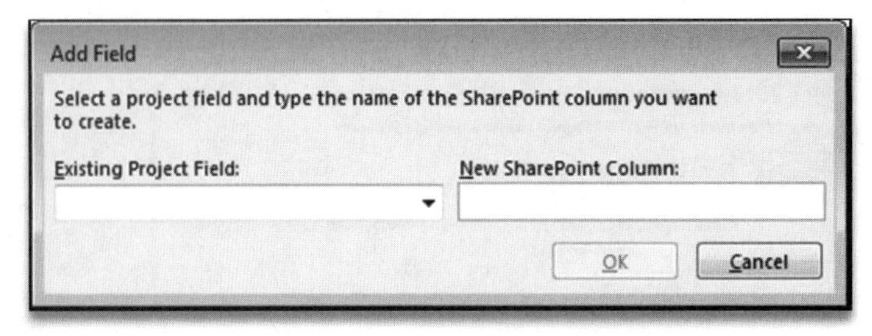

Figure 2 - 14: Add Field dialog

4. In the *Add Field* dialog, click the *Existing Project Field* pick list and select a default or custom field in Project 2013. The system enters the name of the field in the *New SharePoint Column* field automatically.
5. In the *Add Field* dialog, optionally edit the field name in the *New SharePoint Column* field and then click the *OK* button.
6. Repeat steps #3-5 for every field you want to add to the synchronization process.
7. Click the *OK* button to close the *Map Fields* dialog.

If you add certain fields in the *Map Fields* dialog, such as the *Actual Start* or *Actual Finish* fields, the software may display a warning dialog like the one shown in Figure 2 - 15. This warning indicates that Project 2013 will ignore the dates my team members enter in the *Actual Start* field in the SharePoint site, and will override the *Actual Start* date with the current *Start* date instead during each synchronization cycle. In essence, this dialog reveals it is **totally useless** to add fields like *Actual Start, Actual Finish,* or *Actual Work* to the SharePoint synchronization process!

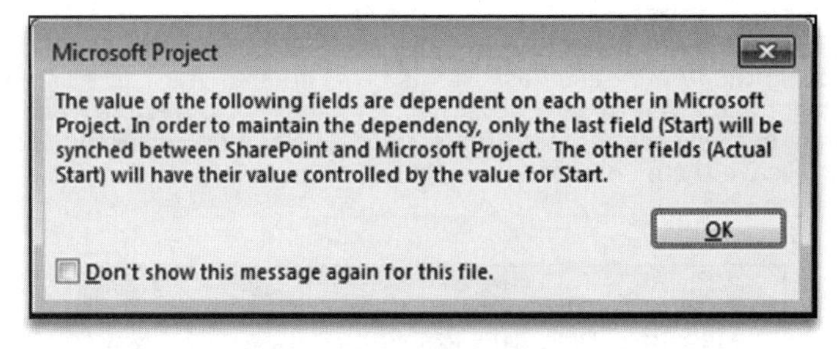

Figure 2 - 15: Warning dialog

Information: The default method of tracking progress in the SharePoint site is very simple. Your team members can update their progress by entering dates in the *Start* and *Finish* fields, and can update their progress by entering a number in the *% Complete* field. The system ignores information they add to fields that are more accurate for tracking progress, such as the *Actual Start* and *Actual Finish* fields.

8. In the *Save and Sync Your Project* section of the *Info* page, click the *Save* button.

Information: You can also synchronize your project with SharePoint by clicking the *Save* button on your *Quick Access Toolbar*.

When Project 2013 completes the synchronization process with SharePoint, the software automatically adds the new fields you select in the *Map Fields* dialog to the SharePoint site. This behavior alone is a major improvement over Project 2010, which required the project manager to manually edit the Project site so that users could see and use the new fields.

Hands On Exercise

Exercise 2 - 4

Open the project from the SharePoint site and add new fields to the synchronization process.

1. Leave your Internet Explorer application window open and return to your Project 2013 application.
2. Click the *File* tab and then click the *Close* button in the *Backstage*.
3. Leave your Project 2013 application window open and return to your Internet Explorer application window.
4. Click the *Site Assets* link in the *Quick Launch* menu.
5. On the *Site Assets* page, click the *Open Menu* button (the ... symbol) to the right of the project file name and select the *EDIT* item in the shortcut menu.
6. In the *Downloading* dialog, monitor the progress of the file download, and in the *Sync with Tasks List* dialog in Project 2013, monitor the progress of the synchronization process.
7. If you see a warning dialog about resources that do not exist in the SharePoint server, click the *OK* button.
8. Click the *File* tab and then click the *Info* tab in the *Backstage*, if necessary.
9. In the *Save and Sync Your Project* section of the *Info* page, click the *Map Fields* button.
10. In the *Map Fields* dialog, click the *Add Field* button.
11. In the *Add Field* dialog, click the *Existing Project Field* pick list and select the *Notes* field, and then click the *OK* button.
12. In the *Map Fields* dialog, click the *OK* button.
13. In the *Save and Sync Your Project* section of the *Info* page, click the *Save* button.
14. In the *Sync with Tasks List* dialog in Project 2013, monitor the progress of the synchronization process.
15. If you see a warning dialog about resources that do not exist in the SharePoint server, click the *OK* button.

Adding Users to the SharePoint Site

Before your team members can collaborate with you on your project using the SharePoint site, they must have permission to access the site. If your team members do not already have access, you can grant them access to the site by completing the following steps:

1. Launch your Internet Explorer application and navigate to the *Home* page of your SharePoint site.

2. In the *Get started with your site* section of the *Home* page, click the *Share your site* button in the carousel. SharePoint displays the *Share* dialog shown in Figure 2 - 16.

Figure 2 - 16: Share dialog

3. To see the list of users who currently have access to the SharePoint site, click the *lots of people* link in the upper left corner of the *Share* dialog. SharePoint displays the *Shared With* dialog shown in Figure 2 - 17. Notice that Dale Howard, Gary Chefetz, and John White currently have access to the SharePoint site, along with the domain users group.

Information: If you click the *INVITE PEOPLE* link in the *Shared With* dialog shown in Figure 2 - 17, SharePoint displays the *Share* dialog shown previously in Figure 2 - 16. If you click the *EMAIL EVERYONE* link, the software creates a new e-mail message, adds the name of the site in the *Subject* line, and adds each current user in the *To* line of the message. If you click the *ADVANCED* link, the software displays the *Permissions* page for your SharePoint site. Because setting custom SharePoint permissions is beyond the scope of this book, I do not show this page, nor do I discuss it.

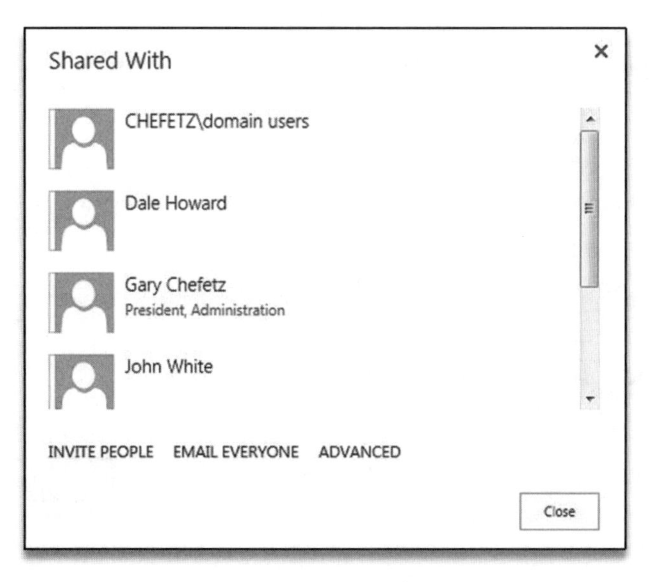

Figure 2 - 17: Shared With dialog

4. Click the *Close* button to close the *Shared With* dialog after you determine which users currently have access to the SharePoint site.

5. In the *Invite people to 'Edit'* section of the *Share* dialog, enter the Windows network user ID, the e-mail address, or the name of the user.

6. As you enter the information for a user, the *Share* dialog displays a pick list of user names corresponding to each user you enter, as shown in Figure 2 - 18. Select a user name from the pick list to add the user.

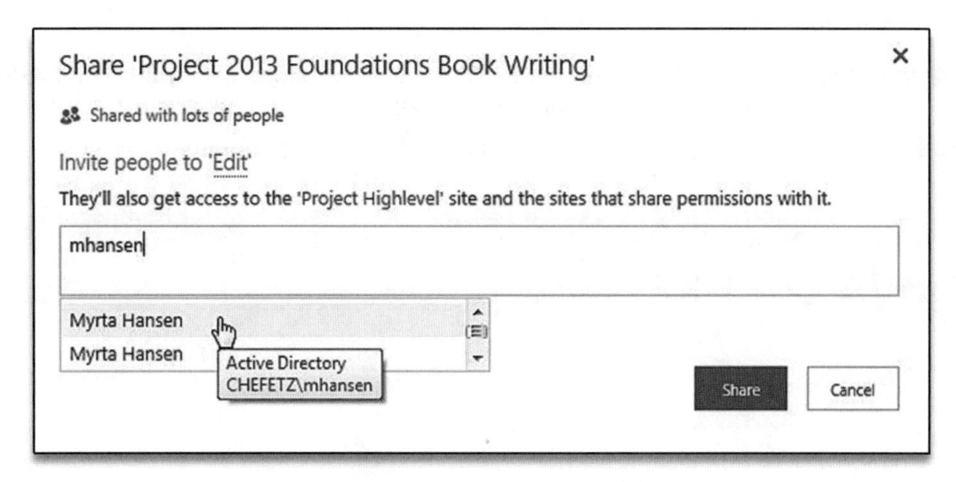

Figure 2 - 18: Share dialog shows available users

7. After adding the names of additional users in the *Share* dialog, click the *SHOW OPTIONS* link in the lower left corner of the dialog. SharePoint expands the dialog to display the *Select a group or permission level* section, as shown in Figure 2 - 19. Notice in the dialog that I want to grant access to the SharePoint site to three additional users: Myrta Hansen, Terry Uland, and Linda Erickson.

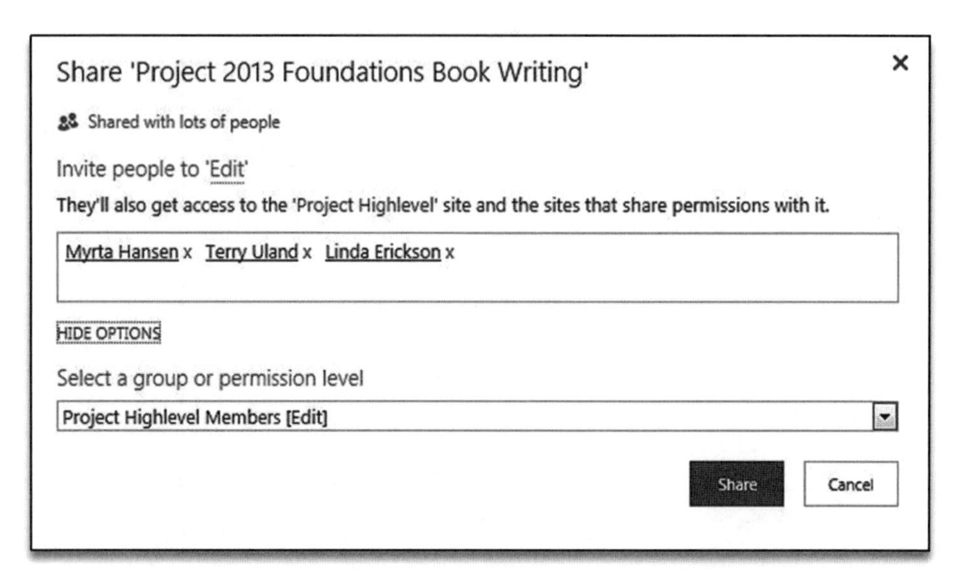

Figure 2 - 19: Share dialog, refreshed to show options

8. Click the *Select a group or permission level* pick list and select a SharePoint group or permission level you want to grant to the additional users. Permission levels include *Excel Services Viewers [View Only]*, *Project Highlevel Members [Edit]*, *Project Highlevel Owners [Full Control]*, and *Project Highlevel Visitors [Read]*. SharePoint selects the *Project Highlevel Members [Edit]* by default.

Information: To see exactly what the *Edit* permission means, float your mouse pointer over the *'Edit'* link in the upper left corner of the dialog. With the *Edit* permission, your new users can add, edit, and delete lists. Your new users can also add, edit, and delete list items and documents. The *Edit* permission, by the way, is the ideal permission for team members.

9. Click the *Share* button.

The software adds the new users to the SharePoint site using the permissions you grant them. After adding users to your site, be sure to open your project in Project 2013 and click the *Save* button on *the Quick Access Toolbar* to synchronize the information in the project with the new users you added to the site.

Hands On Exercise

Exercise 2 - 5

Add your team members to the SharePoint site.

1. Leave your Project 2013 application window open and return to your Internet Explorer application window.
2. At the top of the *Quick Launch* menu, click the *Home* link to return to the *Home* page of the SharePoint site.

3. In the *Getting started with your site* section of the *Home* page, click the *Share your site* button in the carousel.

4. In the *Share* dialog, type the name of your first team member.

5. In the list of users shown at the bottom of the *Share* dialog, select the name of your team member.

6. In the *Share* dialog, repeat the preceding two steps for your second and third team members as well.

7. Click the *Share* button.

8. In the *Getting started with your site* section of the *Home* page, click the *Share your site* button again in the carousel.

9. In the *Share* dialog, click the *lots of people* link in the upper left corner of the dialog.

10. In the *Shared With* dialog, scroll through the list of users who have access to the SharePoint site.

11. Click the *Close* button to close the *Shared With* dialog and then click the *Cancel* button to close the *Share* dialog.

12. Leave your Internet Explorer application window open and return to your Project 2013 application window.

13. In Project 2013, click the *File* tab and then click the *Save* button in the *Backstage*.

Warning: At the end of the synchronization process, you should no longer see a warning dialog about resources that do not exist in the SharePoint server. If you see this dialog again, note the name of the resource shown in the dialog, and then add the resource as a user in the SharePoint site using the preceding steps in this exercise.

Collaborating Using the SharePoint Site

You and the team members in your project can collaborate together about the project using the SharePoint site. Remember that you must add your team members to the SharePoint site before they can access the site. To collaborate with you by reporting task progress, a team member must complete the following steps:

1. Navigate to the *Home* page of the SharePoint site and then click the *Tasks* link in the *Quick Launch* menu. The software displays the *Tasks* list for the project, as shown previously in Figure 2 - 8.

2. Click the name of the task for which to report progress. SharePoint displays the *Tasks* page for the selected task with the *View* ribbon applied. For example, Figure 2 - 20 shows the *Tasks* page for the *Design* task, assigned to a team member named John White. Notice that by default, the software displays only the *Task Name, Start Date, Due Date, Assigned To,* and *% Complete* fields.

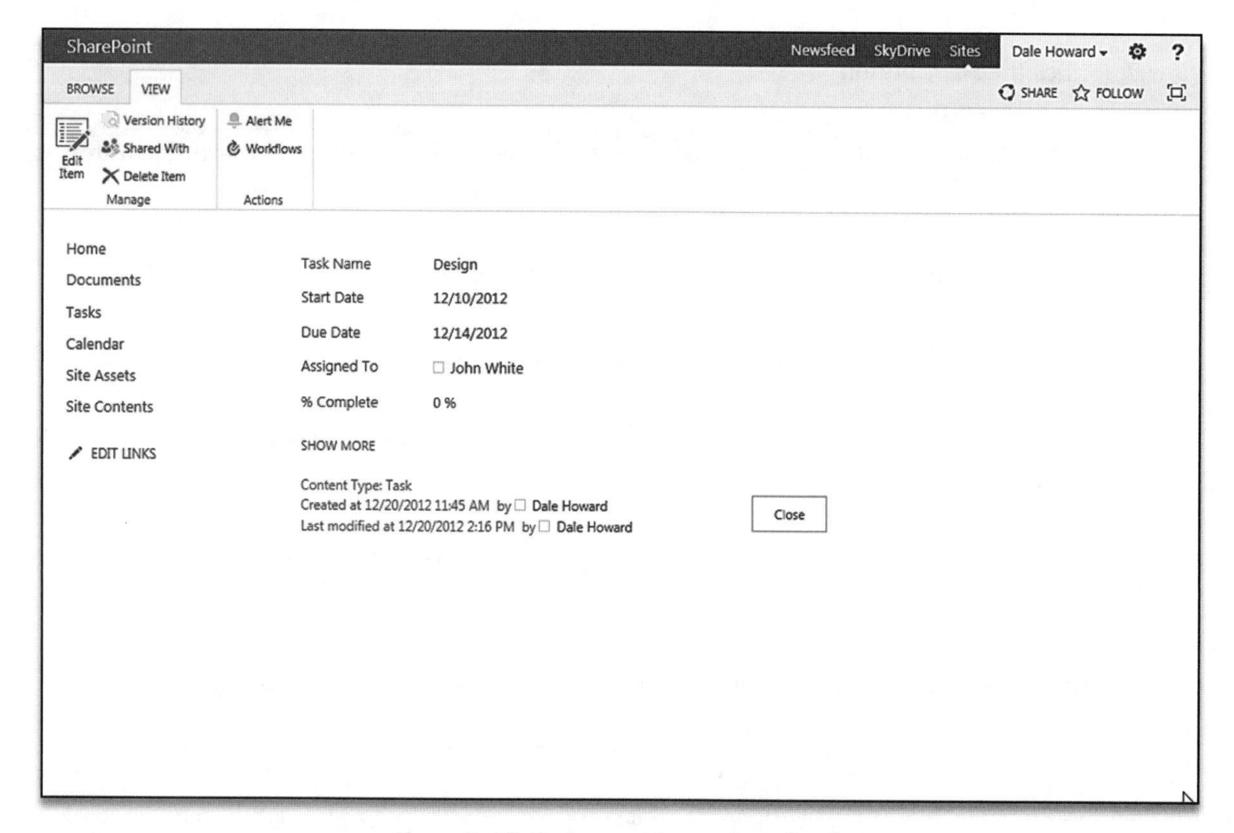

Figure 2 - 20: Tasks page for a selected task

3. In the *Manage* section of the *View* ribbon, click the *Edit Item* button. SharePoint redisplays the *Tasks* page in editing mode with the *Edit* ribbon applied. To see all available fields, click the *SHOW MORE* link near the bottom of the page. The software refreshes the page as shown in Figure 2 - 21. Notice that the *Tasks* page now includes all of the default fields, plus the two custom fields I added, which are the *Actual Start* and *Actual Finish* fields.

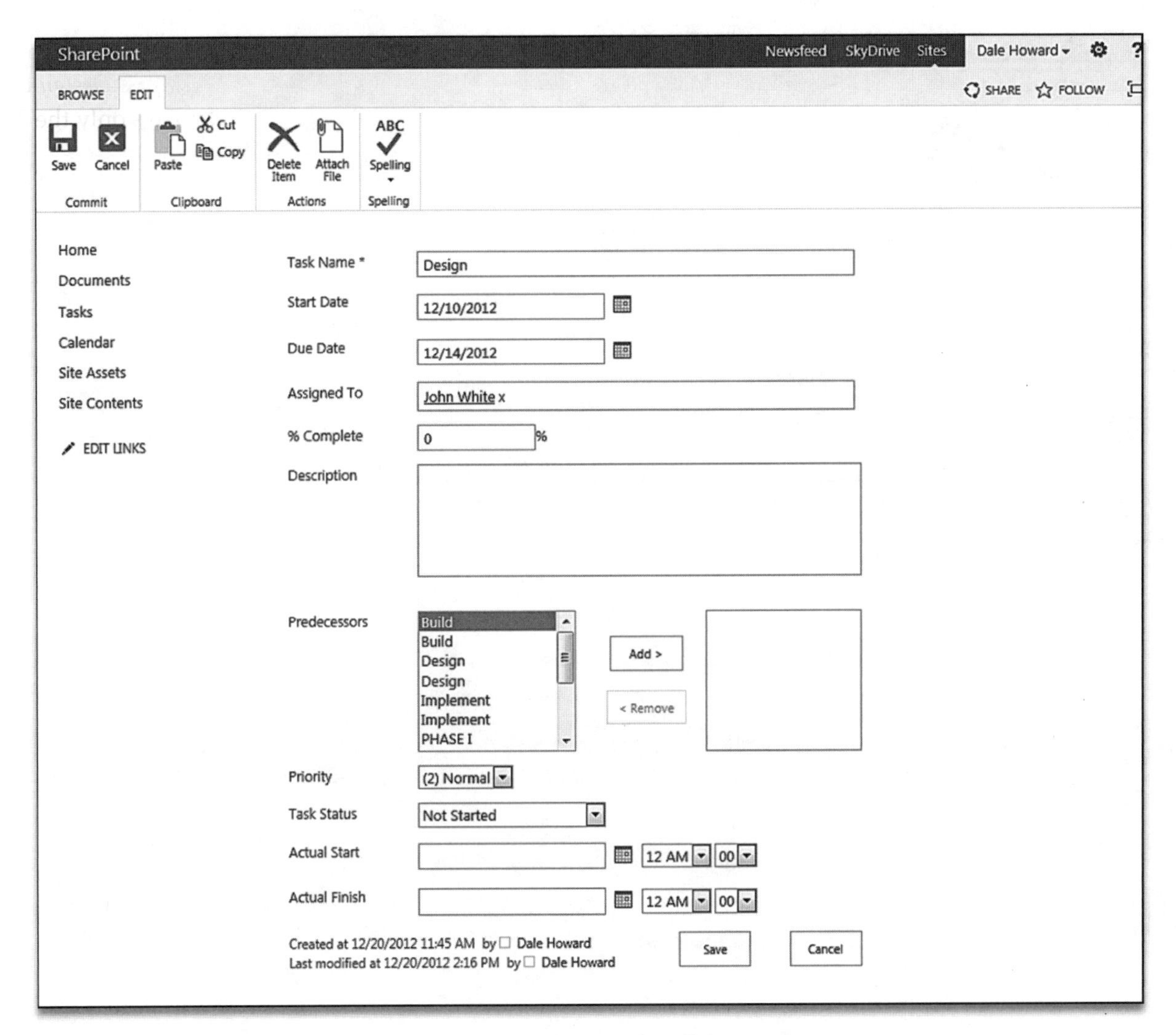

Figure 2 - 21: Tasks page in editing mode

4. Using the fields available on the *Tasks* page, enter progress according to your company's methodology for tracking progress. At a minimum, this means you should enter a *% Complete* value to show your current estimated progress on the task.

5. When finished, click either the *Save* button at the bottom of the page or the *Save* button in the *Commit* section of the *Edit* ribbon. If the team member enters a *100%* value in the *% Complete* field, the software updates the *Tasks* page to show task completion for the selected task. Notice in Figure 2 - 22 that the *Tasks* page shows completion for the *Design* task, indicated by the strikethrough formatting applied to the task name, and with the checkbox selected to the left of the task.

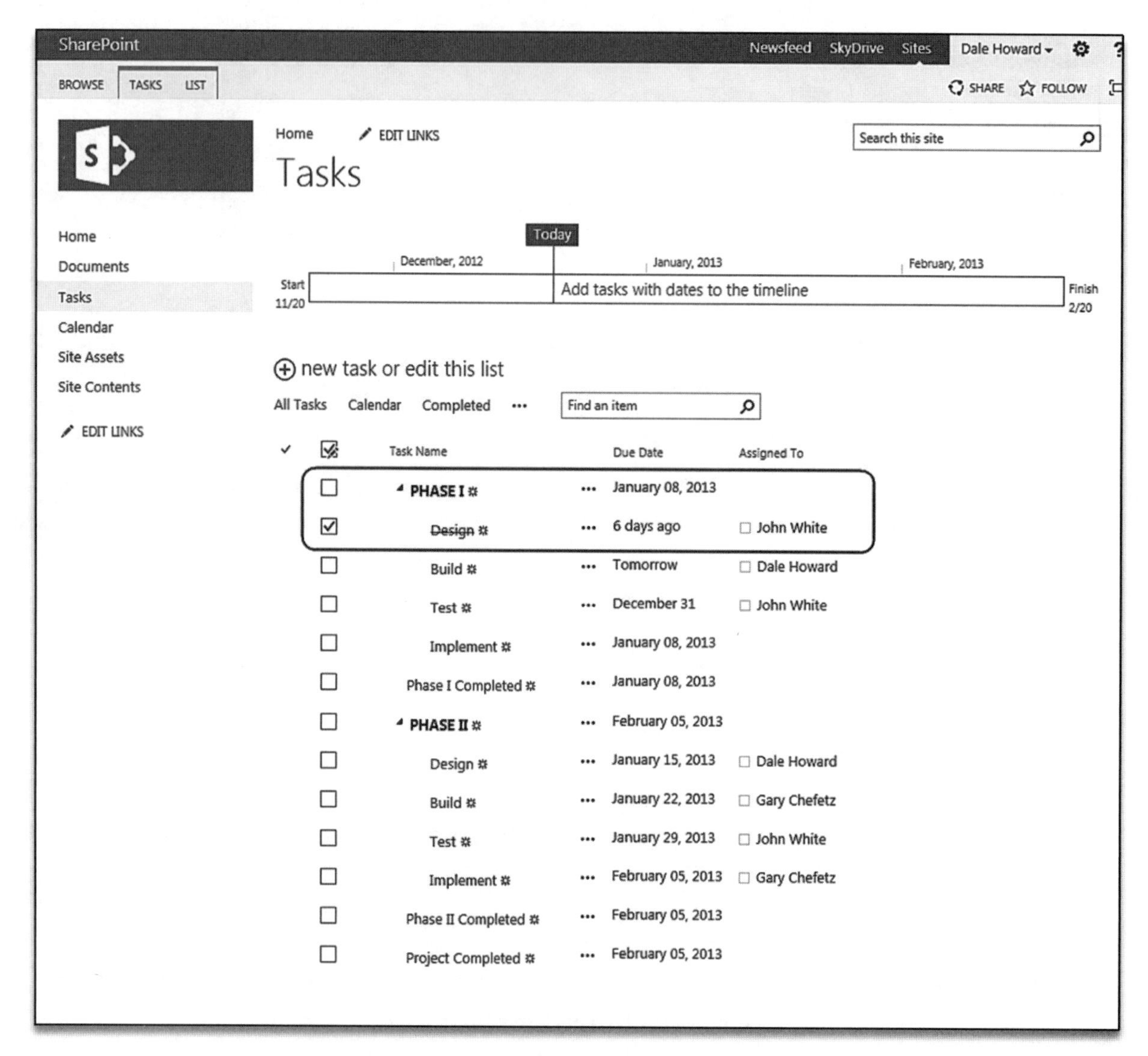

Figure 2 - 22: Design task completed by team member

After team members enter progress in the *Tasks* list in SharePoint, the project manager can open the project in Project 2013 and resynchronize the project to import the updates into the project. Figure 2 - 23 shows the project after synchronizing it with the progress entered by John White in the SharePoint site. Notice that the synchronization progress marked the *Design* task as *100% complete* in the Phase I section of the project.

Warning: If a team member changes the *Start Date* value for the task, SharePoint **does not** update the *Due Date* value correspondingly. For example, if a team member changes the *Start Date* value to a date two days later, the software does not change the *Due Date* value to a date that is two days later. This means that when you accept the task update from your team member into your Project 2013 plan, the software **shortens** the *Duration* of the task by 2 days! Therefore, stress to your team members that they should report progress by only updating the *% Complete* value, and they **should not** change the *Start Date* or *Due Date* values unless absolutely necessary.

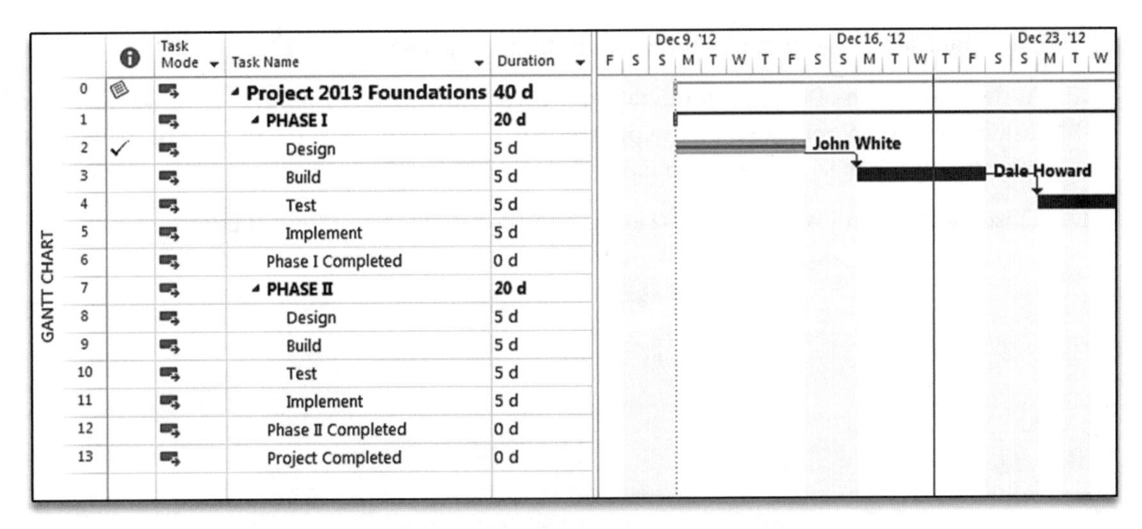

Figure 2 - 23: Project 2013 file updated with progress entered on the Design task by the team member in the SharePoint site

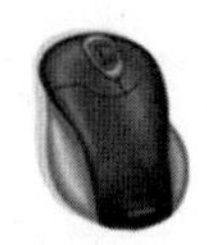

Hands On Exercise

Exercise 2 - 6

Enter progress on a task in the SharePoint site and then synchronize the project.

1. Leave your Project 2013 application window open and return to your Internet Explorer application window.
2. In the *Quick Launch* menu, click the *Tasks* link.
3. On the *Tasks* page of the SharePoint site, examine the list of tasks and the resource assigned to each task.
4. Click the *Order Server* task to display additional details about the task.
5. In the *Manage* section of the *View* ribbon, click the *Edit Item* button.
6. Near the bottom of the page, click the *SHOW MORE* link to display all of the details about the *Order Server* task.
7. Examine the information shown in the *Notes* field at the bottom of the page.
8. In the *% Complete* field, enter the value *100*, and then click the *Save* button in either the *Edit* ribbon or at the bottom of the page.
9. Note that SharePoint indicates that the *Order Server* task is completed using the strikethrough font formatting and by selecting the checkbox to the left of the task.
10. Close your Internet Explorer application window and return to your Project 2013 application window.

11. Click the *File* tab and then click the *Save* button in the *Backstage*.
12. At the conclusion of the synchronization process, notice that Project 2013 shows the *Order Server* task is completed, indicated by the progress line drawn through the middle of the task's Gantt bar, and by the check mark in the *Indicators* column.
13. Close the **Training Advisor 2013-Tasks.mpp** file and then exit Project 2013.

Module 03

Using Project 2013 Day to Day

Learning Objectives

After completing this module, you will be able to:

- Understand how to use the new task filters
- Understand how to see and use the new cumulative fields in the Task Usage and Resource Usage views
- Know the latest possible date available for use in Project 2013
- Use the new Task Path feature
- Understand the improved functionality of the Inactivate Task feature
- Use task pane Office Apps
- Use Lync integration with Project 2013

Inside Module 03

Understanding Date Changes

In all previous versions of the software, from the Project 2000 version through the Project 2010 version, the software would not support *Start* dates earlier than January 1, 1984 or *Finish* dates later than December 31, 2049. A major change in Project 2013 is that the software now allows dates up to **December 31, 2149**. With this simple change, Microsoft added 100 years to the life of any project!

Figure 3 - 1 shows a Project 2010 project in which I specified *December 30, 2049* as the *Start* date of the project. In this project, I added a task named *Design* and attempted to enter a *Duration* value of *5 days*. Notice that the software limits me to a *Duration* value of only *1 day* for the task, and notice that the Timescale shows no dates later than **December 31, 2049**.

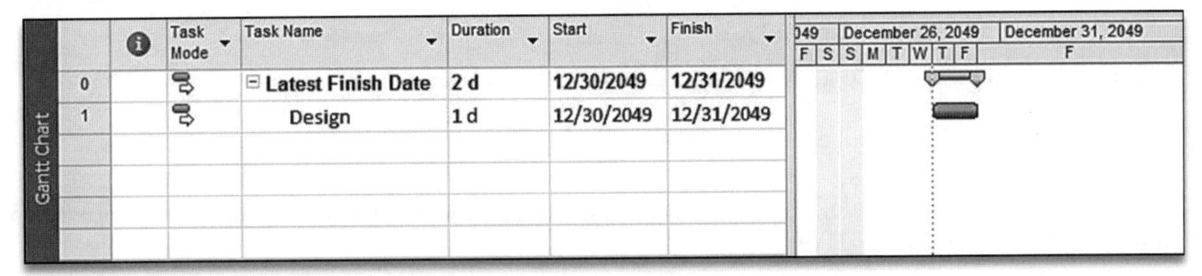

Figure 3 - 1: Latest possible Finish date in Project 2010

Figure 3 - 2 shows a similar project in Project 2013 in which I specified *December 30, 2149* as the *Start* date of the project. In this project, I added a task named *Design* and attempted to enter a *Duration* value of *5 days*. Notice that the software limits me to a *Duration* value of only *2 days*, and notice that the Timescale shows no dates later than **December 31, 2149**.

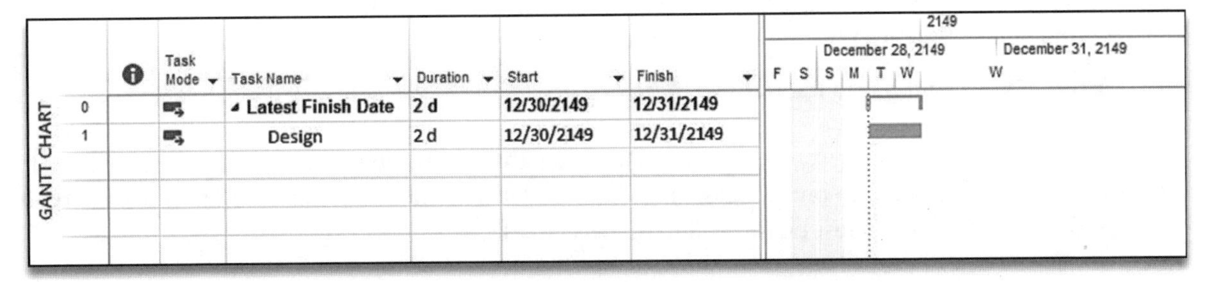

Figure 3 - 2: Latest possible Finish date in Project 2013

If you use the *Project Information* dialog and attempt to enter either a *Start date* or *Finish date* value outside of the acceptable date range in Project 2013, the software displays the warning dialog shown in Figure 3 - 3. Notice that the warning dialog confirms the earliest and latest dates possible in the software.

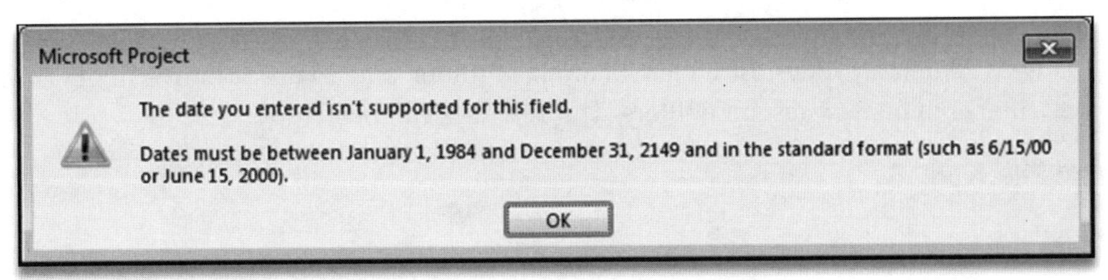

Figure 3 - 3: Date range warning dialog

Hands On Exercise

Exercise 3 - 1

Explore the new date changes in Project 2013.

1. Click the *File* tab and then click the *New* tab in the *Backstage*.
2. On the *New* page in the *Backstage*, click the *Blank Project* icon to create a new blank project.
3. Click the *Project* tab to display the *Project* ribbon.
4. In the *Properties* section of the *Project* ribbon, click the *Project Information* button.
5. In the *Start date* field, enter **3/18/2150** and then click the *OK* button.

Notice that the warning dialog reveals the acceptable range for dates in your project, spanning from January 1, 984 to December 31, 2149.

6. Click the *OK* button to close the warning dialog.
7. In the *Start date* field, enter **12/29/2149** and then click the *OK* button.
8. In the lower left corner of the Project 2013 application window, click the *Default Task Mode* button and select the *Auto Scheduled* item on the menu.
9. Manually enter a new task named *Design*, enter a *Duration* value of *5 days* for this new task, and then press the **Enter** key on your computer keyboard.
10. Drag your split bar to the right so that you can see the *Finish* column, if necessary.

Notice that the software does not allow any date later than December 31, 2149. Because of this, Project 2013 shortens the *Duration* to only *3 days* to calculate a *Finish* date of *December 31, 2149* for the new task. Remember that this is the latest possible date in Project 2013.

11. Click the *File* tab and then click the *Close* tab in the *Backstage*.
12. When prompted in a dialog to save the changes to the new project, click the *No* button.

Using the New Task Filters

Project 2013 ships with 70 default filters, of which 45 are task filters, and 25 are resource filters. The software includes 11 new task filters but no new resource filters. The new task filters include:

- *Completed Milestones*
- *Late Milestones*
- *Milestones Due This Month*

- *No Actuals*
- *No Resources Assigned*
- *Overallocated Tasks*
- *Summary Task with Assigned Resources*
- *Tasks Due This Week*
- *Tasks Starting Soon*
- *Tasks with Durations < 8h*
- *Upcoming Milestones*

Understanding the Completed Milestones Filter

Use the *Completed Milestones* filter to display all completed milestone tasks in your projects. Figure 3 - 4 shows the *Filter Definition* dialog for the new *Completed Milestones* filter. For every task in your project, the filter first determines whether the task is an *Active* task, as opposed to a task you set to *Inactive* status to cancel the task. If the task is an *Active* task, then the filter determines whether the task is a *Milestone* task. If true, then the filter determines if the *% Work Complete* value for the task is *100%*. If all three values are true in the filter criteria for any task, then the filter displays the task.

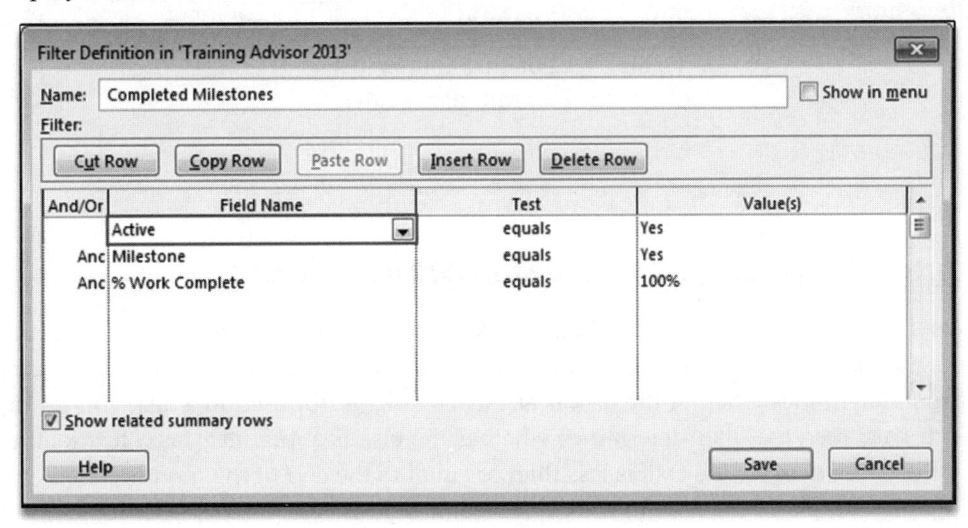

Figure 3 - 4: Filter Definition dialog for the Completed Milestones filter

Understanding the Late Milestones Filter

Use the *Late Milestones* filter to display incomplete *Milestone* tasks that are late. By definition, a **late task** in Project 2013 is any task where the time-phased cumulative percent complete (represented by the black progress line in a Gantt bar) does not reach the *Status Date* you specify for the project. If you do not specify a *Status Date* for your project, then the software uses the *Current Date* to determine whether tasks are late. If any task is a late task, then the software displays a *Late* value in the *Status* field for that task.

Figure 3 - 5 shows the *Filter Definition* dialog for the new *Late Milestones* filter. For every task in your project, the filter first determines whether the task is an *Active* task, as opposed to a task you set to *Inactive* status to cancel the task. If true, then the filter determines whether the task is a *Milestone* task. If true, then the filter determines whether the *Status* field for the task contains a *Late* value. If true, then the filter determines if the *% Work Complete* value for the task is not equal to *100%*. If all four values are true in the filter criteria for any task, then the filter displays the task.

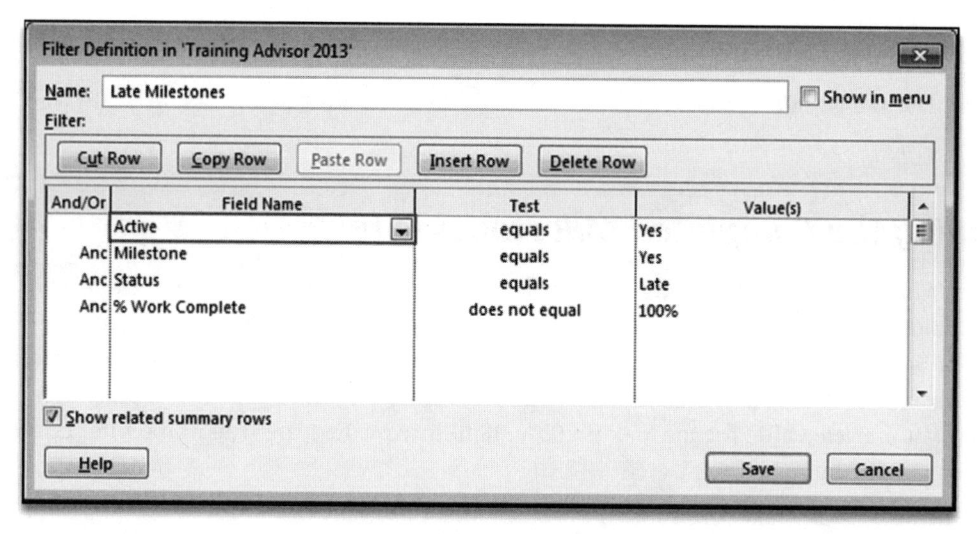

Figure 3 - 5: Filter Definition dialog for the Late Milestones filter

Understanding the Milestones Due This Month Filter

Use the *Milestones Due This Month* filter to display *Milestone* tasks with a *Finish* date occurring this month. Figure 3 - 6 shows the *Filter Definition* dialog for the new *Milestones Due This Month* filter. For each task in your project, the filter first determines whether the task is an *Active* task, as opposed to a task you set to *Inactive* status to cancel the task. If true, then the filter determines whether the task is a *Milestone* task. If true, then the filter determines whether the *Finish* date for the task is less than or equal to the end of the month, based on the date in the *Current Date* field. For example, if the date in the *Current Date* field is June 15, the filter looks for *Milestone* tasks whose *Finish* date is less than or equal to June 30. If true, then the filter determines if the *% Work Complete* value for the task is not equal to *100%*. If all four values are true in the filter criteria for any task, then the filter displays the task.

Warning: The *Milestones Due This Month* filter uses the *Current Date* value to determine the current month and then displays **all incomplete milestones** earlier than the end of the current month. This means that the filter can display milestones that were due **last month** but were not marked as completed.

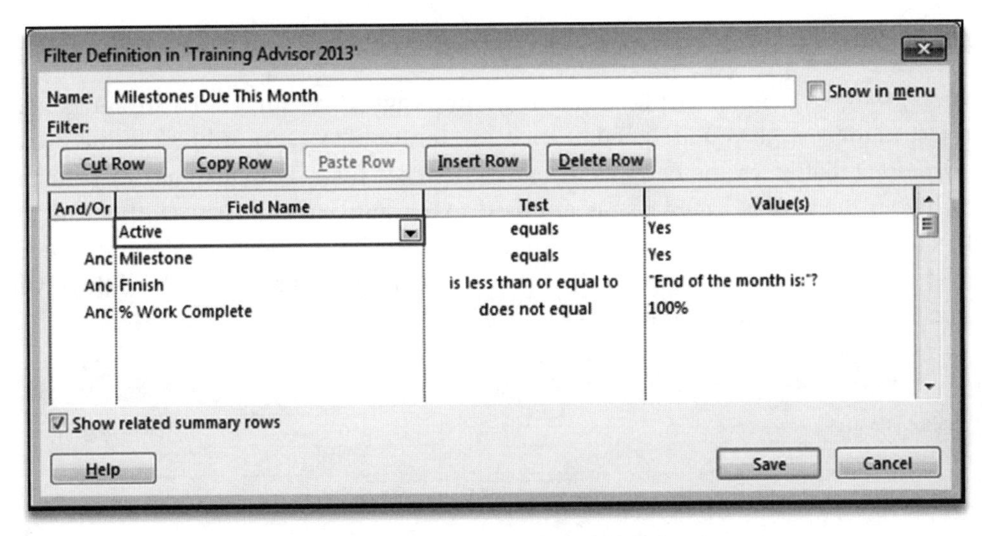

Figure 3 - 6: Filter Definition dialog for the Milestones Due This Month filter

Understanding the No Actuals Filter

Use the *No Actuals* filter to display tasks that contain no actual work to date. Figure 3 - 7 shows the *Filter Definition* dialog for the new *No Actuals* filter. For each task in your project, the filter first determines whether the task is a subtask, as opposed to a summary task. If true, then the filter determines whether the task is a regular task, as opposed to a *Milestone* task. If true, then the filter determines whether the task has 0 hours of *Actual Work* (in other words, the task has no actuals). If true, then the filter determines if the *Start* date of the task is less than today, based on the date in the *Current Date* field. If all four values are true in the filter criteria for any task, then the filter displays the task.

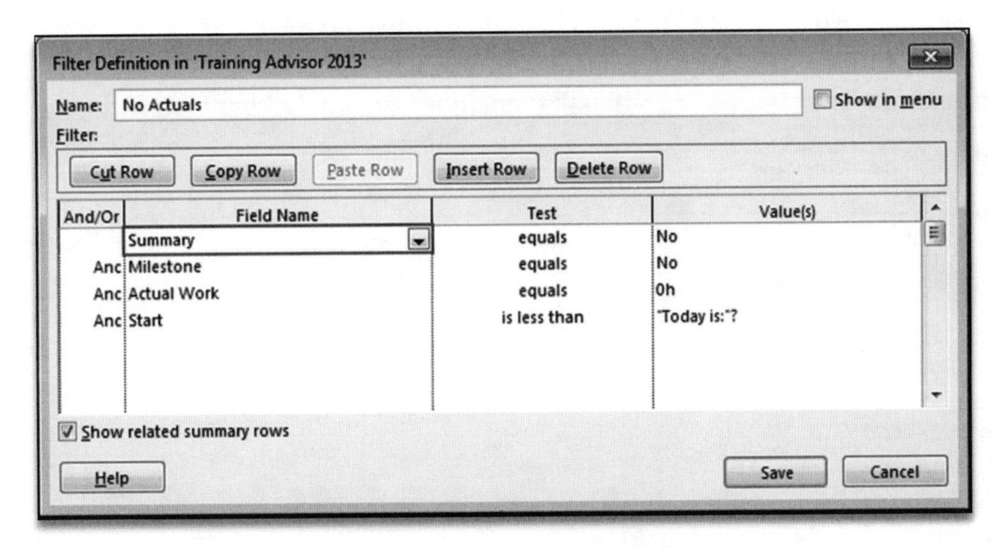

Figure 3 - 7: Filter Definition dialog for the No Actuals filter

Understanding the No Resources Assigned Filter

Use the *No Resources Assigned* filter to display tasks without assigned resources. This filter is very useful when auditing your project to make sure you assigned at least one resource to every subtask in the project. Figure 3 - 8 shows the *Filter Definition* dialog for the new *No Resources Assigned* filter. For each task in your project, the filter first determines whether the task is a subtask, as opposed to a summary task. If true, then the filter determines whether the task is a regular task, as opposed to a *Milestone* task. If true, then the filter determines whether the *Resource Names* field is blank, which indicates that the task has no resources assigned. If all three values are true in the filter criteria for any task, then the filter displays the task.

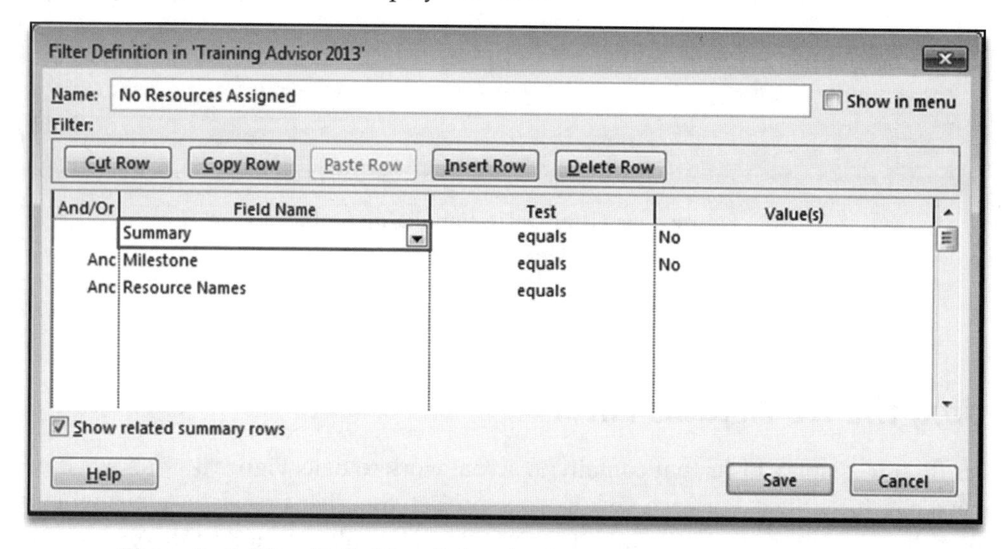

Figure 3 - 8: Filter Definition dialog for the No Resources Assigned filter

Understanding the Overallocated Tasks Filter

Use the *Overallocated Tasks* filter to display tasks assigned to an overallocated resource. Figure 3 - 9 shows the *Filter Definition* dialog for the new *Overallocated Tasks* filter. For each task in your project, the filter determines whether the *Overallocated* field contains a *Yes* value, indicating that you have one or more overallocated resources assigned to the task. If the filter returns a true value for the task, then the filter displays the task.

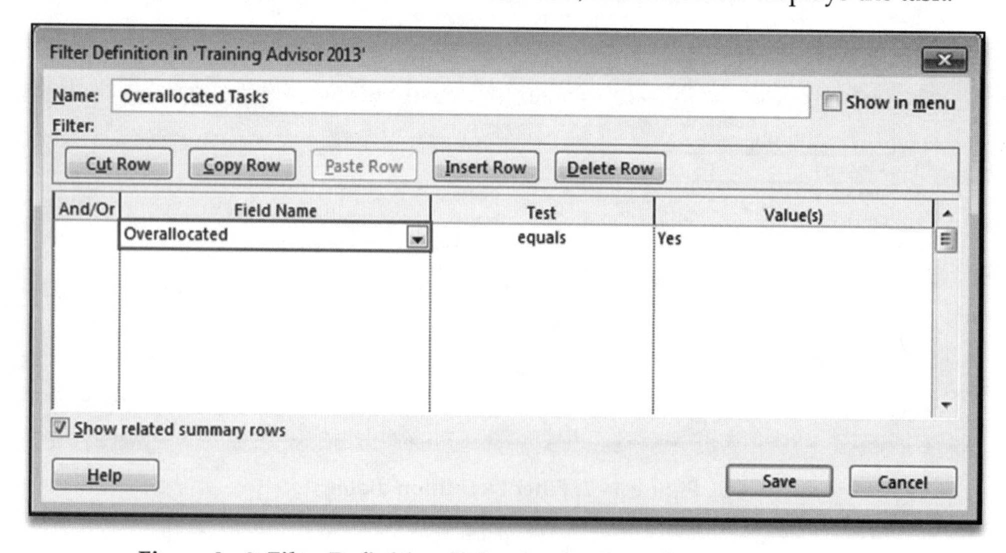

Figure 3 - 9: Filter Definition dialog for the Overallocated Tasks filter

Warning: Because of an unfixed bug in the release (RTM) version of Project 2013, the *Overallocated Tasks* filter **does not** display parallel tasks assigned to an overallocated resource. Instead, this filter only shows tasks in which two specific conditions cause the overallocation: when you assign a resource to the task with a *Units* value greater than the *Max. Units* value for the resource, and when you assign a resource to work on a task during a nonworking time period, such as a weekend. Because of these limitations, the *Overallocated Resource* filter is of very limited practical use.

Understanding the Summary Task with Assigned Resources Filter

Use the *Summary Task with Assigned Resources* filter to display summary tasks to which you assigned resources. Because assigning resources to a summary task is very bad practice, this new filter is very useful when auditing your project to make sure you have no resources assigned to summary tasks. Figure 3 - 10 shows the *Filter Definition* dialog for the new *Summary Task with Assigned Resources* filter. For each task in your project, the filter first determines whether the task is a summary task. If true, then the filter determines if the *Resource Names* field is not blank, indicating that you have at least one resource assigned to the task. If both values are true in the filter criteria for any task, then the filter displays the task.

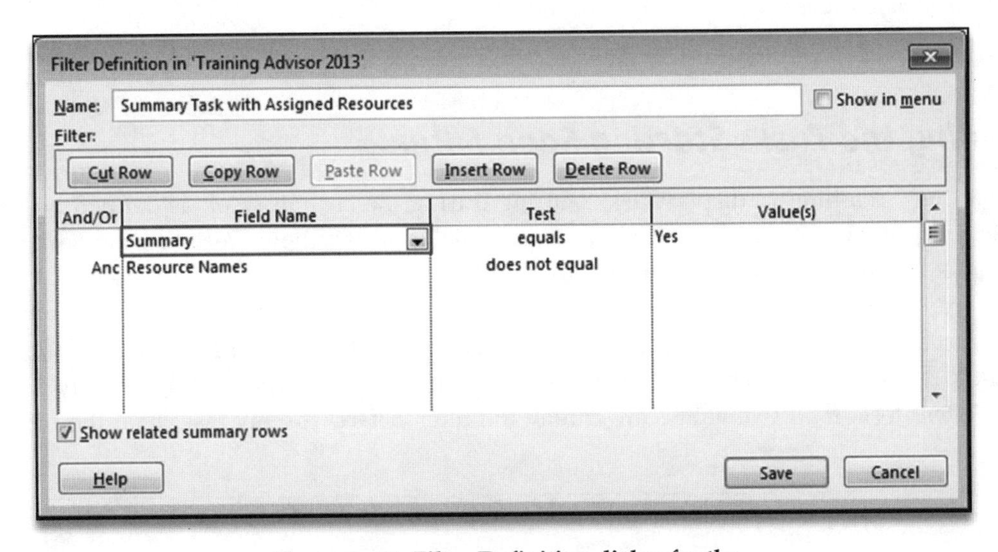

Figure 3 - 10: Filter Definition dialog for the Summary Task with Assigned Resources filter

Understanding the Tasks Due This Week Filter

Use the *Tasks Due This Week* filter to display tasks with a *Finish* date during the current week as defined by the date in the *Current Date* field. Figure 3 - 11 shows the *Filter Definition* dialog for the new *Tasks Due This Week* filter. For each task in your project, the filter first determines whether the task is an *Active* task, as opposed to a task you set to *Inactive* status to cancel the task. If true, then the filter uses the next two criteria to determine whether the *Finish* date for the task occurs in the current week, as defined by the date in the *Current Date* field. If true, then the filter determines if the *% Work Complete* value for the task is not equal to *100%*. If true, the filter finally determines if the task is not a *Milestone* task. If all five values are true in the filter criteria for any task, then the filter displays the task.

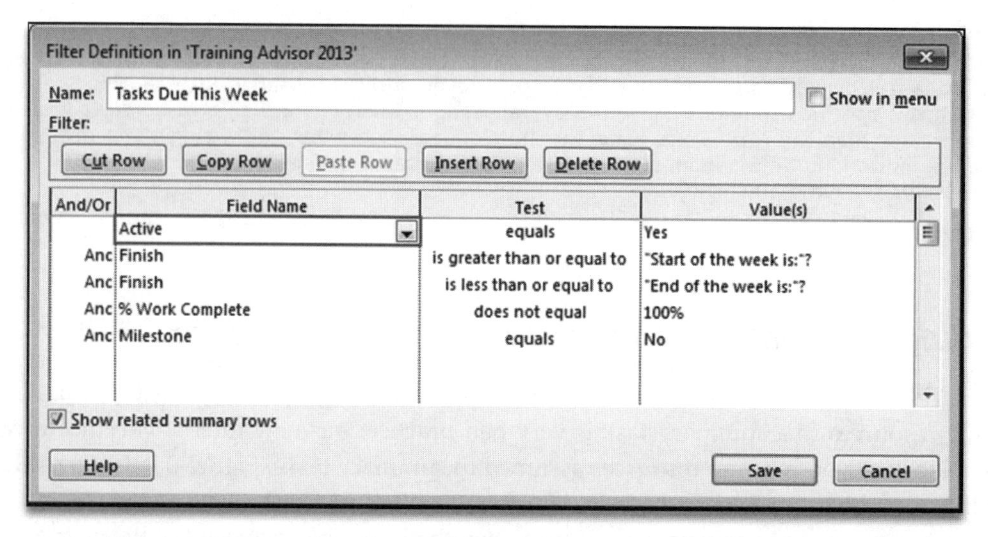

Figure 3 - 11: Filter Definition dialog for the Tasks Due This Week filter

Warning: The *Tasks Due This Week* filter uses the *Current Date* value to determine the current week and then displays **all incomplete tasks** earlier than the end of the current week. This means that the filter can display tasks that were due last week but were not completed.

Understanding the Tasks Starting Soon Filter

Use the *Tasks Starting Soon* filter to display tasks starting during the current week as defined by the date in the *Current Date* field. Figure 3 - 12 shows the *Filter Definition* dialog for the new *Tasks Starting Soon* filter. For each task in your project, the filter first determines whether the task is an *Active* task, as opposed to a task you set to *Inactive* status to cancel the task. If true, then the filter uses the next two criteria to determine whether the *Start* date for the task occurs in the current week, as defined by the date in the *Current Date* field. If true, then the filter determines if the *% Work Complete* value for the task is not equal to *100%*. If true, the filter finally determines if the task is not a *Milestone* task. If all five values are true in the filter criteria for any task, then the filter displays the task.

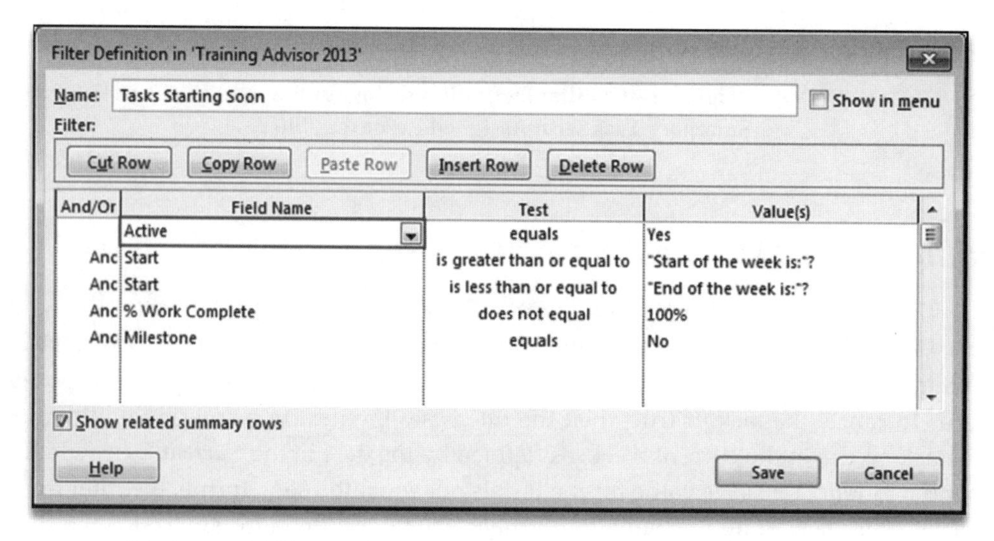

Figure 3 - 12: Filter Definition dialog for the Tasks Starting Soon filter

Understanding the Tasks with Duration < 8h Filter

Some organizations use a methodology that does not allow a project manager to specify a task *Duration* value less than *1 day*. If your organization uses a methodology such as this, use the *Tasks with Duration < 8h* filter to display tasks with a *Duration* value of less than *1 day*. Figure 3 - 13 shows the *Filter Definition* dialog for the new *Tasks with Duration < 8h* filter. For each task in your project, the filter determines if the *Scheduled Duration* value is less than *8 hours*. If the filter returns a true value for the task, then the filter displays the task.

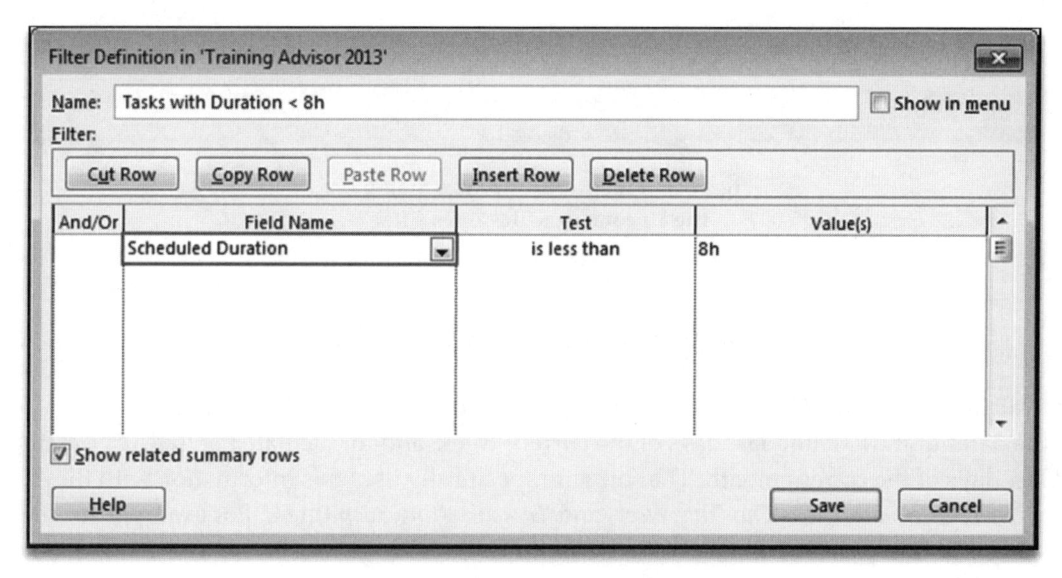

Figure 3 - 13: Filter Definition dialog for the Tasks with Durations < 8h filter

Information: The *Tasks with Duration < 8h* filter uses the *Scheduled Duration* field instead of the *Duration* field so that it can correctly filter both *Manually Scheduled* tasks and *Auto Scheduled* tasks.

Understanding the Upcoming Milestones Filter

Use the *Upcoming Milestones* filter to see all incomplete *Milestone* tasks in your project. Figure 3 - 14 shows the *Filter Definition* dialog for the new *Upcoming Milestones* filter. For each task in your project, the filter first determines whether the task is a *Milestone* task. If true, then the filter determines if the *% Work Complete* value does not equal *100%*. If both values in the filter criteria are true for any task, then the filter displays the task.

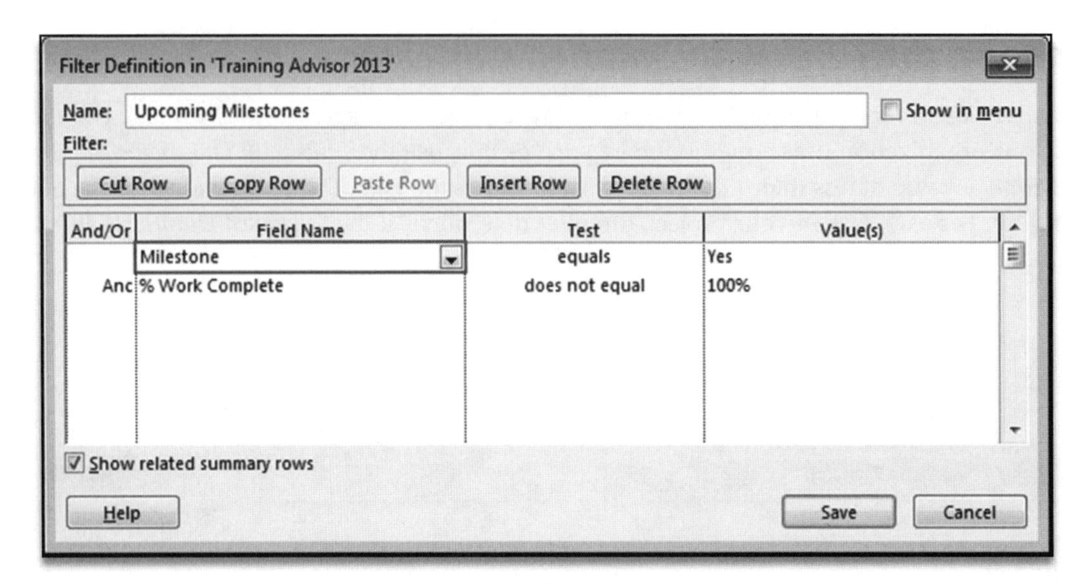

Figure 3 - 14: Filter Definition dialog for the Upcoming Milestones filter

> **Understanding the New Date Filters**
>
> A new feature in Project 2013 is that the software uses the date in the *Current Date* field to calculate the dates of the first and last days of the current week, and to calculate the dates of the first and last days of the current month. The software specifically uses this information with the *Milestones Due This Month, Tasks Due This Week,* and *Tasks Starting Soon* filters. For example, for the *Milestones Due This Month* filter, the software captures the date in the *Current Date* field, calculates the date of the last day of the month, and then filters for any *Milestone* task with a *Finish* date less than the date of the last day of the month.

Displaying the New Filters on the Filter and Highlight Filter Pick Lists

By default, Project 2013 **does not** display any of these eleven new filters in either the *Filter* pick list or the *Highlight Filter* pick list in the *Data* section of the *View* ribbon. If you want to see one of these filters on the *Filter* and *Highlight Filter* pick lists for all of your projects, complete the following steps:

1. Open the project you want to filter.
2. Click the *View* tab to display the *View* ribbon.
3. In the *Data* section of the *View* ribbon, click the *Filter* pick list and select the *More Filters* item.
4. In the *More Filters* dialog, select the filter you want to display on both the *Filter* and *Highlight Filter* pick lists and then click the *Edit* button.
5. In the *Filter Definition* dialog, select the *Show in menu* checkbox in the upper right corner of the dialog and then click the *Save* button.
6. In the *More Filters* dialog, click the *Organizer* button.

7. In the *Organizer* dialog, select the filter you edited in the current project (in the list on the right) and then click the *Copy* button to copy this filter to your Global.mpt file (in the list on the left).
8. In the warning dialog, click the *Yes* button to overwrite the existing filter.
9. Click the *Close* button to close the *Organizer* dialog.

Hands On Exercise

Exercise 3 - 2

Explore the new filters in Project 2013.

Information: To reduce the number of steps required to complete this Hands On Exercise, I modified the sample file so that you can see each of the new filters on both the *Filter* pick list and the *Highlight Filter* pick list. To do this, I followed the steps listed in the *Displaying the New Filters on the Filter and Highlight Filter Pick Lists* topical section immediately preceding this Hands On Exercise.

1. Open the **Using New Filters, Fields, and Task Path.mpp** sample file from your sample files folder.
2. Click the *Project* tab to display the *Project* ribbon.
3. In the *Properties* section of the *Project* ribbon, click the *Project Information* button.
4. In the *Project Information* dialog, enter **02/02/15** in the *Current date* field (**not** the *Start date* field) and then click the *OK* button.

I ask you to do the preceding step to temporarily "trick" Project 2013 into believing that today is actually Monday, February 2, 2015. After you save and close this sample project, the next time you open the project the *Current Date* value automatically reverts back to the date displayed on the system clock in your computer.

5. Click the *View* tab to display the *View* ribbon.
6. In the *Data* section of the *View* ribbon, click the *Filter* pick list and select the new *Completed Milestones* filter.

Using the *Completed Milestones* filter, notice how the software displays one completed milestone in the INSTALLATION phase of the project, and one completed milestone in the TRAINING phase of the project. You can determine that each milestone is completed by the blue check mark indicator shown in the *Indicators* column for each task.

7. Press the **F3** function key on your computer keyboard to clear the current filter.
8. Click the *Filter* pick list again and select the new *Late Milestones* filter.

Using the *Late Milestones* filter, notice how the software displays only the *Training Materials Created* milestone in the TRAINING phase of the project. Project 2013 determines that this milestone task is late because it is an incomplete milestone task that occurs earlier than the current date.

9. Press the **F3** function key on your computer keyboard to clear the current filter.
10. Click the *Filter* pick list again and select the new *Milestones Due This Month* filter.

When you use the *Milestones Due This Month* filter, Project 2013 uses the *Current Date* value to determine the current month. In this example, the software determines the current month is February 2015. Using this new filter, notice how the software displays two milestones due on February 1 (during the current month). Notice also that the software displays the late milestone task in the TRAINING phase. Remember that this filter displays milestones that occur during the current month, plus incomplete milestones in the past.

11. Press the **F3** function key on your computer keyboard to clear the current filter.
12. Click the *Filter* pick list again and select the new *No Actuals* filter.

Notice that the software displays the *Perform Server Stress Test* task in the INSTALLATION phase and the *Create Training Module 03* task in the TRAINING phase of the project. The *No Actuals* filter displays these two tasks because each of them is an unstarted task with a *Start* date earlier than the current date.

13. Press the **F3** function key on your computer keyboard to clear the current filter.
14. Click the *Filter* pick list again and select the new *No Resources Assigned* filter.

Notice that the software displays only the *Provide End User Training* task in the TRAINING phase of the project. The *No Resource Assigned* filter displays this task because the project manager forgot to assign team members to this task.

15. Press the **F3** function key on your computer keyboard to clear the current filter.

Before you apply the *Overallocated Tasks* filter, visually scan the *Indicators* column and look for any task on which an overallocated resource is assigned, shown using the "burning man" (red stick figure) indicator. You should see that there are four tasks with an overallocated resource assigned to them.

16. Click the *Filter* pick list again and select the new *Overallocated Tasks* filter.

Using the *Overallocated Tasks* filter, notice that the software displayed only **two** of the four tasks with overallocated resources assigned. Remember that this is due to an unfixed bug in the RTM version of Project 2013. The filter correctly shows Mike Andrews is overallocated on the *Perform Server Stress Test* task because this task occurs during nonworking time (on a weekend). The filter correctly shows Ruth Andrews is overallocated on the *Create Training Module 03* task because she is assigned at a *Units* value of *150%* on this task.

17. Press the **F3** function key on your computer keyboard to clear the current filter.
18. Click the *Filter* pick list again and select the new *Summary Task with Assigned Resources* filter.

Notice that the software displays the *Create Training Materials* summary task in the TRAINING phase. The *Summary Task with Assigned Resources* filter correctly displays the *Create Training Materials* summary task because the project manager accidently assigned a resource to this summary task.

19. Press the **F3** function key on your computer keyboard to clear the current filter.

20. Click the *Filter* pick list again and select the new *Tasks Due This Week* filter.

When you use the *Tasks Due This Week* filter, Project 2013 uses the *Current Date* value to determine the current week. In this example, the software determines the current week is February 1-7, 2015. Using this new filter, notice how the software displays two tasks due to finish during the current week. Notice that the *Perform Server Stress Test* task in the INSTALLATION phase is due to finish on February 1, while the *Conduct Skills Assessment* task in the TRAINING phase is due to finish on February 6.

21. Press the **F3** function key on your computer keyboard to clear the current filter.

22. Click the *Filter* pick list again and select the new *Tasks Starting Soon* filter.

When you use the *Tasks Starting Soon* filter, Project 2013 uses the *Current Date* value to determine the current week. In this example, the software determines the current week is February 1-7, 2015. Using this new filter, notice how the software displays two tasks scheduled to start during the current week. Notice also that the *Install Training Advisor Clients* task in the INSTALLATION phase and the *Conduct Skills Assessment* task in the TRAINING phase are both scheduled to start on February 2.

23. Press the **F3** function key on your computer keyboard to clear the current filter.

24. Click the *Filter* pick list again and select the new *Tasks with Duration < 8h* filter.

Using the *Tasks with Duration < 8h* filter, notice that the software displays only the milestone tasks in the project, along with their associated summary tasks. This is because we have no tasks with a *Duration* value less than 8 hours.

25. Press the **F3** function key on your computer keyboard to clear the current filter.

26. Click the *Filter* pick list again and select the new *Upcoming Milestones* filter.

Using the *Upcoming Milestones* filter, notice that the software identifies three incomplete milestones earlier than the current date (in the past) and three milestone tasks later than the current date (in the future). Remember that this filter displays **all** incomplete milestones, regardless of whether they are scheduled in the past or in the future.

27. Press the **F3** function key on your computer keyboard to clear the current filter.

28. Save but **do not** close your **Using New Filters, Fields, and Task Path.mpp** sample file.

Understanding the New Cumulative Fields

In earlier versions of Project, such as the 2010 version, the software offered cumulative fields for use in the timephased grid of either the *Task Usage* view or *Resource Usage* view. Cumulative task fields included *Cumulative Cost, Cumulative Percent Complete,* and *Cumulative Work.* Cumulative resource fields included *Cumulative Cost* and *Cumulative Work* only.

In Project 2013, the software continues to offer these previous cumulative fields, but now offers a new set of cumulative fields intended for use with new reports, such as a *Burn Down* report. You can use the *Burn Down* report, by the way, to see a "glide path" or "trajectory" for the completion of project work. The software now includes the following new cumulative fields in either the *Task Usage* view or *Resource Usage* view:

- *Baseline Cumulative Work*
- *Baseline Remaining Cumulative Work*
- *Baseline Remaining Tasks* (available only in the *Task Usage* view)
- *Cumulative Actual Work*
- *Remaining Actual Tasks* (available only in the *Task Usage* view)
- *Remaining Cumulative Actual Work*
- *Remaining Cumulative Work*
- *Remaining Tasks* (available only in the *Task Usage* view)

For the *Baseline Cumulative Work, Baseline Remaining Cumulative Work,* and *Baseline Remaining Tasks* fields, the software includes a corresponding field for each of the 10 additional sets of baseline fields. This means that you also have the *Baseline1 Cumulative Work* to *Baseline10 Cumulative Work* fields, the *Baseline1 Remaining Cumulative Work* to *Baseline10 Remaining Cumulative Work* fields, and the *Baseline1 Remaining Tasks* to *Baseline10 Remaining Tasks* fields.

To access and use any of these new cumulative fields, navigate to either the *Task Usage* view or the *Resource Usage* view in your project, right-click anywhere in the timephased grid on the right side of the view, and then select the *Detail Styles* item on the shortcut menu. The software displays the *Detail Styles* dialog shown in Figure 3 - 15. You find the new cumulative fields in the *Available fields* list on the left side of the *Detail Styles* dialog. Notice that I selected the new *Baseline Cumulative Work* field in the *Available fields* list.

Information: Project 2013 offers you several other methods for displaying the *Detail Styles* dialog in either the *Task Usage* or *Resource Usage* view. The first method is to double-click in any working day cell in the timephased grid. The second method is to click the *Format* tab to display the *Format* ribbon, and then to click the *Add Details* button in the *Details* section of the *Format* ribbon.

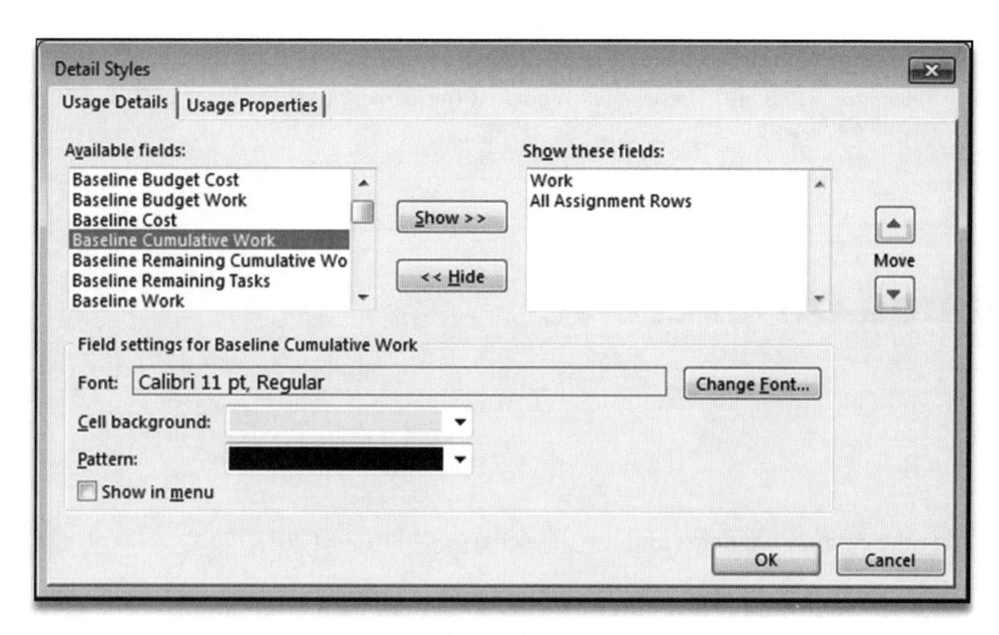

Figure 3 - 15: Detail Styles dialog in the Task Usage view

To add one of these new cumulative fields as a row in the timephased grid, select the field in the *Available fields* list and then click the *Show* button to add the field to the *Show these fields* list. Additionally, you can change the order of the fields in the *Show these fields* list by clicking the *Move* buttons (up and down arrows) to the right of the list. Click the *OK* button when finished to see the new fields in the timephased grid. For example, Figure 3 - 16 shows the *Task Usage* view with the *Baseline Work* field and the new *Baseline Cumulative Work* field added to the timephased grid. You can easily see the new functionality of the *Baseline Cumulative Work* field by examining the numbers in the timephased grid for the Project Summary Task (Row 0) or for the *Perform Initial Planning* summary task.

	Task Mode	Task Name	Work	Details	Mar 31, '13 S	M	T	W	T	F	S
0		**Annual Audit Preparation FY2012**	**720 h**	Base. Work		16h	8h	24h	24h	8h	
				Base. Cum. Work		16h	24h	48h	72h	80h	80h
1		**Perform Initial Planning**	**88 h**	Base. Work		16h	8h	24h	24h	8h	
				Base. Cum. Work		16h	24h	48h	72h	80h	80h
2		Review lessons learned from last year	16 h	Base. Work		16h					
				Base. Cum. Work		16h	16h	16h	16h	16h	16h
		Gary Chefetz	*8 h*	Base. Work		8h					
				Base. Cum. Work		8h	8h	8h	8h	8h	8h
		Tim Clark	*8 h*	Base. Work		8h					
				Base. Cum. Work		8h	8h	8h	8h	8h	8h
3		Confirm changes, if any, to financial reporting requirements	8 h	Base. Work			8h				
				Base. Cum. Work			8h	8h	8h	8h	8h
		Tim Clark	*8 h*	Base. Work			8h				
				Base. Cum. Work			8h	8h	8h	8h	8h
4		Identify Annual Report Theme and Section Requirements	24 h	Base. Work				24h			
				Base. Cum. Work				24h	24h	24h	24h
		Cliff Wener	*8 h*	Base. Work				8h			
				Base. Cum. Work				8h	8h	8h	8h
		Gary Chefetz	*8 h*	Base. Work				8h			
				Base. Cum. Work				8h	8h	8h	8h
		Marlene Roth	*8 h*	Base. Work				8h			
				Base. Cum. Work				8h	8h	8h	8h

TASK USAGE

Figure 3 - 16: Task Usage view with a new cumulative field

Information: Project 2013 calculates the data in all of these new cumulative fields from January 1, 1984 through December 31, 2149. These dates represent the earliest possible *Start* date and latest possible *Finish* date in the software.

Hands On Exercise

Exercise 3 - 3

Explore the new cumulative fields and the date changes in Project 2013.

1. Return to your **Using New Filters, Fields, and Task Path.mpp** sample file, if necessary.
2. In the *Task Views* section of the *View* ribbon, click the *Task Usage* button to display the *Task Usage* view.
3. Click the *Format* tab to display the *Format* ribbon.
4. In the *Details* section of the *Format* ribbon, click the *Add Details* button.
5. In the *Available fields* section of the *Detail Styles* dialog, select the following fields and then click the *Show* button:
    - *Baseline Cumulative Work*
    - *Baseline Remaining Cumulative Work*
6. Click the *OK* button to close the *Detail Styles* dialog.
7. In the timephased grid on the right side of the view, double-click the right edge of the *Details* column header to widen this column.
8. For the *INSTALLATION* summary task, examine how Project 2013 timephases the data in the new *Baseline Cumulative Work* and *Baseline Remaining Cumulative Work* cumulative fields.
9. Save but **do not** close your **Using New Filters, Fields, and Task Path.mpp** sample file.

Using the New Task Path Feature

Over the years, several common questions asked by many project managers include the following:

- What is the task path of all predecessor tasks for a task in my project?
- Which task is the driving predecessor for a task in my project?
- What is the task path of all successors for a task in my project?
- Which task is the driven successor to a task in my project?

No version of the software earlier than Project 2013 offered a default feature to answer any of these questions. In fact, the only way to answer either question was to use a custom macro written in the VBA programming language by a fellow Project MVP named Jack Dahlgren. With the release of Project 2013, however, you can use the new *Task Path* feature to determine the answer to all four common questions.

Before you can use this new *Task Path* feature, your project must contain a list of tasks with dependencies set between all tasks. To use the feature, apply any Gantt-based view, such as the *Gantt Chart* view, and then select a task. Click the *Format* tab to display the *Format* ribbon with the *Gantt Chart Tools* applied. In the *Bar Styles* section of the *Format* ribbon, click the *Task Path* pick list button and select one of four options on the menu, as shown in Figure 3 - 17.

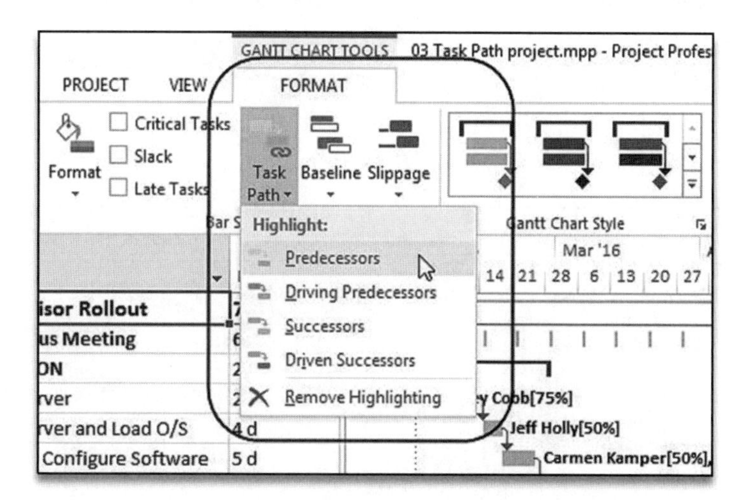

Figure 3 - 17: Task Path menu on the Format ribbon

Your options on the *Task Path* menu include:

- **Predecessors** – Select this option to display the complete task path of all predecessors for the selected task.
- **Driving Predecessors** – Select this option to display only those predecessors that directly affect the schedule of the selected task.
- **Successors** – Select this option to display the complete task path of all successors for the selected task.
- **Driven Successors** – Select this option to display only those successors whose schedule is directly affected by the selected task.
- **Remove Highlighting** – Select this option to remove all of the *Task Path* highlighting currently applied.

Information: When you select the *Predecessors* option on the *Task Path* menu, Project 2013 displays **all** predecessor tasks including completed tasks, which are predecessors for the selected task. When you select the *Driving Predecessors* option, however, the software displays **only** the last completed task in the chain of completed tasks, plus all other incomplete tasks that are driving predecessors for the selected task. When you select the *Successors* option, Project 2013 displays all successor tasks including completed tasks, which are successors of the selected task. When you select the *Driven Successors* option, however, the software **does not** display any completed tasks and only displays incomplete tasks, which are driven successors of the selected task.

If you select the *Predecessors* option on the *Task Path* menu, Project 2013 formats the Gantt bars of all predecessor tasks using a light orange color. For example, Figure 3 - 18 shows all predecessor tasks for task ID #35, the *Create Training Schedule* task, which include every task in the *INSTALLATION* and *TESTING* phases, along with the first five tasks in the *TRAINING* phase.

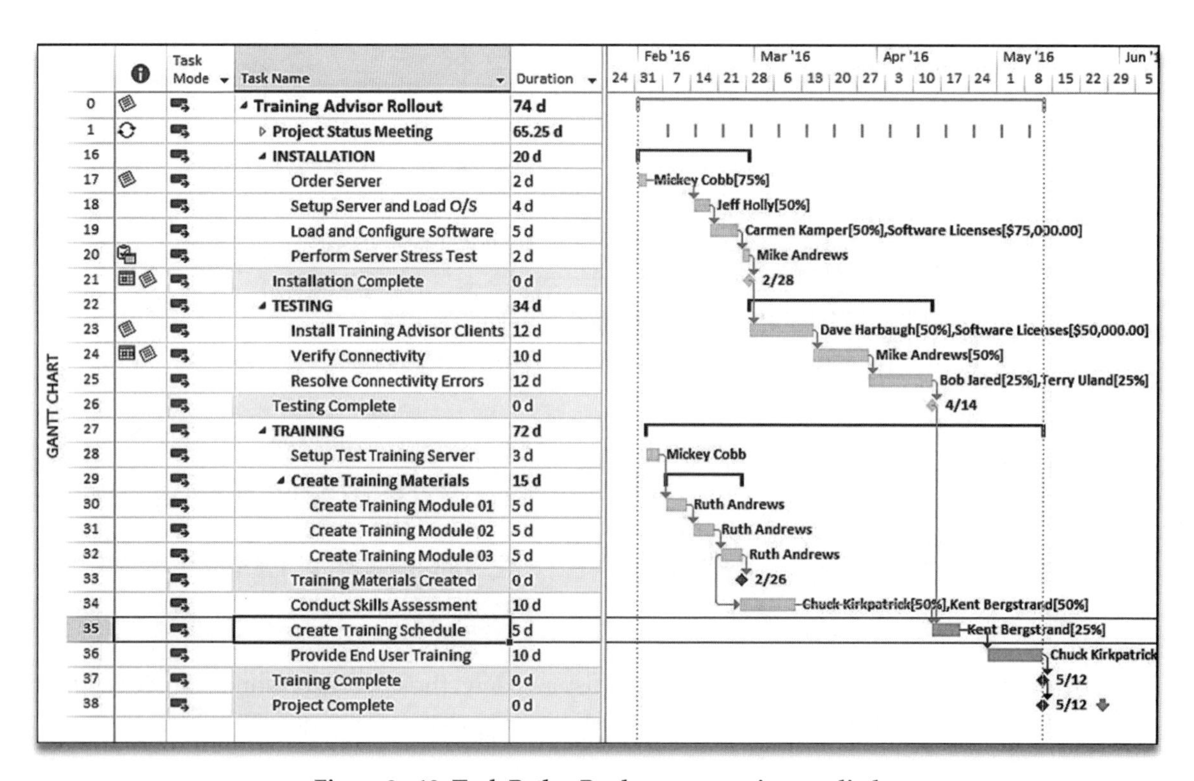

Figure 3 - 18: Task Path – Predecessors option applied

If you select the *Driving Predecessors* option on the *Task Path* menu, Project 2013 formats the Gantt bars of all driving predecessor tasks using a dark orange color. Remember that driving predecessors are only those predecessor tasks that directly affect the schedule of the selected task. For example, Figure 3 - 19 shows all of the driving predecessor tasks for task ID #35, the *Create Training Schedule* task. Notice that the software reveals that the driving predecessors include only the tasks in the *INSTALLATION* and *TESTING* phases, and do not include any of the tasks in the *TRAINING* phase.

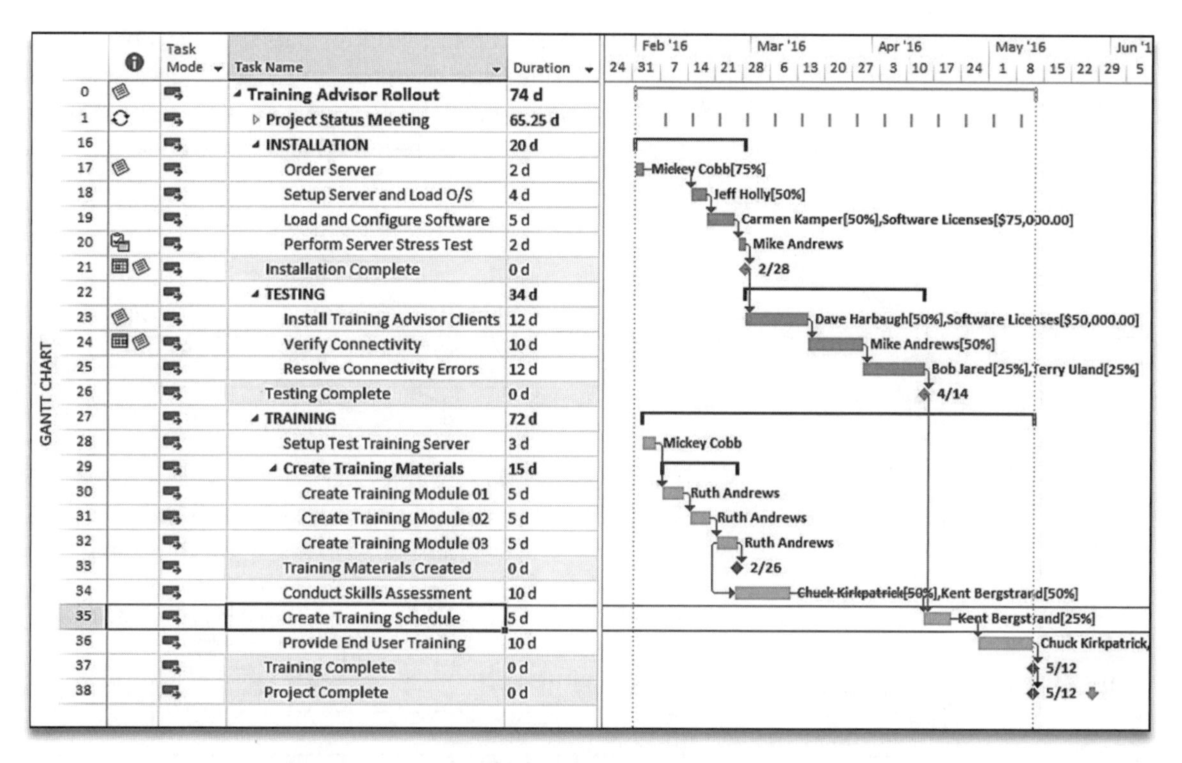

ID	Task Name	Duration
0	Training Advisor Rollout	74 d
1	Project Status Meeting	65.25 d
16	INSTALLATION	20 d
17	Order Server	2 d
18	Setup Server and Load O/S	4 d
19	Load and Configure Software	5 d
20	Perform Server Stress Test	2 d
21	Installation Complete	0 d
22	TESTING	34 d
23	Install Training Advisor Clients	12 d
24	Verify Connectivity	10 d
25	Resolve Connectivity Errors	12 d
26	Testing Complete	0 d
27	TRAINING	72 d
28	Setup Test Training Server	3 d
29	Create Training Materials	15 d
30	Create Training Module 01	5 d
31	Create Training Module 02	5 d
32	Create Training Module 03	5 d
33	Training Materials Created	0 d
34	Conduct Skills Assessment	10 d
35	Create Training Schedule	5 d
36	Provide End User Training	10 d
37	Training Complete	0 d
38	Project Complete	0 d

Figure 3 - 19: Task Path – Driving Predecessors option applied

If you select the *Successors* option on the *Task Path* menu, Project 2013 formats the Gantt bars of all successor tasks using a light purple color. For example, Figure 3 - 20 shows all successor tasks for task ID #28, the *Setup Test Training Server* task. Notice that the software reveals that the successors include all of the other tasks in the *TRAINING* phase of the project.

ID	Task Name	Duration
0	Training Advisor Rollout	74 d
1	Project Status Meeting	65.25 d
16	INSTALLATION	20 d
17	Order Server	2 d
18	Setup Server and Load O/S	4 d
19	Load and Configure Software	5 d
20	Perform Server Stress Test	2 d
21	Installation Complete	0 d
22	TESTING	34 d
23	Install Training Advisor Clients	12 d
24	Verify Connectivity	10 d
25	Resolve Connectivity Errors	12 d
26	Testing Complete	0 d
27	TRAINING	72 d
28	Setup Test Training Server	3 d
29	Create Training Materials	15 d
30	Create Training Module 01	5 d
31	Create Training Module 02	5 d
32	Create Training Module 03	5 d
33	Training Materials Created	0 d
34	Conduct Skills Assessment	10 d
35	Create Training Schedule	5 d
36	Provide End User Training	10 d
37	Training Complete	0 d
38	Project Complete	0 d

Figure 3 - 20: Task Path – Successors option applied

If you select the *Driven Successors* option on the *Task Path* menu, Project 2013 formats the Gantt bars of all driven successor tasks using a dark purple color. Remember that driven successors are only those successor tasks whose schedule is directly affected by the selected task. For example, Figure 3 - 21 shows all driven successor tasks for task ID #28, the *Setup Test Training Server* task. Notice that the software reveals that the driven successor tasks include only the next four tasks in the *TRAINING* phase and do not include the last two tasks in this phase.

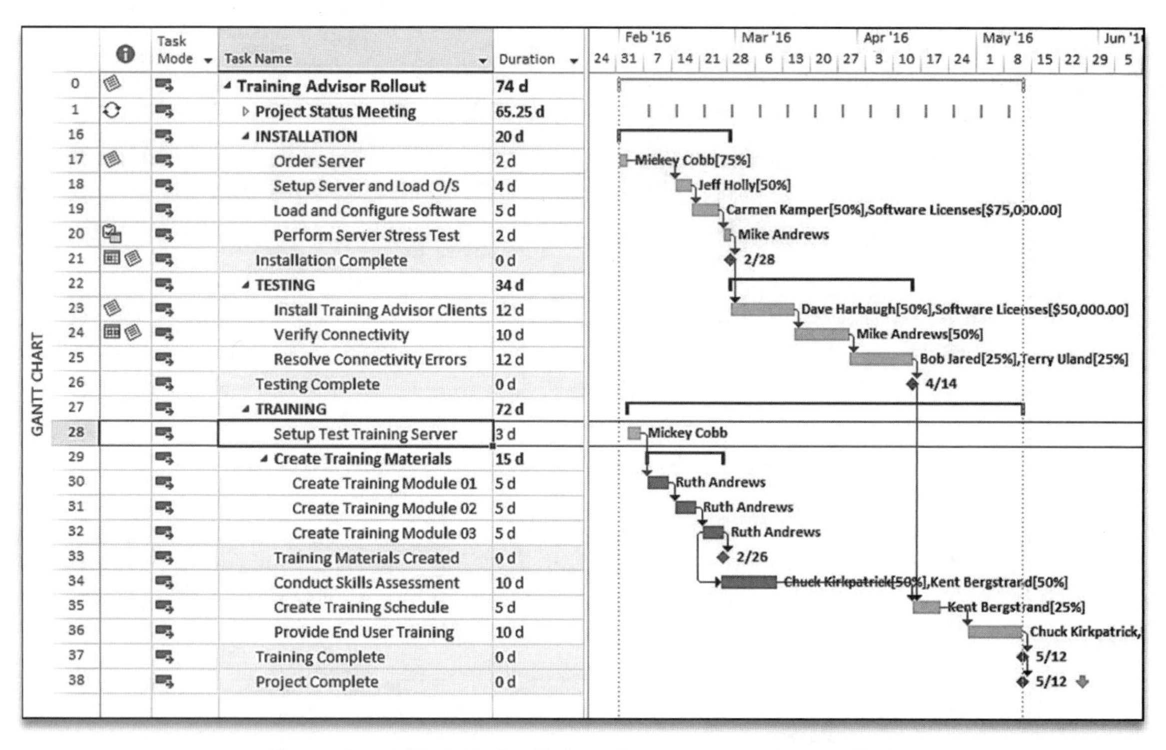

Figure 3 - 21: Task Path – Driven Successors option applied

Information: When you select one of the four options on the *Task Path* menu, Project 2013 leaves the option selected until you remove it. This allows you to select a series of tasks individually to see the *Predecessors* or *Successors* for each of the tasks you select. Beyond this, the software also allows you to select multiple items on the *Task Path* menu. For example, if you select both the *Predecessors* and *Driving Predecessors* options, the software allows you to determine which tasks are *Predecessors* and which tasks are *Driving Predecessors*, based on the colors of the Gantt bars.

To clear a selected option on the *Task Path* menu, click the *Task Path* button and deselect the selected item. To clear one or more items on the *Task Path* menu simultaneously, click the *Task Path* button and then click the *Remove Highlighting* item on the menu.

Hands On Exercise

Exercise 3 - 4

Experiment with the new Task Path feature in Project 2013.

1. Return to your **Using New Filters, Fields, and Task Path.mpp** sample file, if necessary.
2. Click the *Task* tab to display the *Task* ribbon.
3. In the *View* section of the *Task* ribbon, click the *Gantt Chart* pick list button and select the *Gantt Chart* view.
4. Click the *Format* tab to display the *Format* ribbon.
5. Select task ID #9, the *Testing Phase Begins* milestone task.
6. In the *Bar Styles* section of the *Format* ribbon, click the *Task Path* pick list button and select the *Predecessors* item on the menu.

Notice that Project 2013 uses a light orange color to highlight the Gantt bars of all of the tasks in the *INSTALLATION* phase of the project.

7. Click the *Task Path* pick list button again, leave the *Predecessors* item still selected on the menu, and select the *Direct Predecessors* item.

Notice that the software uses a dark orange color to highlight the Gantt bars of only three direct predecessor tasks. These highlighted tasks include the two incomplete tasks (the *Perform Server Stress Test* task and the *Installation Complete* milestone task) plus only the last completed task (the *Load and Configure Software* task). Remember that when you select the *Direct Predecessors* option, Project 2013 highlights only incomplete tasks and the last completed task in the chain of completed tasks.

8. Click the *Task Path* pick list button and select the *Remove Highlighting* item on the menu.
9. Select task ID #10, the *Install Training Advisor Clients* task.
10. Click the *Task Path* pick list button again and select the *Successors* item on the menu.

Notice that Project 2013 uses a light purple color to highlight the Gantt bars of all seven of the successor tasks (four regular tasks and three milestone tasks) in the *TESTING* and *TRAINING* phases of the project.

11. Click the *Task Path* pick list button again, leave the *Successors* item still selected on the menu, and select the *Driven Successors* item.

Notice that the software uses a dark purple color to highlight the Gantt bars of four tasks (three regular tasks and one milestone task) that are the driven tasks in the schedule. These are the tasks whose schedule is directly driven by the selected task.

12. Click the *Task Path* pick list button and select the *Remove Highlighting* item on the menu.
13. Save but **do not** close your **Using New Filters, Fields, and Task Path.mpp** sample file.

Using the Improved Inactivate Task Feature

Introduced originally in Project 2010, the *Inactivate Task* feature allows you to cancel unneeded tasks. Microsoft improved the functionality of this feature in Project 2013. Keep in mind that this feature is only available in the **Professional** version of Project 2013; if you use the **Standard** version of the software, this feature **is not** available to you.

To cancel tasks by setting them to *Inactive* status in Project 2013, select one or more tasks, and then click the *Inactivate* button in the *Schedule* section of the *Task* ribbon. When you cancel a task using the *Inactivate* button, Project 2013 does the following:

- The software formats the text of the *Inactive* task using the strikethrough font effect and the gray font color.
- The software formats the Gantt bar of the *Inactive* task using a hollow (unfilled) pattern.
- The software treats the *Inactive* task as if it has *0h* of *Remaining Work*. This means the *Inactive* task no longer affects resource availability for resources assigned to it.
- The software **cancels** the dependency relationship between the *Inactive* task and its successor task, and schedules the successor task as if it is linked to the last predecessor task **before** the *Inactive* task.

The last bullet point in the preceding list describes the new functionality in Project 2013. When you cancel a task using the previous version of the software (Project 2010), the software cancels the dependency relationship between the *Inactive* task and its successor task, and schedules the successor task to start on the *Start* date of the project. Figure 3 - 22 shows a project in which I cancelled a task by setting it to *Inactive* status using Project 2010. Notice that after I set the *Test* task to *Inactive* status, the software cancels the dependency between the *Test* task and the *Implement* task, and then reschedules the *Implement* task to start on the *Start* date of the project. To rectify this situation, I must link the *Build* task to the *Implement* task to show the correct task sequence.

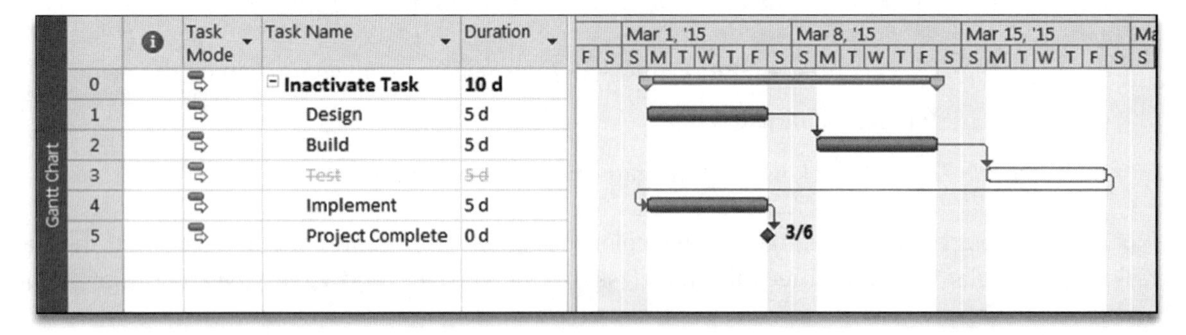

Figure 3 - 22: Task set to Inactive status using Project 2010

Figure 3 - 23 shows the same project in which I cancelled a task by setting it to *Inactive* status, except this time using Project 2013. Notice that after I set the *Test* task to *Inactive* status, the software cancels the dependency between the *Test* task and the *Implement* task, but the software reschedules the *Implement* task to start immediately after the finish of the *Build* task. In other words, the software treats the *Implement* task as if it is linked with a Finish-to-Start dependency to the *Build* task. If you prefer, you can manually link these two tasks, but the software does not require you to do so.

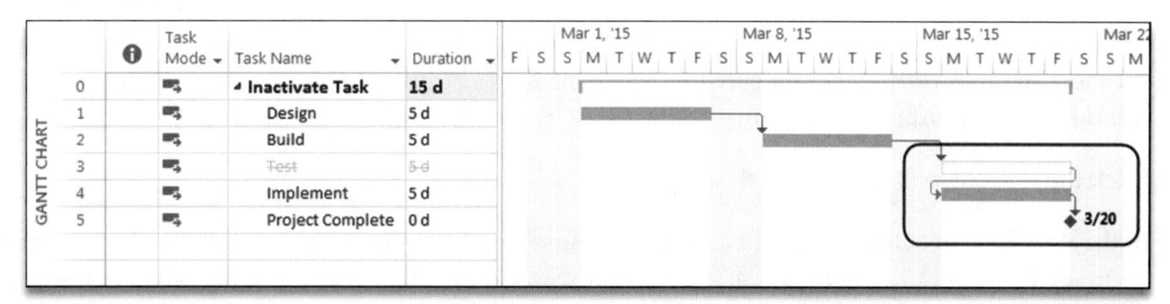

Figure 3 - 23: Task set to Inactive status using Project 2013

Hands On Exercise

Exercise 3 - 5

Team members report that a task is no longer needed in the project; therefore, cancel the unneeded task by setting its status to *Inactive*.

Warning: You can only perform this Hands On Exercise if you use the **Professional** version of Project 2013. If you use the **Standard** version, you must skip this exercise.

1. Open the **Inactivate a Task 2013.mpp** sample file.
2. Click the *View* tab to display the *View* ribbon.
3. In the *Zoom* section of the *View* ribbon, click the *Timescale* pick list, and then select the *Days* level of zoom.
4. Click the *Task* tab to display the *Task* ribbon.
5. Select task ID #21, the *Re-test modified code* task.
6. In the *Editing* section of the *Task* ribbon, click the *Scroll to Task* button to scroll the Gantt bar into view for the selected task.
7. In the *Schedule* section of the *Task* ribbon, click the *Inactivate* button.

Notice that Project 2013 schedules the *Testing Complete* milestone task immediately after the finish of the *Modify code* task. You can see that the software treats the *Testing Complete* milestone task as if it is linked with a Finish-to-Start dependency to the *Modify code* task.

8. Save and close the **Inactivate a Task 2013.mpp** sample file.

Using Task Pane Office Apps

Introduced as a new feature in Office 2013, Office Apps are simply web pages loaded in a pane inside an Office 2013 application. In Project 2013, you can only use task pane Office Apps to help you work with a project file. Before you can use an Office App, you must first connect to it by completing the following steps:

1. Click the *Project* tab to display the *Project* ribbon.

2. In the *Apps* section of the *Project* ribbon, click the *Apps for Office* button. Project 2013 displays a menu similar to the one shown in Figure 3 - 24. If you connected to any Office Apps recently, you see the app listed in the *Recently Used Apps* section at the top of the menu. Otherwise, you see *a No apps have been used recently* message at the top of the menu. Notice in Figure 3 - 24 that I used the *SharkPro SharePoint Insite for Project* app recently.

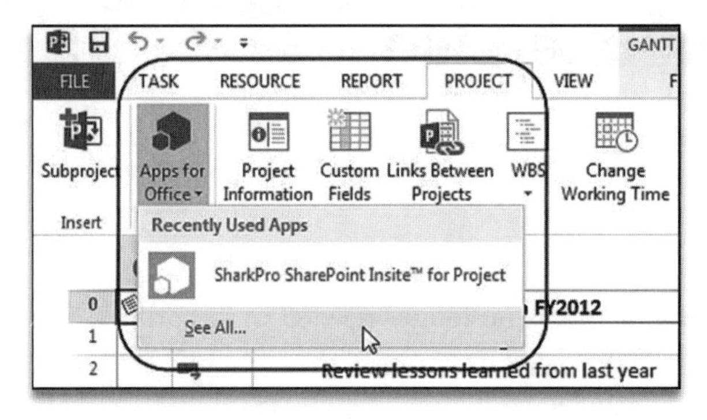

Figure 3 - 24: Apps for Office menu

3. If you recently used an Office App and want to use it again, click the name of the Office App in the *Recently Used Apps* section at the top of the menu. Otherwise, click the *See All* item at the bottom of the menu. The software displays the *Apps for Office* dialog with the *MY APPS* page selected by default, as shown in Figure 3 - 25. As the name implies, the *MY APPS* page shows Office Apps you used previously in Project 2013.

Figure 3 - 25: Apps for Office dialog, MY APPS page

4. In the upper left corner of the *Apps for Office* dialog, click the *FEATURED APPS* link to see Office Apps featured by Microsoft. The *FEATURED APPS* page normally displays a few of the Office Apps available for Project 2013, including both free and commercial apps. For example, notice that the *FEATURED APPS* page shown in Figure 3 - 26 shows two commercial apps and one free app.

Figure 3 - 26: Apps for Office dialog, FEATURED APPS page

Information: Notice that the *Apps for Office* dialog shown previously in Figure 3 - 26 includes a third tab: the *MY ORGANIZATION* tab. You use the *MY ORGANIZATION* page of the dialog if your organization creates Office Apps for you to use, and lists them in your organization's apps catalog.

5. To see all of the currently available Office Apps, click the *Find more apps at the Office Store* link in the lower left corner of the *MY APPS* page in the dialog, or click the *More apps* link in the upper left corner of the *FEATURED APPS* page. Project 2013 launches your Internet Explorer browser and navigates to the *Office Store* website.

Information: If the *MY APPS* page contains no recently used Office Apps, click the *Office Store* button to navigate to the *Office Store* website.

6. Click the *Apps for Office and SharePoint* link at the top of the page and select *Apps for Project* to display the *Apps for Project* page shown in Figure 3 - 27. Notice that the available Office Apps listed on this page include both free and commercial apps, including apps for both Project 2013 and SharePoint 2013. Microsoft displays SharePoint apps on this page because you can use Project 2013 in conjunction with SharePoint when you sync a project with a *Tasks* list in SharePoint, and when you use Project 2013 with Project Server 2013.

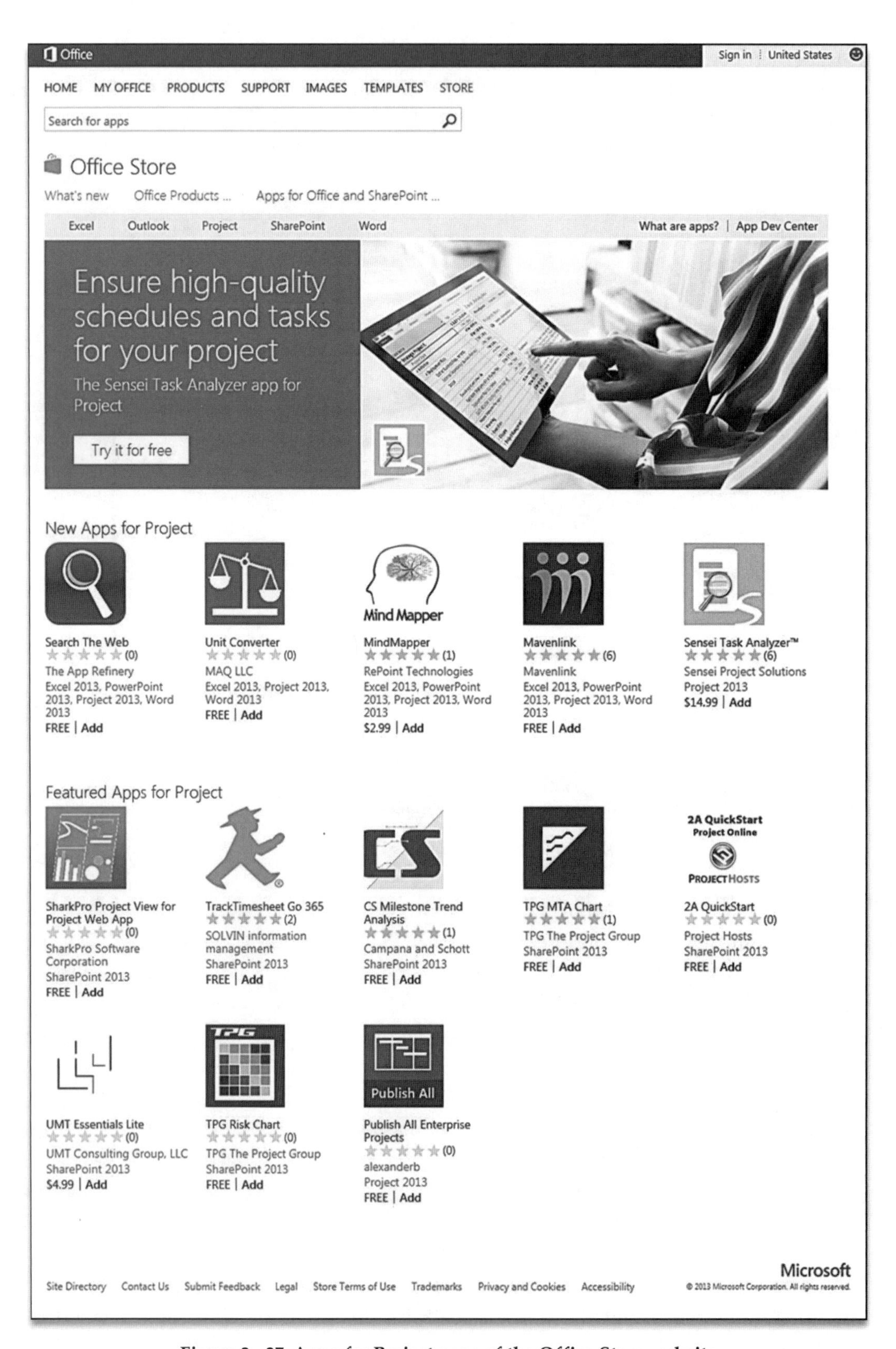

Figure 3 - 27: Apps for Project page of the Office Store website

7. On the *Apps for Project 2013* page, click the icon for the Office App you want to use. The software navigates to the *Home* page of the selected Office App in the *Office Store* website as shown in Figure 3 - 28. Notice that I want to install the Office App called *Search the Web.*

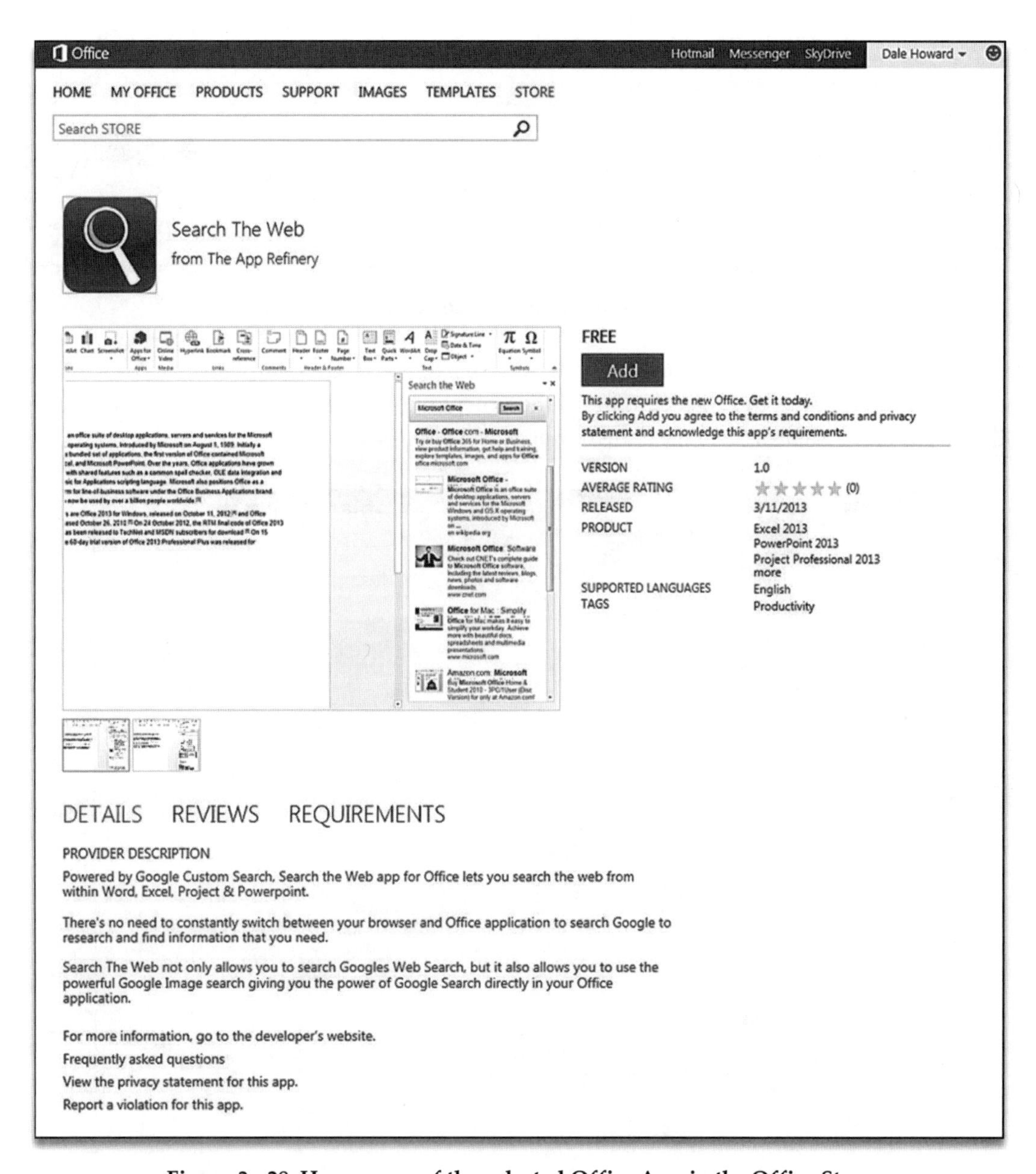

Figure 3 - 28: Home page of the selected Office App in the Office Store

8. Click the *Add* button to connect to the selected Office App. The software displays a confirmation page similar to the one shown in Figure 3 - 29.

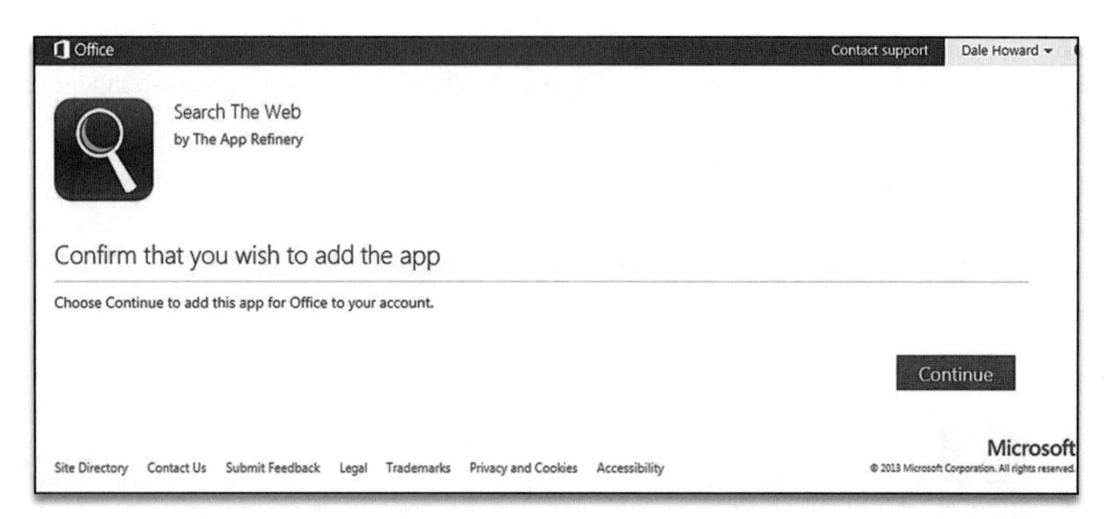

Figure 3 - 29: Confirmation page to add an Office App

9. On the confirmation page, click the *Continue* button. The software completes the process of connecting your selected Office App to Project 2013 and then displays a page with additional information about using the Office App, such as the page shown in Figure 3 - 30.

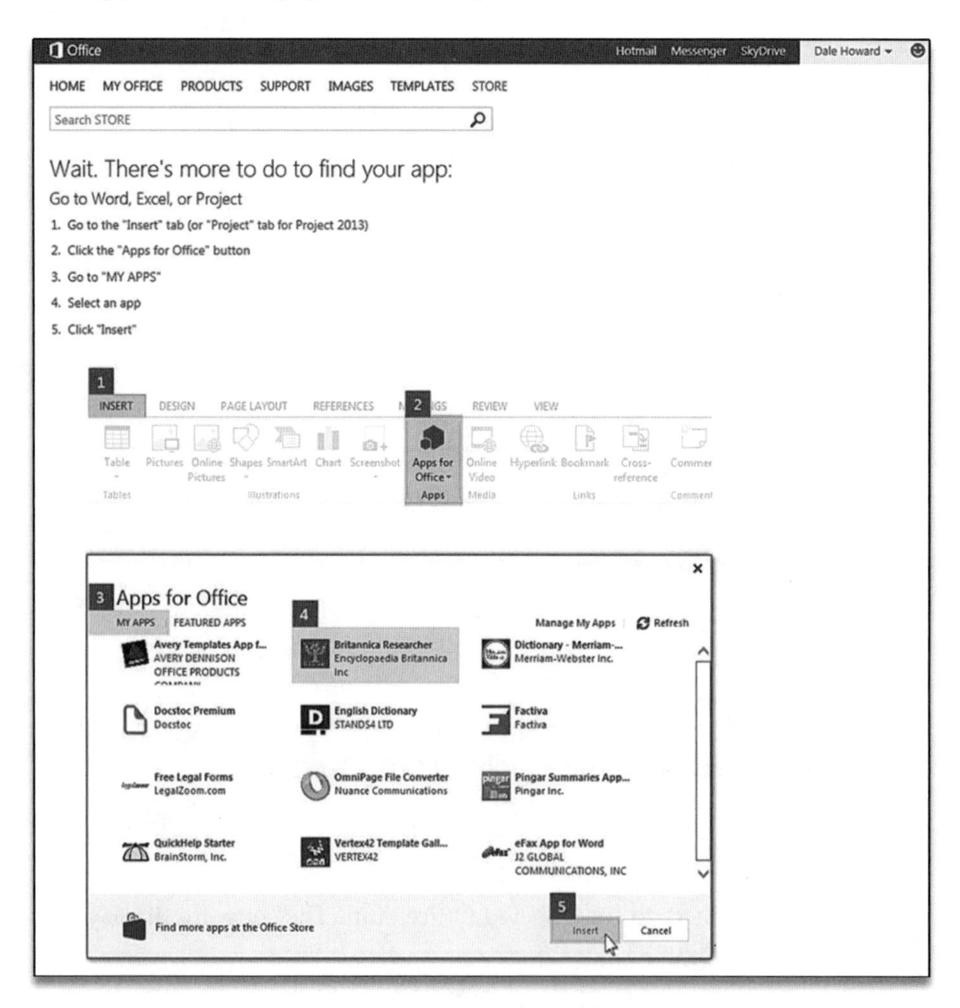

Figure 3 - 30: Additional information about how to use the Office App

10. Close your Internet Explorer browser and then return to Project 2013.

11. In the *Apps* section of the *Project* ribbon, click the *Apps for Office* button again, and click the *See All* link again.

12. On the *MY APPS* page of the *Apps for Office* dialog, you should now see the new Office App to which you just connected. If you do not see your Office App, click the *Refresh* button in the upper right corner of the dialog.

13. In the *Apps for Office* dialog, select the name of the Office App to which you just connected and then click the *Insert* button. Project 2013 displays the new Office App in a task pane on the right side of the application window, such as the free *Search the Web* Office App shown in Figure 3 - 31.

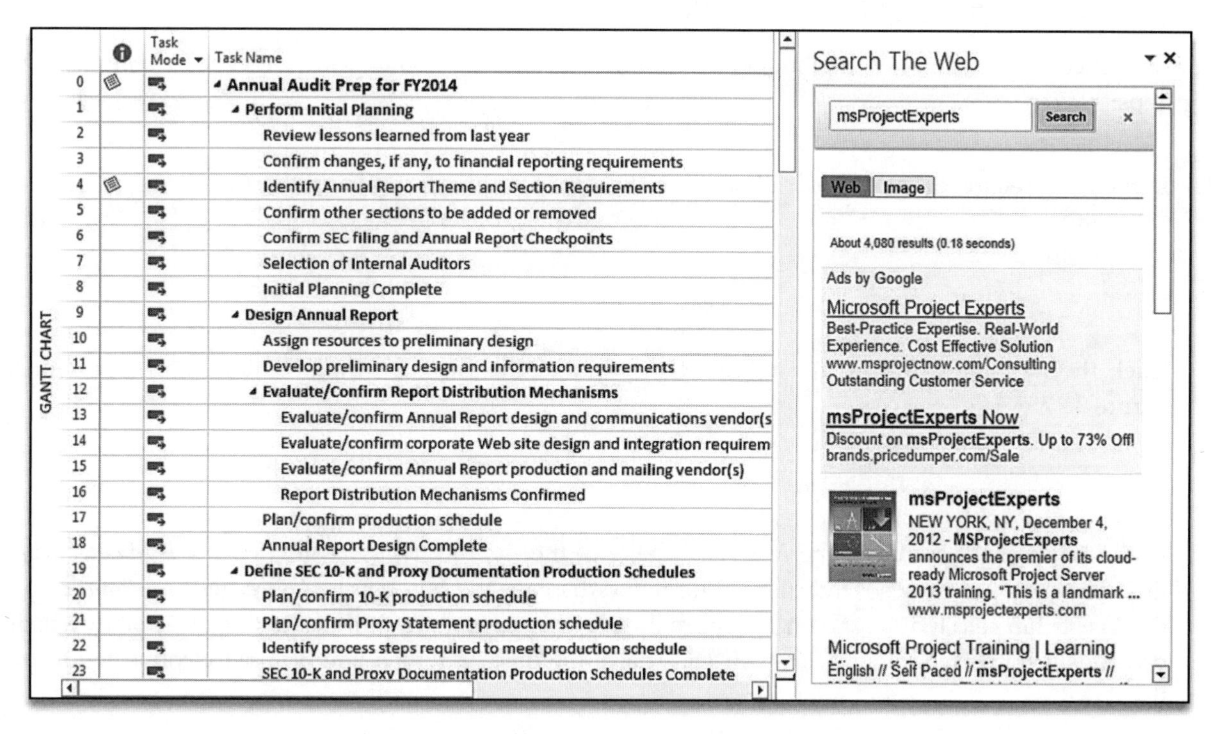

Figure 3 - 31: Office App displayed in a task pane

Once you display the Office App in a task pane, you can use the Office App in conjunction with your project file. In addition, after you use the Office App for the first time, you can see and select the Office App in the *Recently Used Apps* section of the *Apps for Office* menu. For example, notice that the *Apps for Office* menu now shows four Office Apps in the *Recently Used Apps* section, as shown in Figure 3 - 32.

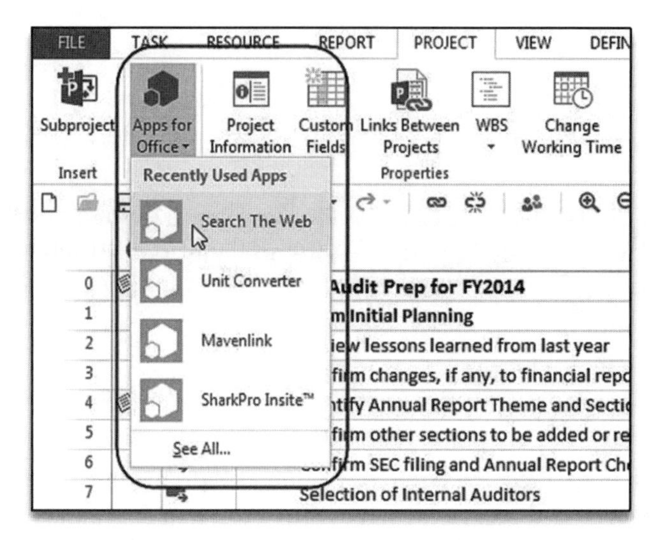

Figure 3 - 32: Updated Apps for Office menu

Hiding and Unhiding an Office App

To hide an Office App so that you no longer see it on the *Apps for Office* menu in Project 2013, complete the following steps:

1. In the *Apps* section of the *Project* ribbon, click the *Apps for Office* button and then select the *See All* item on the menu.

2. Click the *MY APPS* link in the upper left corner of the *Apps for Office* dialog shown previously in Figure 3 - 25.

3. In the upper right corner of the *MY APPS* page of the *Apps for Office* dialog, click the *Manage My Apps* link. The software launches Internet Explorer and displays the *My Apps for Office and SharePoint* page with the *Visible* tab selected, as shown in Figure 3 - 33. This page shows all of the Office Apps to which you previously connected, along with their status and the date on which you originally connected to the Office App.

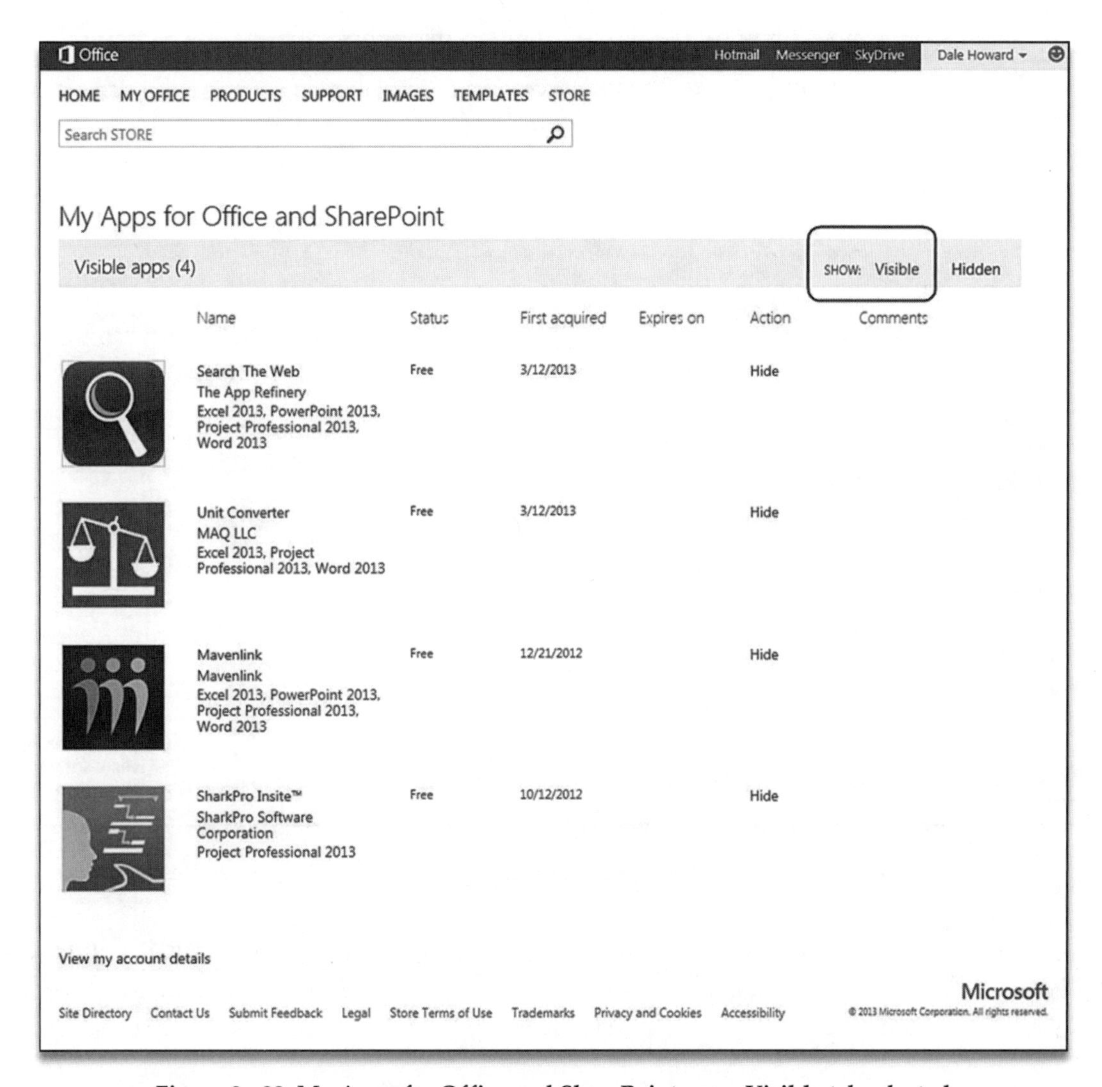

Figure 3 - 33: My Apps for Office and SharePoint page, Visible tab selected

4. In the *Action* column to the right of the Office App you want to hide, click the *Hide* link. After hiding two of my Office Apps, the *My Apps for Office and SharePoint* page refreshes as shown in Figure 3 - 34. Notice that the page shows that I currently have only visible apps.

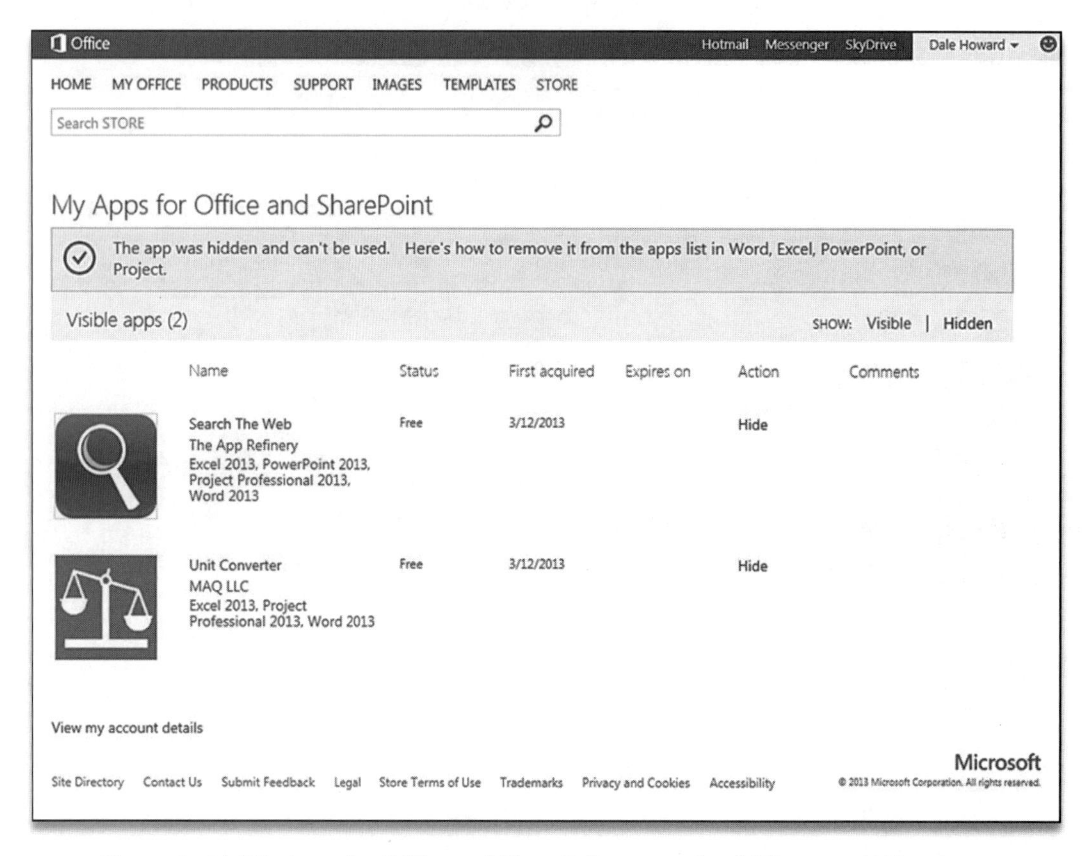

Figure 3 - 34: My Apps for Office and SharePoint page after hiding two Office Apps

5. After hiding Office Apps, return to the *Apps for Office* dialog in Project 2013 and click the *Refresh* link in the upper right corner of the dialog. The software no longer displays the hidden Office App in the *Apps for Office* dialog, and hides the Office App in the *Recently Used Apps* section of the *Apps for Office* menu.

Warning: Because of an unfixed bug in the release (RTM) version of Project 2013, when you hide an Office App, the software does not hide the Office App on the *Apps for Office* pick list. Instead, the software displays a *Failed to load app details* link on the *Apps for Office* pick list for each hidden Office App.

To unhide a hidden Office App, complete the following steps:

1. In the *Apps* section of the *Project* ribbon, click the *Apps for Office* button and then select the *See All* item on the menu.

2. In the *Apps for Office* dialog, click the *Manage My Apps* link in the upper right corner of the dialog. The software launches Internet Explorer and displays the *My Apps for Office And SharePoint* page with the *Visible* tab selected, as shown previously in Figure 3 - 34.

3. Click the *Hidden* tab at the top of the *My Apps for Office And SharePoint* page. The software displays the *Hidden* page shown in Figure 3 - 35. Notice that I previously hid two Office Apps.

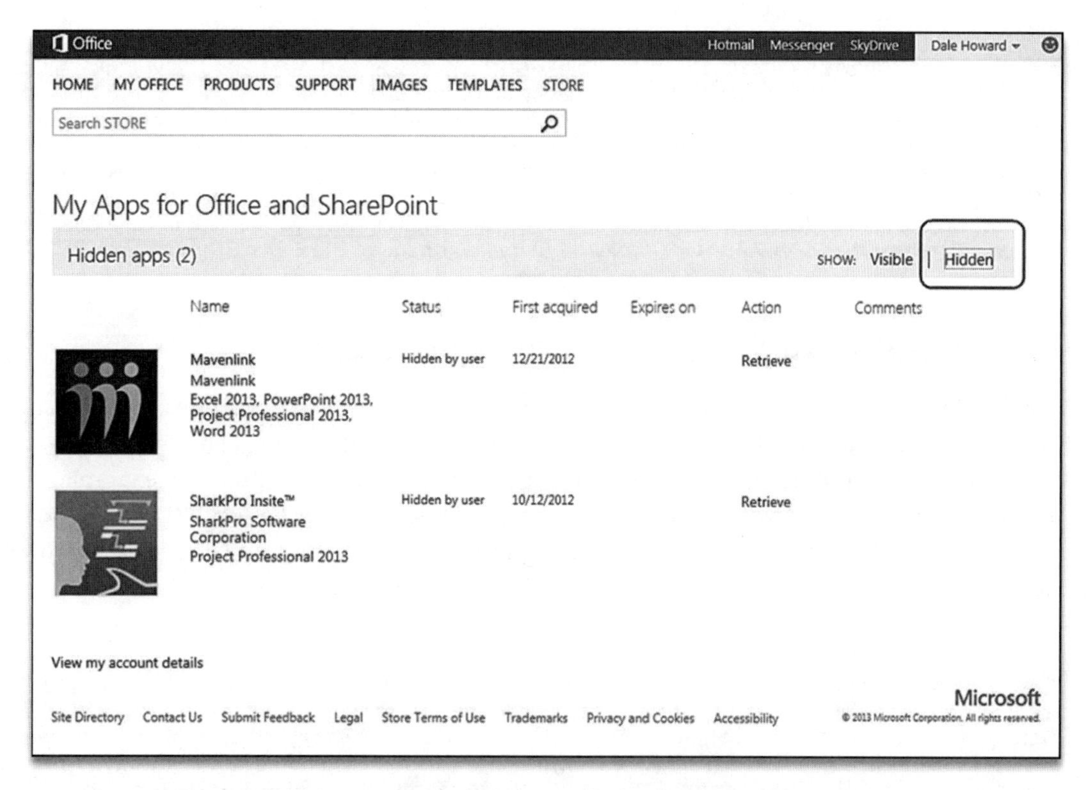

Figure 3 - 35: My Apps for Office and SharePoint, Hidden tab selected

4. In the *Action* column to the right of the Office App you want to unhide, click the *Retrieve* link. The *My Apps for Office and SharePoint* page refreshes as shown in Figure 3 - 36 with the *Hidden* tab selected. After unhiding both of the hidden Office Apps, notice that the page indicates that I currently have no hidden Office Apps.

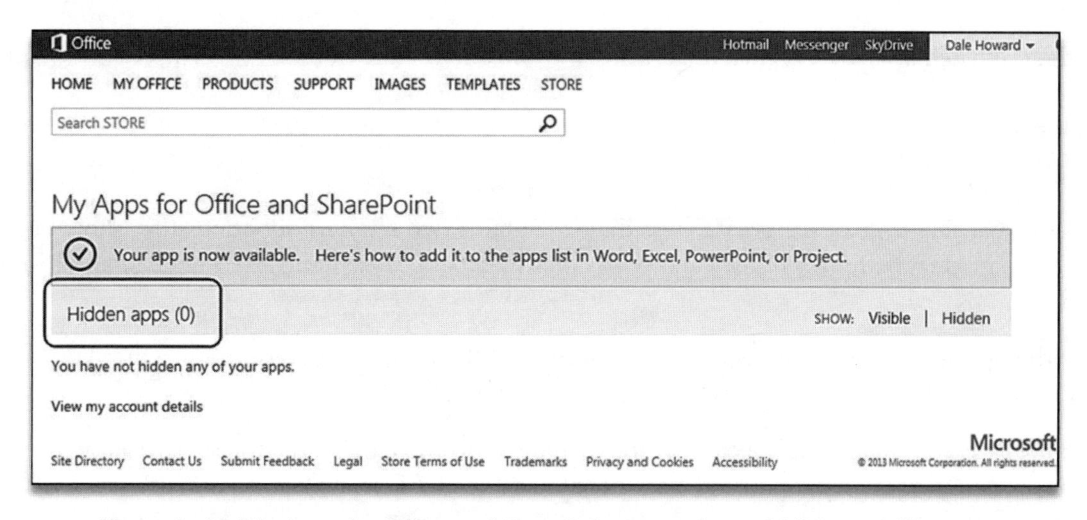

Figure 3 - 36: My Apps for Office and SharePoint page after unhiding an Office App

5. After unhiding the Office App, return to the *Apps for Office* dialog and click the *Refresh* link in the upper right corner of the dialog. The software redisplays Office App in both the *Apps for Office* dialog and the *Recently Used Apps* section of the *Apps for Office* menu.

Warning: Because of an unfixed bug in the release (RTM) version of Project 2013, if you hide all of your Office Apps, Project 2013 no longer displays a *Manage My Apps* link on the *MY APPS* page of the *Apps for Office* dialog shown previously in Figure 3 - 25. To return to the *My Apps for Office And SharePoint* website, click the *Office Store* button on the *MY APPS* page of the *Apps for Office* dialog. The software launches Internet Explorer and navigates you to the *Office Store* website. On the home page of the *Office Store* website, click the *MY OFFICE* link in the upper left corner of the page. In the *Sign in to Office.com* dialog, log in with your Microsoft account. On the *MY OFFICE* page of the *Office Store* website, click the *My Apps* link in the upper right corner of the page to return to the *My Apps for Office And SharePoint* page of the *Office Store* website.

Controlling the Auto Launch Behavior of Office Apps

Using the *Trust Center* dialog, you can control whether Project 2013 launches Office Apps automatically whenever you launch Project 2013 and open a file used with one of your Office Apps. In fact, using this dialog, you actually control how **all** Office 2013 applications interact with their respective Office Apps. For example, suppose you navigate to the *Office Store and Apps* website and connect to one Office App for Project 2013 and connect to another Office App for Excel 2013. Using the *Trust Center* dialog in Project 2013, you can set up these two Office Apps so that they launch automatically whenever you launch their respective Office application and open a file used with the respective Office App.

Information: When you set up trusted Office Apps in the *Trust Center* dialog in Project 2013, the Office 2013 system enters the same information in the *Trust Center* dialog of **every** other application in the Office 2013 suite of tools, including applications such as Word 2013, Excel 2013, and PowerPoint 2013. When you remove a trusted catalog in the *Trust Center* dialog in Project 2013, the Office 2013 system removes the trusted catalog from the *Trust Center* dialog of **every** other application in the Office 2013 suite.

To set up Office Apps to launch with their respective Office 2013 applications automatically, complete the following steps:

1. Click the *File* tab and then click the *Options* tab in the *Backstage*.

2. In the *Project Options* dialog, click the *Trust Center* tab and then click the *Trust Center Settings* button.

3. In the *Trust Center* dialog, click the *Trusted App Catalogs* tab to display the *Trusted App Catalogs* page shown in Figure 3 - 37.

The *Trusted App Catalogs* page of the *Trust Center* dialog contains two sections of options that allow you to control how Office Apps interact with Project 2013 and with other members of the Office 2013 suite of applications. These sections include:

- Use the options in the *Trusted App Catalogs* section of the dialog to determine whether your Office Apps launch automatically when open a project that uses the Office App.

- Use the *Trusted Catalogs Table* section of the dialog to add the URL of each website from which you access your Office Apps. For example, you may want to add the URL of the *Office Store* website.

In the *Trusted App Catalogs* section at the top of the *Trust Center* dialog shown in Figure 3 - 37, notice that the dialog offers two options. You can select only the *Don't allow apps from the Office Store to start* option to prevent Office Apps from the *Office Store and Apps* website from auto launching when you launch Project 2013. With this option selected, the software can auto launch Office Apps from other trusted catalogs, but does not auto launch Office Apps from the *Office Store* website. Alternately, you can select the *Don't allow any apps to start* option to prevent the software from auto launching all Office Apps, regardless of their location.

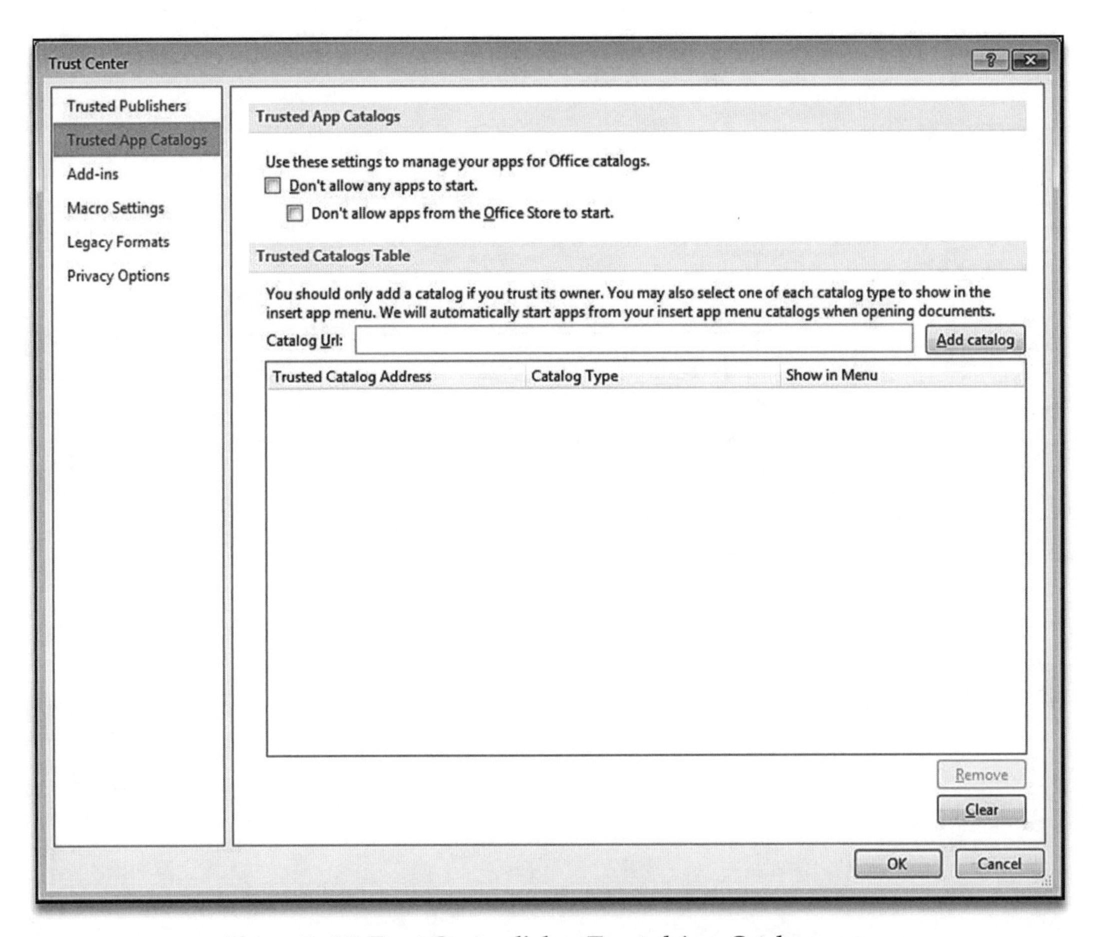

Figure 3 - 37: Trust Center dialog, Trusted App Catalogs page

4. In the *Catalog Url* field, enter the URL of the source of the Office App. For example, the URL of the *Office Store* website is **https://office.microsoft.com/en-us/store**.

5. Click the *Add catalog* button. The software refreshes the *Trust Center* dialog to show the new Office Apps catalog in the *Trusted Catalogs Table* section, as shown in Figure 3 - 38.

Warning: Project 2013 does not allow you to add a URL beginning with **http://** in the *Catalog URL* field, displaying a *Manage App Catalogs* error dialog if you attempt to do so. The error dialog states that the URLs you enter must begin with **https://**, indicating the catalog is in a secure Internet zone.

6. Select the *Show in Menu* checkbox to the right of the URL for the new trusted catalog if you want the catalog to appear in the *Apps for Office* dialog. When you select the *Show in Menu* checkbox, Project 2013 displays a *MY ORGANIZATION* tab in the *Apps for Office* dialog, shown previously in Figure 3 - 25.

7. To remove an existing trusted catalog, select the URL in the *Trust Catalogs Table* section of the dialog and then click the *Remove* button.

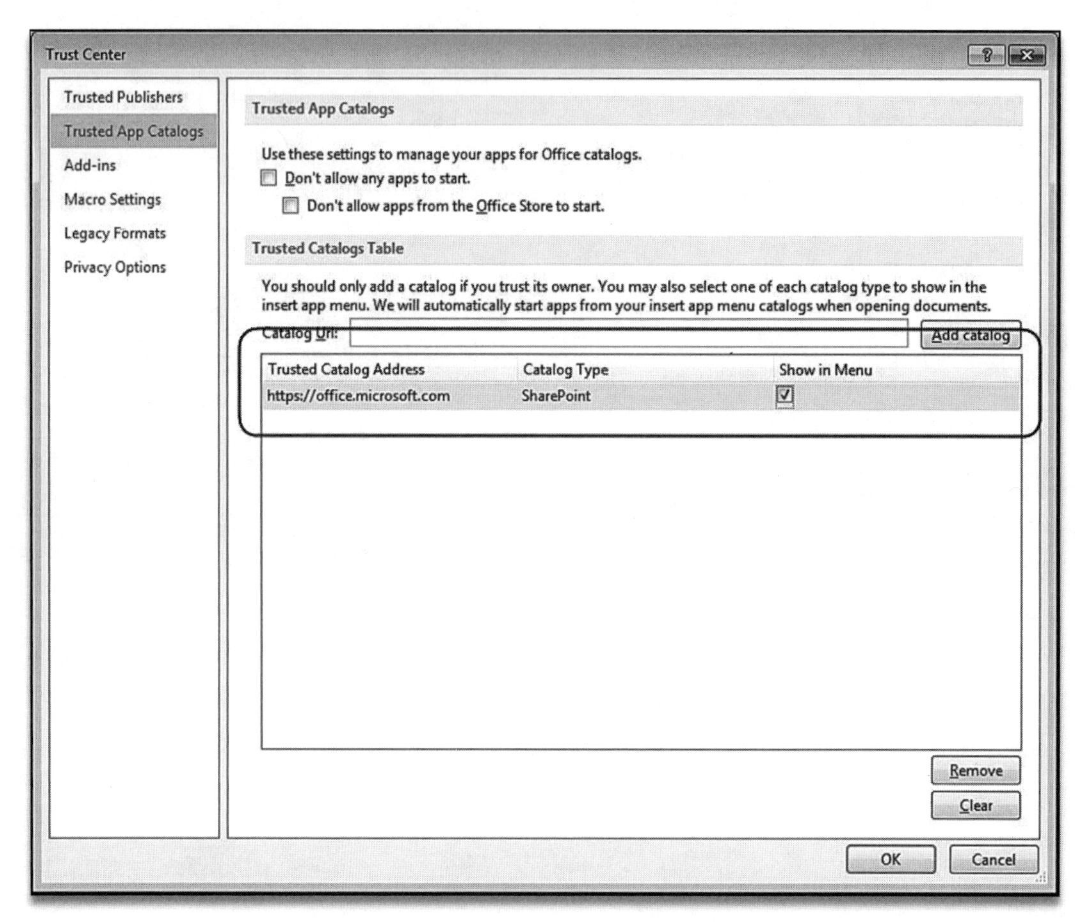

Figure 3 - 38: New catalog added on the Trusted App Catalogs page

8. Click the *OK* button. If you select the *Show in Menu* checkbox for a new trusted app catalog, the software displays the *Manage App Catalogs* dialog shown in Figure 3 - 39.

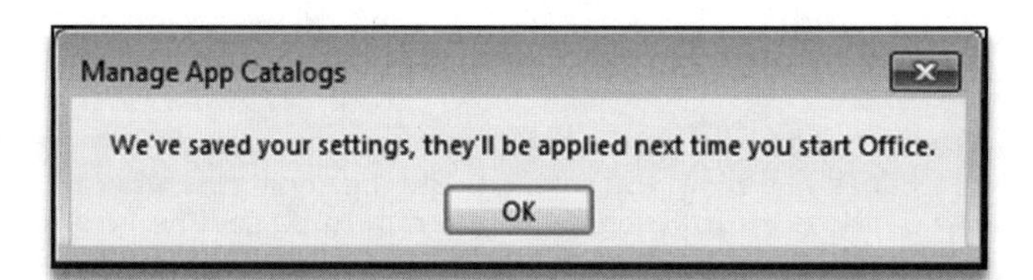

Figure 3 - 39: Manage App Catalogs dialog

9. Click the *OK* button to close the *Manage App Catalogs* dialog and then click the *OK* button to close the *Project Options* dialog.

10. Exit Project 2013 and then relaunch the application so that the software can apply the changes made in the *Trust Center* dialog.

Using Lync Integration with Project 2013

Lync is an enterprise-ready unified communications platform created by Microsoft. The Lync software offers features like instant messaging (IM), online meetings, and voice communication. In order to use the Lync integration feature with Project 2013, your organization must use the Lync software. In addition, you must meet the following requirements:

- You must enter the name of each team member in the *Resource Name* field in the *Resource Sheet* view of your project.

- You must enter the e-mail address of each team member in the *Email* field in the *Resource Sheet* view of your project.

- You must install the Lync client software on the computer running Project 2013 and you must have the Lync client software application running.

You use the new Lync integration to foster communication between you and your team members. Lync integration is available in most resource views in Project 2013, in any task view that displays resources, such as the *Gantt Chart* view with the *Entry* table applied, and even in the *Assign Resources* dialog. You can also use Lync integration in any SharePoint page that displays the names of team members.

To use the new Lync integration feature, float your mouse pointer over the name of any team member in either Project 2013 or in SharePoint. The software displays a Lync floating dialog that allows you to use the software to communicate with the team member. For example, Figure 3 - 40 shows the Lync floating dialog for John White, accessed by floating my mouse pointer over his name in the *Gantt Chart* view.

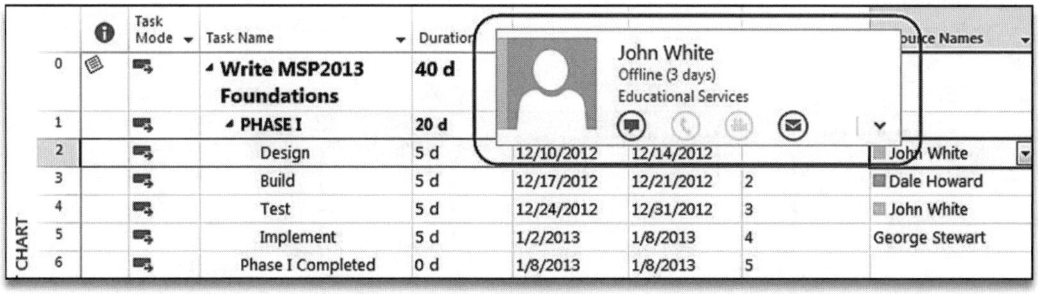

Figure 3 - 40: Lync floating dialog in the Gantt Chart view

The Lync floating dialog displays the name of the resource, their current status according to their Outlook calendar, and their job title. At the bottom of this floating dialog, click one of the four buttons to use the Lync application to send the user an instant message, to call the user, to start a video call with the user, or send an e-mail message to the user. You can also open the Lync contact card for the user by clicking the down arrow button (**v**) in the lower right corner of the floating dialog. If you click the first button to send an instant message, for example, Project 2013 displays the Lync instant message dialog shown in Figure 3 - 41, ready for you to compose and send an instant message to the user about the project.

Figure 3 - 41: Lync instant message dialog

Figure 3 - 42 shows the Lync floating dialog for John White in the *Assign Resources* dialog in Project 2013.

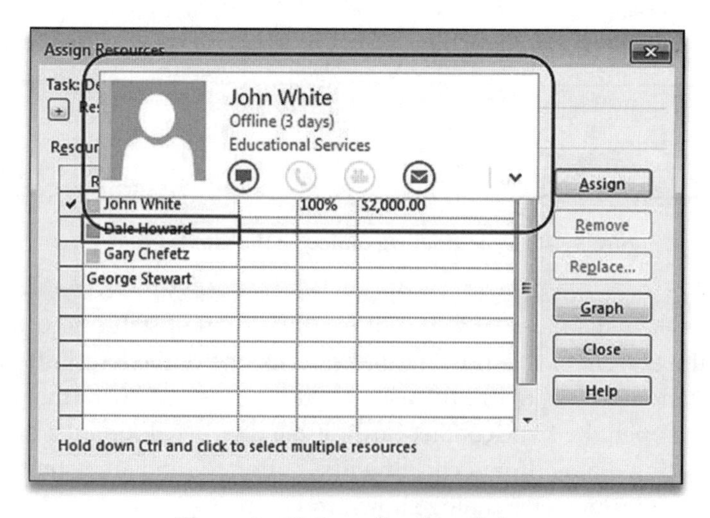

Figure 3 - 42: Lync floating dialog in the Assign Resources dialog

Figure 3 - 43 shows the Lync floating dialog in the *Team Planner* view in Project 2013.

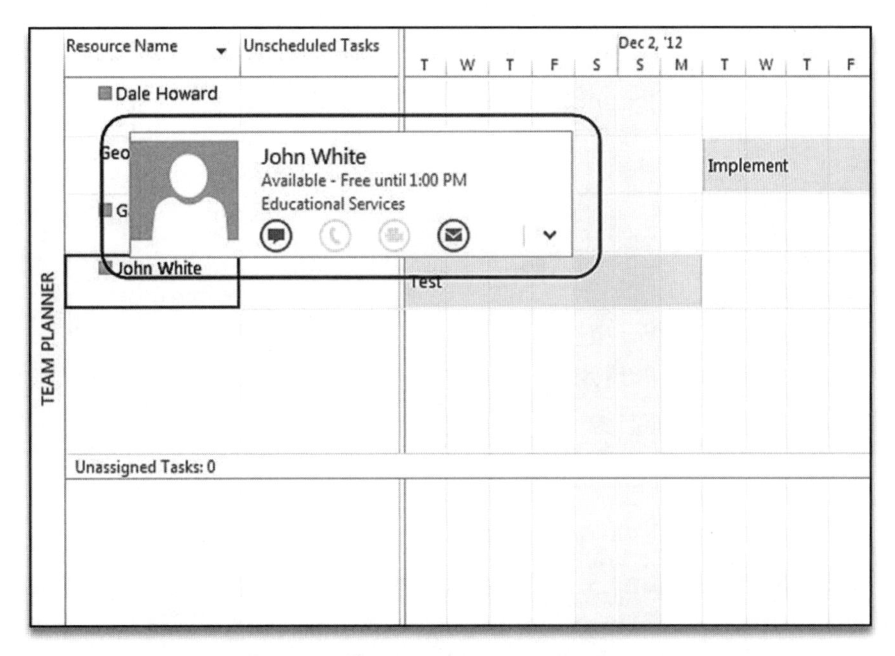

Figure 3 - 43: Lync floating dialog in the Team Planner view

Information: If you double-click the name of a resource in either the *Resource Sheet* view or the *Resource Usage* view, Project 2013 displays a Lync dialog that lists all of the contact information for the resource, including the resource's e-mail address, phone numbers, current location, company, and Instant Messenger account.

Module 04

Project Reporting Changes

Learning Objectives

After completing this module, you will be able to:

- Understand the new reports added to Project 2013
- Customize an existing report
- Customize a chart and a table
- Add a new chart or table in an existing report
- Create a new report
- Print a report
- Delete an existing report
- Share a report with another Microsoft Office application

Inside Module 04

Understanding the New Reports

Prior to Project 2013, all previous versions of the software offered six categories of built-in reports. Although the software allowed users to preview and print reports, the reports feature had two significant limitations:

- Users cannot export the report data to other Microsoft Office applications, such as to Excel or PowerPoint.
- The reports contain textual data only, such as the type of data you might find in an Excel workbook, but the reports do not include any type of graphical data, such as charts.

For example, Figure 4 - 1 shows the *Project Summary* report in *Print Preview* mode in Project 2010. Notice how the report contains only textual data. My only choice is to print this report to paper since the software does not allow me to export it to Excel.

SE Region Office Renovation
msProjectExperts
Gary Chefetz
as of 12/24/12

Dates			
Start:	4/7/14	Finish:	8/21/14
Baseline Start:	4/7/14	Baseline Finish:	7/24/14
Actual Start:	4/7/14	Actual Finish:	NA
Start Variance:	0 d	Finish Variance:	19.5 d

Duration			
Scheduled:	96.5 d	Remaining:	62 d
Baseline:	77 d	Actual:	34.5 d
Variance:	19.5 d	Percent Complete:	36%

Work			
Scheduled:	1,170 h	Remaining:	800 h
Baseline:	1,118 h	Actual:	370 h
Variance:	52 h	Percent Complete:	32%

Costs			
Scheduled:	$62,090	Remaining:	$41,535
Baseline:	$59,975	Actual:	$20,555
Variance:	$2,115		

Task Status		Resource Status	
Tasks not yet started:	54	Work Resources:	14
Tasks in progress:	4	Overallocated Work Resources:	0
Tasks completed:	19	Material Resources:	1
Total Tasks:	77	Total Resources:	15

Notes
Project to vacate our offices, completely renovate the office complex, and then return to our offices.

Figure 4 - 1: Print preview in Project 2010 of the Project Summary report

With the introduction of Project 2013, the software now offers a powerful new reporting engine that generates graphical dashboard reports, which you can view, print, or export to another Microsoft Office application. To use any of these new reports, click the *Report* tab to display the *Report* ribbon shown in Figure 4 - 2. Notice that the *View Reports* section of the *Report* ribbon contains eight pick list buttons that allow you to work with the new reporting feature.

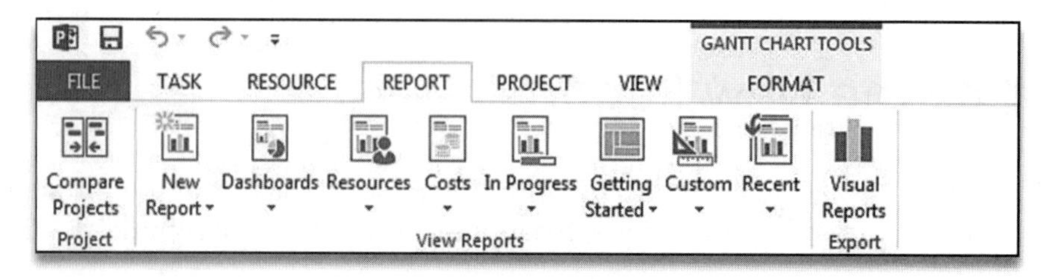

Figure 4 - 2: Report ribbon

Viewing a Report

Project 2013 organizes the default reports into five categories: *Dashboards, Resources, Costs, In Progress,* and *Getting Started.* To view a report, click one of these five pick list buttons and select a report, or click the *Recent* pick list button and select a recently used report. For example, to view an overview report about key data in your project, click the *Dashboards* pick list button and select the *Project Overview* report.

Figure 4 - 3 shows the new *Project Overview* report in Project 2013. Notice that the software displays the name of the report vertically along the left side of the report. Notice also that the report shows you a graphical table with a summary of the current *% Complete* for the project (*36%*), with a chart that shows the *% Complete* by first level tasks, along with two tables that show milestones due (not yet completed) and late tasks. If you compare the two *Project Overview* reports shown in Figure 4 - 1 and Figure 4 - 3, the difference between the two is absolutely striking!

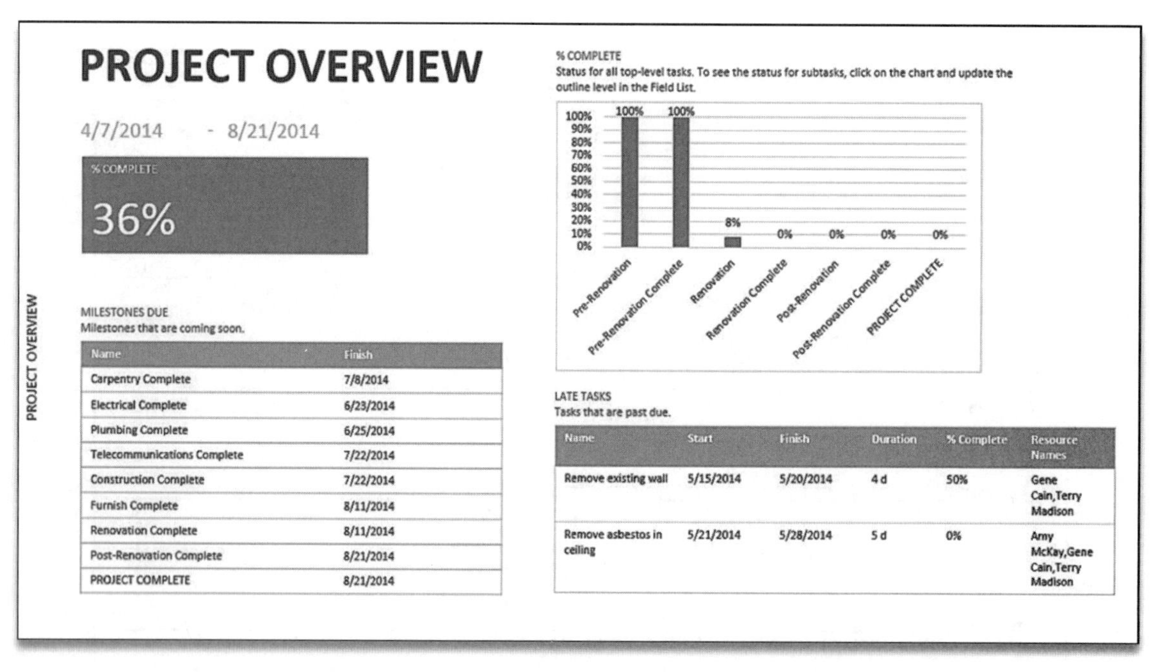

Figure 4 - 3: Project Overview report in Project 2013

Another way to view a report is to click the *Custom* pick list button and select the *More Reports* item on the pick list. You can also select the *More Reports* item at the bottom of the *Dashboards, Resources, Costs, In Progress, Getting Started,* or *Recent* pick lists. Project 2013 displays the *Reports* dialog with the *Custom* tab selected. Click one of the tabs along the left side of the dialog to see reports in that section. For example, Figure 4 - 4 shows the *Reports* dialog with the *Costs* tab selected. To view any report using the *Reports* dialog, select the report and then click the *Select* button.

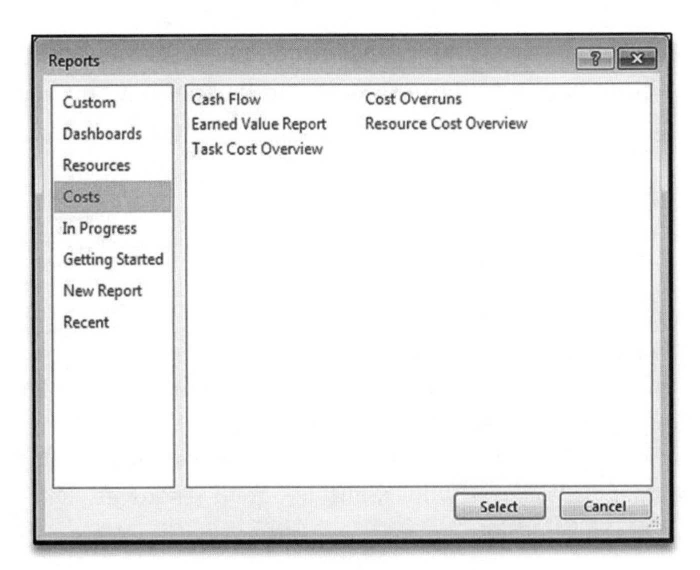

Figure 4 - 4: Reports dialog

When you view one of the new reports in Project 2013, the software displays a new *Design* ribbon with the *Report Tools* applied as shown in Figure 4 - 5. The software organizes the *Design* ribbon into five sections. Use the buttons in the *View* section to apply a view or a different report. Use the buttons in the *Themes* section to apply a set of theme colors, fonts, and effects to your report. Use the buttons in the *Insert* section to insert a graphical image, a graphical shape, a new chart, a new table, or a text box. Use the buttons in the *Report* section to manage your reports or to copy the current report to the Windows clipboard so that you can export the report data to another Microsoft Office application. Use the buttons in the *Page Setup* section to prepare your report for printing.

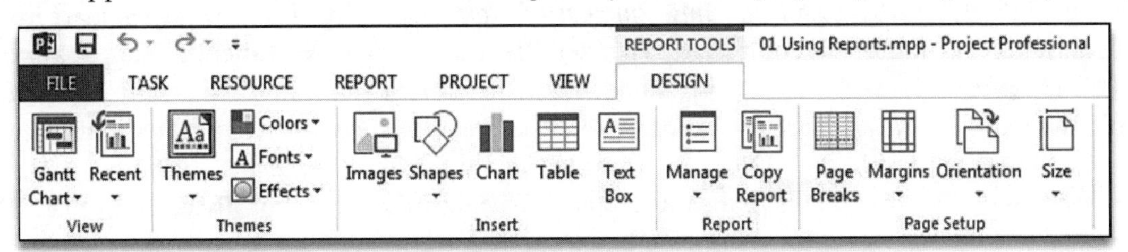

Figure 4 - 5: Design ribbon with the Report Tools applied

Every report in Project 2013 can contain any of the following types of objects:

- **Text boxes** – The software uses text boxes to show the title of the report, plus additional information about other objects in the report. For example, the *Project Overview* title shown previously in Figure 4 - 3 is a text box, as are the *Milestones Due* and *Late Tasks* labels, along with their descriptions.

- **Fields** – The software uses fields to display project data in a format similar to text boxes. You find two fields immediately below the title of the *Project Overview* report, which are the *Start* and *Finish* dates fields.

- **Tables** – The software uses tables to display data from project fields. For example, the *% Complete* value you see in the upper left corner of the *Project Overview* report is actually a table. In addition, you also see tables containing project data in the *Milestones Due* and *Late Tasks* sections of the *Project Overview* report.

- **Charts** – The software uses charts to graphically display data about your project. You see a *% Complete* chart about first level tasks in the upper right corner of the *Project Overview* report.

- **Hyperlinks** – The software uses hyperlinks to direct you to a *Help* article in Office.com that is relevant to the type of report currently displayed. For example, the *Burndown* report contains a *Try setting a baseline* hyperlink in an information text section at the bottom of the report.

Understanding Dashboard Reports

Click the *Dashboards* pick list button to see the five default dashboard reports that display project data in a dashboard format. These new dashboard reports include the following:

- *Project Overview* report shown previously in Figure 4 - 3 includes three tables and one chart that display high-level summary information about your project. The table in the upper left corner of the report shows the current *Percent Complete* for the project. The *Milestones Due* table displays a list of upcoming milestone tasks along with their *Finish* dates. The *Late Tasks* table displays a list of late tasks, along with their *Start* date, *Finish* date, *Duration*, *% Complete* values, and assigned resources. The *% Complete* chart shows the *Percent Complete* for all first level tasks.

Information: In Project 2013, a **late task** is any task with a *Late* value in the *Status* field. By default, the software sets a *Late* value in the *Status* field when the time-phased cumulative percent complete (represented by the black progress line in a Gantt bar) does not reach the *Status Date* you specify for the project. If you do not specify a *Status Date*, then the software uses the *Current Date* to determine late tasks.

- The *Burndown* report shown in Figure 4 - 6 contains two charts arranged horizontally. The *Work Burndown* chart is a line chart that compares the completed work with remaining work, timephased at the two-week level. This chart displays the information using the new *Remaining Cumulative Actual Work, Remaining Cumulative Work,* and *Baseline Remaining Cumulative Work* fields. The *Task Burndown* chart is a line chart that compares the number of completed tasks with the remaining tasks, timephased at the two-week level. This chart uses the new *Baseline Remaining Tasks, Remaining Tasks,* and *Remaining Actual Tasks* fields. Below the *Work Burndown* chart, the report displays a *Try setting a baseline* hyperlink that points to the *Set and save a baseline* page in the Office.com website. Below the *Task Burndown* chart, the report displays a *Learn more* hyperlink that points to the *Create a burndown report* page in the Office.com website.

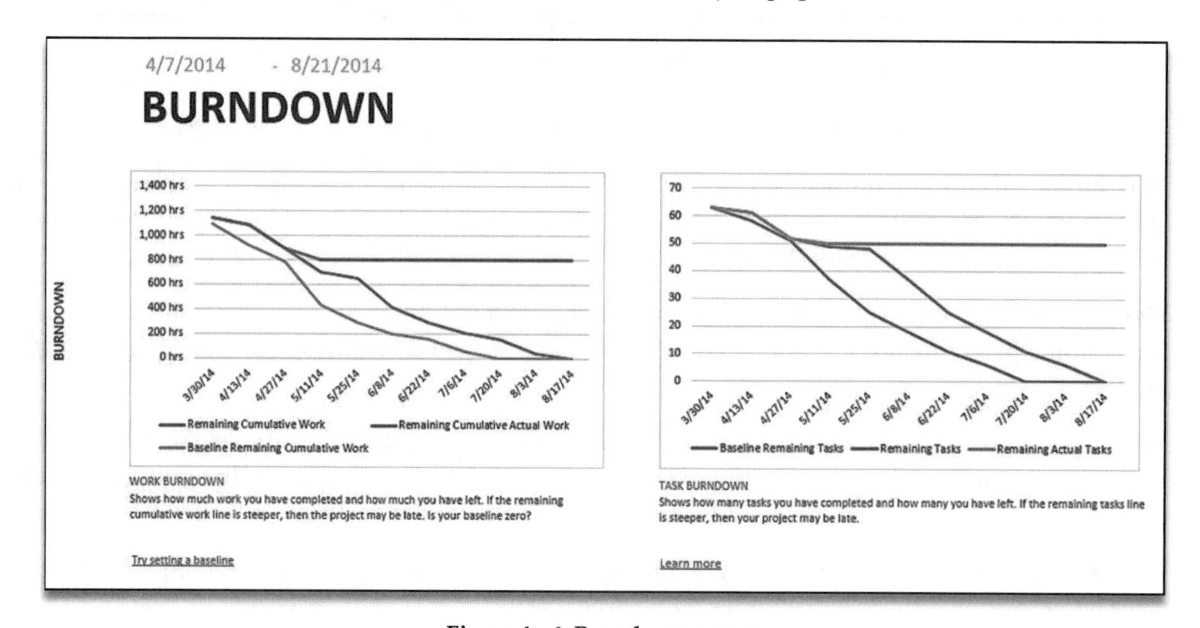

Figure 4 - 6: Burndown report

Warning: Due to the small size of the *Work Burndown* and *Task Burndown* charts, Project 2013 does not display the dates properly on the X-axis of each chart. To display the dates properly, you must edit each chart by changing the date format. I discuss how to customize a chart in the *Customizing a Chart* topical section later in this module.

- The *Cost Overview* report shown in Figure 4 - 7 contains four tables and two charts that display cost-related information about your project. The upper left corner of the report includes three tables, which display the current values in the *Cost, Remaining Cost,* and *% Complete* fields for the entire project. The *Cost Status* table shows you the current cost-related fields for every first level task. These fields include the *Actual Cost, Remaining Cost, Baseline Cost, Cost,* and *Cost Variance* fields. The *Progress Versus Cost* chart is a line chart that compares the *Cumulative Percent Complete* field with the *Cumulative Cost* field, timephased at the two-week level. The *Cost Status* chart is a combination chart that shows stacked columns for *Remaining Cost* and *Actual Cost,* with a line for *Baseline Cost.* This chart shows the data for all first level tasks. In the description section of the *Cost Status* chart, the report displays a *Try setting a baseline* hyperlink pointing to the *Set and save a baseline* page in the Office.com website.

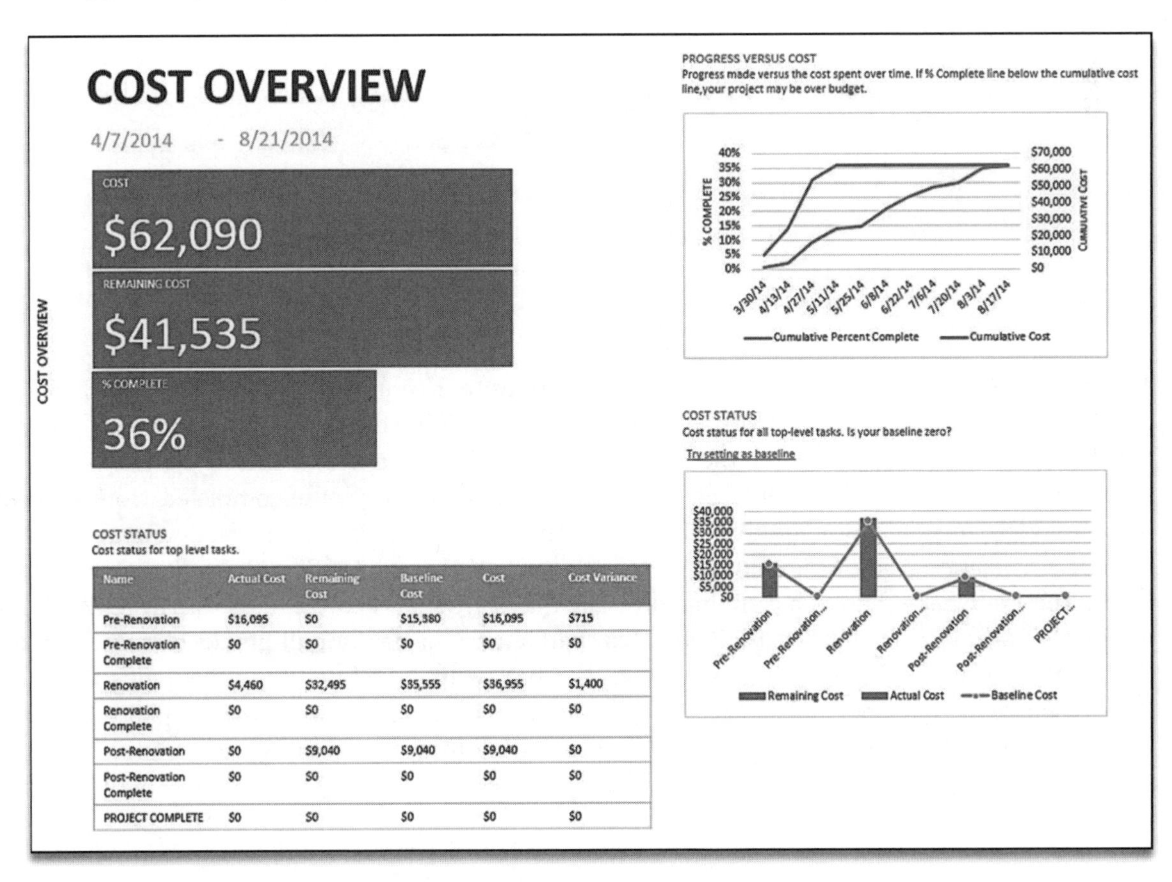

Name	Actual Cost	Remaining Cost	Baseline Cost	Cost	Cost Variance
Pre-Renovation	$16,095	$0	$15,380	$16,095	$715
Pre-Renovation Complete	$0	$0	$0	$0	$0
Renovation	$4,460	$32,495	$35,555	$36,955	$1,400
Renovation Complete	$0	$0	$0	$0	$0
Post-Renovation	$0	$9,040	$9,040	$9,040	$0
Post-Renovation Complete	$0	$0	$0	$0	$0
PROJECT COMPLETE	$0	$0	$0	$0	$0

Figure 4 - 7: Cost Overview report

- The *Upcoming Tasks* report shown in Figure 4 - 8 contains two tables and one chart that display task-related information about your project. The table in the upper left corner of the dialog shows the total *% Work Complete* value for the entire project. The *Tasks Starting Soon* table shows any task scheduled to start during the current week, based on the date in the *Current Date* field, and includes the *Resource Names, Start, Finish,* and *Work* fields. The *Remaining Tasks* chart is a column chart, which displays the *% Complete* value for any task scheduled to finish this week, based on the date in the *Current Date* field.

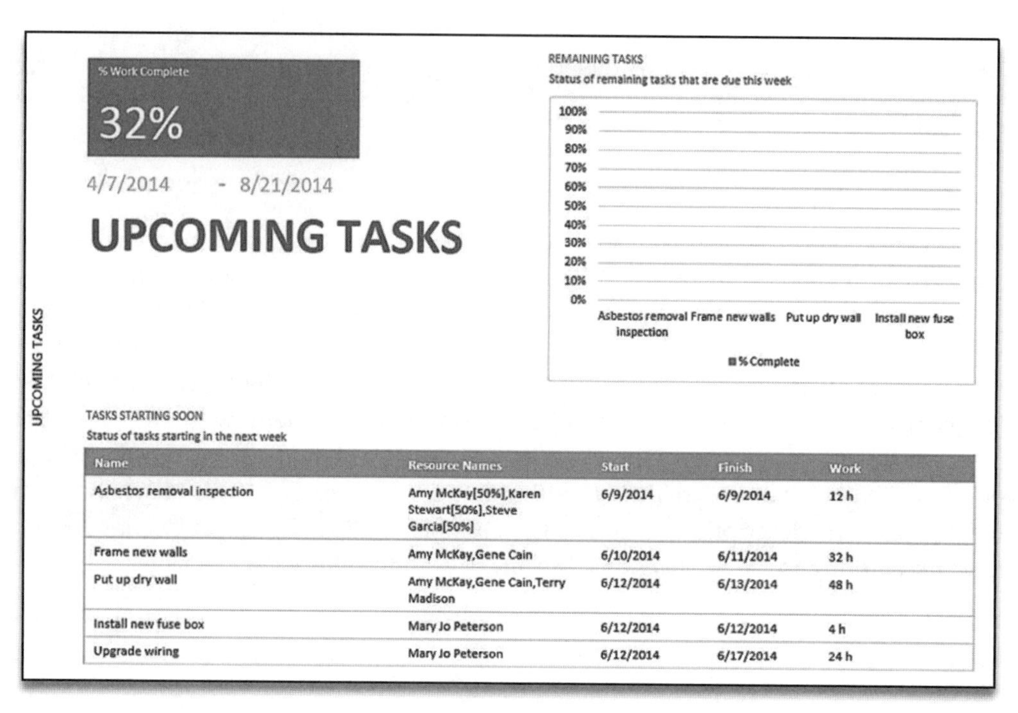

Name	Resource Names	Start	Finish	Work
Asbestos removal inspection	Amy McKay[50%],Karen Stewart[50%],Steve Garcia[50%]	6/9/2014	6/9/2014	12 h
Frame new walls	Amy McKay,Gene Cain	6/10/2014	6/11/2014	32 h
Put up dry wall	Amy McKay,Gene Cain,Terry Madison	6/12/2014	6/13/2014	48 h
Install new fuse box	Mary Jo Peterson	6/12/2014	6/12/2014	4 h
Upgrade wiring	Mary Jo Peterson	6/12/2014	6/17/2014	24 h

Figure 4 - 8: Upcoming Tasks report

- The *Work Overview* report shown in Figure 4 - 9 includes four charts and three tables that display information about task and resource work in your project. The right side of the report contains three tables, which display the current values in the *% Work Complete, Remaining Work,* and *Actual Work* fields for the entire project. The *Work Burndown* chart is a line chart that compares the completed work with the remaining work, timephased at the two-week level. This chart displays the information using the new *Remaining Cumulative Work, Remaining Cumulative Actual Work,* and *Baseline Remaining Cumulative Work* fields. The *Work Stats* chart is a combination chart that shows stacked columns for *Actual Work* and *Remaining Work,* with a line for *Baseline Work.* This chart shows the data for all first level tasks. The *Resource Stats* chart is a stacked bar chart that shows stacked bars with *Actual Work* and *Remaining Work* for each *Work* resource in your project. The *Remaining Availability* chart is a line chart that displays the *Remaining Availability,* timephased at the two-week level for each *Work* resource in your project.

Warning: Due to the small size of the *Remaining Availability* chart, Project 2013 can only show a small number of resources in the chart. To limit the number of resources shown in the *Remaining Availability* chart, you must customize the chart to filter for only the resources you want to see displayed in the chart. I discuss how to customize a chart in the *Customizing a Chart* topical section later in this module.

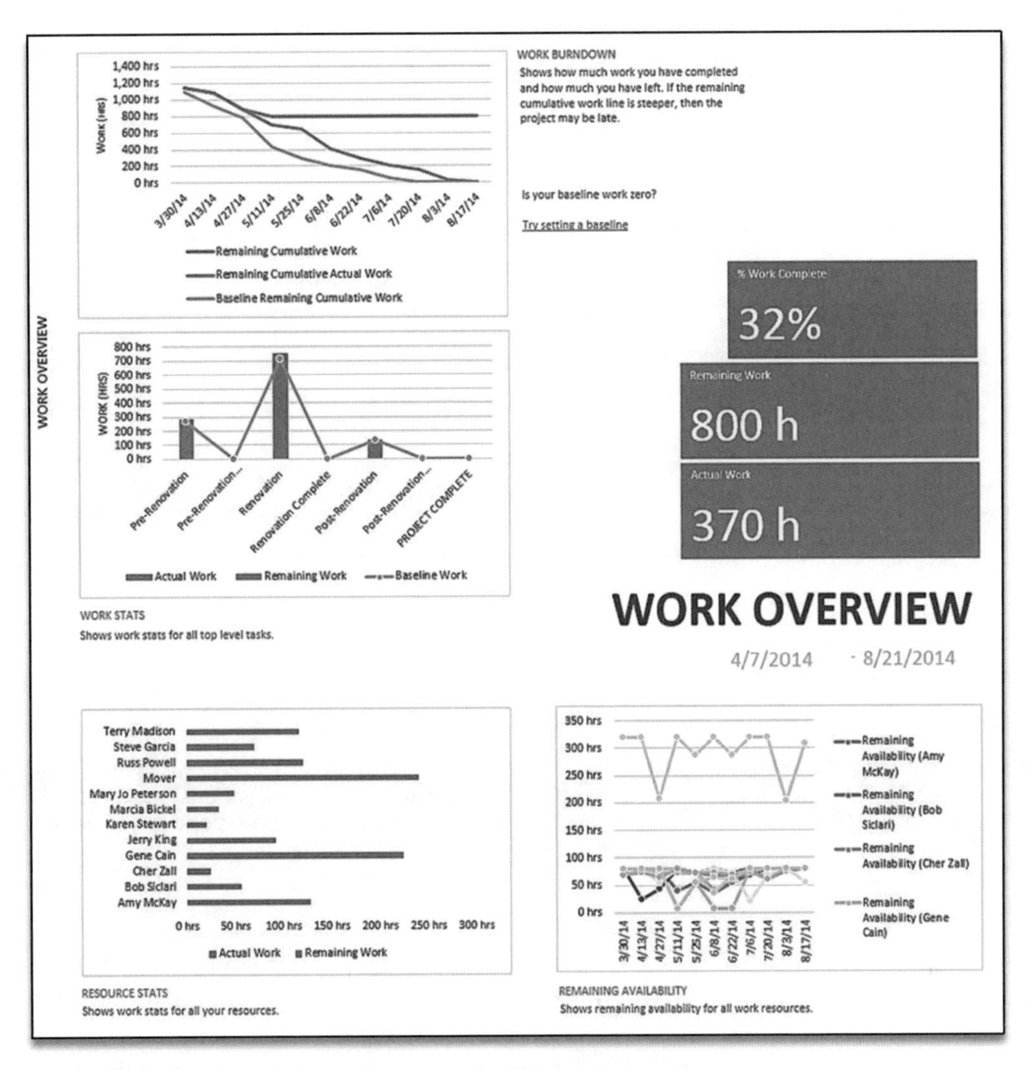

Figure 4 - 9: Work Overview report

Understanding Resource Reports

Click the *Resources* pick list button to see the two default resource reports that display information about the resources in your project team. These new resource reports include the following:

- The *Overallocated Resources* report shown in Figure 4 - 10 contains two charts that display information about overallocated resources in your project team. The *Work Status* chart is a stacked column chart that shows the *Actual Work* and *Remaining Work* for each overallocated resource. The *Overallocation* chart is a line chart that shows the total *Overallocation* for each overallocated resource, timephased at the daily level, from the *Start* date to the *Finish* date of the project.

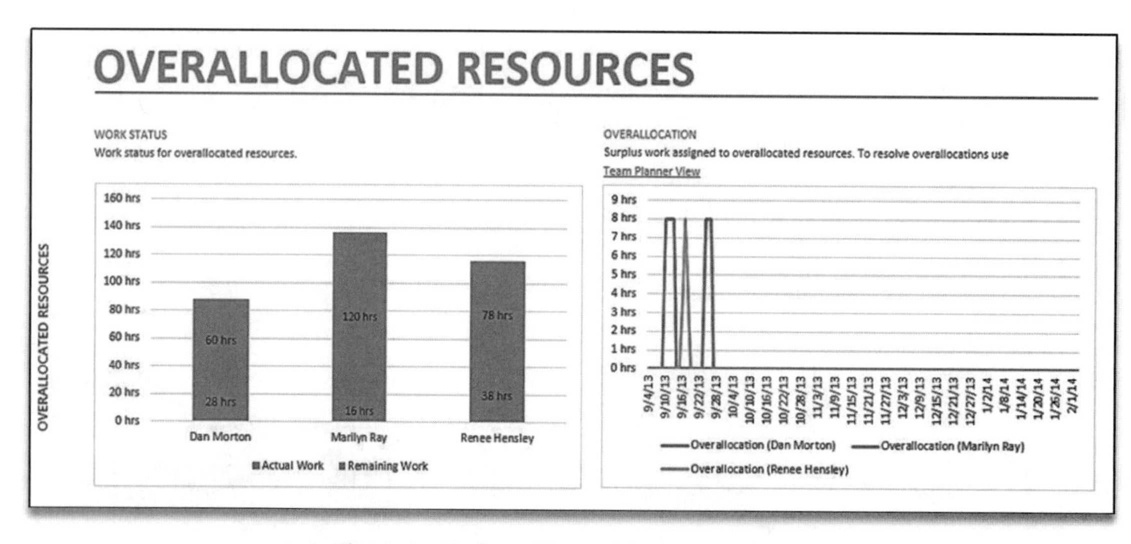

Figure 4 - 10: Overallocated Resources report

Warning: Due to the small size of the *Overallocation* chart, Project 2013 compresses the time periods shown along the X-axis of the chart. If you want to limit the number of time periods shown in the *Overallocation* chart, you must edit the *Time* category to format the timescale with the time periods you want to see. I discuss how to customize a chart in the *Customizing a Chart* topical section later in this module.

- The *Resource Overview* report shown in Figure 4 - 11 contains two charts and one table that display work-related information about each of the *Work* resources in your project team. The *Resource Stats* chart is a combination chart that shows stacked columns for *Actual Work* and *Remaining Work,* with a line for *Baseline Work* for each of the *Work* resources in your project team. The *Work Status* chart is a column chart that shows the *% Work Complete* for each of the *Work* resources in your project team. The *Resource Status* table shows the status of *Remaining Work* for each resource and includes the *Start, Finish,* and *Remaining Work* fields.

Information: In the *Resource Status* table, the *Start* field contains the earliest *Start* date of any task assigned to each resource, while the *Finish* field contains the latest *Finish* date of any task assigned to each resource. The *Remaining Work* field shows the total *Remaining Work* for all tasks assigned to each resource.

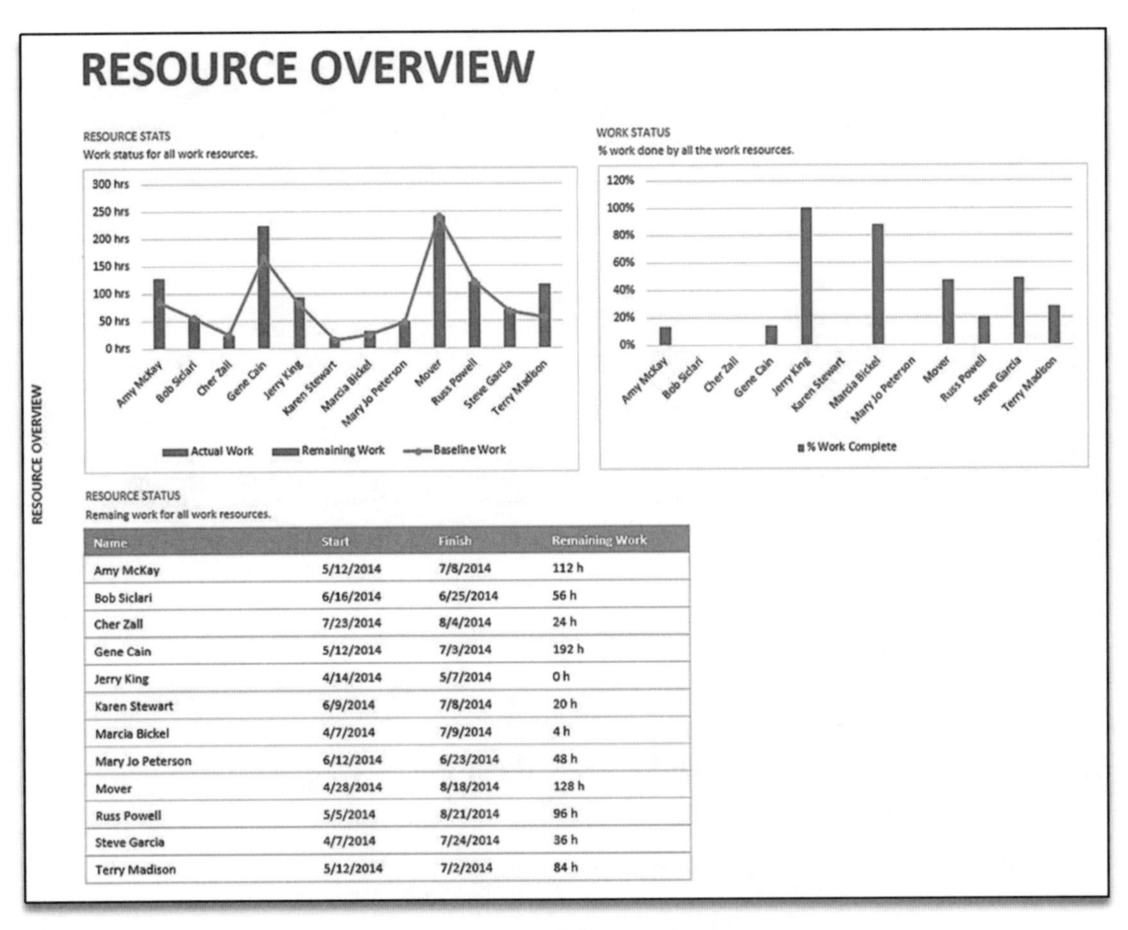

Name	Start	Finish	Remaining Work
Amy McKay	5/12/2014	7/8/2014	112 h
Bob Siclari	6/16/2014	6/25/2014	56 h
Cher Zall	7/23/2014	8/4/2014	24 h
Gene Cain	5/12/2014	7/3/2014	192 h
Jerry King	4/14/2014	5/7/2014	0 h
Karen Stewart	6/9/2014	7/8/2014	20 h
Marcia Bickel	4/7/2014	7/9/2014	4 h
Mary Jo Peterson	6/12/2014	6/23/2014	48 h
Mover	4/28/2014	8/18/2014	128 h
Russ Powell	5/5/2014	8/21/2014	96 h
Steve Garcia	4/7/2014	7/24/2014	36 h
Terry Madison	5/12/2014	7/2/2014	84 h

Figure 4 - 11: Resource Overview report

Understanding Cost Reports

Click the *Costs* pick list button to see the five default cost reports that display project cost information. These new cost reports include the following:

- The *Cash Flow* report shown in Figure 4 - 12 contains a chart, two tables, and an informational text box. The table at the top of the report, shown as a gray-shaded box, displays the *Actual Cost, Baseline Cost, Remaining Cost,* and *Cost Variance* fields for the entire project. The chart is a combination chart that shows a column for *Cost* and a line for *Cumulative Cost,* timephased by quarters for the entire project. The table at the bottom of the report shows you the current cost and earned value data for every first level task. The fields in the table include the *Remaining Cost, Actual Cost, Cost, ACWP (Actual Cost of Work Performed), BCWP (Budgeted Cost of Work Performed),* and *BCWS (Budgeted Cost of Work Scheduled)* fields. The informational text box to the right of the chart explains the meaning of the data in the chart and the table at the bottom of the report.

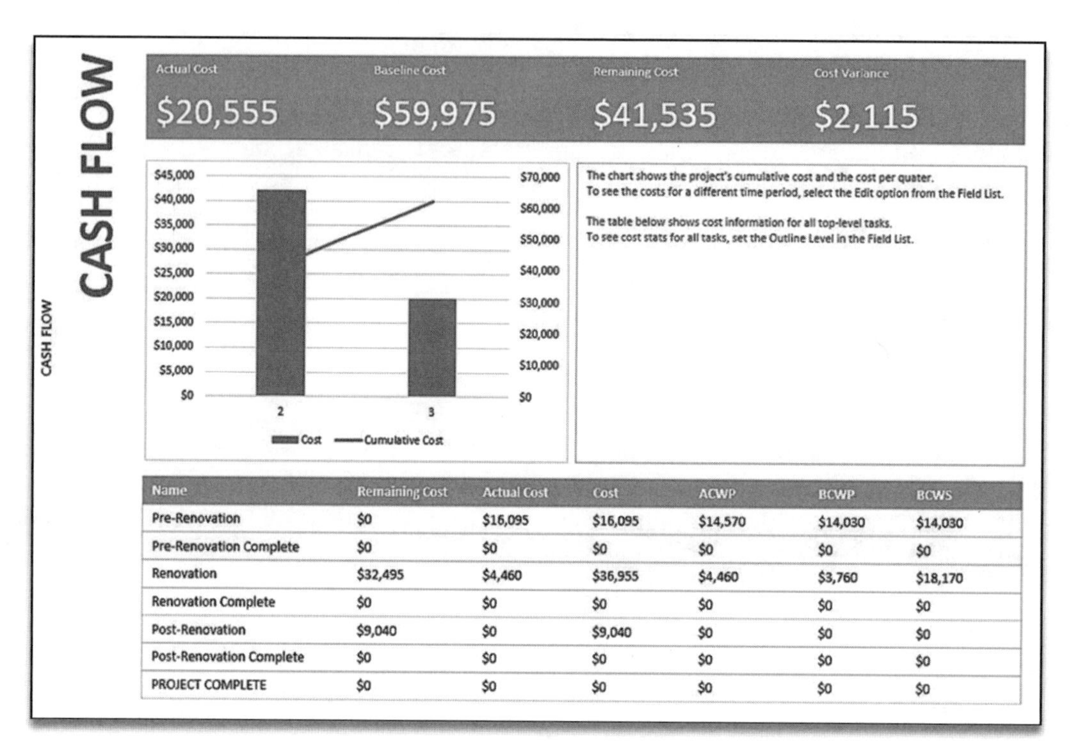

Name	Remaining Cost	Actual Cost	Cost	ACWP	BCWP	BCWS
Pre-Renovation	$0	$16,095	$16,095	$14,570	$14,030	$14,030
Pre-Renovation Complete	$0	$0	$0	$0	$0	$0
Renovation	$32,495	$4,460	$36,955	$4,460	$3,760	$18,170
Renovation Complete	$0	$0	$0	$0	$0	$0
Post-Renovation	$9,040	$0	$9,040	$0	$0	$0
Post-Renovation Complete	$0	$0	$0	$0	$0	$0
PROJECT COMPLETE	$0	$0	$0	$0	$0	$0

Figure 4 - 12: Cash Flow report

- The *Cost Overruns* report shown in Figure 4 - 13 contains two charts and two tables. The *Task Cost Variance* chart is a line chart that shows the *Cost Variance* data for every first level task in the project. The table immediately below this chart shows you the status and current cost data for every first level task. The fields in the table include the *% Work Complete, Cost, Baseline Cost,* and *Cost Variance* fields. The *Resource Cost Variance* chart is a column chart that shows the *Cost Variance* for every *Work* and *Cost* resource in your project team. The table immediately below this chart shows you the cost information for every *Work* resource in your project team. The fields in this table include the *Cost, Baseline Cost,* and *Cost Variance* fields.

Information: The table immediately below the *Resource Cost Variance* chart displays only the *Work* resources in your project team. If you use *Cost* and *Material* resources in your project, in addition to *Work* resources, you may want to customize this table to filter for all resources. I discuss how to customize a table in the *Customizing a Table* topical section later in this module.

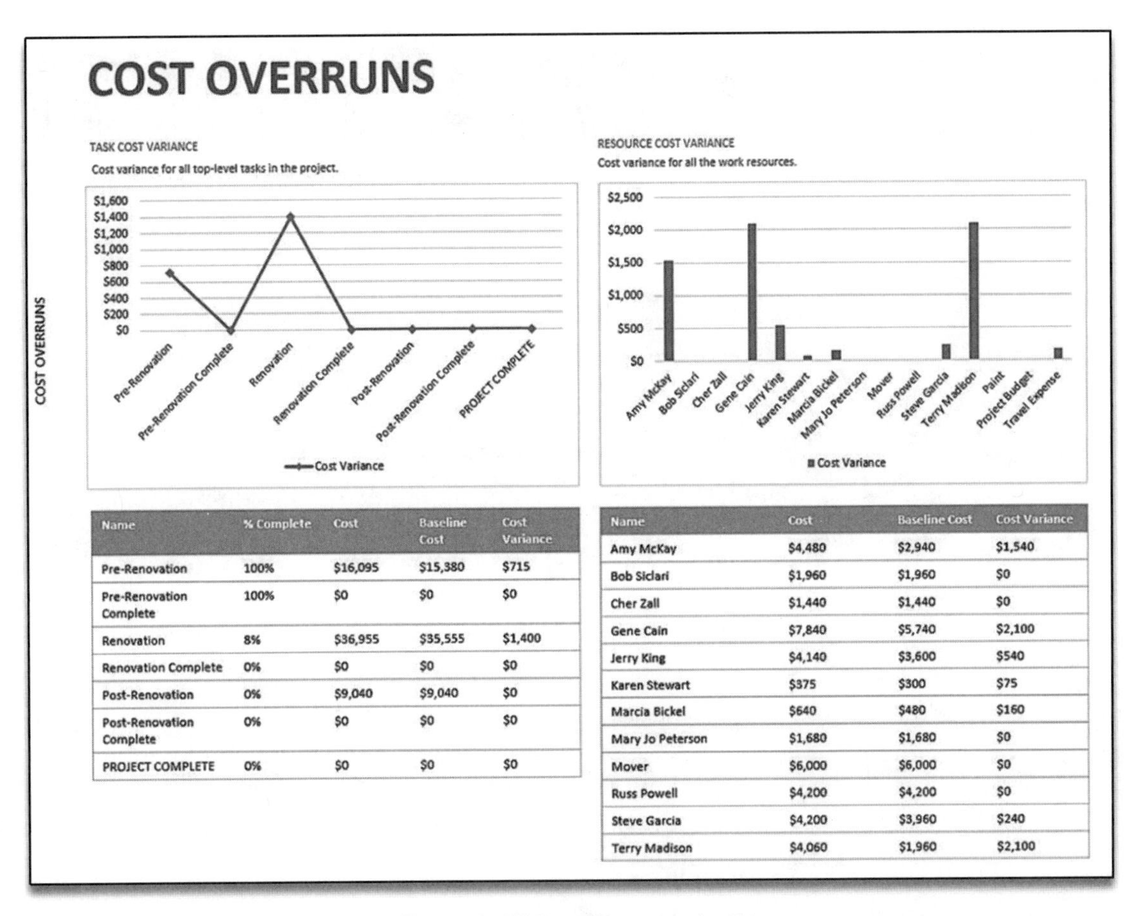

Name	% Complete	Cost	Baseline Cost	Cost Variance
Pre-Renovation	100%	$16,095	$15,380	$715
Pre-Renovation Complete	100%	$0	$0	$0
Renovation	8%	$36,955	$35,555	$1,400
Renovation Complete	0%	$0	$0	$0
Post-Renovation	0%	$9,040	$9,040	$0
Post-Renovation Complete	0%	$0	$0	$0
PROJECT COMPLETE	0%	$0	$0	$0

Name	Cost	Baseline Cost	Cost Variance
Amy McKay	$4,480	$2,940	$1,540
Bob Siclari	$1,960	$1,960	$0
Cher Zall	$1,440	$1,440	$0
Gene Cain	$7,840	$5,740	$2,100
Jerry King	$4,140	$3,600	$540
Karen Stewart	$375	$300	$75
Marcia Bickel	$640	$480	$160
Mary Jo Peterson	$1,680	$1,680	$0
Mover	$6,000	$6,000	$0
Russ Powell	$4,200	$4,200	$0
Steve Garcia	$4,200	$3,960	$240
Terry Madison	$4,060	$1,960	$2,100

Figure 4 - 13: Cost Overruns report

- The *Earned Value* report shown in Figure 4 - 14 contains one table, three charts, and one informational text box. The table at the top of the report, shown as a blue-shaded box, displays the *EAC (Estimate at Completion), ACWP (Actual Cost of Work Performed),* and *BCWP (Budgeted Cost of Work Performed)* fields for the entire project. The *Earned Value Over Time* chart is a line chart that shows the *ACWP (Actual Cost of Work Performed), BCWP (Budgeted Cost of Work Performed),* and *BCWS (Budgeted Cost of Work Scheduled)* fields, timephased at the weekly level. In the description section of the *Earned Value Over Time* chart, the report contains a *Learn more about earned value* hyperlink that points to the *Earned value analysis, for the rest of us* page in the Office.com website. The *Variance Over Time* chart is a line chart that shows the *CV (Cost Variance)* and *SV (Schedule Variance)* fields, timephased at the weekly level. The *Indices Over Time* chart is a line chart that shows the *SPI (Schedule Performance Index)* and *CPI (Cost Performance Index)* fields, timephased at the weekly level. The informational text box to the left of the charts briefly explains the concept of earned value management.

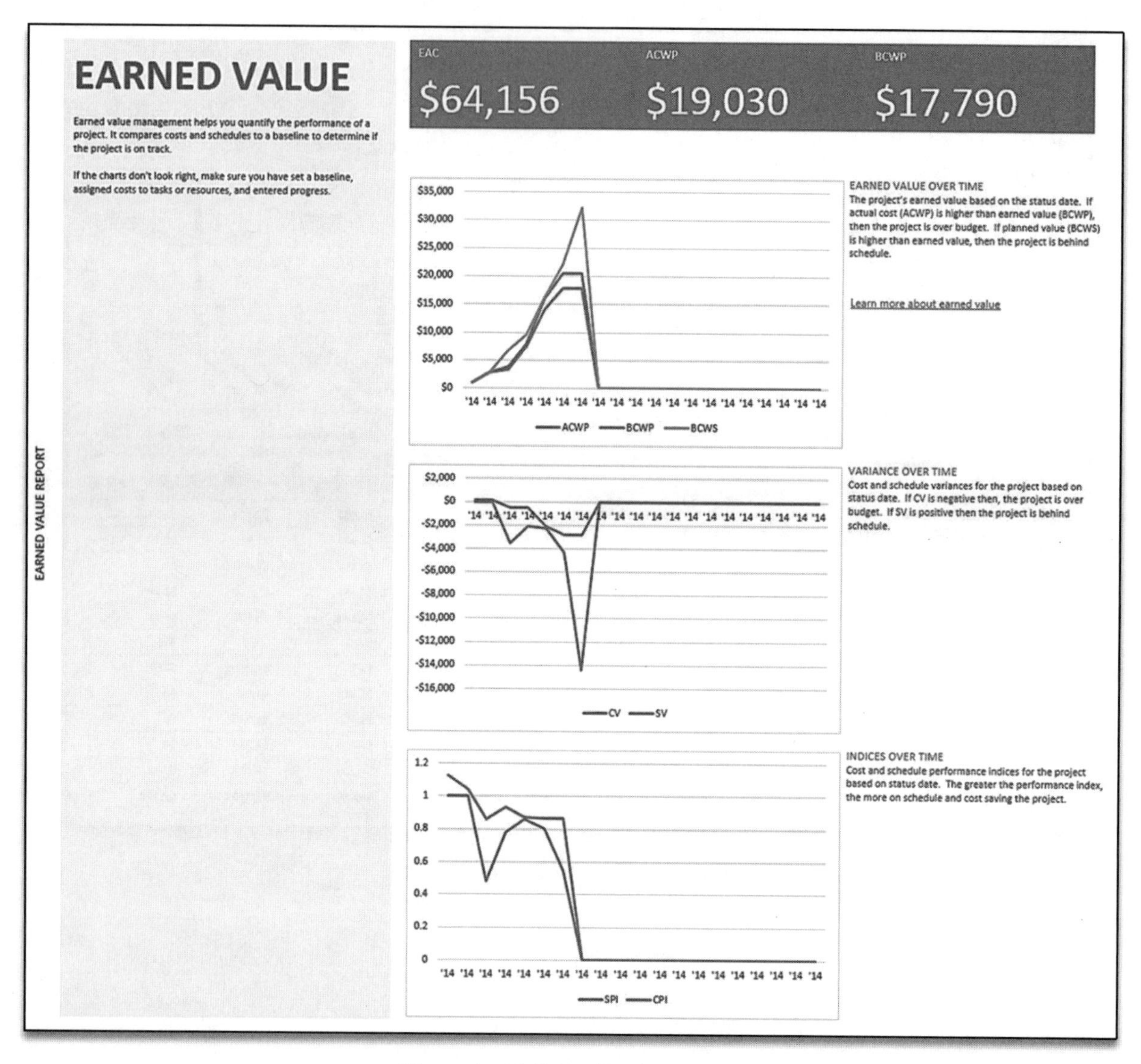

Figure 4 - 14: Earned Value report

- The *Resource Cost Overview* report shown in Figure 4 - 15 contains two charts and one table. The *Cost Status* chart is a combination chart that displays stacked columns for *Actual Cost* and *Remaining Cost,* with a line for *Baseline Cost.* The *Cost Distribution* chart is a pie chart that displays *Cost* information distributed by resource type for *Work, Material,* and *Cost* resources. The *Cost Details* table shows work and cost information for each *Work* resource in your project team, and includes the *Actual Work, Actual Cost,* and *Standard Rate* columns.

Warning: Because of the small size of the *Cost Status* chart, Project 2013 overlaps the resource names on the X-axis over the *Legend* element at the bottom of the chart. To resolve this situation, you must edit the chart to display the *Legend* element at the top of the chart. I discuss how to customize a chart in the *Customizing a Chart* topical section later in this module.

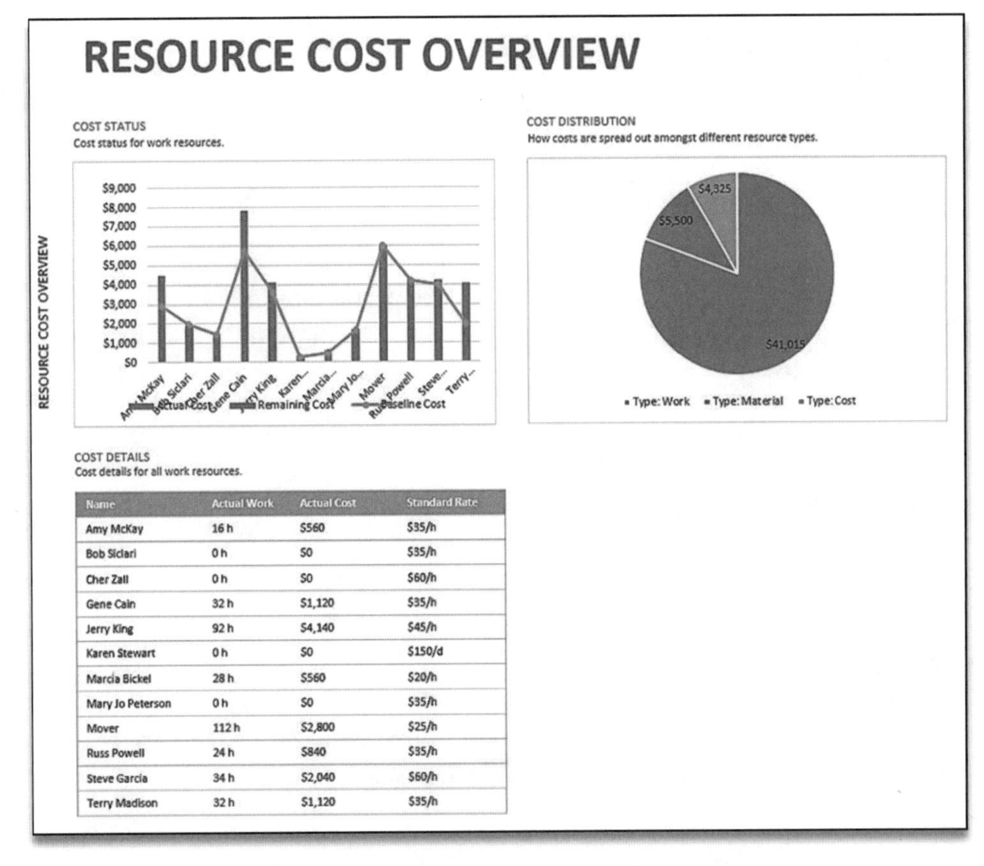

Name	Actual Work	Actual Cost	Standard Rate
Amy McKay	16 h	$560	$35/h
Bob Siclari	0 h	$0	$35/h
Cher Zall	0 h	$0	$60/h
Gene Cain	32 h	$1,120	$35/h
Jerry King	92 h	$4,140	$45/h
Karen Stewart	0 h	$0	$150/d
Marcia Bickel	28 h	$560	$20/h
Mary Jo Peterson	0 h	$0	$35/h
Mover	112 h	$2,800	$25/h
Russ Powell	24 h	$840	$35/h
Steve Garcia	34 h	$2,040	$60/h
Terry Madison	32 h	$1,120	$35/h

Figure 4 - 15: Resource Cost Overview report

Information: The *Cost Details* table displays only the *Work* resources in your project team. If you use *Cost* and *Material* resources in your project, in addition to *Work* resources, you may want to customize this table to filter for all resources. I discuss how to customize a table in the *Customizing a Table* topical section later in this module.

- The *Task Cost Overview* report shown in Figure 4 - 16 contains two charts and a table that display information about the cost of tasks in your project. The *Cost Status* chart is a combination chart that shows stacked columns for *Actual Cost* and *Remaining Cost*, with a line for *Baseline Cost*. This chart shows the data for all first level tasks. The *Cost Distribution* chart is a pie chart that displays *Cost* distribution based on the *Status* value for every task in the project. The *Status* field determines whether a task is completed, on schedule, a future task, or a late task. The *Cost Status* table shows you the current cost-related fields for every first level task. These fields include the *Fixed Cost, Actual Cost, Remaining Cost, Cost, Baseline Cost,* and *Cost Variance* fields.

Information: Remember that a **late task** is any task with a *Late* value in the *Status* field. By default, the software sets a *Late* value in the *Status* field when the time-phased cumulative percent complete (represented by the black progress line in a Gantt bar) does not reach the *Status Date* you specify for the project. If you do not specify a *Status Date*, then the software uses the *Current Date* to determine late tasks.

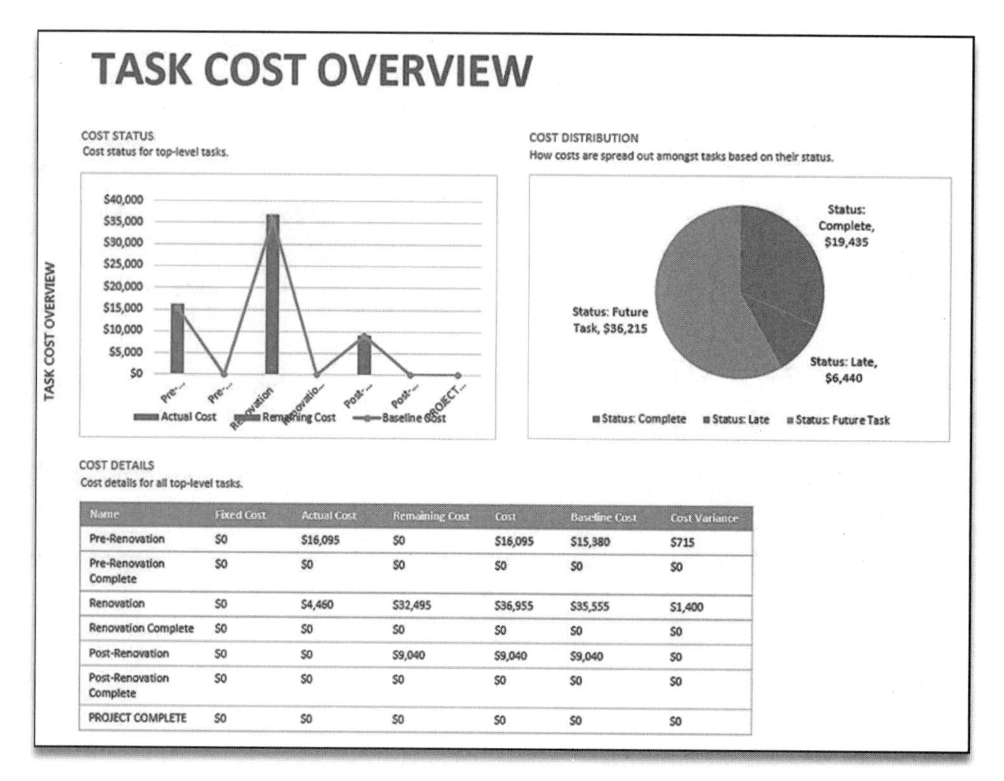

Name	Fixed Cost	Actual Cost	Remaining Cost	Cost	Baseline Cost	Cost Variance
Pre-Renovation	$0	$16,095	$0	$16,095	$15,380	$715
Pre-Renovation Complete	$0	$0	$0	$0	$0	$0
Renovation	$0	$4,460	$32,495	$36,955	$35,555	$1,400
Renovation Complete	$0	$0	$0	$0	$0	$0
Post-Renovation	$0	$0	$9,040	$9,040	$9,040	$0
Post-Renovation Complete	$0	$0	$0	$0	$0	$0
PROJECT COMPLETE	$0	$0	$0	$0	$0	$0

Figure 4 - 16: Task Cost Overview report

Warning: Because of the small size of the *Cost Status* chart, Project 2013 overlaps the task names on the X-axis over the *Legend* element at the bottom of the chart. To resolve this situation, you must edit the chart to display the *Legend* element at the top of the chart. I discuss how to customize a chart in the *Customizing a Chart* topical section later in this module.

Understanding In Progress Reports

Click the *In Progress* pick list button to see the four default reports that display progress information about tasks in your project. These new *In Progress* reports include the following:

- The *Critical Tasks* report shown in Figure 4 - 17 contains a chart and a table. The chart in the upper left corner of the report is a pie chart that displays *Cost* distribution based on the *Status* value for every task in the project. The *Status* field determines whether a task is completed, on schedule, a future task, or a late task. The table displays schedule-related information about every *Critical* task in the project, and includes the *Start, Finish, % Complete, Remaining Work,* and *Resource Names* columns. In the description section of table, the report contains a *Learn more about managing your project's critical path* hyperlink that points to the *Show the critical path of your project* page in the Office.com website.

Information: The table in the *Critical Tasks* report does not display any completed tasks. Remember that Project 2013 does not consider completed tasks to be *Critical* tasks. By definition, a *Critical* task is any uncompleted task with a *Total Slack* value of 0 days.

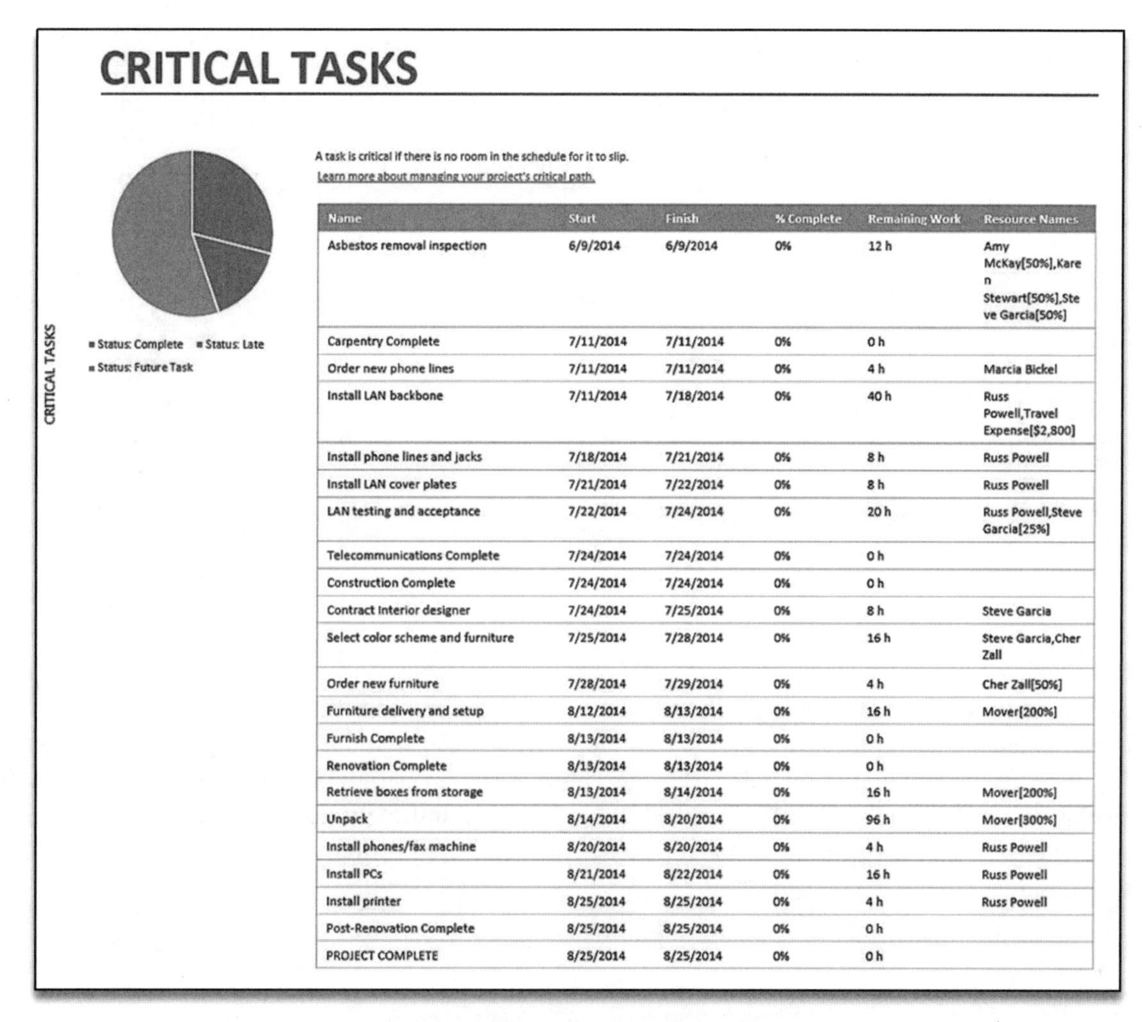

CRITICAL TASKS

A task is critical if there is no room in the schedule for it to slip.
Learn more about managing your project's critical path.

Name	Start	Finish	% Complete	Remaining Work	Resource Names
Asbestos removal inspection	6/9/2014	6/9/2014	0%	12 h	Amy McKay[50%],Karen Stewart[50%],Steve Garcia[50%]
Carpentry Complete	7/11/2014	7/11/2014	0%	0 h	
Order new phone lines	7/11/2014	7/11/2014	0%	4 h	Marcia Bickel
Install LAN backbone	7/11/2014	7/18/2014	0%	40 h	Russ Powell,Travel Expense[$2,800]
Install phone lines and jacks	7/18/2014	7/21/2014	0%	8 h	Russ Powell
Install LAN cover plates	7/21/2014	7/22/2014	0%	8 h	Russ Powell
LAN testing and acceptance	7/22/2014	7/24/2014	0%	20 h	Russ Powell,Steve Garcia[25%]
Telecommunications Complete	7/24/2014	7/24/2014	0%	0 h	
Construction Complete	7/24/2014	7/24/2014	0%	0 h	
Contract interior designer	7/24/2014	7/25/2014	0%	8 h	Steve Garcia
Select color scheme and furniture	7/25/2014	7/28/2014	0%	16 h	Steve Garcia,Cher Zall
Order new furniture	7/28/2014	7/29/2014	0%	4 h	Cher Zall[50%]
Furniture delivery and setup	8/12/2014	8/13/2014	0%	16 h	Mover[200%]
Furnish Complete	8/13/2014	8/13/2014	0%	0 h	
Renovation Complete	8/13/2014	8/13/2014	0%	0 h	
Retrieve boxes from storage	8/13/2014	8/14/2014	0%	16 h	Mover[200%]
Unpack	8/14/2014	8/20/2014	0%	96 h	Mover[300%]
Install phones/fax machine	8/20/2014	8/20/2014	0%	4 h	Russ Powell
Install PCs	8/21/2014	8/22/2014	0%	16 h	Russ Powell
Install printer	8/25/2014	8/25/2014	0%	4 h	Russ Powell
Post-Renovation Complete	8/25/2014	8/25/2014	0%	0 h	
PROJECT COMPLETE	8/25/2014	8/25/2014	0%	0 h	

Figure 4 - 17: Critical Tasks report

- The *Late Tasks* report shown in Figure 4 - 18 contains a chart and a table. The chart in the upper left corner of the report is a pie chart that displays *Cost* distribution based on the *Status* value for every task in the project. The *Status* field determines whether a task is completed, on schedule, a future task, or a late task. The table displays schedule-related information about every *Late* task in the project, and includes the *Start, Finish, % Complete, Remaining Work,* and *Resource Names* columns.

Information: Remember that in Project 2013, a **late task** is any task with a *Late* value in the *Status* field. By default, the software sets a *Late* value in the *Status* field when the time-phased cumulative percent complete (represented by the black progress line in a Gantt bar) does not reach the *Status Date* you specify for the project. If you do not specify a *Status Date*, then the software uses the *Current Date* to determine late tasks.

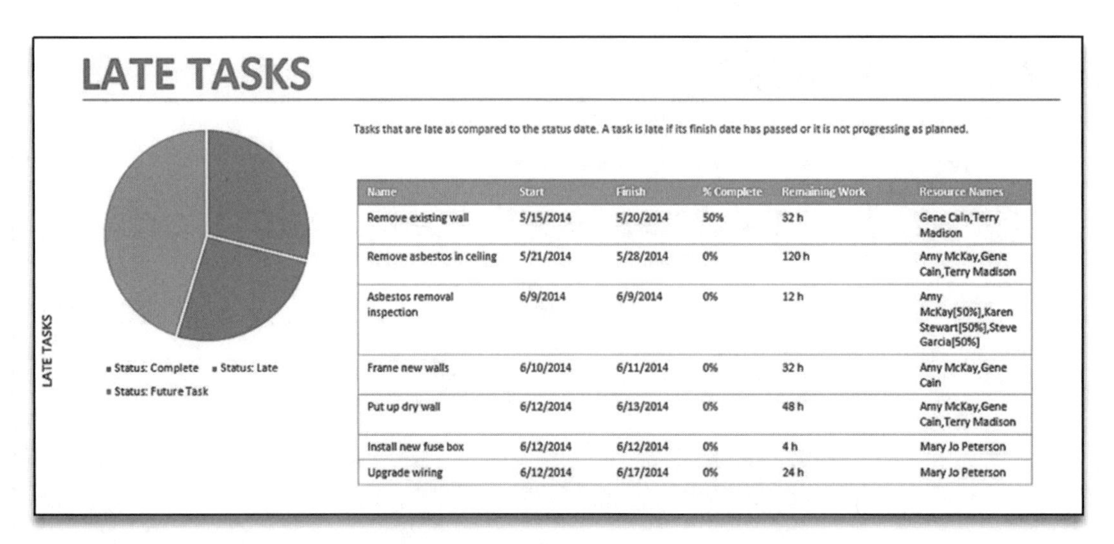

Name	Start	Finish	% Complete	Remaining Work	Resource Names
Remove existing wall	5/15/2014	5/20/2014	50%	32 h	Gene Cain,Terry Madison
Remove asbestos in ceiling	5/21/2014	5/28/2014	0%	120 h	Amy McKay,Gene Cain,Terry Madison
Asbestos removal inspection	6/9/2014	6/9/2014	0%	12 h	Amy McKay[50%],Karen Stewart[50%],Steve Garcia[50%]
Frame new walls	6/10/2014	6/11/2014	0%	32 h	Amy McKay,Gene Cain
Put up dry wall	6/12/2014	6/13/2014	0%	48 h	Amy McKay,Gene Cain,Terry Madison
Install new fuse box	6/12/2014	6/12/2014	0%	4 h	Mary Jo Peterson
Upgrade wiring	6/12/2014	6/17/2014	0%	24 h	Mary Jo Peterson

Figure 4 - 18: Late Tasks report

- The *Milestone Report* shown in Figure 4 - 19 contains three tables and one chart. The *Late Milestones* table displays any milestone task whose *Status* value is *Late,* and includes the *Finish* date of the milestone task. The *Milestones Up Next* table displays uncompleted milestones in the past or milestones that are due during the current month, and includes the *Finish* date of the milestone task. The *Completed Milestones* table displays all milestones with a *% Complete* value of *100%,* and includes the *Finish* date of the milestone task. The chart on the right side of the report is a line chart that shows data from the new *Remaining Tasks* and *Remaining Actual Tasks* fields.

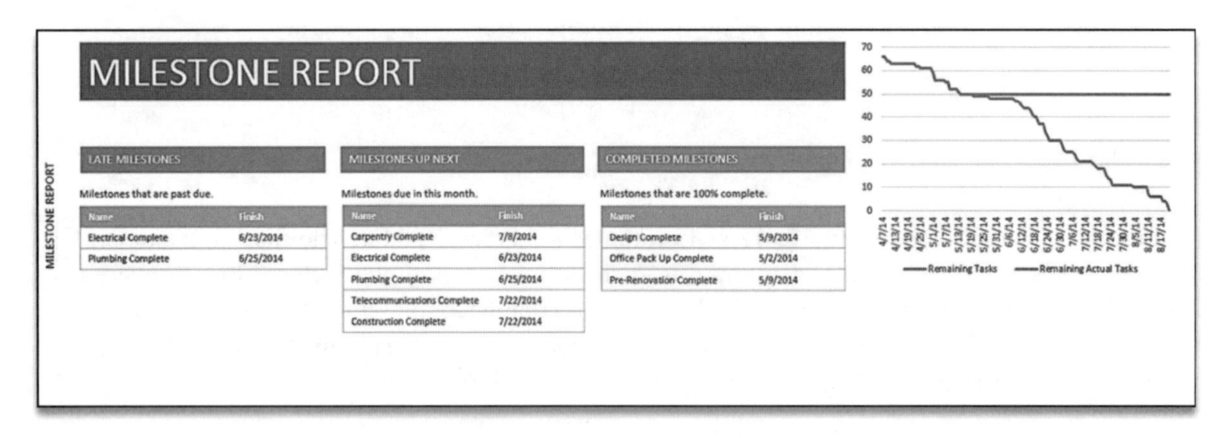

LATE MILESTONES — Milestones that are past due.

Name	Finish
Electrical Complete	6/23/2014
Plumbing Complete	6/25/2014

MILESTONES UP NEXT — Milestones due in this month.

Name	Finish
Carpentry Complete	7/8/2014
Electrical Complete	6/23/2014
Plumbing Complete	6/25/2014
Telecommunications Complete	7/22/2014
Construction Complete	7/22/2014

COMPLETED MILESTONES — Milestones that are 100% complete.

Name	Finish
Design Complete	5/9/2014
Office Pack Up Complete	5/2/2014
Pre-Renovation Complete	5/9/2014

Figure 4 - 19: Milestone Report

- The *Slipping Tasks* report shown in Figure 4 - 20 contains a chart and a table. The chart in the upper left corner of the report is a line chart that shows data from the new *Remaining Cumulative Work* and *Remaining Cumulative Actual Work* fields. The table displays all slipping tasks, and includes the *Start, Finish, % Complete, Remaining Work,* and *Resource Names* columns. Remember that by definition in Project 2013, a slipping task is any uncompleted task whose *Finish* date is later than its *Baseline Finish* date. This means that a completed task cannot be a slipping task.

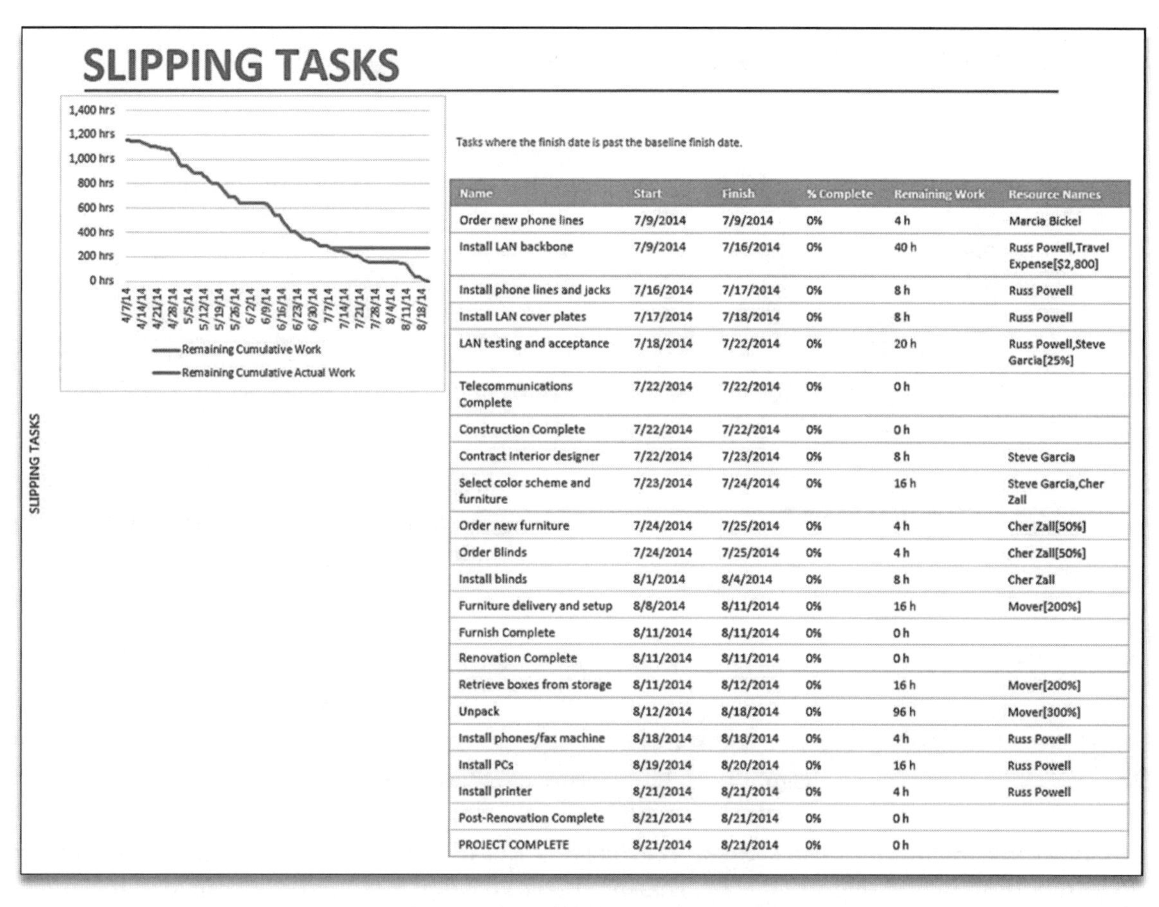

Name	Start	Finish	% Complete	Remaining Work	Resource Names
Order new phone lines	7/9/2014	7/9/2014	0%	4 h	Marcia Bickel
Install LAN backbone	7/9/2014	7/16/2014	0%	40 h	Russ Powell,Travel Expense[$2,800]
Install phone lines and jacks	7/16/2014	7/17/2014	0%	8 h	Russ Powell
Install LAN cover plates	7/17/2014	7/18/2014	0%	8 h	Russ Powell
LAN testing and acceptance	7/18/2014	7/22/2014	0%	20 h	Russ Powell,Steve Garcia[25%]
Telecommunications Complete	7/22/2014	7/22/2014	0%	0 h	
Construction Complete	7/22/2014	7/22/2014	0%	0 h	
Contract interior designer	7/22/2014	7/23/2014	0%	8 h	Steve Garcia
Select color scheme and furniture	7/23/2014	7/24/2014	0%	16 h	Steve Garcia,Cher Zall
Order new furniture	7/24/2014	7/25/2014	0%	4 h	Cher Zall[50%]
Order Blinds	7/24/2014	7/25/2014	0%	4 h	Cher Zall[50%]
Install blinds	8/1/2014	8/4/2014	0%	8 h	Cher Zall
Furniture delivery and setup	8/8/2014	8/11/2014	0%	16 h	Mover[200%]
Furnish Complete	8/11/2014	8/11/2014	0%	0 h	
Renovation Complete	8/11/2014	8/11/2014	0%	0 h	
Retrieve boxes from storage	8/11/2014	8/12/2014	0%	16 h	Mover[200%]
Unpack	8/12/2014	8/18/2014	0%	96 h	Mover[300%]
Install phones/fax machine	8/18/2014	8/18/2014	0%	4 h	Russ Powell
Install PCs	8/19/2014	8/20/2014	0%	16 h	Russ Powell
Install printer	8/21/2014	8/21/2014	0%	4 h	Russ Powell
Post-Renovation Complete	8/21/2014	8/21/2014	0%	0 h	
PROJECT COMPLETE	8/21/2014	8/21/2014	0%	0 h	

Figure 4 - 20: Slipping Tasks report

Understanding Getting Started Reports

Click the *Getting Started* pick list button to see the five default reports that help you to get started using Project 2013 as your project scheduling tool. These new *Getting Started* reports include the following:

- The *Best Practices Analyzer* report shown in Figure 4 - 21 contains two charts and two tables. Use this report to make sure that your project follows four best practices for task and assignment planning. The *Remaining Work* chart is a column chart that shows the *Remaining Work* for every unstarted task that has a *Start Date* earlier than the *Current Date*. The *Unassigned Work* chart is a column chart that shows the *Work* value for every task that has no resources assigned to it. The *Tasks with Durations Less Than 8 Hours* table shows every task with a *Duration* value less than *8 hours*, even if the task is completed, and includes the *Scheduled Duration* and *Work* columns. The *Summary Tasks with Assigned Resources* table displays every summary task with at least one resource assigned to it. In a project that you plan and manage well, you should not see data in the charts or the tables in this report.

Warning: Because of an unfixed bug in the release (RTM) version of Project 2013, the *Summary Tasks with Assigned Resources* table **does not** show any data, even if you assigned resources to summary tasks in the project. To work around this bug, click one of the column headers in the *Summary Tasks with Assigned Resources* table to display the *Field List* sidepane on the right side of the report. In the *Field List* sidepane, select the *Show Hierarchy* checkbox option at the bottom of the sidepane. Click anywhere outside the table to hide the *Field List* sidepane.

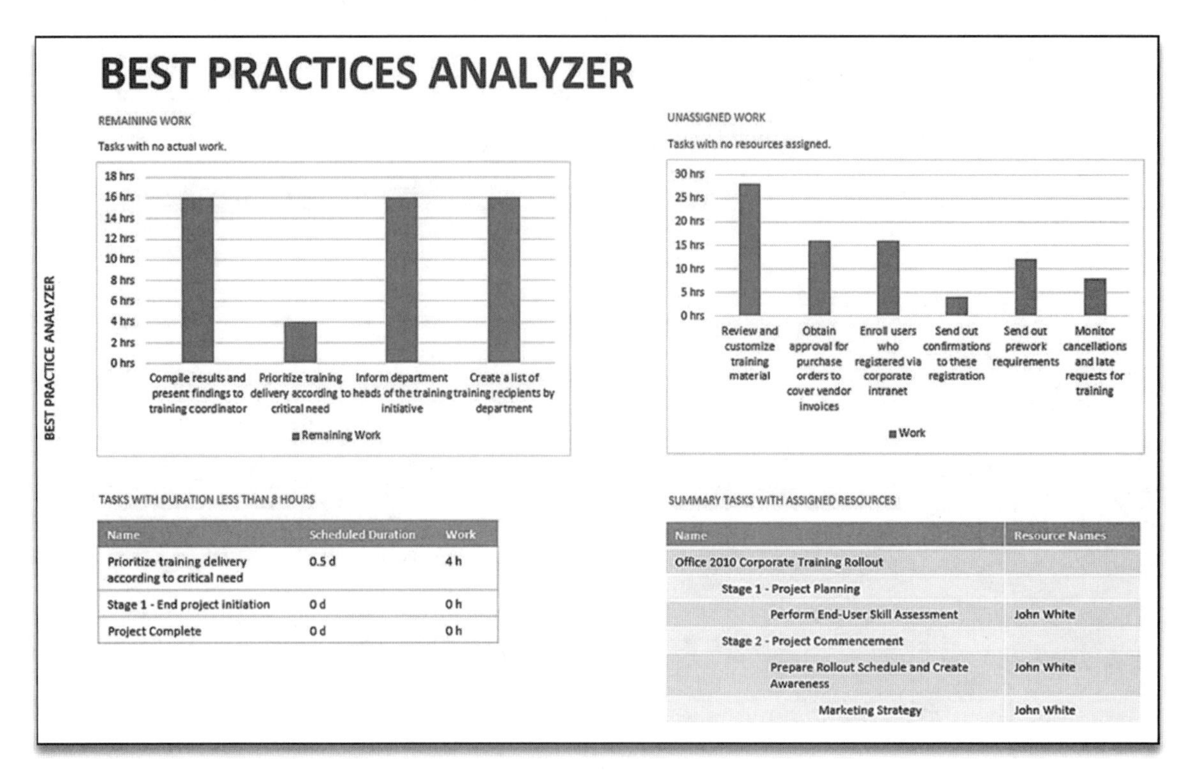

Figure 4 - 21: Best Practices Analyzer report

- On the *Getting Started* pick list, select the *Getting Started with Project* item to display the *Welcome to Project 2013* report shown in Figure 4 - 22. This report is actually a wizard you can use to advance your knowledge about how to organize tasks, create reports, and share project data with your project team. If you click the *Start* button or click the *Organize tasks* button in this report, Project 2013 displays the *Organize Tasks* report shown in Figure 4 - 23. If you click the *Create reports* button, the software displays the *Create Reports* report shown in Figure 4 - 24. If you click the *Share with your team* button, the software displays the *Share with your Team* report shown in Figure 4 - 25. If you click the *Skip Intro* button, the software exits the report and displays a *Gantt with Timeline* view of your project.

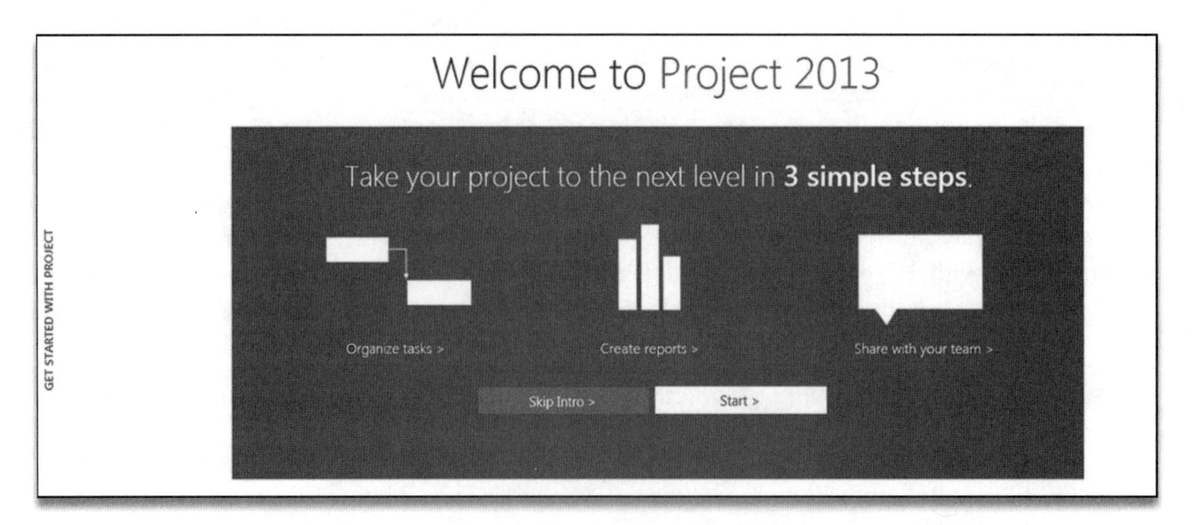

Figure 4 - 22: Welcome to Project 2013 report

- On the *Getting Started* pick list, select the *Organize Tasks* item to display the *Organize Tasks* report shown in Figure 4 - 23. The *Organize Tasks* report provides a brief tutorial on how to add task details, measure progress in your project, and manage task dependencies. At the bottom of each topical section, click the *Learn more* hyperlink to see more information about that topic. For example, if you click the *Learn more* hyperlink at the bottom of the *Add task details* section of the report, the software displays the *Change a task duration* page in the Office.com website. If you click the *Skip & go to your tasks* hyperlink in the upper right corner of the report, the software exits the *Organize Tasks* report and displays the *Gantt with Timeline* view in your project. Otherwise, you can click the *Next* button to display the *Create Reports* report shown in Figure 4 - 24.

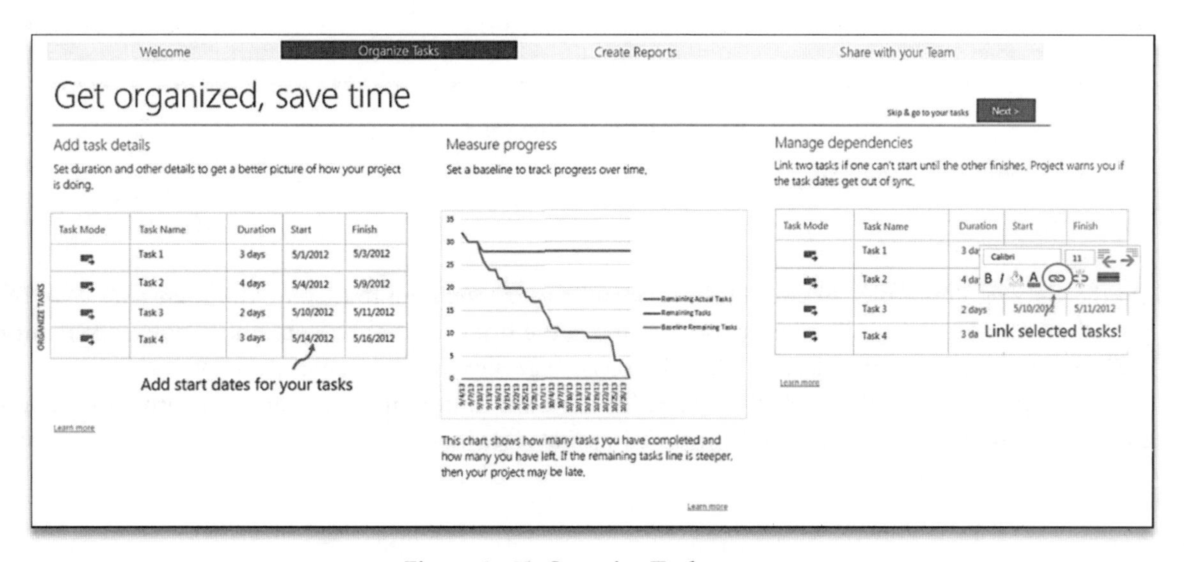

Figure 4 - 23: Organize Tasks report

- On the *Getting Started* pick list, select the *Create reports* item to display the *Create Reports* report shown in Figure 4 - 24. This report continues the brief tutorial by explaining the new reporting feature in Project 2013. The *Create Reports* report contains one table and two charts. The table in the upper left corner of the report displays the *% Complete* value for the entire project. The *Task Burndown* chart is a line chart that compares the number of completed tasks with the remaining tasks, timephased at the weekly level. Remember that this chart uses the new *Baseline Remaining Tasks, Remaining Tasks,* and *Remaining Actual Tasks* fields. The *Work Status* chart is a stacked column chart that shows the *Actual Work* and *Remaining Work* for each *Work* resource in your project team. Click the *Learn how to create a burndown* hyperlink to navigate to the *Create a burndown report* page in the Office.com website. If you click the *Skip & go to your tasks* hyperlink in the upper right corner of the report, the software exits the *Create Reports* report and displays the *Gantt with Timeline* view in your project. Otherwise, you can click the *Next* button to display the *Share with your Team* report shown in Figure 4 - 25.

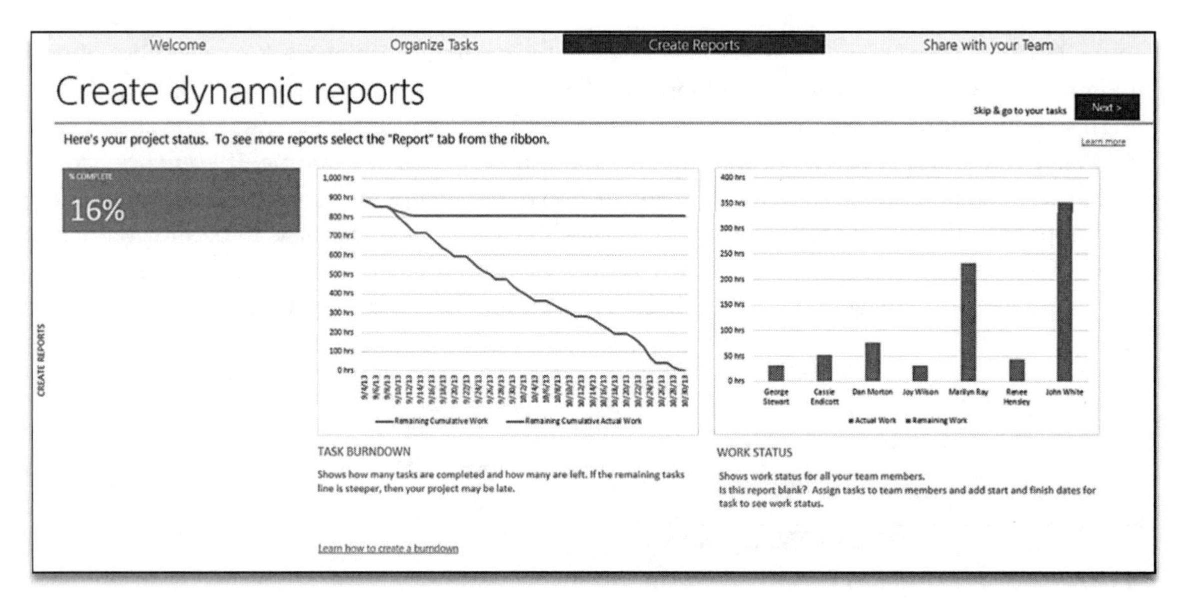

Figure 4 - 24: Create Reports report

- On the *Getting Started* pick list, select the *Share with your team* item to display the *Share with your Team* report shown in Figure 4 - 25. This report continues the brief tutorial by explaining how to synchronize a project with a SharePoint tasks list. Click the *Learn more hyperlink* to view a video on the *Collaborating with your Team* page in the Office.com website. Click the *Done* button in the upper right corner of the report to exit the report and navigate to the *Gantt with Timeline* view in your project.

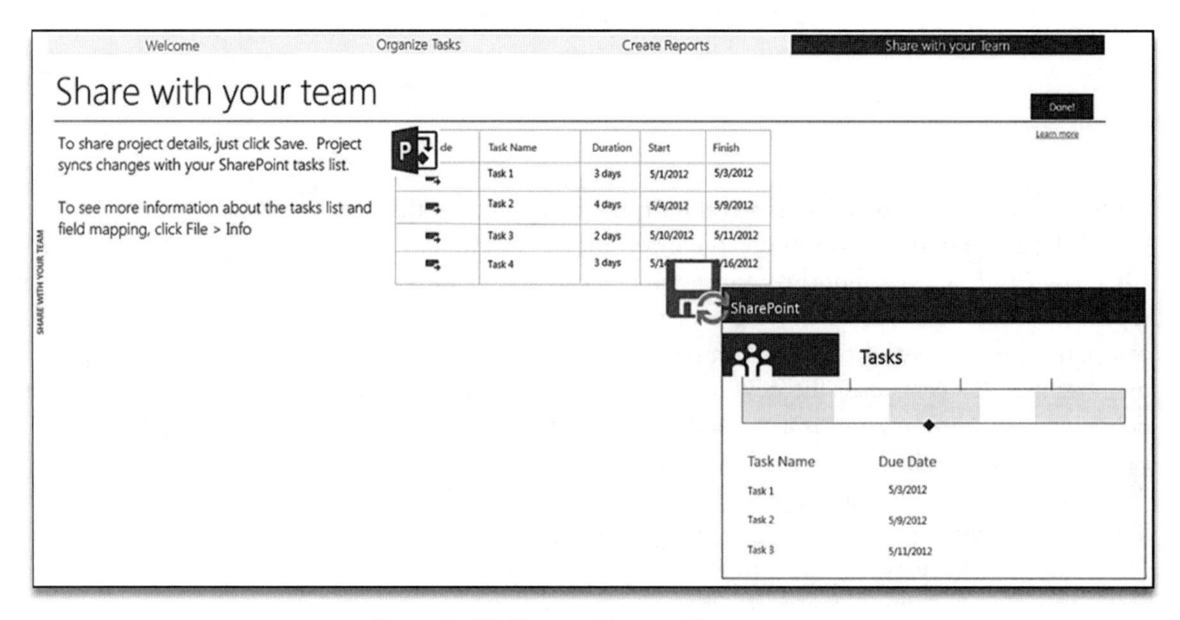

Figure 4 - 25: Share with your Team report

Hands On Exercise

Exercise 4 - 1

Explore the new reports in Project 2013.

1. Open the **Office Renovation 2013.mpp** sample file from your sample files folder.
2. Click the *Report* tab to display the *Report* ribbon.
3. In the *View Reports* section of the *Report* ribbon, click the *Dashboards* pick list button and select the *Project Overview* item in the pick list.

Notice how Project 2013 displays the *Design* ribbon with the *Report Tools* applied.

4. Click anywhere in the *Milestones Due* table and notice how the software displays the *Field List* sidepane on the right side of the page.

Information: If you do not see the *Field List* sidepane when you click in the *Milestones Due* table, click the second *Design* tab to display the *Design* ribbon with the *Table Tools* applied. In the *Show/Hide* section of the *Design* ribbon, click the *Table Data* button to display the *Field List* sidepane on the right side of the report.

5. Examine the selected options in the *Field List* sidepane on the right side of the report, including the fields selected in the *Select Fields* section of the sidepane, along with the items selected on the *Filter, Group By, Outline Level,* and *Sort By* pick lists.
6. Click anywhere in the *% Complete* chart and then examine the selected options in the *Field List* sidepane.
7. Click the *Report* tab to display the *Report* ribbon again.
8. In the *View Reports* section of the *Report* ribbon, click the *Resources* pick list button and select the *Resource Overview* item in the pick list.
9. Study the data shown in the *Resource Stats* and the *Work Status* charts, along with the data shown in the *Resource Status* table.
10. Click anywhere in the *Resource Stats* chart and examine the fields selected in the *Select Fields* section of the *Field List* sidepane.
11. Click the *Report* tab to display the *Report* ribbon again.
12. In the *View Reports* section of the *Report* ribbon, click the *Costs* pick list button and select the *Task Cost Overview* item in the pick list.
13. Examine the data shown in the *Cost Status* and the *Cost Distribution* charts, along with the data shown in the *Cost Details* table.
14. Click the *Report* tab to display the *Report* ribbon again.

15. In the *View Report* section of the *Report* ribbon, click the *In Progress* pick list button and select the *Critical Tasks* item in the pick list.

16. Examine the data shown in the pie chart, along with the tasks shown in the table.

17. Click the *Learn more about managing your project's critical path* hyperlink at the top of the table.

18. Study the information shown on the *Show the critical path of your project* page in the Office.com website and then close the Internet Explorer when finished.

19. Save but **do not** close the **Office Renovation 2013.mpp** sample file.

Customizing an Existing Report

Project 2013 offers you multiple ways to customize an existing report. These methods include: customizing a chart, customizing a table, customizing a text box, adding a new chart, adding a new table, and adding a new text box. In addition, you can also add new images and new shapes to the report, and you can move and resize all report objects.

Customizing a Chart

To customize a chart in your report, click one time in the chart you want to customize. The software refreshes the user interface as shown in Figure 4 - 26. Notice that when I select the *% Complete* chart in the *Project Overview* report, the user interface includes the following elements:

- On the far right side of the report, the software displays the *Field List* sidepane.

- To the right of the selected chart, the software displays three formatting buttons: the *Chart Elements, Chart Styles,* and *Chart Filters* buttons.

- At the top of the user interface, the software displays the *Design* and *Format* ribbon tabs with the *Chart Tools* applied.

You can use any of these three options to customize a chart, plus you can double-click any chart element to edit that individual element. I discuss each of these chart customization options individually.

Information: Customizing a chart in Project 2013 is nearly identical to customizing a chart in Excel 2013. The more experience you have with formatting an Excel chart, the better you will be at formatting a Project chart.

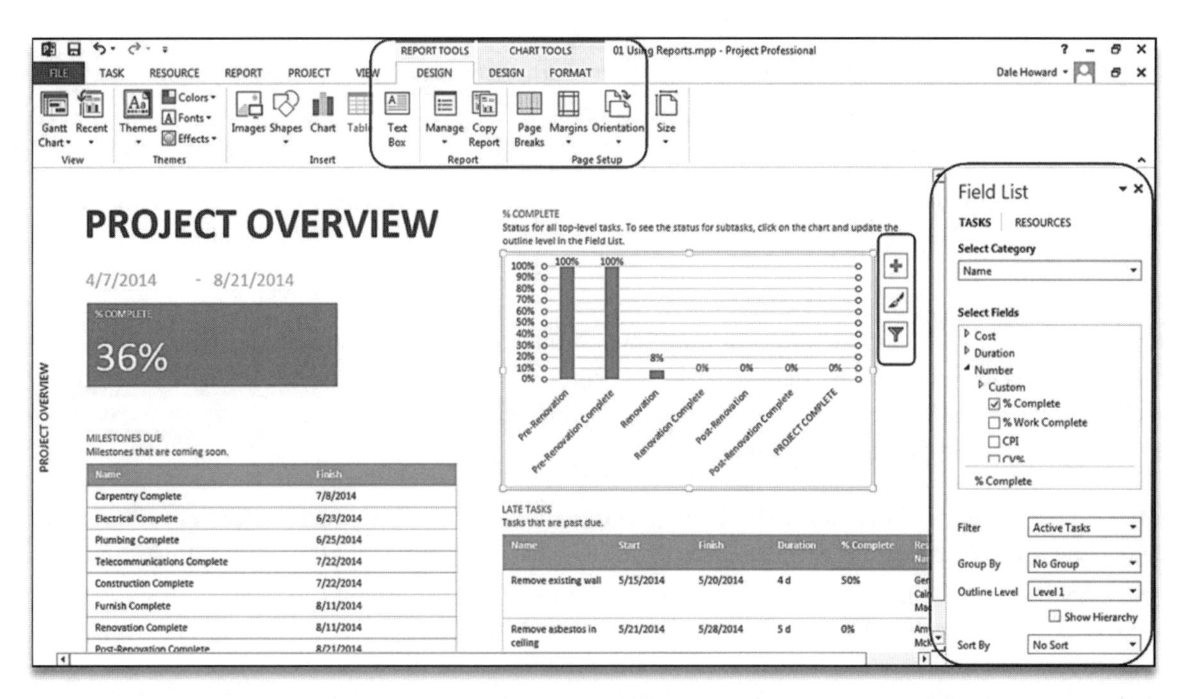

Figure 4 - 26: Select a chart for customization

Using the Field List sidepane

In the upper left corner of the *Field List* sidepane on the right side of the report, Project 2013 displays two tabs: the *Tasks* and *Resources* tab. The software selects the correct tab for the type of data shown in the chart. For example, notice in Figure 4 - 26 shown previously that the software selects the *Tasks* tab since the *% Complete* chart displays task data.

Warning: If you click the *Resources* tab while you have a task chart selected, or if click the *Tasks* tab while you have a resource chart selected, the software automatically removes all of the chart data and forces you to create a totally new chart from scratch for the type of data selected.

Click the *Select Category* pick list to select the type of fields you want displayed at the bottom of the selected chart. For the *% Complete* chart, the available categories include the *Time, ID, Name, Resource Names,* and *Unique ID* fields. By default, the software selects the *Name* field in the *Select Category* pick list, which displays the name of each task shown in the chart.

The *Select Fields* section of the sidepane displays the types of fields available for display in the selected chart, which include *Cost, Duration, Number,* and *Work* fields for a task chart. By default, the software expands the types of fields used in the selected chart. In the *% Complete* chart, the software expands the *Number* type, which shows the list of available *Number* fields for inclusion in the report. To expand any other type of field to see the available fields of that type, click the *Expand* symbol (white arrow button) to the left of the field type. In the bottom half of the *Select Fields* section, the software displays the fields currently included in the chart. By default, the *% Complete* chart includes only the *% Complete* field. To include any other fields in the chart, expand the field type and select the checkboxes for the fields you want to add. For example, I need to add the *% Work Complete* field in the *Number* section. To remove any current fields from the chart, deselect the checkbox for any field you want to omit.

Information: If you add additional fields to your chart, you can change the display order of the fields by manually dragging the fields up and down in the list of selected fields shown at the bottom of the *Select Fields* section of the *Field List* sidepane. If you right-click the name of any displayed field in the bottom half of the *Select Fields* section, the software displays a shortcut menu. On this shortcut menu, select the *Move Up* or *Move Down* item on the shortcut menu to move the field in the selected chart. Select the *Remove Field* item on the shortcut menu to remove the field from the selected chart. Select the *Field Settings* item on the shortcut menu to display the *Field Settings* dialog, in which you can apply a label or display name for the field in the selected chart.

The bottom of the *Field List* sidepane offers you options to filter, group, sort, and display the outline level of task data shown in the selected chart. By default, the *% Complete* chart includes the *Active Tasks* filter, the *No Group* item selected in the *Group By* pick list, the *Outline Level* option set to *Level 1*, with the *Show Hierarchy* checkbox option deselected, and the *Sort By* option set to *No Sort*.

Because the default filtering shows all *Active* tasks at outline level 1, and because I prefer to outdent milestones at the same outline level as the summary tasks they represent, the *% Complete* chart shows both summary tasks and milestone tasks. My reporting requirement, however, is to show **only** summary tasks at both outline level 1 and outline level 2. To meet this reporting requirement, I must complete the following steps:

1. Click the *Filter* pick list and select the *Summary Tasks* filter. Project 2013 displays only summary tasks at outline level 1.

2. Click the *Outline Level* pick list and select the *Level 2* item. The software displays only summary tasks at outline level 2; but at this point, I cannot see the outline level 1 summary tasks.

3. Select the *Show Hierarchy* checkbox.

The software displays Level 1 and Level 2 summary tasks in the chart. In the *% Complete* chart shown in Figure 4 - 27, the Level 1 summary tasks are the *Pre-Renovation* and *Renovation* tasks on the bottom row, while the Level 2 summary tasks are the *Design, Office Pack Up, Construction,* and *Furnish* tasks in the top row.

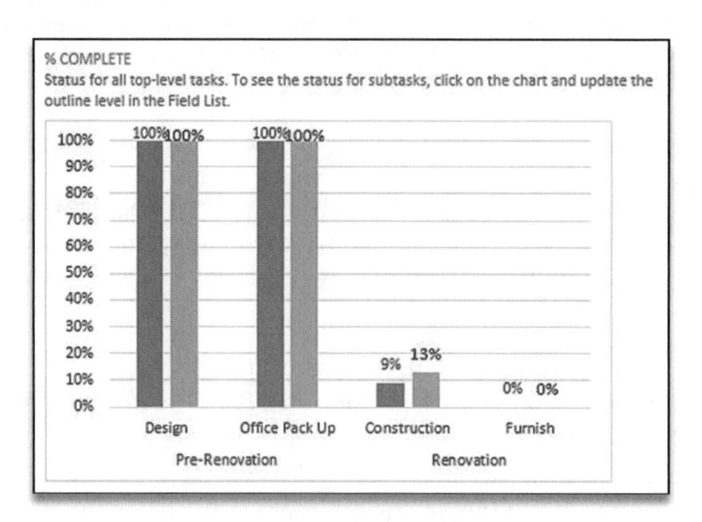

Figure 4 - 27: Updated % Complete chart

Edit the selected chart using the *Filter, Group By, Outline Level,* and *Sort By* pick lists, along with selecting the *Show Hierarchy* checkbox option as needed. When you finish editing the selected chart, click anywhere outside of the chart to close the *Field List* sidepane.

Information: If you close the *Field List* sidepane by clicking the *Close* button (**X**) in the upper right corner of the sidepane, Project 2013 offers you two methods to redisplay it. To use the first method, click the *Design* tab with the *Chart Tools* applied and then click the *Chart Data* button in the *Show/Hide* section of the *Design* ribbon. To use the second method, right-click anywhere in the selected chart and then click the *Show Field List* item at the bottom of the shortcut menu.

Using the Formatting Buttons

If you click the *Chart Elements* button on the right side of the chart, Project 2013 displays the *Chart Elements* menu shown in Figure 4 - 28. In the *Chart Elements* menu, select the checkboxes of any additional elements you want to add to the chart, and deselect the checkboxes for any elements you do not want to show. For example, notice in Figure 4 - 28 that the software selects the *Axes, Data Labels,* and *Gridlines* chart elements by default.

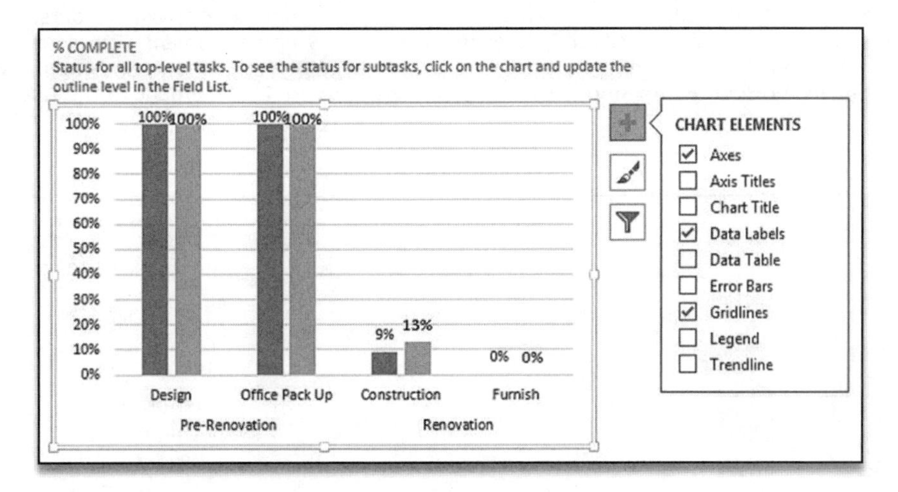

Figure 4 - 28: Chart Elements menu

When you select the checkbox to show an additional element in the chart or float your mouse pointer over the element, the software displays a right-arrow button at the end of the line. When you click this right-arrow button for any chart element, the software displays a flyout menu with additional options that control how to display the element. For example, if I click the right-arrow button to the right of the *Chart Title* element, Project 2013 displays the flyout menu shown in Figure 4 - 29. Notice that the flyout menu includes the *Above Chart, Centered Overlay,* and *More Options* items, which I can use to control where to display the *Chart Title* element in the chart.

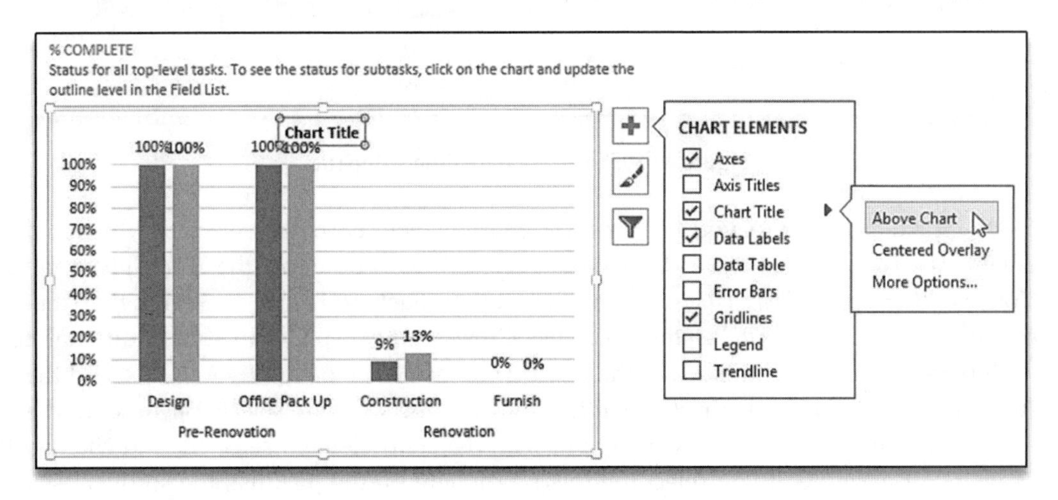

Figure 4 - 29: Flyout menu for the Chart Title element

Warning: If you select the *More Options* item on the *Chart Title* flyout menu and you still have the *Field List* sidepane open, the software displays an additional *Format Chart Title* sidepane to the right of the *Field List* sidepane. With two sidepanes open at the same time, you may want to close the *Field List* sidepane by clicking the *Close* button (**X**) in the upper right corner of the sidepane.

If I select the *More Options* item on the *Chart Title* flyout menu, the software adds the *Chart Title* element at the top of the chart, and then displays the *Format Chart Title* sidepane on the right side of the report. Figure 4 - 30 shows the *Format Chart Title* sidepane for the *Chart Title* chart element in the *% Complete* chart.

Information: If you add the *Chart Title* element to a chart, you must rename it, and you may also need to move it to a new location in the chart so that it does not cover up other chart data. To rename the *Chart Title* element, right-click anywhere in the element and select the *Edit Text* item on the shortcut menu. In the *Chart Title* element, delete the old name and enter a new title, and then click anywhere outside of the element. For example, I need to rename the *Chart Title* element to its new name, *Percent Complete Comparison*. To move the *Chart Title* element, click and hold anywhere on the edge of the element, and then drag and drop the element in its new location. For example, I need to move the *Chart Title* element to the upper right corner of the chart.

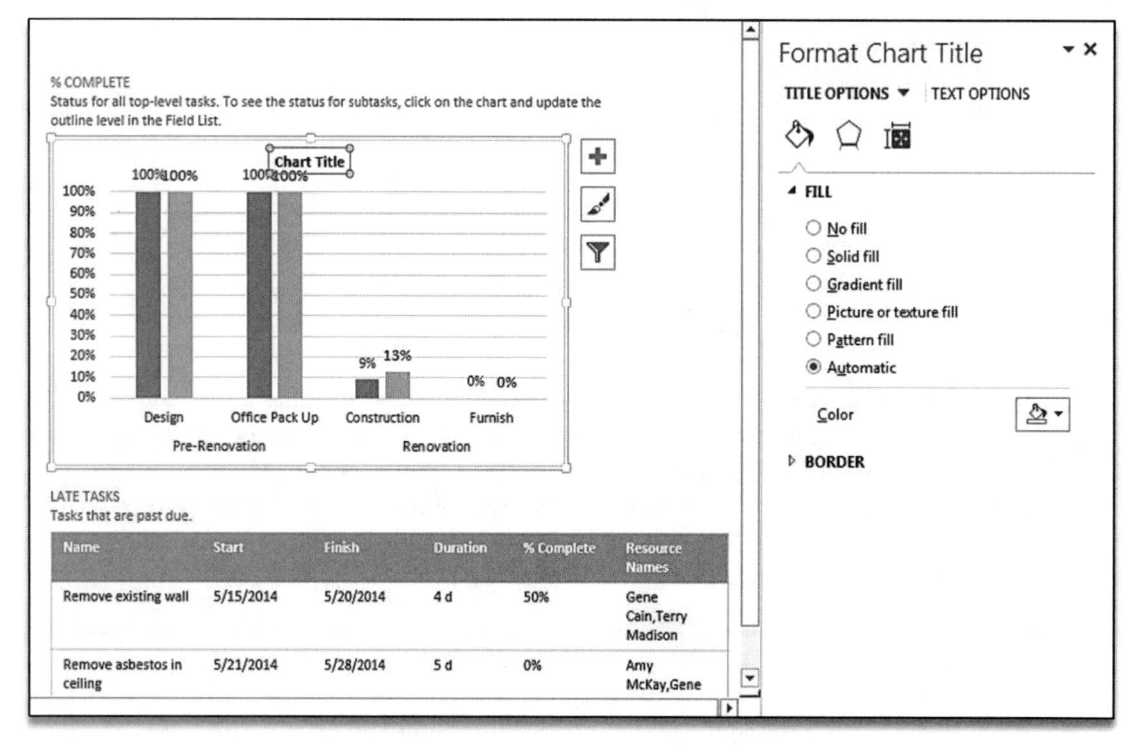

Figure 4 - 30: Format Chart Title sidepane

The *Format Chart Title* sidepane allows you to format the chart element currently selected, which in this case is the *Chart Title* element. The *Format Chart Title* sidepane includes two tabs at the top: the *Title Options* tab and the *Text Options* tab. Notice in the *Format Chart Title* sidepane shown previously in Figure 4 - 30 that the *Title Options* tab is actually a pick list. If you click the *Title Options* pick list, Project 2013 displays a list of additional items you can format in the sidepane, including items such as the *Chart Area*, the *Horizontal (Category) Axis*, and the *Vertical (Value) Axis*. If you select any other item on the *Title Options* pick list, the software selects the new chart element in the chart, changes the name of the sidepane to correspond with the chart element selected, and changes the name of the pick list as well. For example, if you select the *Chart Area* item on the pick list, the software selects the *Chart*

Area element in the chart, changes the name of the sidepane to *Format Chart Area*, and changes the name of the pick list to *Chart Options*.

Click either of the two tabs at the top of the sidepane to see a set of buttons that indicate the available options for formatting the selected chart element. With the *Chart Title* element selected, when you click the *Title Options* tab, the software offers you the following buttons, which you can use to format the title:

- Click the *Fill & Line* button to display options for formatting the fill color and background, as well as formatting the borders of the *Chart Title* element. With the *Fill & Line* button selected, the sidepane displays two formatting sections: the *Fill* and *Border* sections. You may need to click the *Expand* indicator to the left of a section to see the settings in that section. Using the options available in the *Fill* and *Border* sections, specify your formatting options for the *Chart Title* element.

- Click the *Effects* button to see all available effects options. With the *Effects* button selected, the sidepane displays four sections of effects options: the *Shadow, Glow, Soft Edges,* and *3-D Format* sections. To view the available options in any of these four sections, you must first click the *Expand* indicator to the left of the section. Use the options in any of these four sections to apply various effects to the *Chart Title* element.

- Click the *Size & Properties* button to see the available options for size and alignment of the selected chart element. With the *Size & Properties* button selected, the sidepane displays only one section, the *Alignment* section. Use the options in the *Alignment* section of the sidepane to format the size and alignment of the *Chart Title* element.

Information: If you click the *Title Options* pick list and select either the *Horizontal (Category) Axis* item or the *Vertical (Value) Axis* item, Project 2013 displays an additional button called *Axis Options*. With the *Axis Options* button selected, the sidepane displays four sections of axis options: the *Axis Options*, *Tick Marks*, *Labels*, and *Numbers* sections. If you select one of the *Series* items on the *Title Options* pick list, such as the *Series % Complete* item, the software displays an additional button called *Series Options*. With the *Series Options* button selected, the sidepane displays only one section, the *Series Options* section.

When you click the *Text Options* tab at the top of the *Format Chart Title* sidepane, Project 2013 offers you the following buttons, which you can use to format the title text:

- Click the *Text Fill & Outline* button to display the options for formatting the fill color and outline of the text in the selected element. With the *Text Fill & Outline* button selected, the sidepane displays two formatting sections: the *Text Fill* and *Text Outline* sections. Using the options available in the *Text Fill* and *Text Outline* sections, specify your formatting options for the text in the *Chart Title* element.

- Click the *Text Effects* button to see all available effects options for formatting text. With the *Text Effects* button selected, the sidepane displays six sections of effects options: the *Shadow, Reflection, Glow, Soft Edges, 3-D Format,* and *3-D Rotation* sections. To view the available options in any of these six sections, you must first click the *Expand* indicator to the left of the section. Use the options in any of these six sections to apply various effects to the text in the *Chart Title* element.

- Click the *Text Box* button to see the available options for the alignment and direction of the text box used for the selected chart element. With the *Text Box* button selected, the sidepane displays only one section, the *Text Box* section. Use the options in the *Text Box* section of the sidepane to format the alignment and text direction of the *Chart Title* element.

If you click the *Chart Styles* button on the right side of the selected chart, Project 2013 displays the *Chart Styles* menu shown in Figure 4 - 31. This menu includes two tabs at the top, the *Style* tab and the *Color* tab with the *Style* tab selected by default. The *Style* page of the menu displays 16 pre-formatted styles, labeled *Style 1* through *Style*

16, which you can apply to your chart. You see the label, by the way, when you float your mouse pointer over the style preview. Select any style in the list, as needed. When you initially apply a style, the software applies a gray color theme by default to all of the elements in the selected chart.

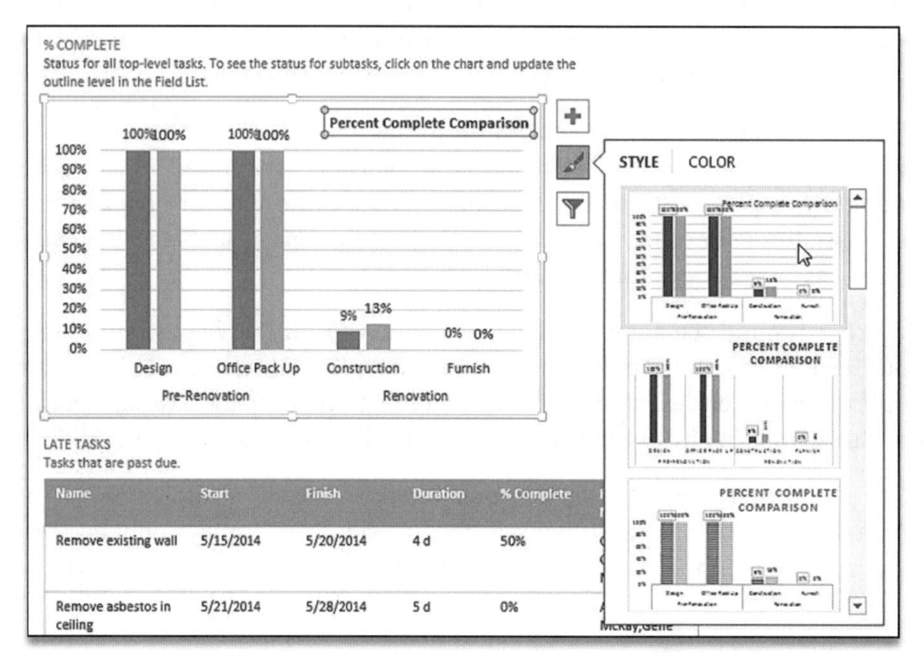

Figure 4 - 31: Chart Styles menu, Style tab selected

If you select a pre-formatted style on the *Style* page of the menu, you may want to change the color theme from the default gray colors. To do so, click the *Color* tab to display the *Color* page of the menu. Figure 4 - 32 shows the *Color* page of the menu after I applied the *Style 5* style to my chart. The *Color* page offers you two sections of theme colors, which you can apply to the selected chart. Select one of the theme colors in either the *Colorful* section or the *Monochromatic* section to apply the theme colors to the elements in the selected chart.

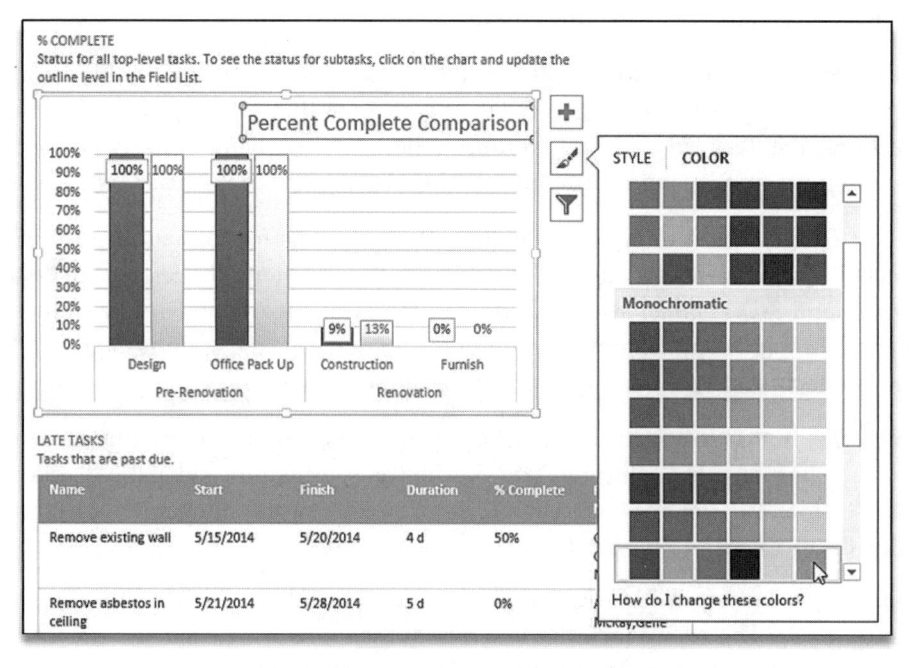

Figure 4 - 32: Chart Styles menu, Color tab selected

Information: If you float your mouse pointer over the *How do I change these colors* hyperlink at the bottom of the *Color* page in the *Chart Styles* menu, Project 2013 displays the *Change Theme Colors* tooltip that explains how to change the colors used in the report.

If you click the *Chart Filters* button on the right side of the chart, Project 2013 displays the *Values* menu. Figure 4 - 33 shows the *Values* menu after I applied the *Color 4* theme colors to my chart. The *Values* menu offers you a number of checkboxes organized into a *Series* section and a *Categories* section. The checkboxes in the *Series* section generally represent numerical fields, such as the *% Complete* and *% Work Complete* fields used in the *% Complete* chart, and show the data on the Y-axis of the chart. The checkboxes in the *Categories* section generally represent task or resource data, such as the first level tasks used in the *% Complete* chart, and show this data on the X-axis of the chart. You can select or deselect any of the checkboxes, as needed, to apply filtering to the data shown in the selected chart. Select the checkboxes for only the data you want to display in your chart and then click the *Apply* button. Click anywhere outside the *Values* menu to hide the menu.

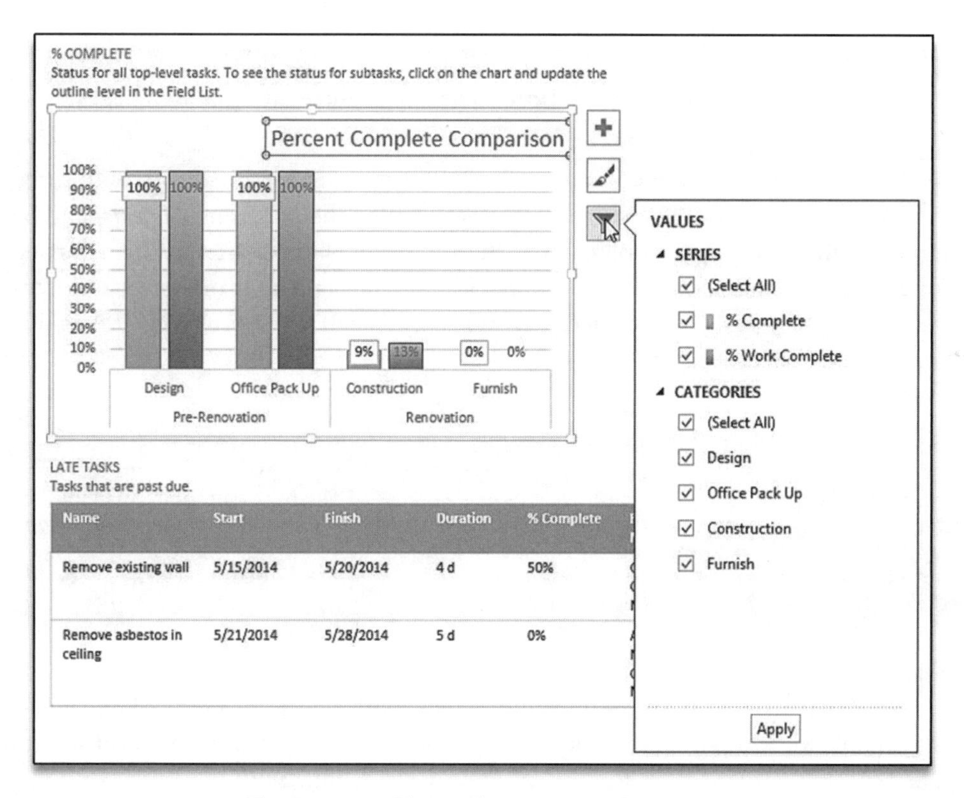

Figure 4 - 33: Chart Filter menu, Values page

Using Other Format Sidepanes

If you double-click any element in a chart, Project 2013 displays a *Format* sidepane for the selected chart element. For example, if I double-click one of the columns in the *% Complete* chart, the software displays the *Format Data Point* sidepane with the *Series Options* button selected, as shown in Figure 4 - 34.

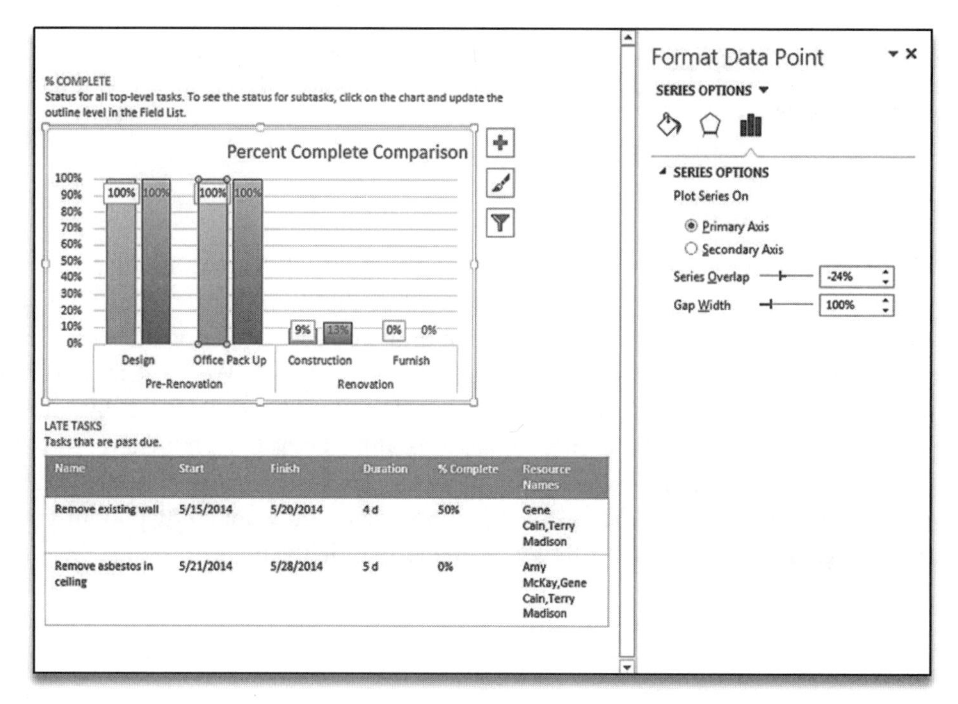

Figure 4 - 34: Format Data Point sidepane

Notice that the *Format Data Point* sidepane contains a *Series Options* pick list at the top, with three options buttons immediately below the pick list. Click these three buttons to display the *Fill & Line, Effects,* and *Series Options* pages in the sidepane. Click the *Series Options* pick list at the top of the sidepane to see the chart elements available for formatting. For example, in the *% Complete* chart, the *Series Options* pick list offers the following chart elements for formatting: *Chart Area, Chart Title, Horizontal (Category) Axis, Plot Area, Vertical (Value) Axis, Vertical (Value) Axis Major Gridlines, Series "% Complete", Series "% Complete" Data Labels, Series "% Work Complete",* and *Series "% Work Complete" Data Labels.*

Information: The *Series Options* pick list contains the list of all chart elements available for formatting in the selected chart. This means that you may see different pick list items depending on the type of chart you format. For example, when formatting the *Cost Distribution* chart in the *Task Cost Overview* report, the *Series Options* pick list contains only the following elements for formatting: *Chart Area, Legend, Plot Area, Series "Cost",* and *Series "Cost" Data Labels.*

If you select any other chart element on the *Series Options* pick list, Project 2013 redisplays the *Format* sidepane to show the options available for formatting the selected chart element. For example, when I select the *Plot Area* element on the pick list, the software displays the *Format Plot Area* sidepane with the *Effects* option selected. Use any of these available options to format the elements in the cart.

Using the Design Ribbon with the Chart Tools Applied

If you click the rightmost of the two *Design* tabs at the top of your Project 2013 application window, the software displays the *Design* ribbon with the *Chart Tools* applied, as shown in Figure 4 - 35. The software divides the *Design* ribbon into four sections: the *Chart Layouts, Chart Styles, Show/Hide,* and *Type* sections.

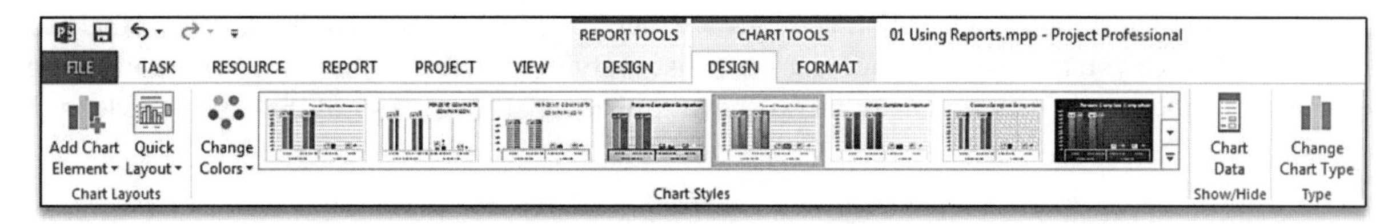

Figure 4 - 35: Design ribbon with the Chart Tools applied

When you click the *Add Chart Element* pick list button in the *Chart Layouts* section of the *Design* ribbon, the software shows you a pick list of available chart elements, including elements such as the *Axes, Axis Titles, Chart Title,* and *Legend* elements. The elements available on the *Chart Elements* pick list are identical to the elements on the *Chart Elements* menu shown previously in Figure 4 - 28. Use the *Add Chart Element* pick list button to add and position any additional elements to the selected chart.

If you click the *Quick Layout* pick list button in the *Chart Layouts* section of the *Design* ribbon, the software offers you 11 pre-defined layouts labeled *Layout 1* through *Layout 11*. Use these quick layouts to quickly lay out all of the elements in the selected chart. For example, the *Layout 2* quick layout centers the *Chart Title* and *Legend* elements across the top of the chart, and resizes the *Plot Area* element, as needed. Figure 4 - 36 shows the *% Complete* chart formatted using the *Layout 2* item on the *Quick Layout* pick list.

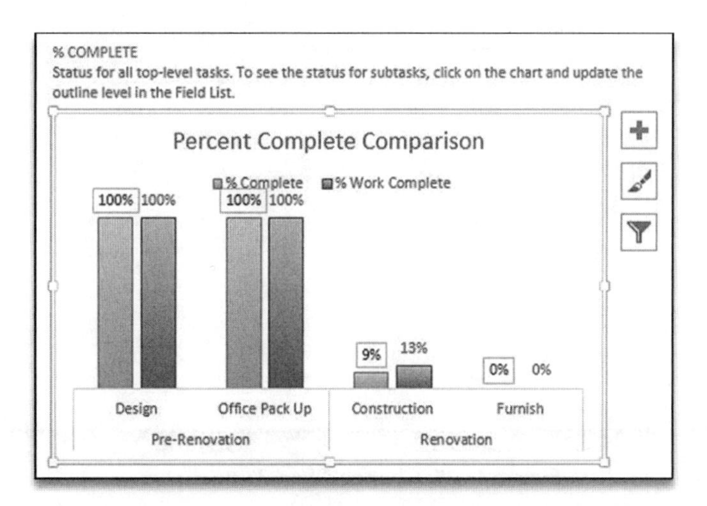

Figure 4 - 36: Layout 2 quick format applied

Information: If your chart does not already include the elements used in the selected *Quick Layout* item, Project 2013 automatically adds the missing elements. For example, if you did not include the *Legend* element in your chart, and then you select the *Layout 2* item on the *Quick Layout* pick list, the software adds this element for you automatically.

Information: After you apply an option on the *Quick Layout* pick list, Project 2013 allows you to use "drag and drop" to manually place the chart elements in a new location, if necessary.

The *Chart Styles* section of the *Design* ribbon contains a gallery of 16 pre-formatted chart styles, labeled *Style 1* through *Style 16,* which you can apply to your chart. The list of styles available in the *Chart Styles* gallery are identical to the list of styles on the *Style and Color* menu shown previously in Figure 4 - 31. Select any style in the gallery, as needed.

Click the *Chart Data* button in the *Show/Hide* section of the *Design* ribbon to display or hide the *Field List* sidepane shown previously in Figure 4 - 26. Click the *Change Chart Type* button in the *Type* section of the *Design* ribbon to change the type of chart displayed in your report. Project 2013 displays the *Change Chart Type* dialog shown in Figure 4 - 37.

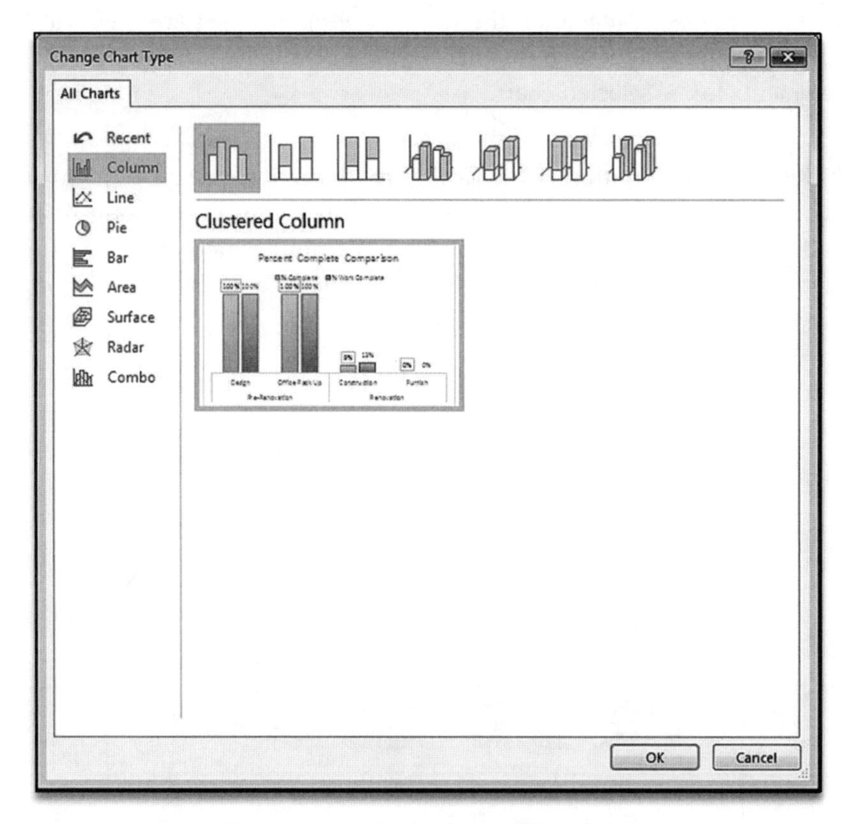

Figure 4 - 37: Change Chart Type dialog

The *Change Chart Type* dialog allows you to select any type of chart available in the software. In the list of chart types on the left side of the dialog, the software allows you to choose from among the *Column, Line, Pie, Bar, Area, Surface, Radar,* and *Combo* chart types. The dialog also includes the *Recent* item in the list to allow you to choose a recently applied chart type. Select a chart type in the list on the left side of the *Change Chart Type* dialog and the software displays a list of sub-types across the top of the dialog. For example, if you select the *Bar* chart type, Project 2013 offers you 6 sub-types, including the *Clustered Bar, Stacked Bar, 100% Stacked Bar, 3-D Clustered Bar, 3-D Stacked Bar,* and the *3-D 100% Stacked Bar* sub-types.

To change the chart type, select a chart type in the list on the left side of the dialog, and then select a sub-type in the list across the top of the *Change Chart Type* dialog. The software shows you a preview of the selected chart type in the middle of the dialog. To see a magnified preview of the chart type you select, float your mouse pointer over the preview image. Click the *OK* button to apply the new chart type to the selected chart. For example, Figure 4 - 38 shows the *% Complete* chart with the *3-D Clustered Bar* chart type applied.

Information: Because of the extremely small size of the *% Complete* chart, notice in Figure 4 - 38 how the data labels (percentages at the right of each bar) overlap each other and how the words in the axis labels (summary tasks on the left side of the chart) do not wrap correctly. To resolve this problem, you must increase the size of the *% Complete* chart. I discuss how to increase the size of a chart later in this module.

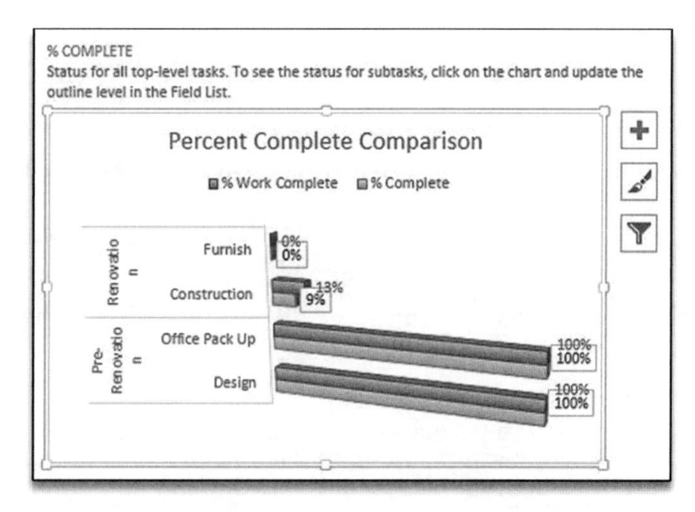

Figure 4 - 38: % Complete chart with 3-D Clustered Bar chart type applied

Using the Format Ribbon with the Chart Tools Applied

If you click the *Format* tab, Project 2013 displays the *Format* ribbon with the *Chart Tools* applied, as shown in Figure 4 - 39. The software divides the *Format* ribbon into six sections: the *Current Selection, Insert Shapes, Shape Styles, WordArt Styles, Arrange,* and *Size* sections.

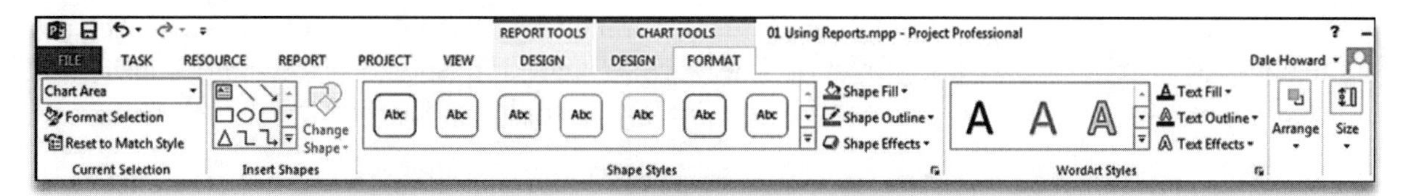

Figure 4 - 39: Format ribbon with the Chart Tools applied

To use the features in the *Current Selection* section of the *Format* ribbon, first click the *Chart Elements* pick list and select the chart element you want to format. For example, you might select the *Chart Title* element for formatting. To format the selected chart element, click the *Format Selection* button. The software displays the *Format* sidepane for the selected element. This means that if you select the *Chart Title* element and then click the *Format Selection* button, Project 2013 displays the *Format Chart Title* sidepane, such as the one shown previously in Figure 4 - 30. Apply the formatting you want in the sidepane and then close the sidepane when finished. If you do not like the current formatting of any element in the selected chart, select the element and then click the *Reset to Match Style* button. The software clears the current formatting on the selected element and then resets the element back to the current visual style applied to the chart.

The *Insert Shapes* section of the *Format* ribbon offers a gallery of available shapes. Click the *More* button in the lower right corner of the *Insert Shapes* gallery to see all of the available shapes that you can insert into the selected chart. The software organizes the shapes in the gallery into the *Recently Used Shapes, Lines, Rectangles, Basic Shapes, Block Arrows, Equation Shapes, Flowchart, Stars and Banners,* and *Callouts* sections. When you select a shape in the gallery, Project 2013 changes your mouse pointer into an *Insert Shape* crosshair pointer. Using this crosshair pointer, click and hold the mouse button and trace an outline of the size of the shape you want in the location where you want the shape. When you release the mouse button, the software creates the new shape and displays the *Format* ribbon with the *Drawing Tools* applied, as shown in Figure 4 - 40.

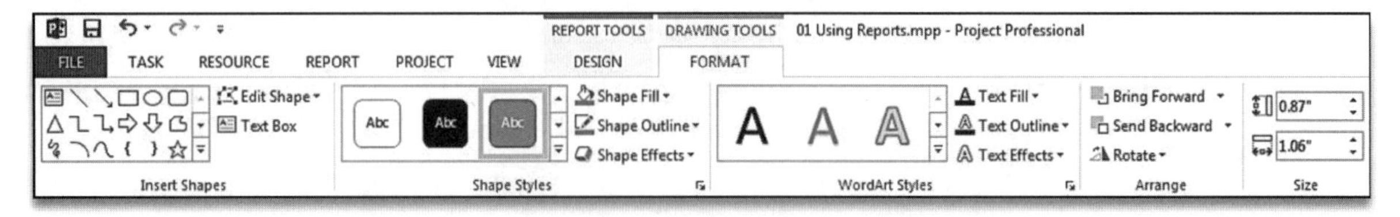

Figure 4 - 40: Format ribbon with the Drawing Tools applied

After inserting the new shape, you can resize and move the shape as needed. You can also type explanatory text into the shape by clicking in the shape and then typing the text. Beyond this, the software offers you all of the features in the *Format* ribbon with the *Drawing Tools* applied to further format the shape to your reporting specifications.

Information: Because I do not intend this book to be a reference book on Excel charting, I do not provide an in-depth discussion of the features in the *Format* ribbon with the *Drawing Tools* applied. On the other hand, keep in mind that this ribbon contains many of the same features as the *Format* ribbon with the *Chart Tools* applied.

Click anywhere in the chart and then return to the *Format* ribbon with the *Chart Tools* applied. The *Shape Styles* section offers a gallery of available shape styles, with additional buttons for formatting the fill, outline, and effects used with a shape. Before you can use any of these shape styles options, you must first select an element in your chart, such as the *Chart Title* element. After selecting the element, click the *More* button in the lower right corner of the *Shape Styles* gallery to see all 42 of the available shape styles. Select one of the shape styles in the gallery, as needed. Click the *Shape Fill* button to add a fill color, a picture, a gradient, or a texture to the selected chart element. Click the *Shape Outline* button to apply a color to the outline around the selected element, as well as to control the thickness of the outline and the type of outline, such as solid or dashed. Click the *Shape Effects* button to apply an effect to the selected element such as adding a shadow or applying beveling.

Information: To add a shadow to your chart, select the chart, and then click the *Shape Effects* pick list button and select one of the effects in the *Shadow* section of the flyout menu.

The *WordArt Styles* section of the *Format* ribbon offers a gallery of available WordArt styles, with additional buttons for formatting the fill, outline, and text effects used with a WordArt shape. Before you can use any of these WordArt options, you must first select any element containing text in your chart, such as the chart title or the chart legend. After selecting the element, click the *More* button in the lower right corner of the *WordArt Styles* gallery to see all 20 of the available WordArt styles, or to remove the current WordArt style. Select one of the WordArt styles in the gallery, as needed. Click the *Text Fill* button to add a fill color, a picture, a gradient, or a texture to the selected text element. Click the *Text Outline* button to apply a color to the outline around the selected text element, as well as to control the thickness of the outline and the type of outline, such as solid or dashed. Click the *Text Effects* button to apply an effect to the selected text element such as adding a shadow or applying beveling.

If you add two or more shapes to the selected chart, you can use the features in the *Arrange* section of the *Format* ribbon to layer the shapes. Before you can use these features, however, you must first select one of the shapes. When you click the *Bring Forward* pick list button, you can choose whether to bring the shape forward or to bring the shape to the front of all of the other shapes. When you click the *Send Backward* pick list button, you can choose whether to send the shape backward or to send the shape to the back of all of the other shapes.

The *Size* section of the *Format* ribbon allows you to control the precise size of the selected chart. Use the spin controls (up and down arrows) in the *Height* and *Width* fields to specify the exact dimensions of the selected chart. For example, you might want to increase the size of the chart to increase the readability of the chart data.

Moving and Resizing a Chart

The final step in modifying an existing chart is to move or resize the chart, as needed. To move a chart to a new location in the report, click anywhere the chart, then click and hold the mouse button to "grab" the chart. Drag the chart to a new location in the report and then release the mouse button to "drop" the chart into its new location. To resize the chart, you can use the *Height* and *Width* fields in the *Size* section of the *Format* ribbon, as I discussed in the previous topical section. Alternately, you can also click the chart to select it and then resize the chart using the "grab handles" in the corners and the sides of the chart. For example, to make a chart wider, click and hold the "grab handle" on the right side of the chart and then drag the chart edge to the right to widen the chart. When you finish formatting the chart, click anywhere outside of the selected chart.

Using Additional Chart Formatting Options

In addition to the chart formatting options presented in the *Customizing a Chart* topical section of this module, Project 2013 also allows you to edit a chart by right-clicking any element in the chart. The software displays a shortcut menu appropriate for the selected element, which offers you even more ways to customize your chart. For example, Figure 4 - 41 shows the shortcut menu when I right-click the Y-axis in the *% Complete* chart. You may need to use this advanced chart editing capability when you mix the types of data displayed in the chart, such as when you include both *Work* and *Cost* data in the same chart.

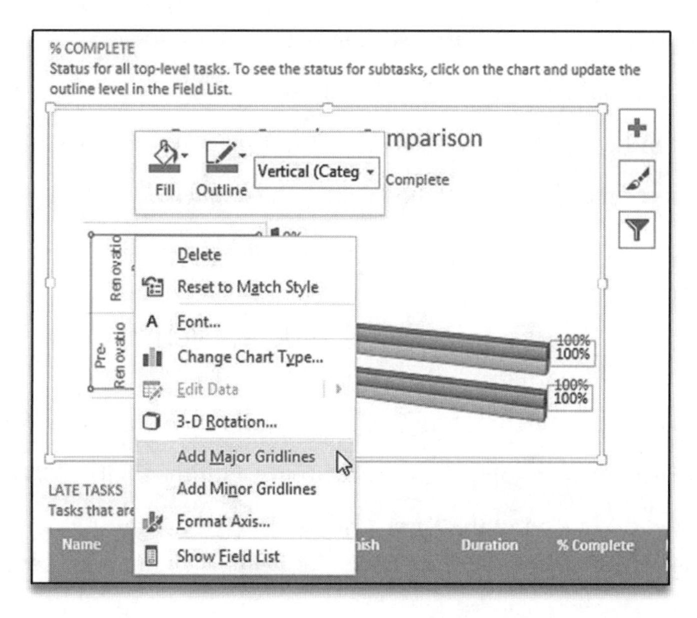

Figure 4 - 41: Shortcut menu to format the Y-axis

Hands On Exercise

Exercise 4 - 2

Customize a chart in a report in Project 2013.

1. Return to the **Office Renovation 2013.mpp** sample file, if necessary.
2. Click the *Report* tab to display the *Report* ribbon.
3. In the *View Reports* section of the *Report* ribbon, click the *Dashboards* pick list button and select the *Work Overview* report.
4. Click anywhere in the *Work Stats* chart to select the chart for editing and to display the *Field List* sidepane.
5. Click the *Chart Elements* button (**+** button) on the right side of the chart and select the checkbox for the *Chart Title* element in the flyout menu.
6. Click anywhere in the new *Chart Title* element in the chart, delete the default text, and enter *Work Comparison by Phase* as the title of the chart.
7. With the *Work Stats* chart still selected, click the *Filter* pick list in the *Field List* sidepane and select the *Summary Tasks* filter.
8. Click the *Chart Styles* button on the right side of the chart and select the *Style 8* item on the flyout menu.
9. Click the *Chart Styles* button again, click the *Color* tab at the top of the flyout menu, and select the *Color 4* color scheme in the *Colorful* section of the flyout menu.
10. Click anywhere in the *Resource Stats* chart to select the chart.
11. Click the second *Design* tab to display the *Design* ribbon with the *Chart Tools* applied.
12. In the *Type* section of the *Design* ribbon, click the *Change Chart Type* button.
13. In the *Change Chart Type* dialog, select the *3-D Stacked Bar* chart type, and then click the *OK* button.
14. With the *Resource Stats* chart still selected, click the *Filter* pick list in the *Field List* sidepane and select the *Group...* filter.
15. In the *Group* dialog, type the name *Construction* and then click the *OK* button.
16. Click the *Format* tab to display the *Format* ribbon with the *Chart Tools* applied.
17. In the *Shape Styles* section of the *Format* ribbon, click the *Shape Effects* pick list button, select the *Shadow* item on the menu, and then select the *Offset Right* item in the *Outer* section of the flyout menu.
18. Save but **do not** close the **Office Renovation 2013.mpp** sample file.

Customizing a Table

To customize a table in your report, click anywhere in the table you want to customize. Project 2013 refreshes the user interface as shown in Figure 4 - 42. Notice that when I click the *Milestones Due* table in the *Project Overview* report, the user interface includes the following elements:

- On the far right side of the report, the software displays the *Field List* sidepane.

- At the top of the user interface, the software adds the *Design* and *Layout* ribbon tabs with the *Table Tools* applied, but leaves selected the *Design* ribbon with the *Report Tools* applied.

You can use either of these two options to customize a table. I discuss these two methods of table customization individually.

Information: Customizing a table in Project 2013 is very similar to customizing a table in Word 2013. The more experience you have with formatting Word tables, the better you will be at formatting a Project table.

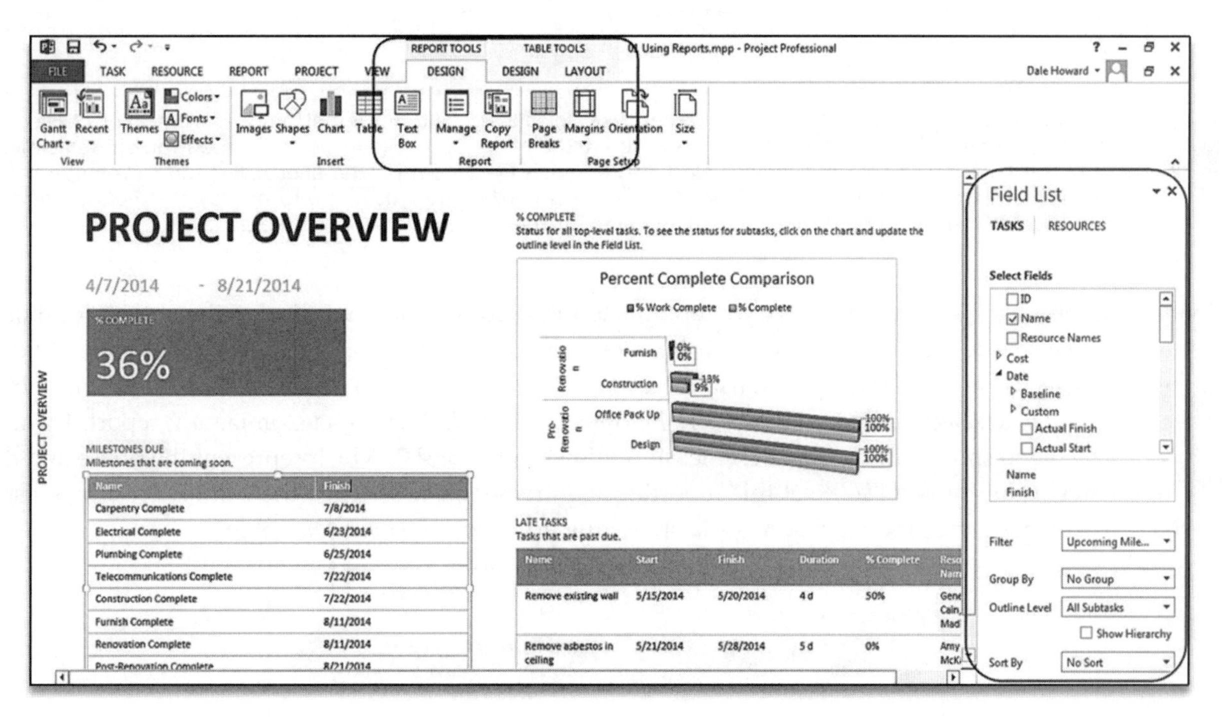

Figure 4 - 42: Select a table for customization

Using the Field List Sidepane

At the top of the *Field List* sidepane on the right side of the report, Project 2013 displays two tabs: the *Tasks* and *Resources* tab. The software selects the correct tab for the type of data shown in the table. For example, notice in Figure 4 - 42 shown previously that the software selects the *Tasks* tab since *Milestones Due* table displays task data.

Warning: If you click the *Resources* tab while you have a task table selected, the software replaces the list of tasks with the names of every resource, but includes all of the columns currently displayed in the table. In addition, the software displays a list of resource fields in the *Select Fields* section of the *Field List* sidepane.

The *Select Fields* section of the sidepane displays the types of fields available for display in the selected table, which include the *ID*, *Name*, and *Resource Names* fields, plus sections for *Cost*, *Date*, *Duration*, *Flag*, *Number*, *Work*, and *Other Fields*. By default, the software expands the types of fields used in the selected table. With the *Milestones Due* table selected, the software expands the *Date* section, which shows the list of available *Date* fields for inclusion in the table. To expand any other type of field to see the available fields of that type, click the *Expand* symbol to the left of the field type.

In the bottom half of the *Select Fields* section, the software displays the fields currently included in the table. By default, the *Milestones Due* table includes only the *Name* and *Finish* fields. To include any other fields in the table, expand the field type and select the checkboxes for the fields you want to add. To remove any current fields from the table, deselect the checkbox for any field you want to omit.

Information: If you add additional fields to your table, you can decrease the width of each column in the table by double-clicking anywhere on the right edge of the column header for the column whose width you want to decrease. You can also change the display order of the fields by moving the fields up and down in the list of selected fields shown at the bottom of the *Select Fields* section of the *Field List* sidepane.

Information: If you right-click on the name of any displayed field in the bottom half of the *Select Fields* section, the software displays a shortcut menu. Select the *Move Up* or *Move Down* item on the shortcut menu to move the field in the selected table. Select the *Remove Field* item on the shortcut menu to remove the field from the selected table. Select the *Field Settings* item on the shortcut menu to display the *Field Settings* dialog, in which you can apply a label or display name for the field in the selected table.

The bottom of the *Field List* sidepane offers you options to filter, group, sort, and display the outline level of task data shown in the selected table. By default, the *Milestones Due* table includes the *Upcoming Milestones* filter, the *No Group* item selected in the *Group By* pick list, the *Outline Level* option set to *All Subtasks*, with the *Show Hierarchy* checkbox option deselected, and with the *Sort By* option set to *No Sort*. To customize my report, I want the *Milestones Due* table to show only those milestones at outline levels 1 and 2, which represent the phase and deliverable milestones in my project. To meet this reporting requirement, I must click the *Outline Level* pick list and select the *Level 2* item on the pick list. Figure 4 - 43 shows the updated *Milestones Due* table.

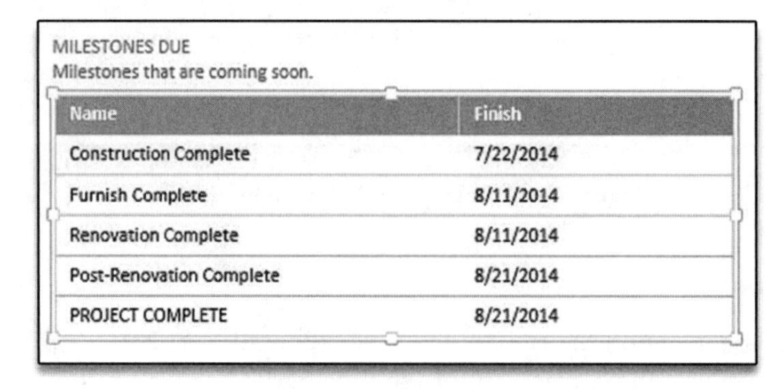

MILESTONES DUE
Milestones that are coming soon.

Name	Finish
Construction Complete	7/22/2014
Furnish Complete	8/11/2014
Renovation Complete	8/11/2014
Post-Renovation Complete	8/21/2014
PROJECT COMPLETE	8/21/2014

Figure 4 - 43: Updated Milestones Due table

Information: If you select the *Show Hierarchy* checkbox at the bottom of the *Field List* sidepane, Project 2013 displays the summary task for each milestone in the table.

Edit the selected table using the *Filter, Group By, Outline Level,* and *Sort By* pick lists, along with selecting the *Show Hierarchy* checkbox option, as needed. If you are finished editing the selected table, click anywhere outside the table to close the *Field List* sidepane.

Information: If you close the *Field List* sidepane by clicking the *Close* button (**X**) in the upper right corner of the sidepane, Project 2013 offers you two methods to redisplay it. To use the first method, click the *Design* tab with the *Table Tools* applied and then click the *Table Data* button in the *Show/Hide* section of the *Design* ribbon. To use the second method, right-click anywhere in the selected table and then click the *Show Field List* item at the bottom of the shortcut menu.

Using the Design Ribbon with the Table Tools Applied

If you click the rightmost of the two *Design* tabs, Project 2013 displays the *Design* ribbon with the *Table Tools* applied, as shown in Figure 4 - 44. The software divides the *Design* ribbon into four sections: the *Table Style Options, Table Styles, WordArt Styles,* and *Show/Hide* sections.

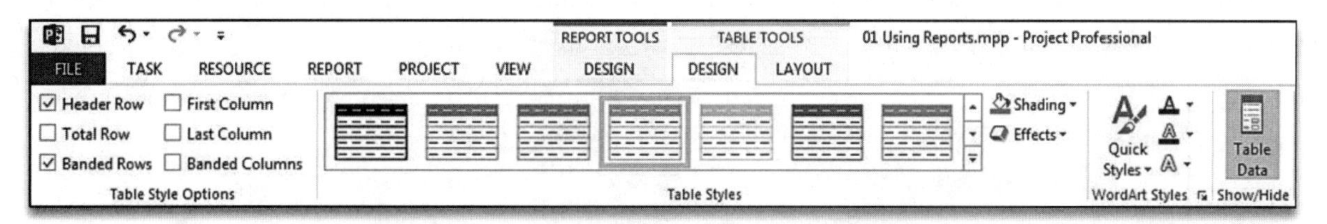

Figure 4 - 44: Design ribbon with the Table Tools applied

In the *Table Style Options* section of the *Design* ribbon, the software selects the *Header Row* and *Banded Rows* options by default. When selected, the *Header Row* option displays the field names as column headers in the first row of the table. I recommend you leave this option selected. When selected, the *Banded Rows* option formats the rows in the table with a gray gridline along the bottom of each row. If desirable, I recommend you leave this option selected as well. If the table contains work or cost information, you can select the *Total Row* to add an additional total row at the bottom of the table. If you select the *First Column* option, the software formats all cells in the first column with *Bold* font formatting. If you select the *Last Column* option, the software formats all cells in the last column with *Bold* font formatting. If you select the *Banded Columns* option, the software formats the columns in the table with a gray gridline along the right edge of each column

Information: The behavior of the options in the *Table Styles Options* section of the *Design* ribbon depends on the table style you choose in the *Table Styles* gallery. For example, if you choose a style in the *Medium* section of the *Table Styles* gallery, selecting the *Banded Rows* option displays alternating light and dark row colors in the selected table. Because of this, you may need to experiment with the settings in these two sections of the *Design* ribbon with the *Table Tools* applied.

The *Table Styles* section of the *Design* ribbon contains a gallery of 74 pre-formatted table styles, which you can apply to the selected table. Project 2013 divides these table styles into sections labeled *Best Match for Document, Light, Medium,* and *Dark*. The default style applied to the *Milestones Due* table is the *Light Style 2 – Accent 3* style. Select any style in the gallery, as needed, to change the style of your table. Select one or more cells in the table and then click the *Shading* pick list button to add a fill color, a picture, a gradient, or a texture to the selected cells. Click the *Effects* button to apply an effect to the selected table, such as adding a shadow or a reflection around the table. On the *Effects* menu, if you click the *Shadow Options* item at the bottom of the *Shadow* flyout menu, or you click the *Reflection Options* item at the bottom of the *Reflection* menu, Project 2013 displays the *Format Shape* sidepane, which gives you access to every option for formatting the shadow and reflection for the selected table.

The *WordArt Styles* section of the *Format* ribbon offers a gallery of available WordArt styles, with additional buttons for formatting the fill, outline, and WordArt effects used with the text in a table. Before you can use any of these WordArt options, you must first select one or more cells in the table. Click the *Quick Styles* pick list button to see all 20 of the available WordArt styles, or to remove the current WordArt style. Select one of the WordArt styles in the gallery, as needed. Click the *Text Fill* pick list button to add a fill color, a picture, a gradient, or a texture to the selected text. Click the *Text Outline* pick list button to apply a color to the outline around the selected text, as well as to control the thickness of the outline and the type of outline, such as solid or dashed. Click the *Text Effects* pick list button to apply an effect to the selected text, such as adding a shadow or applying beveling.

Click the *Table Data* button in the *Show/Hide* section of the *Design* ribbon to display or hide the *Field List* sidepane shown previously in Figure 4 - 42.

Using the Layout Ribbon with the Table Tools Applied

If you click the *Layout* tab, Project 2013 displays the *Layout* ribbon with the *Table Tools* applied, as shown in Figure 4 - 45. The software divides the *Layout* ribbon into five sections: the *Table, Cell Size, Alignment, Table Size,* and *Arrange* sections.

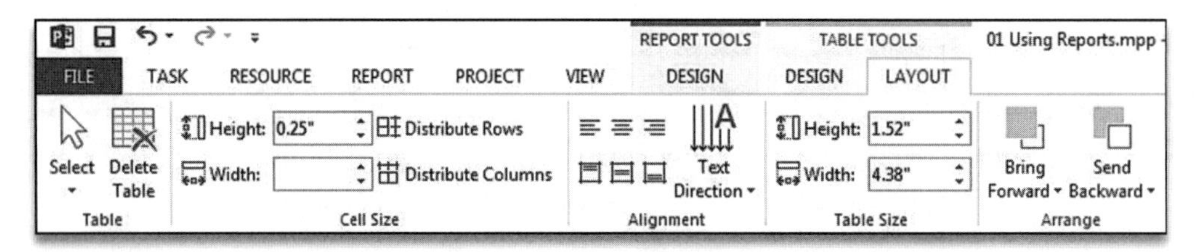

Figure 4 - 45: Layout ribbon with the Chart Tools applied

In the *Table* section of the *Layout* ribbon, click the *Select* pick list button. With any cell selected in the table, you can click the *Select Column* item on the pick list to select all cells in the current column, or click the *Select Row* item to select all cells in the current row. You can also choose the *Select Table* item on the pick list to select the entire table. To delete the selected table, click the *Delete Table* button or press the **Delete** key on your computer keyboard. The software does not warn you about deleting the selected table, but you can undo the deletion by clicking the *Undo* button in the *Quick Access Toolbar*.

Use the commands in the *Cell Size* section of the *Layout* ribbon to change the height and width of any cells in the selected table. Before you use these commands, be sure to select at least one cell in the table. Adjust the number in the *Height* field to adjust the height of the selected row. Adjust the number in the *Width* field to change the width of the selected column. Click the *Distribute Rows* button to set the row height for all rows the same as the tallest row in the selected table. Click the *Distribute Columns* button to set the column width for all columns the same as the widest column in the selected table.

Use the commands in the *Alignment* section of the *Layout* ribbon to control the alignment and text direction of the any cells in the selected table. Before you use these commands, be sure to select at least one cell in the table. Use the *Align Left, Center,* and *Align Right* buttons to align the text horizontally in the selected cells. Use the *Align Top, Center Vertically,* and *Align Bottom* buttons to align the text vertically in the selected cells. Click the *Text Direction* pick list button to set the text direction as horizontal, to rotate the text 90 degrees or 270 degrees, or to stack the text in the selected cells. If you select the *More Options* item at the bottom of the *Text Direction* pick list, Project 2013 displays the *Format Shape* sidepane with the *Text Options* tab selected, which gives you access to every option for formatting the text direction and setting margins in the selected cells.

The *Table Size* section of the *Format* ribbon allows you to control the precise size of the selected table. Use the spin controls (up and down arrows) in the *Height* and *Width* fields to control the height and width of the selected table.

If the selected table overlaps images, shapes, or charts that you added to your report, use the commands in the *Arrange* section of the *Layout* ribbon to layer the selected table with other objects. When you click the *Bring Forward* pick list button, you can choose whether to bring the table forward or to bring the table to the front of all of the other objects. When you click the *Send Backward* pick list button, you can choose whether to send the table backward or to send the table to the back of all of the other objects.

Hands On Exercise

Exercise 4 - 3

Customize a table in a report in Project 2013.

1. Return to the **Office Renovation 2013.mpp** sample file, if necessary.
2. Click the *Report* tab to display the *Report* ribbon.
3. In the *View Reports* section of the *Report* ribbon, click the *Dashboards* pick list button and select the *Project Overview* report.
4. Click anywhere in the *Milestones Due* table to select the table for editing and to display the *Field List* sidepane.
5. In the *Field List* sidepane, do each of the following:
    - Click the *Filter* pick list and select the *Summary Tasks* filter.
    - Click the *Outline Level* pick list and select the *Level 2* item.
    - Select the *Show Hierarchy* checkbox.
6. Click anywhere in the *% Complete* table (orange box in the upper left corner of the report) to select the table for editing and to display the *Field List* sidepane.
7. In the *Select Fields* section of the *Field List* sidepane, select the checkbox for the *% Work Complete* field.
8. Click the second *Design* tab to display the *Design* ribbon with the *Table Tools* applied.
9. In the *Table Styles* section of the *Design* ribbon, select the *Themed Style 1 – Accent 1* color theme in the *Theme Styles* gallery.
10. Click the *Layout* tab to display the *Layout* ribbon with the *Table Tools* applied.
11. Click and drag to select all four cells in the newly-formatted *% Complete* table.

12. In the *Cell Size* section of the *Layout* ribbon, set the *Width* value to *2.2 inches*.
13. Click anywhere in the white part of the *Project Overview* report to deselect the selected table.
14. Save but **do not** close the **Office Renovation 2013.mpp** sample file.

Adding a New Chart

To add a new chart to a report, click anywhere in the white area of the report and then click the *Design* tab to display the *Design* ribbon with the *Report Tools* applied. In the *Insert* section of the *Design* ribbon, click the *Chart* button. The software displays the *Insert Chart* dialog shown in Figure 4 - 46.

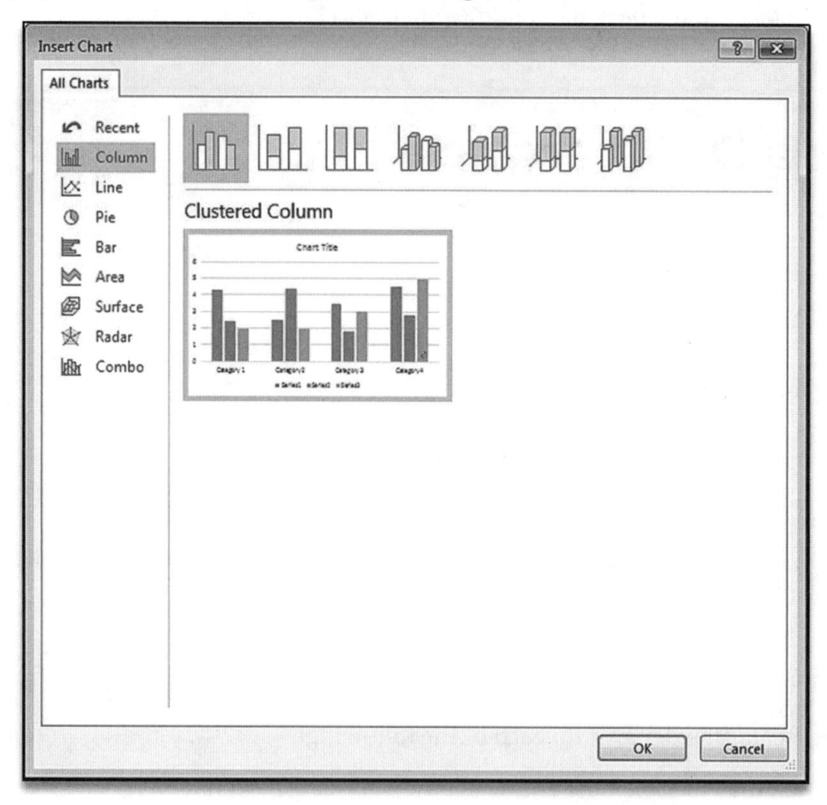

Figure 4 - 46: Insert Chart dialog

Warning: Make sure that you **do not** have an existing chart selected when you click the *Chart* button. If you do have an existing chart selected, the software displays the *Change Chart Type* dialog instead of the *Insert Chart* dialog, and then the software reformats your existing chart with the new chart type you select in the dialog.

The *Insert Chart* dialog allows you to select any type of chart available in the software. In the list of chart types on the left side of the dialog, the software allows you to choose from among the *Column, Line, Pie, Bar, Area, Surface, Radar,* and *Combo* chart types. The dialog also includes the *Recent* item in the list to allow you to choose from among recently used chart types. When you select a chart type in the list on the left side of the *Change Chart Type* dialog, the software displays a list of sub-types across the top of the dialog. For example, if you select the *Pie* chart type, Project 2013 offers you 5 sub-types, including the *Pie, 3-D Pie, Pie of Pie, Bar of Pie,* and the *Doughnut* sub-types.

Information: To make any chart type the default type for all new charts you add to reports, right-click on any of the sub-types at the top of the dialog and select the *Set as Default Chart* item on the shortcut menu.

To insert a new chart, select a chart type in the list on the left side of the dialog and then select a sub-type in the list across the top of the dialog. The software shows you a preview of the selected chart type in the middle of the dialog. To see a magnified preview of the chart type you select, float your mouse pointer over the preview image. Click the *OK* button to create the new chart. Project 2013 displays the new chart in the middle of the report. For example, Figure 4 - 47 shows the new 3-D Pie chart I added to the report. The software also displays the *Design* ribbon with the *Chart Tools* applied and displays the *Field List* sidepane on the right side of the report.

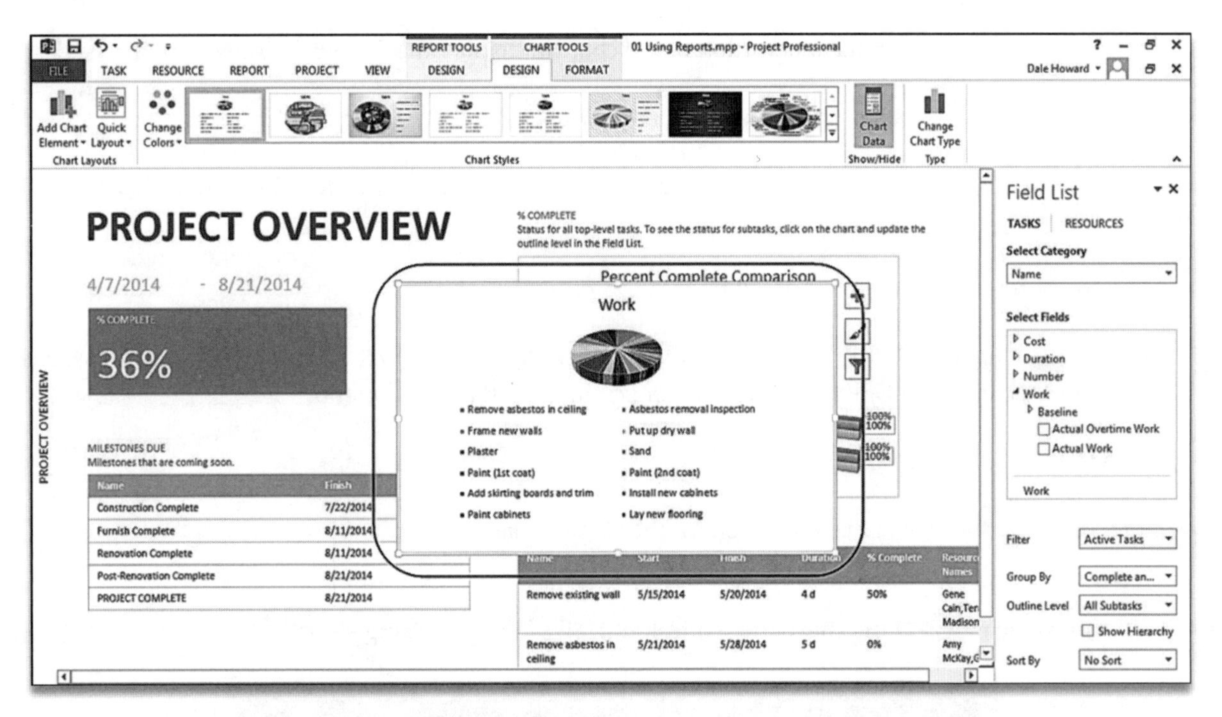

Figure 4 - 47: New 3-D Pie chart inserted in the Project Overview report

To properly format the new chart, you may need to use some or all of the techniques I previously presented in the *Customizing a Chart* topical section in this module. For example, I want to format the new 3-D pie chart to show the total *Work* value by project phase. To show this information in the chart, I must complete the following steps:

1. In the *Field List* sidepane, click the *Filter* pick list and select the *Summary Tasks* filter.
2. In the *Field List* sidepane, click the *Group By* pick list and select the *No Group* item.
3. In the *Field List* sidepane, click the *Outline Level* pick list and select the *Level 1* item. In my projects, summary tasks at the first level of indent represent the phases of the project.
4. Click the *Chart Elements* button on the right of the chart, select the *Data Labels* checkbox, and then select the *More Options* item on the flyout menu.
5. In the *Format Data Labels* sidepane, **select** the *Category Name, Value, Percentage,* and *Legend Key* checkboxes, and then **deselect** the *Show Leader Lines* checkbox.

6. In the *Format Data Labels* sidepane, select the *Outside End* option in the *Label Position* section of the sidepane. When finished, close the *Format Data Labels* sidepane.

7. Reselect the chart, if necessary, then click the *Chart Styles* button on the right side of the chart, and select the *Style 7* item in the *Style* menu.

8. Click the *Chart Elements* button on the right of the chart and then **deselect** the *Legend* checkbox.

9. Click in the *Chart Title* element, delete the existing text, and then change the name of the chart to *Total Work by Phase.*

10. In the *Size* section of the *Format* ribbon, reduce the *Height* value to *2.7"* and reduce the *Width* value to *4.3"*.

11. Double-click anywhere in the pie portion of the chart to display the *Format Data Series* sidepane.

12. In the *Format Data Series* sidepane, change the *Angle of the first slice* value to *90 degrees.*

13. In the *Format Data Series* sidepane, change the *Pie Explosion* value to *5%* and then close the *Format Data series* sidepane.

14. Click the border (outer edge) of the chart to select only the chart.

15. In the *Shape Styles* section of the *Format* ribbon, click the *Shape Effects* pick list button, select the *Shadow* item, and then click the *Offset Diagonal Bottom Left* item on the flyout menu.

16. Close the *Field List* sidepane.

17. Drag and drop the new chart to the right of the *% Complete* chart.

Figure 4 - 48 shows the new 3-D pie chart after completing all of the preceding steps.

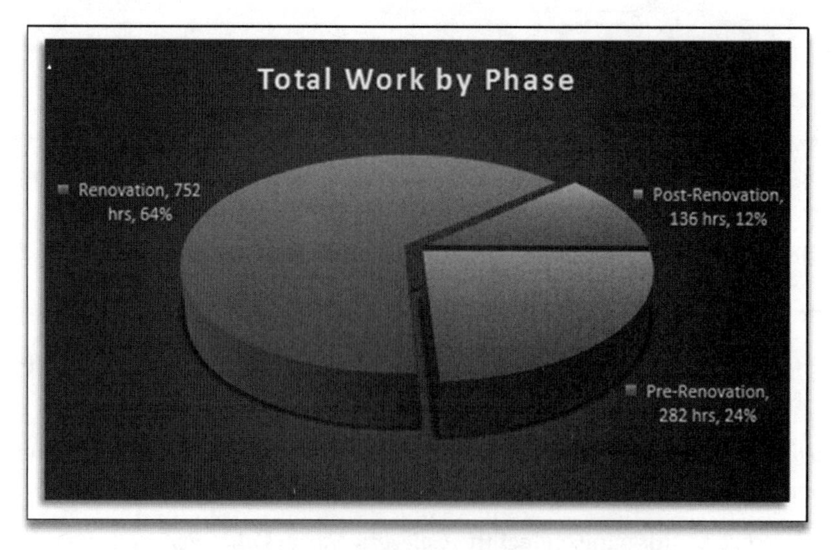

Figure 4 - 48: Completed 3-D pie chart added to the Project Overview report

Hands On Exercise

Exercise 4 - 4

Add a new chart to a report in Project 2013.

1. Return to the **Office Renovation 2013.mpp** sample file, if necessary.
2. Click the *Report* tab to display the *Report* ribbon.
3. In the *View Reports* section of the *Report* ribbon, click the *Dashboards* pick list button and select the *Cost Overview* report.
4. In the *Insert* section of the *Design* ribbon, click the *Chart* button.
5. In the *Insert Chart* dialog, select the *Pie* item on the left side of the dialog, select the *3-D Pie* item at the top of the dialog, and then click the *OK* button.
6. Close the *Field List* sidepane on the right side.
7. Click and hold the new chart and drag it to the right of the *Progress Versus Cost* chart (align the top edges of the new chart with the *Progress Versus Cost* chart).
8. Use your horizontal screen bar to scroll past the right side of the new chart so that you can see the new chart completely when you display the *Field List* sidepane again in step #10.
9. With the new chart still selected, click the second *Design* tab to display the *Design* ribbon with the *Chart Tools* applied.
10. In the *Show/Hide* section of the *Design* ribbon, click the *Chart Data* button to display the *Field List* sidepane again.
11. In the *Field List* sidepane, do each of the following:
    - **Deselect** the *Work* checkbox in the *Select Fields* section of the sidepane.
    - Expand the *Cost* section (click the little white arrow to the left of the *Cost* item) and then **select** the checkbox for the *Cost* field.
    - Click the *Filter* pick list and select the *Summary Tasks* filter.
    - Click the *Group By* pick list and select the *No Group* item.
    - Click the *Outline Level* pick list and select *Level 1.*
12. In the *Chart Styles* section of the *Design* ribbon, click the *Style 3* button in the *Chart Styles* gallery.
13. Close the *Field List* sidepane again.
14. Click anywhere in the *Cost* title in the new chart and change the title to *Cost by Phase.*
15. Right-click anywhere in the pie chart itself and select the *Format Data Labels* item in the shortcut menu.

16. In the *Format Data Labels* sidepane, **select** the *Value* checkbox and then **deselect** the *Percentage* checkbox.

17. Click two separate times (do not do a double-click) in the *Pre-Renovation* slice (blue slice) of the pie chart to display the *Format Data Point* sidepane.

18. In the *Format Data Point* sidepane, set the *Point Explosion* value to *25%*.

19. Right-click anywhere in the *Legend* chart element and then select the *Format Legend* item in the shortcut menu.

20. In the *Format Legend* sidepane, select the *Top* option in the *Legend Options* section of the sidepane.

21. Close the *Format Legend* sidepane.

22. Save but **do not** close the **Office Renovation 2013.mpp** sample file.

Adding a New Table

To add a new table to a report, click anywhere in the white area of the report and then click the *Design* tab to display the *Design* ribbon with the *Report Tools* applied. In the *Insert* section of the *Design* ribbon, click the *Table* button. Project 2013 displays the new table in the middle of the report, as shown in Figure 4 - 49. Notice that the software displays the *Field List* sidepane on the right, and displays the *Design* and *Layout* ribbon tabs with the *Table Tools* applied. To properly format the new table, you may need to use some or all of the techniques I previously presented in the *Customizing a Table* topical section in this module.

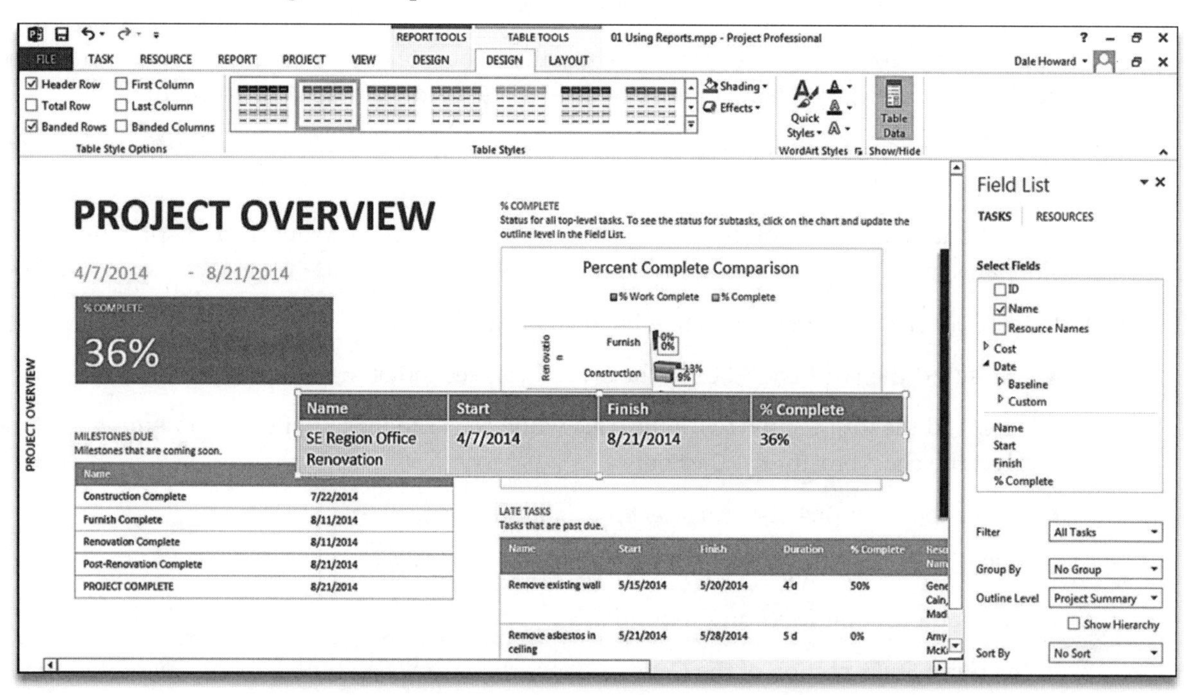

Figure 4 - 49: New table inserted in the Project Overview report

In my new table, I want to show *Work* and *Cost* by level 1 and 2 summary tasks (phase and deliverable sections of the project). To meet this reporting requirement, I must do the following:

1. In the *Field List* sidepane, **deselect** the *Finish, Start,* and *% Complete* checkboxes, and then select the *Work* and *Cost* checkboxes.

2. In the *Field List* sidepane, click the *Filter* pick list and select the *Summary Tasks* filter.

3. In the *Field List* sidepane, click the *Group By* pick list and leave the *No Group* item selected.

4. In the *Field List* sidepane, click the *Outline Level* pick list and select the *Level 2* item, and then select the *Show Hierarchy* checkbox. By selecting the *Show Hierarchy* checkbox, this allows me to show level 2 summary tasks, which represent the deliverables in my project, plus their level 1 summary tasks, which represent the phases of my project.

5. Click the rightmost of the two *Design* tabs to display the *Design* ribbon with the *Table Tools* applied, if necessary.

6. In the gallery in the *Table Styles* section of the *Design* ribbon, select the *Medium Style 2 - Accent 3* style to match the table style applied to the default tables in the *Project Overview* report.

7. Select all of the cells in the table and then click the *Task* tab to display the *Task* ribbon.

8. In the *Font* section of the *Task* ribbon, leave the *Calibri (Body)* font selected in the *Font* pick list, and then select the *9 point* size in the *Font Size* pick list. This allows me to match the font and font size used in the default tables in the *Project Overview* report.

9. Click the *Layout* tab to display the *Layout* ribbon with the *Table Tools* applied.

10. Click anywhere in the *Name* column of the table and then set the *Width* value to 2" in the *Cell Size* section of the *Layout* ribbon.

11. Using the same technique, set the *Width* value of the *Work* and *Cost* columns to *1.2"* each.

12. In the *Table Styles* section of the *Design* ribbon, click the *Effects* pick list button, select the *Shadow* item, and then click the *Offset Diagonal Bottom Left* item on the flyout menu.

13. Drag and drop the new table below the *Milestones Due* table.

14. Close the *Field List* sidepane.

Figure 4 - 50 shows the new table after completing all of the preceding steps.

Name	Work	Cost
Pre-Renovation	282 h	$16,095
Design	156 h	$12,935
Office Pack Up	126 h	$3,160
Renovation	752 h	$36,955
Construction	696 h	$34,155
Furnish	56 h	$2,800
Post-Renovation	136 h	$9,040

Figure 4 - 50: Completed table added to the Project Overview report

Hands On Exercise

Exercise 4 - 5

Add a new table in a report in Project 2013.

1. Return to the **Office Renovation 2013.mpp** sample file, if necessary.
2. Click the *Report* tab to display the *Report* ribbon.
3. In the *View Reports* section of the *Report* ribbon, click the *In Progress* pick list button and select the *Late Tasks* report.
4. In the *Insert* section of the *Design* ribbon, click the *Table* button.
5. In the *Field List* sidepane, do each of the following:
   - **Deselect** the *Finish, Start,* and *% Complete* fields in the *Select Fields* section of the sidepane.
   - Expand the *Duration* section along with its *Baseline* subsection, and then **select** the *Baseline Duration, Duration,* and *Duration Variance* fields.
   - Click the *Filter* pick list and select the *Summary Tasks* filter.
   - Click the *Outline Level* pick list and select *Level 1.*
   - Select the *Show Hierarchy* checkbox.
6. Click and hold anywhere on the edge of the new table and drag it below the table at the top of the report, aligning the left edges of the two tables.
7. Click the second *Design* tab to display the *Design* ribbon with the *Table Tools* applied, if necessary.
8. In the *Table Styles* section of the *Design* ribbon, select the *Light Style 3 – Accent 3* style in the *Light* section of the *Table Styles* gallery.
9. Click the *Task* tab to display the *Task* ribbon.

Warning: Before you complete the next step in this Hands On Exercise, confirm that you have the entire table section and not just one cell in the table. Click anywhere on the edge of the table to select the entire table.

10. In the *Font* section of the *Task* ribbon, click the *Font Size* pick list and select the *9 point* font size.
11. Click and drag all of the cells in the *Baseline Duration, Duration,* and *Duration Variance* columns to select those three columns.
12. Click the *Layout* tab to display the *Layout* ribbon with the *Table Tools* applied.
13. In the *Cell Size* section of the *Format* ribbon, set the *Width* value to *1.5 inches* for the three selected columns.
14. Save but **do not** close the **Office Renovation 2013.mpp** sample file.

Adding a Text Box Shape

When you add a new table or a new chart to your report, you may want to include a title and description for the chart or table. For example, in the *Project Overview* report, Project 2013 includes a title and description for each chart and table in the report. To include a title and description, you must insert a new *Text Box* shape, add the title and description, and then format the shape. The fastest and easiest way to add a *Text Box* shape, however, is to copy any existing *Text Box* shape and then to change the text displayed in the shape. This allows you to duplicate the formatting of the default *Text Box* shapes included in each report.

For example, I want to include a title and description for the new 3-D pie chart and for the new table I added to the *Project Overview* report, shown previously in Figure 4 - 48 and Figure 4 - 50. If I want to go to the bother of manually adding a new title and description, I must complete the following steps:

1. Click the *Design* tab to display the *Design* ribbon with the *Report Tools* applied.
2. In the *Insert* section of the *Design* ribbon, click the *Text Box* button. Project 2013 changes the default mouse pointer into a special *Insert Shape* crosshair pointer.
3. Using this crosshair pointer, click and hold the mouse button and trace an outline of the size of the shape and in the location where I want the *Text Box* shape. When I release the mouse button, the software creates the new shape and displays the *Format* ribbon with the *Drawing Tools* applied, as shown previously in Figure 4 - 40.
4. Enter the required title and description text in the *Text Box* shape and then select the text.
5. Click the *Task* tab to display the *Task* ribbon.
6. Use the features in the *Font* section of the *Task* ribbon to format the text.

Information: To match the formatting of the title text displayed in each default report, format the text in your new *Text Box* shape as follows:

- Font Effect – All Caps
- Font – Calibri (Body)
- Font Size – 9 point
- Font Color – Blue, Accent 1

Information: To match the formatting of the description text displayed in each default report, format the text in your new *Text Box* shape as follows:

- Font – Calibri (Body)
- Font Size – 9 point
- Font Color – White, Background 1, Darker 50%

7. Click and hold anywhere on the edge of the new *Text Box* shape and then drag and drop the shape to its final location, as needed.
8. Narrow the width of the new title to match the width of the table or chart
9. Optionally, I can also use the formatting features in the *Format* ribbon with the *Drawing Tools* applied to apply additional formatting to the *Text Box* shape.

To quickly create a title and description for a new chart or table by copying an existing title and description, I must complete the following steps:

1. Click the *Task* tab to display the *Task* ribbon.
2. Click anywhere in the title and description label to select it.
3. In the *Clipboard* section of the *Task* ribbon, click the *Copy* button.
4. Click anywhere outside of the selected title and description to **deselect** the object.
5. In the *Clipboard* section of the *Task* ribbon, click the *Paste* button. Project 2013 pastes a copy of the selected object slightly below and to the right of the selected object.
6. With the new title and description label still selected, press the **Up-Arrow, Down-Arrow, Left-Arrow,** and **Right-Arrow** keys on your computer keyboard to move the label to its new location.

Information: You can also move the new label by clicking and holding on the outer edge of the selected object and then dragging and dropping it to a new location in the report.

7. Click anywhere in the new label, delete the old text, and then enter the new title and description text.
8. Format the title and description text to match the formatting used in the default labels in the report.
9. Narrow the width of the new label to match the width of the table or chart.

Figure 4 - 51 shows the new title and description for the table I added to the *Project Overview* report.

WORK AND COST
Shows total work and cost by phase and deliverable sections.

Name	Work	Cost
Pre-Renovation	282 h	$16,095
Design	156 h	$12,935
Office Pack Up	126 h	$3,160
Renovation	752 h	$36,955
Construction	696 h	$34,155
Furnish	56 h	$2,800
Post-Renovation	136 h	$9,040

Figure 4 - 51: Title and description added to the new table

If you select any shape, including a title and description label, the *Arrange* section of the *Format* ribbon now contains an additional *Rotate* button not seen when you selected a chart or a table. If you want to rotate a *Text Box* shape or any other type of shape, you can use the *Rotate* pick list button for this purpose. When you click the *Rotate* pick list button, you can choose whether to rotate the shape 90 degrees left or right, or to flip the shape horizontally or vertically. If you click the *More Rotation Options* at the bottom of the *Rotate* pick list, Project 2013 displays the *Format Shape* sidepane, which gives you access to every option for formatting the shape.

Hands On Exercise

Exercise 4 - 6

Use copy and paste to add a title and description text box label in a report in Project 2013.

1. Return to the **Office Renovation 2013.mpp** sample file, if necessary.
2. Click the *Report* tab to display the *Report* ribbon.
3. In the *View Reports* section of the *Report* ribbon, click the *Dashboard* pick list button and select the *Cost Overview* report.
4. Click anywhere in the *Progress Versus Cost* text label and then click anywhere on the edge of the label to select it.
5. Click the *Task* tab to display the *Task* ribbon.
6. In the *Clipboard* section of the *Task* ribbon, click the *Copy* button and then click the *Paste* button.
7. Click and hold anywhere on the edge of the newly-pasted label and then drag the new label immediately above the *Cost By Phase* chart.
8. Edit the text in the new label to display the following:

   COST BY PHASE
   Total cost by first-level summary tasks.

9. Click the *Report* tab to display the *Report* ribbon.
10. In the *View Reports* section of the *Report* ribbon, click the *In Progress* pick list button and select the *Late Tasks* report.
11. Right-click anywhere in the blank part of the *Late Tasks* report and then select the *Keep Source Formatting* item in the *Paste Options* section of the shortcut menu.
12. Click and hold anywhere on the edge of the newly-pasted label and then drag the new label immediately above the new table you added to the *Late Tasks* report.

Warning: Before you can do the preceding step, you may need to drag the new table down in the *Late Tasks* report to make room for the new label text box.

13. Edit the text in the new label to display the following:

    DURATION VARIANCE
    Baseline Duration, Duration, and Duration Variance information for every first-level and second-level summary task in the project.

14. Save but **do not** close the **Office Renovation 2013.mpp** sample file.

Adding Images and Shapes

After adding a new chart and table, as well as adding a title and description label for each, you may also want to add an image or other shapes to your report. To add an image, click the *Design* tab to display the *Design* ribbon with the *Report Tools* applied. In the *Insert* section of the *Design* ribbon, click the *Images* button. Project 2013 displays the *Insert Picture* dialog shown in Figure 4 - 52.

Figure 4 - 52: Insert Picture dialog

In the *Insert Picture* dialog, navigate to the location where you store image files, select an image file, and then click the *Open* button. The software inserts the new image in the middle of the report and then displays the *Format* ribbon with the *Picture Tools* applied, as shown in Figure 4 - 53.

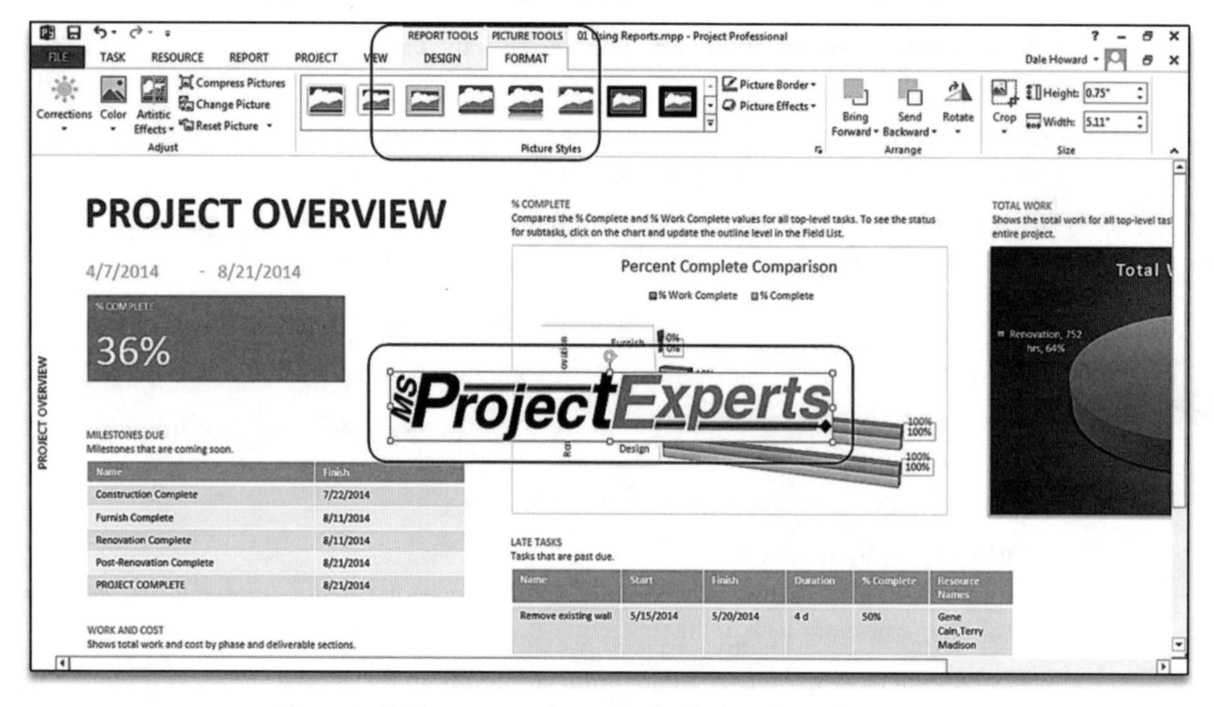

Figure 4 - 53: Insert a new image in the Project Overview report

After inserting the new image, click and hold the image and then drag and drop the image to the desired location in your report. If you want to resize the new image, you can click and hold one of the "grab handles" around the outside edge of the image and then drag the edge to resize the image. If you want to resize the new image proportionately, right-click the image and then select the *Size and Position* item on the shortcut menu. Project 2013 displays the *Format Picture* sidepane, in which you can resize the image proportionately by changing the *Scale Height* and *Scale Width* fields by the same amount, such as changing the value in each field to *75%*.

Information: Keep in mind that you may need to reorganize the layout of current charts and tables to make room for the new image in your report. To quickly "lasso" a block of charts and tables, click and hold anywhere in the white part of the report and then draw an outline of the area you want to select. As you do so, Project 2013 draws a gray shaded box to indicate the block you want to select. When you release the mouse button, the software selects every object in the block. Once selected, you can easily move all of the selected objects as a single block.

To insert a new shape in your report, click the *Design* tab to display the *Design* ribbon with the *Report Tools* applied. In the *Insert* section of the *Design* ribbon, click the *Shapes* pick list button to see the gallery of available shapes. The software organizes the shapes in the gallery into the *Recently Used Shapes, Lines, Rectangles, Basic Shapes, Block Arrows, Equation Shapes, Flowchart, Stars and Banners,* and *Callouts* sections. When you select a shape in the gallery, Project 2013 changes the default mouse pointer into a special *Insert Shape* mouse pointer. Using this special mouse pointer, click and hold the mouse button and trace an outline of the size of the shape you want in the location where you want the shape. When you release the mouse button, the software creates the new shape and displays the *Format* ribbon with the *Drawing Tools* applied, as shown previously in Figure 4 - 40.

After you insert the new shape in your report, click anywhere in the shape and then type the text you want to display in the shape. Select the text and then click the *Task* tab to display the *Task* ribbon. Use the features in the *Font* section of the *Task* ribbon to format the text. Click and hold anywhere on the edge of the new shape and then drag and drop the shape to its final location, as needed. Optionally, you may also want to use the formatting features in the *Format* ribbon with the *Drawing Tools* applied to apply additional formatting to the shape.

Information: Because I do not intend this book to be a reference book on how to edit graphical objects such as shapes, I do not provide an in-depth discussion of the features in the *Format* ribbon with the *Drawing Tools* applied.

If you want to resize the new shape, you can click and hold one of the "grab handles" around the outside edge of the shape and then drag the edge to resize the image. If you want to resize the new image proportionately, right-click the shape and then select the *Format Shape* item on the shortcut menu. In the *Format Shape* sidepane, click the *Size & Properties* button at the top of the sidepane. Project 2013 redisplays the *Format Shape* sidepane. You can resize the image proportionately by changing the *Scale Height* and *Scale Width* fields by the same amount, such as changing the value in each field to *75%*.

Figure 4 - 54 shows the final version of the *Project Overview* report. By the way, I edited this report using all of the features documented in this module.

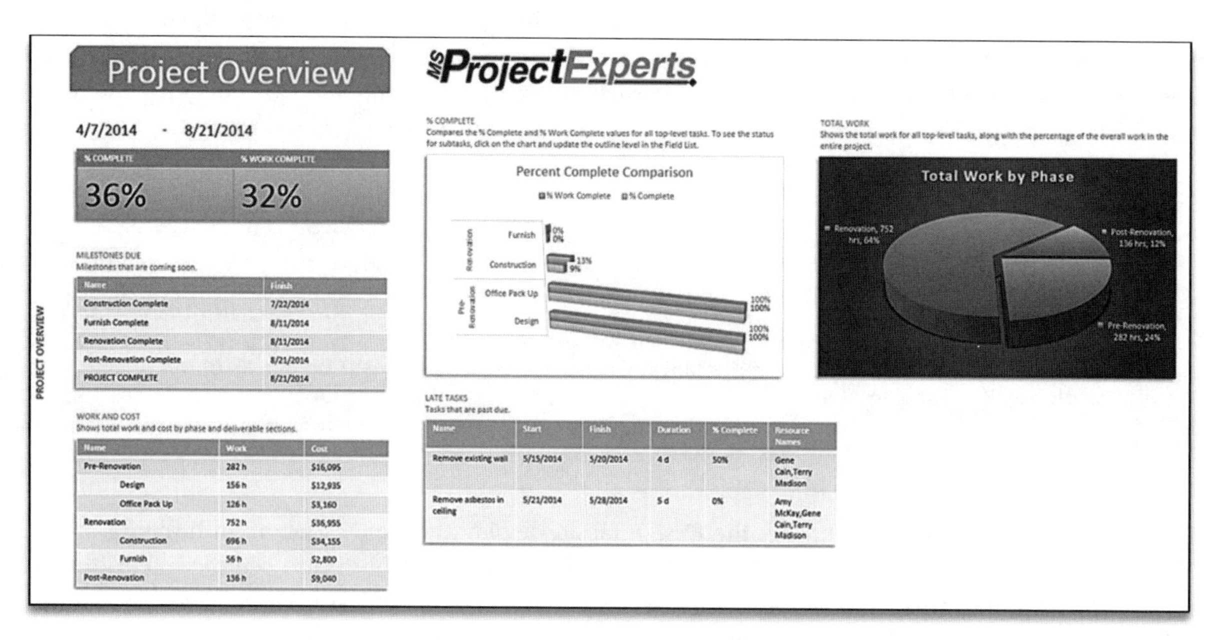

Figure 4 - 54: Final version of the Project Overview report

Notice in Figure 4 - 54 that this new version of the *Project Overview* report includes the following changes:

- At the top of the report, I removed the original *Text Box* title of the report, replaced it with a *Snip Same Side Corner Rectangle* shape, and added the *Project Overview* text as the title.
- I inserted and resized an image file of our company logo at the top of the report.
- I changed the *Font* color to *Black* for the *Start Date* and *Finish Date* fields below the title of the report.
- I added the *% Work Complete* field to the table in the upper left corner of the report and applied the *Themed Style 1 – Accent 1* formatting to the table. In addition, I resized the *Width* value for each column to *2.2 inches.*
- I resized the *% Complete* chart to match the size of the *Total Work* chart.
- I formatted the *Milestones Due* table to display level 2 milestone tasks.
- I added a new *Work and Cost* table in the lower left corner of the report. This table shows the total *Work* and *Cost* by level 1 and level 2 summary tasks (the phases and deliverables in the project).
- I added a title and description to the new *Work and Cost* table, using the same text formatting as in the default tables in the report.
- I added the *% Work Complete* field to the *% Complete* chart, changed the title and layout of the chart, and then formatted the chart to show level 1 and level 2 summary tasks (the phases and deliverables in the project).

- I added a new *Total Work* 3-D pie chart to the report, which shows the total *Work* by only level 1 summary tasks (the phases in the project).
- I added a title and description to the new *Total Work* pie chart, using the same text formatting as in the default tables in the report.
- I applied the same formatting to *Milestones Due, Work and Cost,* and *Late Tasks* tables.
- I rearranged the objects to create a visually pleasing report.

Creating a New Report

In addition to the default reports included in Project 2013, you may want to create new reports to meet your organization's reporting needs. To create a new report, complete the following steps:

1. Click the *Report* tab to display the *Report* ribbon.
2. In the *View Reports* section of the *Report* ribbon, click the *New Report* pick list button to display the *New Report* pick list shown in Figure 4 - 55. Notice that the software offers you four types of reports: a blank report, a report containing a chart, a report containing a table, and a comparison report containing two charts.

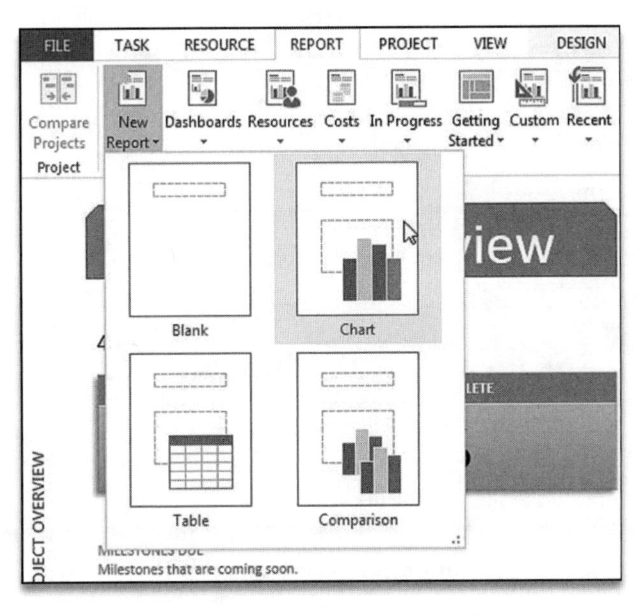

Figure 4 - 55: New Report pick list

Information: To create a new report, you can also click any other pick list button in the *View Reports* section of the *Report* ribbon and then select the *More Reports* item at the bottom of the pick list. The software displays the *Reports* dialog shown previously in Figure 4 - 4. In the *Reports* dialog, click the *New Report* tab to display the same four reports offered on the *New Report* pick list shown previously in Figure 4 - 55.

3. Select one of the available report types on the *New Report* pick list. The software displays the *Report Name* dialog shown in Figure 4 - 56.

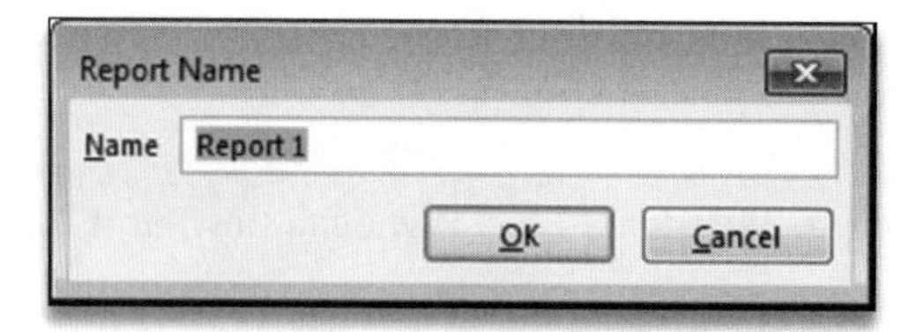

Figure 4 - 56: Report Name dialog

4. Enter a name for your report in the *Report Name* dialog and then click the *OK* button. Project 2013 creates a new report, ready for editing.

When you create a blank report, the software creates the new report similar to the one shown in Figure 4 - 57. Notice that the new report contains only a single *Text Box* shape that displays the name of the report. To set up the new *Blank* report, you must manually add and format all of the required reporting elements, such as charts, tables, shapes, and text boxes. You can manually add each of these elements using the buttons in the *Insert* section of the *Design* ribbon with the *Report Tools* applied, or you can copy and paste these elements from existing reports.

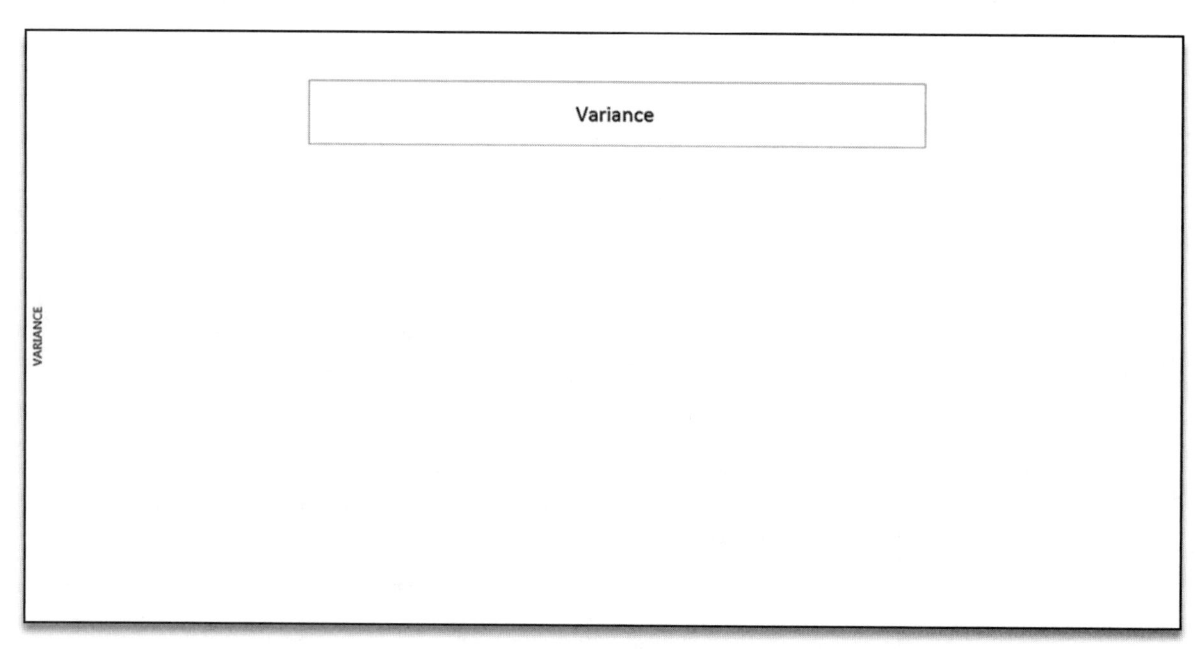

Figure 4 - 57: New blank report

When you create a new *Chart* report, Project 2013 creates the new report similar to the one shown in Figure 4 - 58. As I documented previously in the *Customizing a Chart* section of this module, the software displays the *Field List* sidepane on the right side of the report, displays three formatting buttons to the right of the chart, and displays the *Design* and *Format* ribbon tabs with the *Chart Tools* applied. By default, the chart displays data from the *Actual Work, Remaining Work,* and *Work* fields using the *Clustered Column* chart type. The software also applies the *Active Tasks* filter and sets the *Outline Level* field to *Level 1* in the *Field List* sidepane. To set up the new *Chart* report, you may need to edit the chart, and then you must manually add and format all of the required reporting elements, such as charts, tables, shapes, and text boxes.

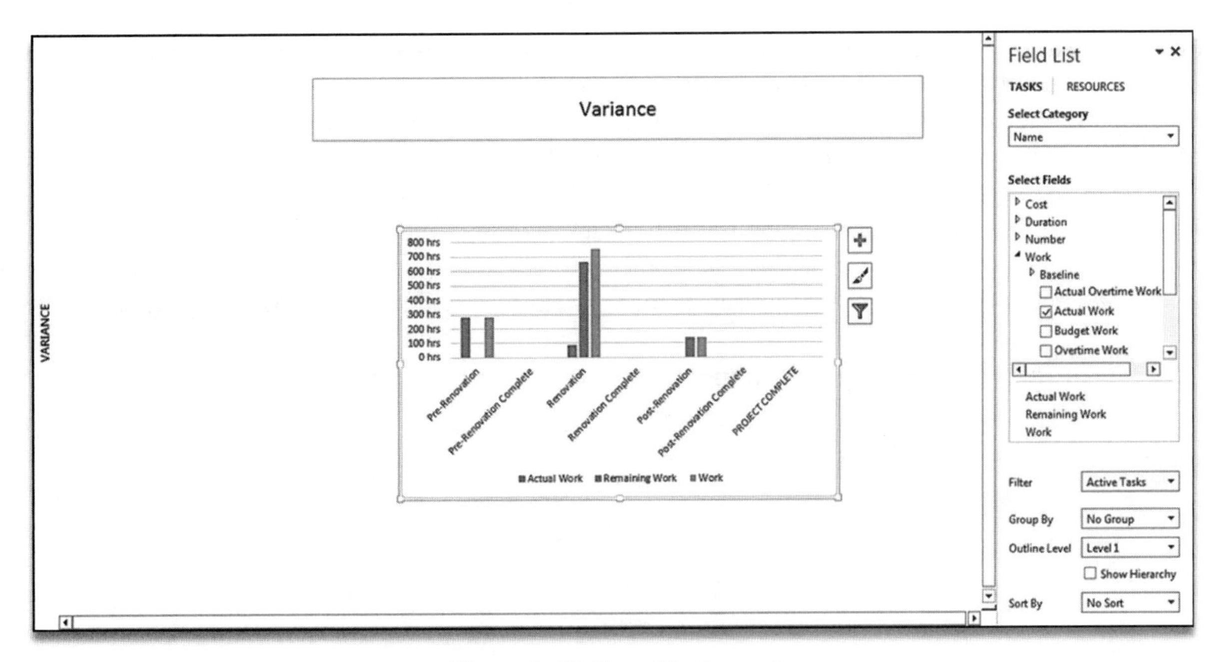

Figure 4 - 58: New Chart report

When you create a new *Table* report, Project 2013 creates a new report similar to the one shown in Figure 4 - 59. As I documented previously in the *Customizing a Table* section of this module, the software displays the *Field List* sidepane on the right side of the report and displays the *Design* and *Layout* ribbon tabs with the *Table Tools* applied. By default, the table displays a single row of data from the *Name, Start, Finish,* and *% Complete* fields with the *Medium Style 2 – Accent 1* style applied to the table. The software also applies the *All Tasks* filter and sets the *Outline Level* field to *Project Summary* in the *Field List* sidepane. To set up the new *Table* report, you may need to edit the table, and then you must manually add and format all of the required reporting elements, such as charts, tables, shapes, and text boxes.

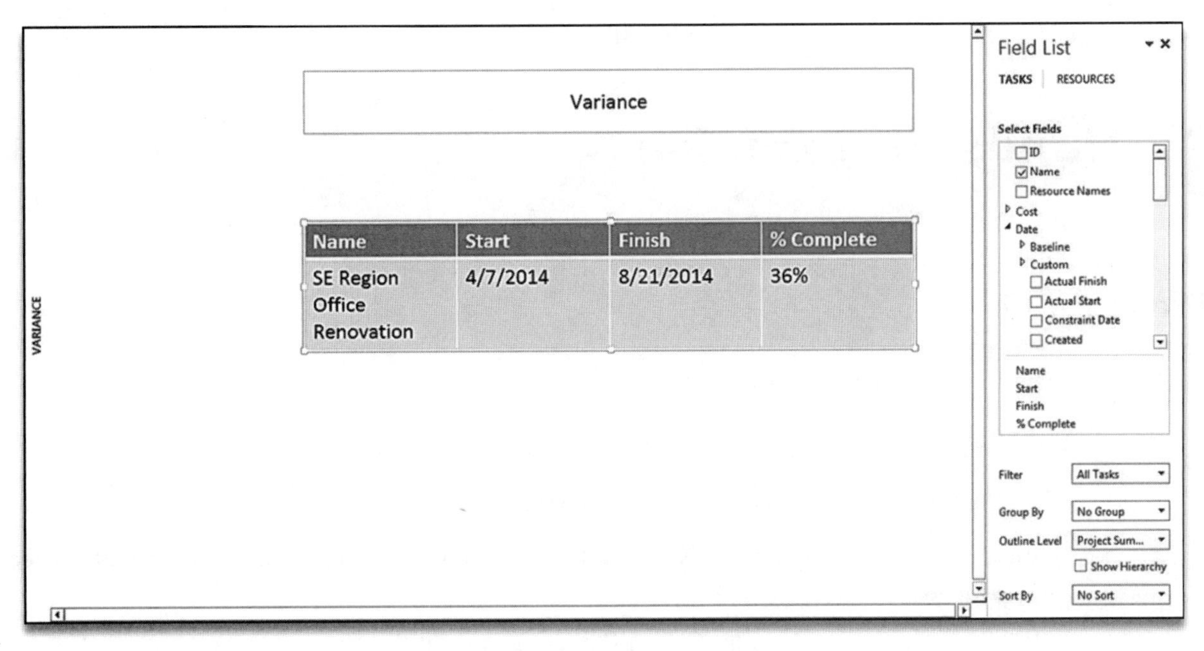

Figure 4 - 59: New Table report

When you create a new *Comparison* report, Project 2013 creates a new report containing two charts, similar to the one shown in Figure 4 - 60. As I documented previously in the *Customizing a Chart* section of this module, the software displays the *Field List* sidepane on the right side of the report, displays three formatting buttons to the right of the first chart, and displays the *Design* and *Format* ribbon tabs with the *Chart Tools* applied. By default, each chart displays data from the *Actual Work, Remaining Work,* and *Work* fields using the *Clustered Column* chart type. For each chart, the software also applies the *Active Tasks* filter and sets the *Outline Level* field to *Level 1* in the *Field List* sidepane. To set up the new *Comparison* report, you may need to edit the chart, and then you may need to manually add and format additional reporting elements, such as charts, tables, shapes, and text boxes.

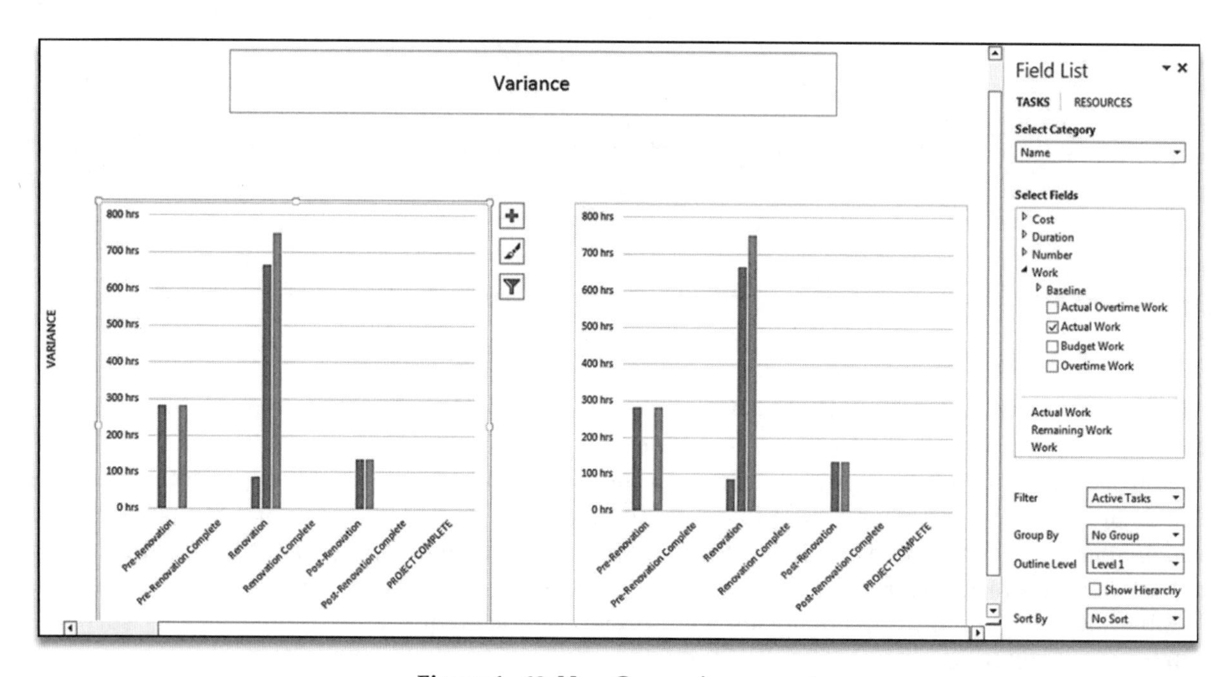

Figure 4 - 60: New Comparison report

Hands On Exercise

Exercise 4 - 7

Create a new comparison report in Project 2013.

1. Return to the **Office Renovation 2013.mpp** sample file, if necessary.
2. Click the *Report* tab to display the *Report* ribbon.
3. In the *View Reports* section of the *Report* ribbon, click the *New Report* pick list button and select the *Comparison* report.
4. In the *Report Name* dialog, enter *Overall Project Variance* in the *Name* field, and then click the *OK* button.

5. With the left-most chart selected, do each of the following in the *Field List* sidepane:
    - **Deselect** the *Actual Work, Remaining Work,* and *Work* fields and then **select** the *Work Variance* field in the *Select Fields* section of the sidepane.
    - Click the *Filter* pick list and select the *Summary Tasks* filter.
6. Click the second *Design* tab to display the *Design* ribbon with the *Chart Tools* applied.
7. In the *Type* section of the *Design* ribbon, click the *Change Chart Type* button.
8. Select the *3-D Clustered Column* item at the top of the dialog and then click the *OK* button.
9. Select the second chart and then do each of the following in the *Field List* sidepane:
    - **Deselect** the *Actual Work, Remaining Work,* and *Work* fields.
    - Expand the *Cost* section and then **select** the *Cost Variance* field.
    - Click the *Filter* pick list and select the *Summary Tasks* filter.
10. In the *Type* section of the *Design* ribbon, click the *Change Chart Type* button.
11. Select the *3-D Clustered Column* item at the top of the dialog and then click the *OK* button.
12. Click anywhere outside of the selected chart in the white part of the new report.
13. In the *Insert* section of the *Design* ribbon, click the *Chart* button.
14. In the *Insert Chart* dialog, select the *3-D Clustered Column* item at the top of the dialog and then click the *OK* button.
15. Do the following in the *Field List* sidepane:
    - **Deselect** the *Actual Work, Remaining Work,* and *Work* fields.
    - Expand the *Duration* section and then **select** the *Duration Variance* field.
    - Click the *Filter* pick list and select the *Summary Tasks* filter.
16. Click the *Format* tab to display the *Format* ribbon with the *Chart Tools* applied.
17. In the *Size* section of the *Format* ribbon, set the *Height* value to *5 inches* and set the *Width* value to *4.5 inches.*
18. Close the *Field List* sidepane.
19. Manually drag and drop the three charts so that they display in one row across the report, with the *Work Variance* chart on the left, the *Cost Variance* chart in the middle, and then *Duration Variance* Chart on the right.
20. Save but **do not** close the **Office Renovation 2013.mpp** sample file.

Exercise 4 - 8

Add a table to the comparison report in Project 2013.

1. Click the *Design* tab to display the *Design* ribbon with the *Report Tools* applied.
2. In the *Insert* section of the *Design* ribbon, click the *Table* button.

3. In the *Field List* sidepane, do each of the following:
    - **Deselect** the *Finish, Start,* and *% Complete* checkboxes.
    - Collapse the *Date* section and then expand the *Cost, Duration,* and *Work* sections.
    - In the relevant sections, **select** the *Start Variance, Finish Variance, Duration Variance, Work Variance,* and *Cost Variance* fields.
    - Click the *Filter* pick list and select the *Summary Tasks* filter.
    - Click the *Outline Level* pick list and select the *Level 2* item.
    - Select the *Show Hierarchy* checkbox.

Information: You find the *Start Variance* and *Finish Variance* fields in the *Duration* section of the *Field List* sidepane. The software includes these two fields in the *Duration* section, rather than the *Date* section, because they display variance as a time span (duration) measured by default in days.

4. Close the *Field List* sidepane, but leave the entire table selected.
5. Click the *Task* tab to display the *Task* ribbon.
6. In the *Font* section of the *Task* ribbon, click the *Font Size* pick list and select the *10 point* size.
7. Click and drag the column headers of the *Start Variance, Finish Variance, Duration Variance, Work Variance,* and *Cost Variance* columns to select those five columns.
8. Click the *Layout* tab to display the *Layout* ribbon with the *Table Tools* applied.
9. In the *Cell Size* section of the *Layout* ribbon, set the *Width* value to *1.6 inches.*
10. Scroll down far enough so that you can see the blank area below the three charts in your *Overall Project Variance* report.
11. Click and hold anywhere on the edge of the table and then drag the table into the blank area immediately below the three charts.
12. If you wish, you may optionally add title and description text fields above or below each of the three charts and the table in the new *Overall Project Variance* report.
13. Save but **do not** close the **Office Renovation 2013.mpp** sample file.

Formatting a New Report

In addition to the capabilities of formatting charts, tables, and shapes, Project 2013 also allows you to format the report itself using the tools in the *Themes* section of the *Design* ribbon with the *Report Tools* applied. Click the *Themes* pick list button to see a gallery of *Custom* and *Office* themes for your report, along with options to browse for additional themes or to save the current theme as a new custom theme. By default, the software applies the *Office* theme to all new reports. Figure 4 - 61 shows the *Themes* gallery with the *Office* theme selected. When you select an alternate theme for your report, the software applies the new theme colors and text styles to all of the elements in your report, including charts, tables, and shapes.

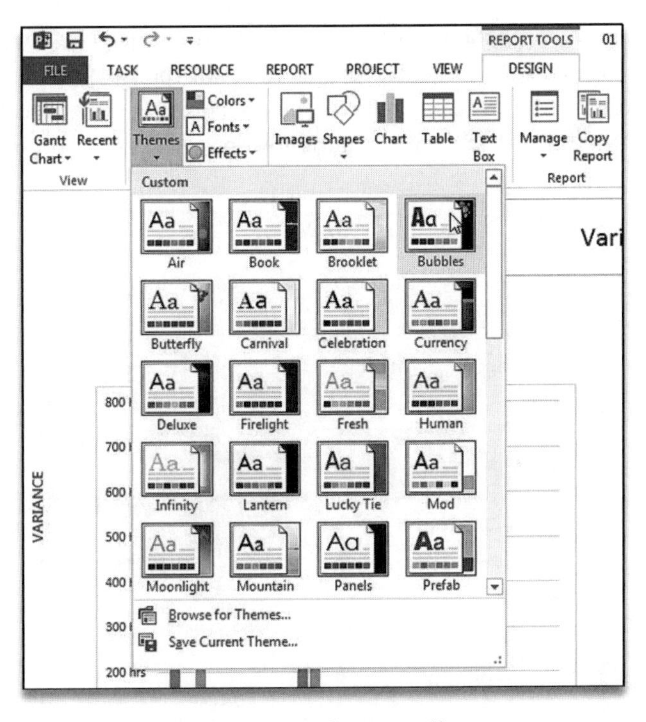

Figure 4 - 61: Themes gallery

Click the *Colors* pick list button to see a gallery of *Custom* and *Office* theme colors for your report, along with the option to create your own set of theme colors. By default, the software applies the *Office* theme to all new reports. Figure 4 - 62 show the *Colors* gallery with the *Bubbles* theme colors selected. When you select an alternate set of theme colors on the *Colors* pick list, Project 2013 changes the colors used in the current theme, but the software does not change the fonts or the effects used in the theme.

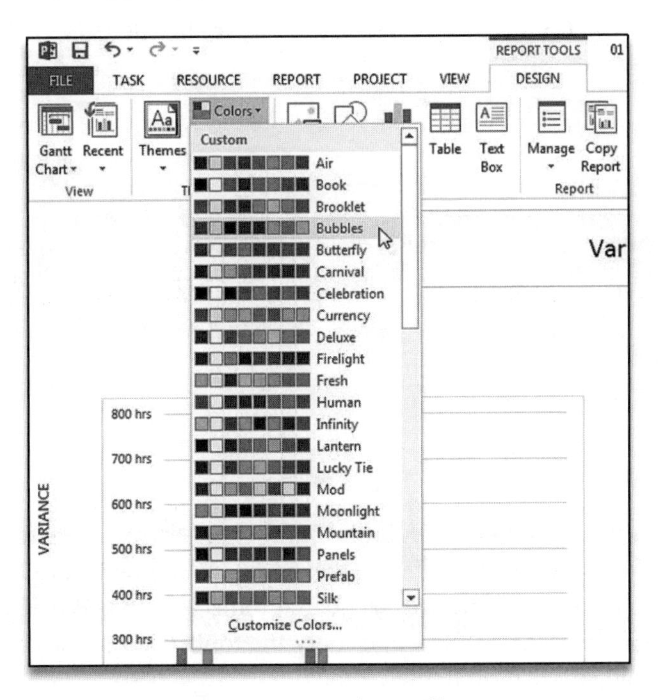

Figure 4 - 62: Colors gallery

If you select the *Customize Colors* item at the bottom of the *Colors* pick list, the software displays the *Create New Theme Colors* dialog shown in Figure 4 - 63. Create your new set of theme colors using the options in the *Theme colors* section of the dialog and view the results in the *Sample* section. To reset the theme colors to their original setting, click the *Reset* button. When finished, enter a name for your new set of theme colors in the *Name* field and then click the *Save* button.

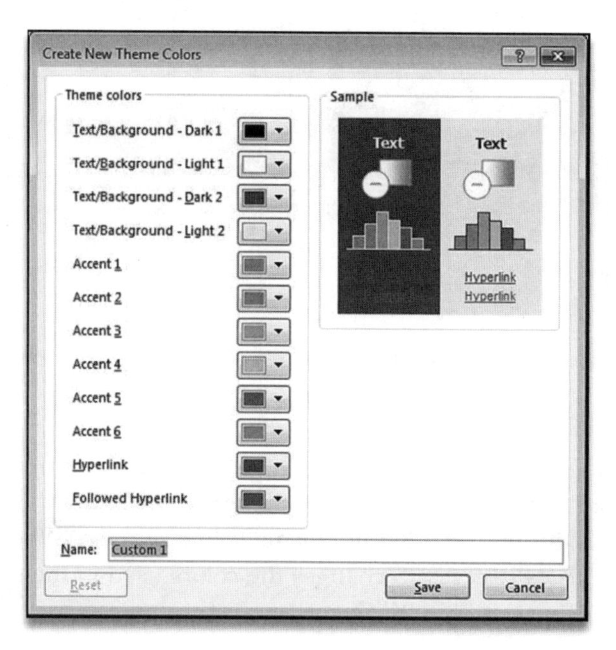

Figure 4 - 63: Create New Theme Colors dialog

Information: When you create a new set of theme colors in Project 2013, the software makes the color theme available to all of the other software applications in the Office 2013 suite of tools.

Click the *Fonts* pick list button to see a gallery of *Custom* and *Office* theme fonts for your report, along with the option to create your own font theme. By default, the software applies the *Office* font to all new reports. Figure 4 - 64 shows the *Font* gallery with the *Bubbles* theme fonts selected. When you select an alternate set of theme fonts on the *Fonts* pick list, Project 2013 changes only the fonts used in the current theme, but the software does not change the colors or the effects used in the theme.

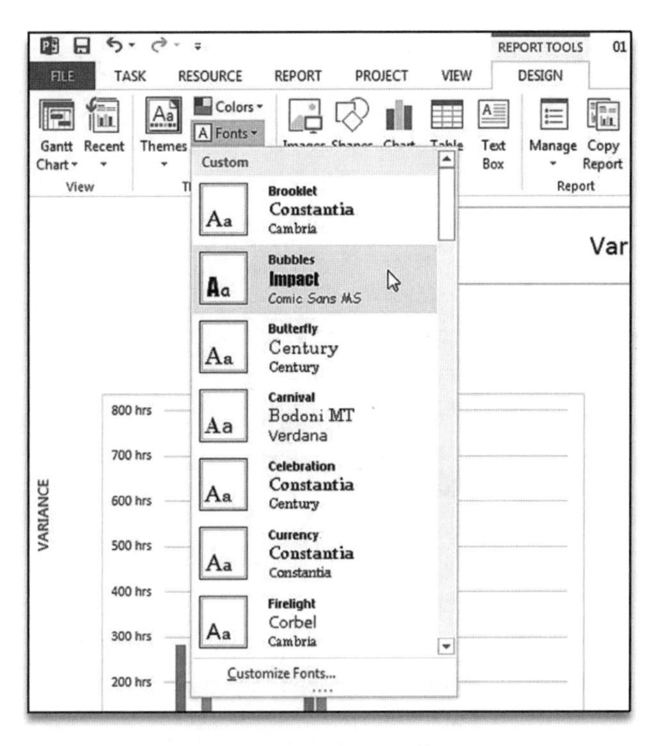

Figure 4 - 64: Font gallery

If you select the *Customize Fonts* item at the bottom of the *Fonts* pick list, the software displays the *Create New Theme Fonts* dialog shown in Figure 4 - 65. Create your new set of theme fonts by selecting the fonts you want to use in the *Heading font* and *Body font* fields. When finished, enter a name for your new set of theme fonts in the *Name* field and then click the *Save* button.

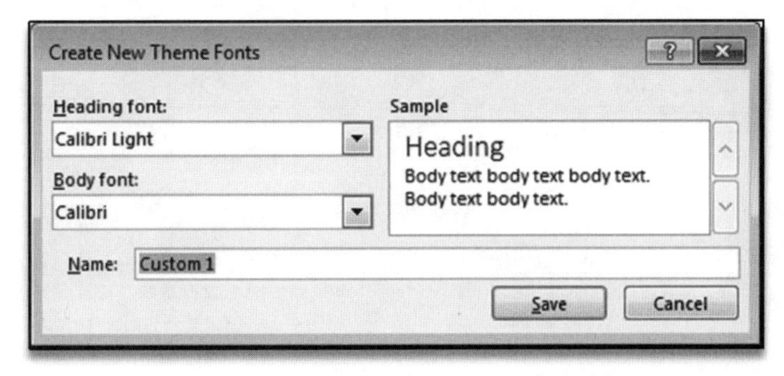

Figure 4 - 65: Create New Theme Fonts dialog

Information: When you create a new set of theme fonts in Project 2013, the software makes the font theme available to all of the other software applications in the Office 2013 suite of tools.

Click the *Effects* pick list to see a gallery of *Custom* and *Office* theme effects for your report. Keep in mind that an **effect** is a set of visual attributes that you can apply to the chart elements in your report. By default, the software applies the *Office* font to all new reports. Figure 4 - 66 shows the *Effects* gallery with the *Bubbles* effects selected. When you select an alternate set of theme effects on the *Effects* pick list, Project 2013 changes only the effects used in the current theme, but the software does not change the colors or the fonts used in the theme.

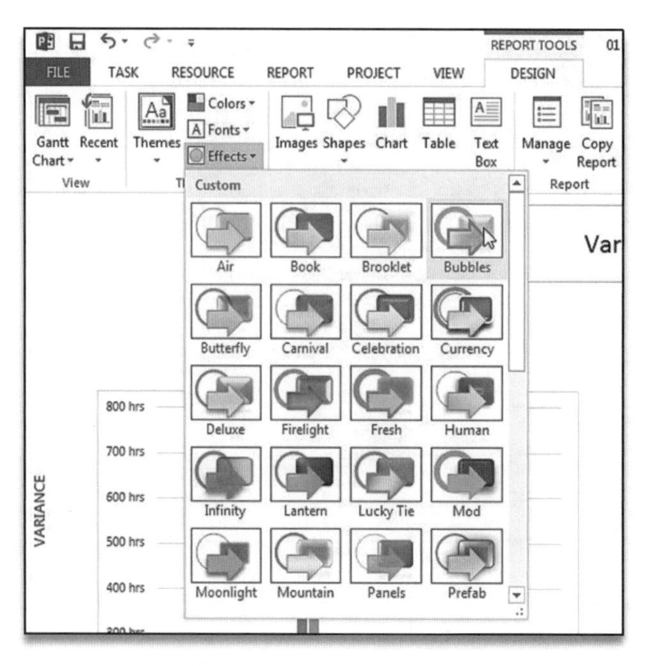

Figure 4 - 66: Effects gallery

If you select a set of theme colors or create a new custom set of theme colors, you select a set of theme fonts or create a new set of theme fonts, and/or you apply an effect, the software allows you to save these custom settings as a new custom theme. When you click the *Themes* pick list and select the *Save Current Theme* item at the bottom of the pick list, the software displays the *Save Current Theme* dialog shown in Figure 4 - 67. Enter a name for the new theme in the *File name* field and then click the *Save* button.

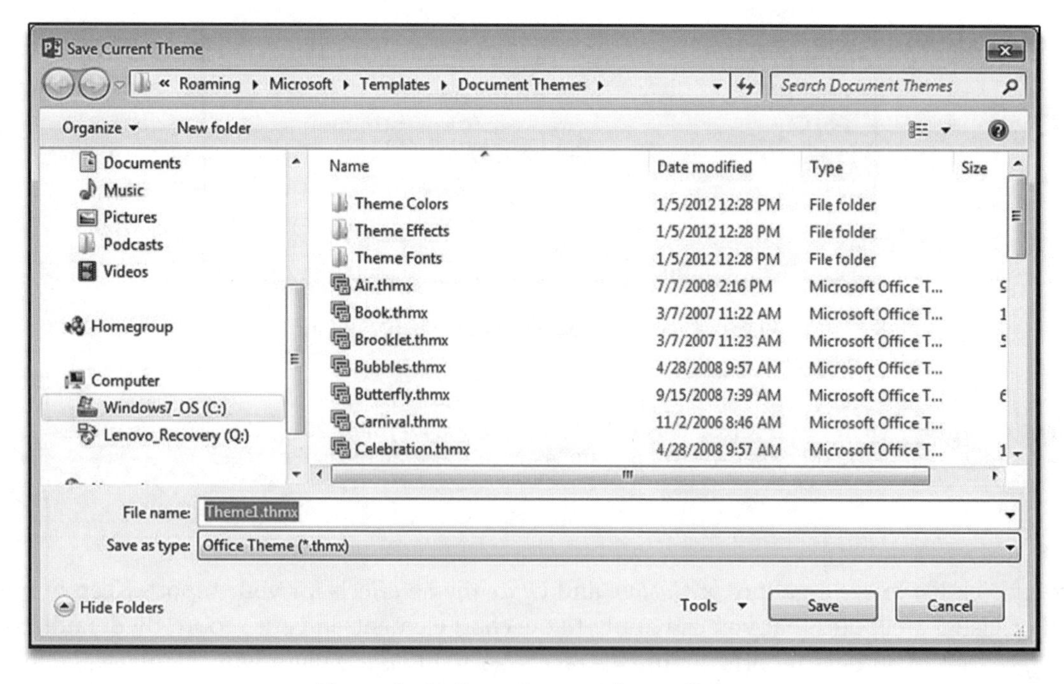

Figure 4 - 67: Save Current Theme dialog

Information: When you create a new theme in Project 2013, the software makes the theme available to all of the other software applications in the Office 2013 suite of tools.

Figure 4 - 68 shows my completed *Variance* report, created as a new *Comparison* report. In the *Work Variance* chart, I selected the *Baseline Work, Work,* and *Work Variance* fields, applied the *3-D Clustered Column* chart type, and then added the *Data Labels* chart element to the *Work Variance* bars. In the *Cost Variance* chart, I selected the *Baseline Cost, Cost,* and *Cost Variance* fields, applied the *3-D Clustered Column* chart type, and then added the *Data Labels* chart element to the *Cost Variance* bars. I added the *Date and Duration Variance* table, selected the *Start Variance, Finish Variance,* and *Duration Variance* fields, and displayed level 1 and level 2 summary tasks (the phases and deliverables in the project.) Notice that I also added a title and a description to both charts and to the table. After creating this new report, I applied the *Metropolitan* theme to the report.

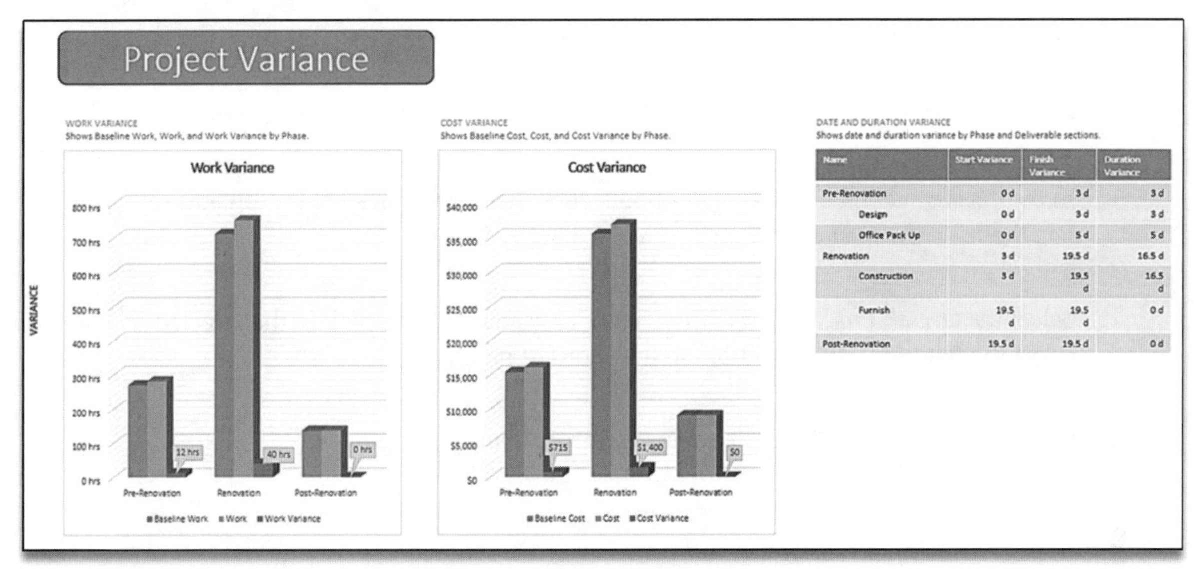

Figure 4 - 68: Variance report

Hands On Exercise

Exercise 4 - 9

Add a custom title and then format the new report in Project 2013.

1. Return to the **Office Renovation 2013.mpp** sample file, if necessary.
2. Click anywhere on the edge of the *Overall Project Variance* title field at the top of the report to select the entire field, and then press the **Delete** key on your computer keyboard.
3. Click the *Design* tab to display the *Design* ribbon with the *Report Tools* applied, if necessary.

4. In the *Insert* section of the *Design* ribbon, click the *Shape* pick list button and select the *Rounded Rectangle* shape in the *Rectangles* section of the pick list.

5. Click and hold your mouse button, and then trace the outline of a new shape in the blank area above the three charts.

6. Double-click anywhere in the new shape to display the *Format* ribbon with the *Drawing Tools* applied.

7. In the *Size* section of the *Format* ribbon, set the *Height* value to *1 inch* and set the *Width* value to *5 inches*.

8. With the new shape still selected, type the words *Overall Project Variance* in the shape.

9. Click the *Design* tab to display the *Design* ribbon with the *Report Tools* applied.

10. In the *Themes* section of the *Design* ribbon, click the *Themes* pick list button and select the *Celebration* theme in the *Custom* section of the pick list.

11. Select the *Overall Project Variance* text in the new shape, right-click in the selected text, and then select the Bold formatting button on the shortcut menu.

12. Save but **do not** close the **Office Renovation 2013.mpp** sample file.

Printing a Report

To prepare a report for printing, click the *Design* tab to display the *Design* ribbon with the *Report Tools* applied. In the *Page* Setup section of the *Design* ribbon, click the *Margins* pick list button. The *Margins* pick list displays three default margins settings: *Normal, Wide,* and *Narrow,* along with a *Custom Margins* option to apply custom margins you specified previously. Select one of the three default margins settings. To specify your own custom margins settings, click the *Custom Margins* item at the bottom of the *Margins* pick list. The software displays the *Page Setup* dialog for the selected report, with the *Margins* tab selected, as shown in Figure 4 - 69. On the *Margins* page of the *Page Setup* dialog, specify your custom margins settings in the *Top, Left, Right,* and *Bottom* fields, and then click the *OK* button when finished.

Click the *Orientation* pick list button to specify the print orientation. The *Orientation* pick list offers two standard orientation options: *Portrait* and *Landscape*. Select your orientation setting on this pick list. Click the *Size* pick list button and then select one of the available options for paper size.

When you finish setting up the report for printing, click the *Page Breaks* button. Project 2013 displays dashed lines in the report to show the current printable area of the report.

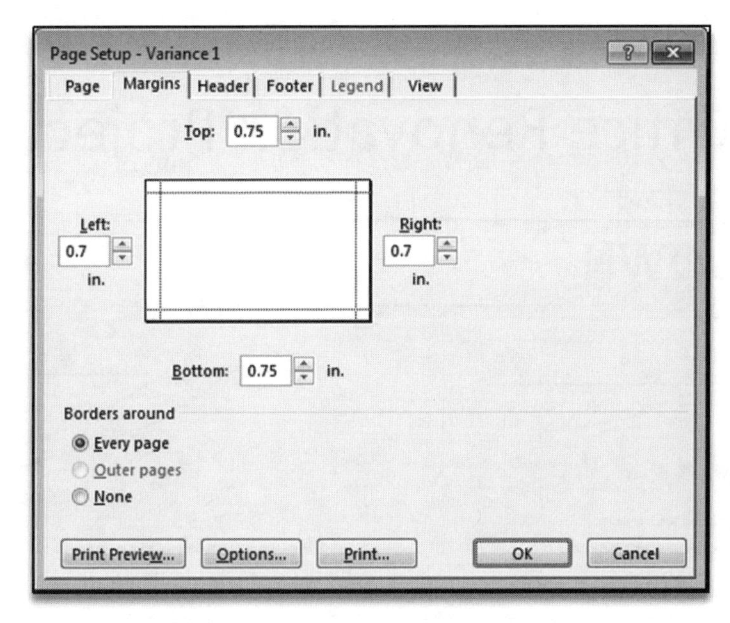

Figure 4 - 69: Page Setup dialog for a report

To print your report, click the *File* tab and then click the *Print* tab in the *Backstage*. The software displays a print preview of your report, and allows you to further customize the printing of your report. For example, if your report is slightly too large to fit on one page, click the *Page Setup* link at the bottom of the *Print* page. In the *Page Setup* dialog, click the *Page* tab, select the *Fit to 1 pages wide by 1 tall* option, and then click the *OK* button. Click the *Print* button to print the report.

Sharing a Report with another Microsoft Application

Another powerful reporting feature in Project 2013 allows you to easily share your reports with another application in the Microsoft Office family of tools, such as with PowerPoint 2013. To share your report with another application, display the report you want to share, and then click the *Design* tab to display the *Design* ribbon with the *Report Tools* applied. In the *Report* section of the *Design* ribbon, click the *Copy Report* button. The software copies the entire report to the Windows Clipboard, ready for you to paste into another Microsoft Office application.

After you launch a Microsoft Office application, set up the document into which you want to paste the report data. For example, in PowerPoint 2013, you might want to insert a new *Blank* slide in your presentation. When ready, click the *Paste* button in the *Clipboard* section of the *Home* ribbon to paste the report data into your selected Microsoft Office application. When you paste the report, the software leaves every object selected in the report, allowing you to see every individual element of the report. For example, Figure 4 - 70 shows the *Burndown* report pasted into a slide in PowerPoint 2013. Notice that you can clearly see every element selected in the report, as evidenced by the outline and "grab handles" around each of the report elements.

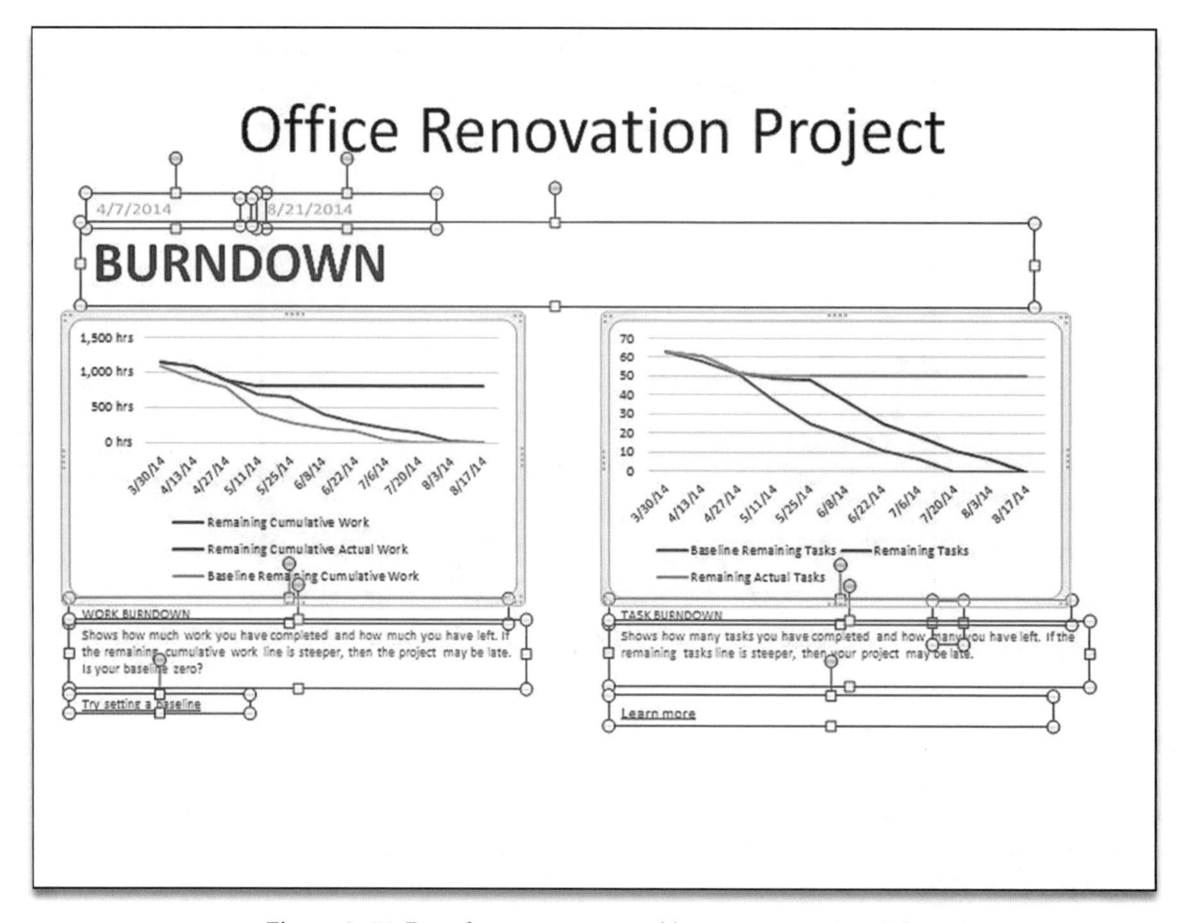

Figure 4 - 70: Burndown report pasted into a PowerPoint slide

Warning: When you paste a report containing multiple tables and/or charts into PowerPoint, the pasted report elements may extend beyond the edges of the slide. In this situation, leave every element selected and then shrink the report elements by completing the following steps:

1. Click the *Format* tab to display the *Format* ribbon with the *Picture Tools* applied.
2. In the lower right corner of the *Size* section of the *Format* ribbon, click the *Size and Position* task pane launcher button (the little arrow button).
3. In the *Format Picture* sidepane on the right side of the PowerPoint 2013 window, select the *Lock aspect ratio* checkbox.
4. In the *Format Picture* sidepane, change the percentage values shown in the *Scale Height* and *Scale Width* fields until the report data fits properly in the slide.
5. Select and move the report elements around in the slide to arrange the elements as needed.

Warning: When you paste a large report containing multiple tables and charts into a Word document, the software stacks the report elements on top of each other even if you set the page orientation to *Landscape* and set the margins to *Narrow* in the document. In response, you must use the same set of steps shown in the preceding *Warning* note to shrink the report elements as a group, and then manually move each report element individually in the document to rearrange the report. Because of the sheer amount of work you must do to rearrange the report elements manually, I do not recommend you paste Project 2013 report data into a Word document.

After pasting the report data into the Microsoft Office application, you can now use the full graphical image editing capabilities of the tool. For example, in the *Burndown* report, use the **Control** key on your computer keyboard to select the *Work Burndown* chart, along with its title and description. With all three elements selected, click the *Format* tab to display the *Format* ribbon with the *Drawing Tools* applied. In the *Arrange* section of the *Format* ribbon, click the *Group* pick list button and then select the *Group* item on the pick list to group all three elements together to form a single element.

Information: To rapidly select a number of report elements simultaneously, "lasso" the elements by clicking and holding your mouse button to trace an imaginary rectangle around all of the elements you want to select.

Hands On Exercise

Exercise 4 - 10

Share a report from Project 2013 with another Microsoft Office application.

1. Return to the **Office Renovation 2013.mpp** sample file, if necessary.
2. Click the *Report* tab to display the *Report* ribbon.
3. In the *View Reports* section of the *Report* ribbon, click the *Dashboards* pick list button and select the *Burndown* item in the pick list.
4. In the *Report* section of the *Report* ribbon, click the *Copy Report* button.
5. Launch PowerPoint 2013 (or any earlier version of the software if you do not have the 2013 version of the software).
6. In the *Slides* section of the *Home* ribbon in PowerPoint, click the *New Slide* pick list and select the *Title Only* layout for the new slide.
7. Click anywhere in the title of the new slide and enter *Office Renovation 2013* as the title.
8. Click anywhere in the blank part of the slide outside of the title field.
9. In the *Clipboard* section of the *Home* ribbon, click the *Paste* button.

Warning: Remember that when you paste a large report containing multiple tables and charts into PowerPoint, the pasted report elements may extend beyond the edges of the slide. To resolve this problem, you must reduce the size of the pasted image.

10. In PowerPoint, click the *Format* tab to display the *Format* ribbon with the *Picture Tools* applied.

11. In the *Size* section of the *Format* ribbon, click the *Size and Position Task Pane Launcher* button (the little arrow in the lower right corner of the section).
12. In the *Format Picture* sidepane on the right side of the PowerPoint 2013 window, select the *Lock aspect ratio* checkbox.
13. In the *Format Picture* sidepane, set the values in the *Scale Height* and *Scale Width* fields to *75%*.
14. Close the *Format Picture* sidepane.

Information: If you have PowerPoint 2010, click the *Size and Position Dialog Launcher* button (little arrow in the lower right corner) in the *Size* section of the *Format* ribbon. In the *Format Picture* dialog, select the *Lock aspect ratio* checkbox, set the values in the *Height* and *Width* fields to *75%*, and then click the *OK* button.

15. With the pasted objects still selected, use the **Down-Arrow** and **Right-Arrow** keys on your computer keyboard to center the pasted image horizontally and vertically as needed.
16. Save the PowerPoint presentation as **Office Renovation Project 2013.pptx** and then close the presentation.
17. Exit your PowerPoint application and return to your Project 2013 application window.

Managing Reports

Project 2013 allows you to manage your default and custom reports several ways, including renaming, copying, and deleting reports. To rename a report, display the report you want to rename and then click the *Design* tab to display the *Design* ribbon with the *Report Tools* applied. In the *Report* section of the *Design* ribbon, click the *Manage* pick list button and select the *Rename* item in the pick list. The software displays the *Rename* dialog shown in Figure 4 - 71. Enter the new name of the report in the dialog and then click the *OK* button to rename the report. The software displays the new name of the report vertically along the left side of the report pane.

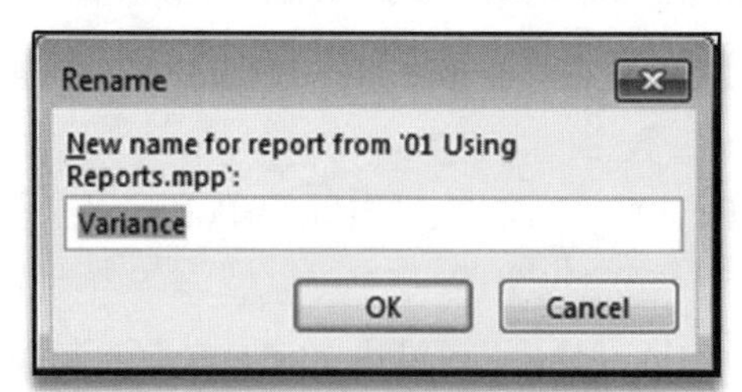

Figure 4 - 71: Rename dialog

To copy or delete a report, click the *Manage* pick list button and then select the *Organizer* item on the pick list. The software displays the *Organizer* dialog with the *Reports* tab selected, as shown in Figure 4 - 72. The *Organizer* dialog shows you the list of all default and custom reports in both the Global.mpt file and in the current project.

Warning: Before you can delete a report using the *Organizer* dialog, you must display a view such as the *Gantt Chart* view, or display any report other than the report you want to delete. This is because Project 2013 prevents you from deleting the report currently displayed.

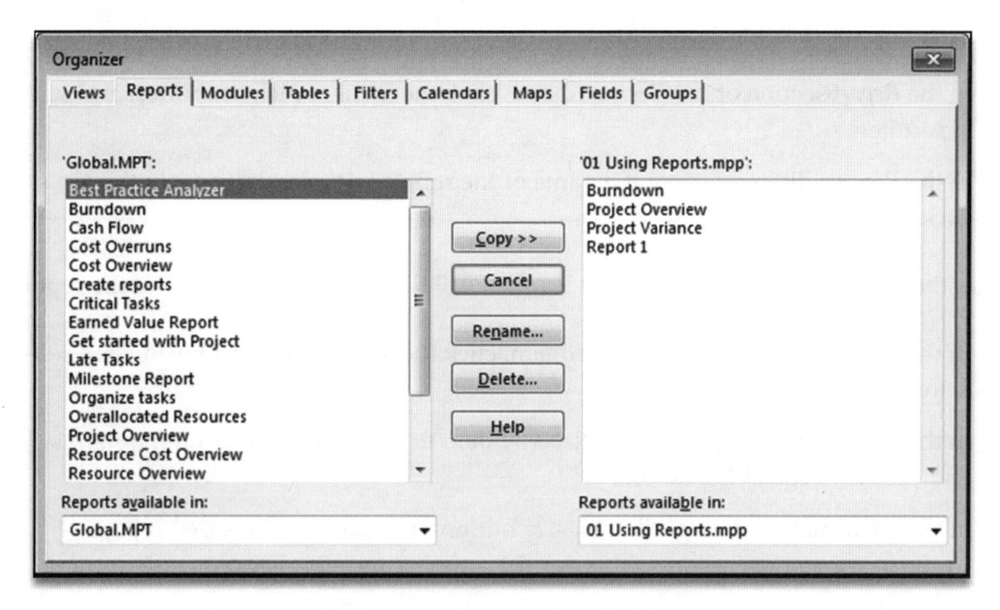

Figure 4 - 72: Organizer dialog

To copy a report from one file to another file, such as from the active project to the Global.mpt file, select the report in the list on the right side of the dialog and then click the *Copy* button. To delete a report, select the report and then click the *Delete* button. Project 2013 displays the confirmation dialog shown in Figure 4 - 73. In the confirmation dialog, click the *Yes* button to complete the deletion of the selected report. Click the *Close* button to close the *Organizer* dialog.

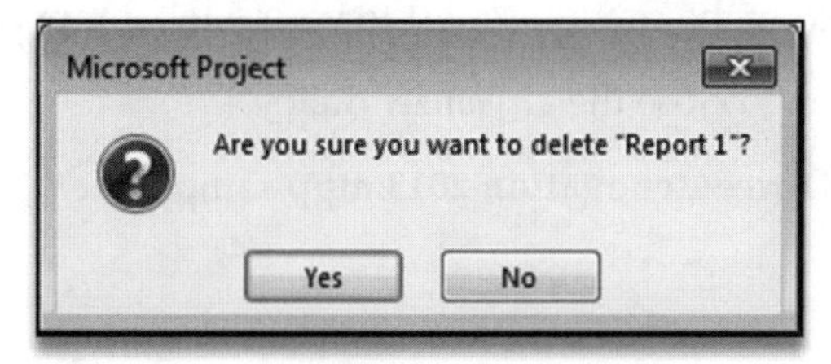

Figure 4 - 73: Confirmation dialog

Hands On Exercise

Exercise 4 - 11

Rename a report and delete a report in Project 2013.

1. Return to the **Office Renovation 2013.mpp** sample file, if necessary.
2. Click the *Report* tab to display the *Report* ribbon.
3. In the *View Reports* section of the *Report* ribbon, click the *Custom* pick list button and select the *Overall Project Variance* report.

4. Click the *Design* tab to display the *Design* ribbon with the *Report Tools* applied, if necessary.
5. In the *Report* section of the *Design* ribbon, click the *Manage* pick list button and select the *Rename Report* item.
6. In the *Rename* dialog, change the name of the report to *Project Variance* in the *Name* field and then click the *OK* button.

Notice on the far left side of the report that Project 2013 displays the new name of the report.

7. In the *Report* section of the *Design* ribbon, click the *Manage* pick list button and select the *Organizer* item.
8. In the *Organizer* dialog, select the *Report 1* item in the list of reports on the right side of the dialog, and then click the *Delete* button.
9. In the confirmation dialog, click the *Yes* button to delete the unneeded report.

Information: My goal for you in completing Exercise 4 - 10 and Exercise 4 - 11 is to create a project variance report that you can use with your real projects. If you believe you can use the *Project Variance* report in your daily work with Project 2013, complete the next step in this Hands On Exercise. Completing the next step copies the new custom report to your Global.mpt file, making the new report available to every current and future project you manage. If you do not want to keep the custom *Project Variance* report, skip the next step in this Hands On Exercise.

10. In the list of reports on the right side of the dialog, select the *Project Variance* report, and then click the *Copy* button to copy the custom report to your Global.mpt file.
11. Click the *Close* button to close the *Organizer* dialog.
12. Save and close the **Office Renovation 2013.mpp** sample file.

Index

A

B

C

D

E

F

I

L

N

O

S

T

V

W

Y